D1570737

Assimilation and Contrast in Social Psychology

Assimilation and Contrast in Social Psychology

Edited by

Diederik A. Stapel and Jerry Suls

Psychology Press
Taylor & Francis Group
NEW YORK AND HOVE

Published in 2007
by Psychology Press
270 Madison Avenue
New York, NY 10016
www.psypress.com

Published in Great Britain
by Psychology Press
27 Church Road
Hove, East Sussex BN3 2FA
www.psypress.com

Psychology Press is an imprint of the Taylor & Francis Group, an informa business

Typeset by RefineCatch Limited, Bungay, Suffolk, UK
Printed in the USA by Edwards Brothers, Inc. on acid-free paper
Cover design by Design Deluxe

10 9 8 7 6 5 4 3 2 1

Library of Congress Cataloging in Publication Data

Assimilation and contrast in social psychology / edited by Diederik A. Stapel and Jerry Suls.
    p. cm.
    Includes bibliographical references and index.
    ISBN 978–1–84169–449–8 (hardback : alk. paper)   1. Social psychology.   I. Stapel, Diederik A.   II. Suls, Jerry M.
    HM1033.A79 2006
303.48′2—dc22   2006037983

ISBN: 978-1-84169-449-8 (hbk)

Contents

About the Editors

Diederik A. Stapel received his PhD in Social Psychology from the University of Amsterdam in 1997. He had appointments at the University of Amsterdam and the University of Groningen before he accepted a position as Research Professor of Consumer Science and became Director of the Tilburg Institute for Behavioral Economics Research (TIBER) at Tilburg University in 2006. He has published widely in social psychology on context effects, the affect–cognition interface, social comparison, and unconscious processes, and has received grants from the Dutch National Science Foundation. In the past, he served as Associate Editor of the *British Journal of Social Psychology*. Currently, he is Associate Editor of *Personality and Social Psychology Bulletin* and *Psychological Science*.

Jerry Suls received his PhD in Social Psychology from Temple University in 1973. He had appointments at Georgetown University and the State University of New York at Albany before moving to the University of Iowa as Professor of Psychology. He has published widely in both social psychology and health psychology and received grants from the National Institutes of Health and National Science Foundation. From 1998 to 2001, he served as Editor of *Personality and Social Psychology Bulletin*.

Contributors

Monica Biernat
Department of Psychology
University of Kansas
Lawrence, KS, USA

Herbert Bless
Faculty of Social Sciences
University of Mannheim
Mannheim, Germany

Rosalind M. Chow
Graduate School of Business
Stanford University
Stanford, CA, USA

Ronald A. Elizaga
Department of Psychology
Ohio University
Athens, OH, USA

Jens Förster
School of Humanities and
    Social Sciences
International University Bremen
Bremen, Germany

Jack Glaser
The Goldman School of
    Public Policy
University of California,
    Berkeley
Berkeley, CA, USA

Susanne K. Hicklin
Department of Psychology
University of South Carolina
Columbia, SC, USA

Colin Wayne Leach
Department of Psychology
University of Sussex
Brighton, UK

Nira Liberman
Department of Psychology
Tel Aviv University
Tel Aviv, Israel

Melvin Manis
Department of Psychology
University of Michigan
Ann Arbor, MI, USA

Keith D. Markman
Department of Psychology
Ohio University
Athens, OH, USA

Leonard L. Martin
Department of Psychology
University of Georgia
Athens, GA, USA

Matthew N. McMullen
Department of Psychology
Montana State University-Billings
Billings, MT, USA

Nobuko Mizoguchi
Department of Psychology
Ohio University
Athens, OH, USA

Thomas Mussweiler
Department of Psychology
University of Cologne
Cologne, Germany

Paula M. Niedenthal
Laboratory of Social and Cognitive
    Psychology
CNRS and Blaise Pascal University
Clermont-Ferrand, France

Jennifer J. Ratcliff
Department of Psychology
Ohio University
Athens, OH, USA

François Ric
Laboratory of Social Psychology
University of Paris 5
Paris, France

Norbert Schwarz
Institute for Social Research
University of Michigan
Ann Arbor, MI, USA

Steve Shirk
Department of Psychology
University of Georgia
Athens, GA, USA

Laura O. Smarandescu
Marketing Department
Univerisy of South Carolina
Columbia, SC, USA

Russell Spears
School of Psychology
Cardiff University
Cardiff, UK
Department of Social Psychology
University of Amsterdam
Amsterdam, The Netherlands

Diederik A. Stapel
Tilburg Institute for Behavioral
    Economics Research
    (TIBER)
Tilburg University
Tilburg, The Netherlands

Jerry Suls
Department of Psychology
Spence Laboratories
University of Iowa
Iowa City, IA, USA

Larissa Z. Tiedens
Graduate School of Business
Stanford University
Stanford, CA, USA

Miguel M. Unzueta
Anderson School of Business
University of California,
    Los Angeles
Los Angeles, CA, USA

Michael L. W. Vliek
Department of Social Psychology
University of Amsterdam
Amsterdam, The Netherlands

Douglas H. Wedell
Department of Psychology
University of South Carolina
Columbia, SC, USA

Ladd Wheeler
School of Psychology
Macquarie University
Sydney, Australia

Introduction

JERRY SULS and DIEDERIK A. STAPEL

> There was a girl beside him. Her hair was a lovely shade of dark red and she had a distant smile on her lips and over her shoulders she had a blue mink that almost made the Rolls Royce look like just another automobile. It didn't quite. Nothing can.
>
> (Raymond Chandler, 1953, *The Long Goodbye*, p. 1)

Assimilation and contrast are pervasive phenomena in social perception, social judgment, and social behavior. For example, Western religions espouse a common humanity—an assimilative vision. Racism and xenophobia, however, seem to stem in part from the tendency to perceive members of other groups as more different from ourselves than they are in reality—a contrastive outcome. Many real-life examples and empirical demonstrations of assimilation and contrast are described in this volume. Although contrast and assimilation were first investigated by psychological researchers of sensation and perception in the 19th century, they have been a continual source of theoretical and empirical interest to psychologists since that time. One of the fundamental contributions of the social sciences has been its recognition, appreciation, and delineation of the important role of context. In recent years, the study of assimilation and contrast has been especially active among social psychologists (Biernat, 2005).

This seemed to be an appropriate time to create a contemporary compendium of social psychological perspectives on assimilation and contrast by the leading researchers in the field. Not surprisingly, researchers from across the globe are represented—another indication of the significance and interest of this topic. Classic issues in social psychology have recently been reinvigorated with the increased recognition of the roles of assimilation and contrast and new areas of relevance and application are being discovered. As building blocks of social psychology and with connections to many other areas of psychological science, assimilation and contrast were perceived by us to deserve a volume of their own.

The book is organized into three major sections with the first presenting "Classic, Perceptual, and Judgmental Perspectives." Suls and Wheeler begin by surveying the history of assimilation and contrast with its cross-cutting traditions in early experimental psychology, sensation and perception, cognitive psychology, and social psychology. Important contributions of the Gestalt psychologists, psycho-physicists, Sherif and Asch, social cognition, and social comparison are reviewed, and two "lessons" acquired by the authors, while assembling this challenging history, also are presented.

Wedell, Hicklin, and Smarandescu provide a tutorial on the psychophysics of assimilation and contrast. The authors' treatment is guided by the idea that examination of the basic constituent processes hypothesized by the different psychophysical models to produce contrast or assimilation should provide insight into the applicability of the models across different situations and the boundary conditions under which they operate.

Biernat and Manis describe their "shifting standards model," with its strong roots in psychophysics, and with significant implications for understanding stereotyping. The authors elaborate upon and review research evidence relevant to this shifting standards model of judgment, with a particular emphasis on what the model predicts about assimilation and contrast effects in judging individual members of stereotyped groups. Biernat and Manis' general perspective is that social judgments may show evidence of assimilation to *or* contrast from social stereotypes, depending on the nature of the judgment at hand. Contrary to common belief, they demonstrate that stereotyping is not strictly an assimilative phenomenon.

The first section concludes with Ric and Niedenthal's contribution. In this chapter the authors present their perspective on emotion and assimilation–contrast effects beginning with discussion of *direct* assimilation and contrast effects of affect on mood judgments. These effects are described as *direct* because the judgment is made with direct reference to the affect currently experienced by the judge. The authors then review their studies showing that these "direct" effects can be fundamentally modified when other information, such as the target's category membership, is provided. These are considered *indirect effects* of affect on judgment that are consistent with recent "information-as-affect" theory (Clore et al., 2001). Ric and Niedenthal also consider whether assimilation and contrast effects of affect are specifically due to affective state or to a more general kind of conceptual priming. The authors propose that the effects of affect can be reduced neither to evaluative nor to conceptual priming—leading to their proposal for a discrete affective states level of analysis.

The second section presents "Social Cognitive Perspectives," beginning with the influential inclusion/exclusion model originally introduced by Schwarz and Bless. According to their perspective, how representations of the target and standard are mentally represented determines whether assimilation or contrast effects result. Certain kinds of information used in construing the target give rise to assimilation, while certain kinds of information used in construing the standard give rise to contrast effects. Schwarz and Bless also describe the implications of mental construal processes for three applied issues: asymmetries in public opinion, the dynamics of stereotype change, and brand extensions.

Whereas the inclusion/exclusion perspective represents a broad spectrum approach to social judgment, the next two chapters by Stapel and by Mussweiler focus on judgment effects through processes like interpretation, comparison, and hypothesis testing. These models share a social cognitive perspective and emphasize the importance of cognitive accessibility, but highlight different fundamental processes and draw somewhat different conclusions and implications for self-evaluation.

Stapel describes his Interpretation Comparison Model (ICM) and reviews pertinent empirical evidence. The ICM attempts to give a comprehensive perspective on the effects of accessible knowledge by focusing on the way such knowledge is used during impression formation. A major assumption is that when people are unaware of the influence of such information, using accessible information as an interpretation frame is more likely to result in assimilation, whereas using such information as a reference frame is more likely to result in contrastive comparison effects—given that the primed information is sufficiently extreme and that there is prime–target similarity.

In the next chapter, Mussweiler outlines his Selective Accessibility Model of social comparison. His perspective also suggests that comparisons may lead to assimilation as well as contrast. However, which is the outcome depends on whether similarity or dissimilarity with the comparison target is expected. Similarity testing leads to assimilation, whereas dissimilarity testing leads to contrast. As a consequence, any factor that induces judges to focus on similarities between target and context information fosters assimilative context effects. Any factor that induces judges to focus on differences fosters contrast.

In the next chapter, Markman and his co-authors, Ratcliff, Mizoguchi, Elizaga, and McMullen, examine when and how *mental simulation*—the consideration of alternatives to present reality—produces emotional responses that reflect either contrast or assimilation. The chapter begins with a description of a comparison domain that is most commonly associated with mental simulation—counterfactual thinking. Then the authors consider how mental simulation plays a critical role in determining assimilative and contrastive responses to other type of comparisons. Markman et al. conclude with presentation of a model of mental simulation-based comparison processes and describe its relationship to other contemporary comparison models.

In the concluding chapter of the second section, Martin and Shirk review the major tenets of the Set/Reset Model of assimilation–contrast and then describe how it may lend insight about failures in self-regulation. In reset contrast, individuals attempt to partial out from their judgment of the target stimulus any reactions they perceive to be coming from nontarget sources (e.g., contextual stimuli, their mood). Because this "partialling" can be difficult to calibrate precisely, it sometimes leads to overcorrection. That is, people partial out aspects of their genuine reaction to the target and turn what would have been a judgment biased toward the implications of the inappropriate reaction (assimilation) into one that is biased away from that reaction (contrast). Martin and Shirk note that there is a similarity in the area of self-control (e.g., dieting) where shifts from self-control to overindulgence frequently can be observed. Both assimilation–contrast and self-regulation reflect a kind of overcorrection. In their chapter, the authors examine this similarity and the implications for both phenomena.

Motivation is not ignored in the previous sections, but the third section of this volume is more focused on motivated influences. Glaser considers the role of automatic evaluation and contrast effects in stereotyping, noting there has been the presumption that for contrast effects to occur, via some adaptation or correction, there must be a degree of awareness of the potentially biasing prime or context. Evidence of contrast in measures of automatic processes, however, challenge this assumption and provide evidence of a more comprehensive unconscious. Glaser reviews evidence of contrast (i.e., reverse priming) effects in sequential priming automatic evaluation studies and that people seem capable of correcting for an evaluation (of the prime) of which they are not consciously aware. The evidence reviewed by Glaser indicates that humans are capable of being nonconsciously vigilant for biasing information and can take proactive, and yet unconscious, action to redress such bias.

Tiedens, Chow, and Unzueta describe how Interpersonal Theory (Kiesler, 1983; Wiggins, 1982) can inform and extend understanding of assimilation–contrast. In particular, they argue that assimilation and contrast can help people to achieve their goals. The authors draw connections between contrast and assimilation to the phenomenon of interpersonal complementarity. They then argue from various forms of evidence that when people engage in perceptual or behavioral complementary contrast and assimilation (contrast for control and assimilation for affiliation) their social relationships are facilitated. The relationship becomes more enjoyable, more comfortable, and more sustainable, and coordination between relationship partners is facilitated.

Förster and Liberman observe that, like the operation of correction and adjustment in producing contrast (described in earlier chapters), inhibition at an early stage of information processing can play an important role. In particular, the strength of the motivation to work on a task, the completion of a goal, or the parallel operation of competing goals can render certain kinds of information inaccessible so it is not used for judgments and behavior. Such (unconscious) inhibitory processes may prevent assimilation effects. Also, because different factors mediate inhibition than anchoring or correction, failures to find assimilation effects in the laboratory may be due to the fact that the process of inhibition was given insufficient consideration.

In their chapter, Vliek, Leach, and Spears seek to integrate research on interpersonal assimilation–contrast and its role in individual self-evaluation with research on intergroup assimilation–contrast and its role in group self-evaluation (Pettigrew, 1967). The authors' reintegration of these traditions involves a focus on a level of analysis at which interpersonal and intergroup assimilation–contrast intersect—the "intragroup dimension." This "meso" level of analysis between the interpersonal and intergroup is irreducible to either the interpersonal or intergroup level. By adopting this distinctive level of analysis, Vliek et al. present a better understanding of how individuals assimilate and contrast themselves in relation to the successful others who are most relevant to self-evaluation.

In volumes of this kind, it is common to conclude with a commentary by the editors or a widely respected sage. The editors decided, however, to adopt a different approach. As Alice in *Alice's Adventures in Wonderland* said, "What's the use of a book . . . without pictures or conversations?" (Carroll, 1865/1898).

Although we did not provide pictures (excepting scientific figures), we devised four key questions and asked each of the contributors to share their thoughts and reactions via e-mail. In this way, we tried to approximate the kind of conversation we would hope for if we discussed these four questions with all of the authors assembled. Only the reader can decide whether this "virtual" commentary in the final chapter improves upon the more conventional format.

It is the hope of the editors that by the time the reader has read all of the chapters, he or she should have a much better idea about the factors that shift perceptions, evaluations, and emotions toward or away from the immediate context, that they gain a greater appreciation of the connections to other social psychological domains, and that some readers pursue those connections in future research.

ACKNOWLEDGMENTS

The editors wish to thank the funding sources that partly supported their editorial efforts. Diederik A. Stapel was supported in part by a "Pionier" grant from the Dutch Science Foundation (Nederlandse Organisatie voor Wetenschappelijk Onderzoek). Jerry Suls was supported by a grant from the National Science Foundation (BCS-99–10592).

REFERENCES

Biernat, M. (2005). *Standards and expectations: Contrast and assimilation in judgments of self and others*. New York: Psychology Press/Taylor & Francis Group.

Carroll, L. (1898). *Alice's adventures in wonderland*. New York: Macmillan. (Original work published 1865)

Chandler, R. (1953). *The long goodbye*. New York: Houghton Mifflin.

Clore, G. L., Wyer, R. S., Dienes, B., Gasper, K., Gohm, C., & Isbell, L. (2001). Affective feelings as feedback: Some cognitive consequences. In L. L. Martin & G. L. Clore (Eds.), *Theories of mood and cognition: A user's guidebook* (pp. 27–62). Mahwah, NJ: Lawrence Erlbaum Associates, Inc.

Kiesler, D. (1983). The 1982 interpersonal circle: A taxonomy for complementarity in human transactions. *Psychological Review*, 90, 185–214.

Pettigrew, T. (1967). Social evaluations theory: Convergences and applications. In D. Levine (Ed.), *Nebraska symposium on motivation* (Vol. 15, pp. 241–311). Lincoln, NE: University of Nebraska Press.

Wiggins, J. S. (1982). Circumplex models of interpersonal behavior in clinical psychology. In P. C. Kendall & J. K. Butcher (Eds.), *Handbook of research methods in clinical psychology* (pp. 183–221). New York: Wiley.

Section I

Classic, Perceptual, and Judgmental Perspectives

1

Psychological Magnetism: A Brief History of Assimilation and Contrast in Psychology

JERRY SULS and LADD WHEELER

We begin with two passages to provide concrete examples of assimilation and contrast. The first, which illustrates contrast, is an editorial from the *New York Times* (2006): "We thought President Bush's two recent Supreme Court nominees set new lows when it came to giving vague and meaningless answers to legitimate questions, but Attorney General Alberto Gonzales made them look like models of openness when he testified before the Senate Judiciary Committee on Monday about domestic spying" (p. A-22). The second, which illustrates both contrast and assimilation, is from a description of a character in novelist Edith Wharton's *House of Mirth*: ". . . the heroine Lily Bart—no longer as young as she once was, the financial promises made to her failing to pan out, her prospects at marriage dwindling daily, has a friend named Gerty Farish. Gerty is also unmarried. Gerty has no annuity. Gerty takes her meals in public dining rooms with other single women. And she does so good-naturedly. Every time Lily sees Gerty, she experiences an interval of panic. Wharton writes: '. . . the restrictions of Gerty's life, which once has the charm of contrast, now reminded [Lily] too painfully of the limits to which her own existence was shrinking' " (Rakoff, 2001, p. 60).

Assimilation and *contrast* are concepts that arise together frequently in contemporary psychology, but in the past they often have been researched as distinct phenomena and their historical trails can be difficult to track (see Biernat, 2005, for an excellent book-length treatment of the subject). In this chapter, we review the history of psychological conceptions about assimilation and contrast to provide a context for the contemporary approaches presented by the other contributors to this volume. We begin with some definitions and then sketch the relevant developments from 19th-century experimental psychology, Gestalt psychology, the psychophysics of the mid-20th century, the social psychological research of Sherif, Asch, and Festinger, the eras of attitude change and attribution theory, to the present day of social cognition. This history is offered with the hope that familiarization with past ideas and conceptions from other areas might help to uncover connections and confusions overlooked by current researchers. In the concluding section, we take the liberty to make some observations and offer some advice.

DEFINITIONS

Our preferred definition of contrast refers to situations whereby perceptions or judgments of a stimulus are displaced from the context. For example in *Gulliver's Travels*, Gulliver seems to tower as a giant in the land of the diminutive Lilliputians, but seems like a midget among the giant Brobdingnagians. Assimilation refers to situations whereby perception and judgment are displaced toward the context. For example, a baseball player will be perceived as more skilled if he plays for the New York Yankees (0.596% wins in 2005) than if he plays for the Kansas City Royals (0.346% wins in 2005). Assimilation can be thought of as a kind of magnetic-like attraction toward and contrast as a kind of repulsion from a context or standard.[1] Assimilation and contrast are descriptive terms; they describe the phenomena but do not explain how these different outcomes come about.

The above definitions are pretty general and allow for considerable latitude in terms of the types of judgments being made. Other writers' definitions are even broader, however. For example Bless, Schwarz, and Wänke (2003) refer to "assimilation effects whenever the judgment reflects a positive relation between the implications of some piece of information and the judgment, and to contrast effects whenever the judgment reflects a negative (inverse) relationship between the judgment and the implications of some piece of information" (pp. 180–181). Thus, Bless et al. also allow for displacements in affect, mood, and behavior, in addition to perception. In describing the history of assimilation and contrast, we try to be as inclusive as possible although we will note later when we think more specificity might be desirable.

EARLY EXPERIMENTAL PSYCHOLOGY

Contrast for von Helmholtz, Hering, and Wundt

The term *contrast* was first used by von Helmholtz (1866) to describe the phenomena of perceptual distortions associated with the exaggeration of sensory differences. In the early decades of experimental psychology, contrast was demonstrated for several sensory dimensions—color, brightness, size, shape, and direction. For example, a small gray square will look dark on a white background, light on a black background, blue on yellow, and reddish on green. A more contemporary example is when a sports announcer of average height (e.g., 5 feet 10 inches) appears to be much shorter than average when interviewing a group of basketball players, but taller than average when interviewing a group of racehorse jockeys.

Early experimental psychologists actively pursued the study of sensory contrast phenomena. An account by Hering (1874) proposed a peripheral effects theory in which activity of one retinal area induces an opposed activity—a complementary chemical reaction—in the adjacent area. He conceived sensory contrast as a function of physiological responses that were innate to the organism at the local sensory level. Hering's emphasis on complementary local (excitatory or inhibitory) physiological processes became a legacy in the study of several types of sensory contrast, notably in vision research.

Peripheral physiological processes, however, are unlikely to explain some instances of contrast that must involve encoding or judgment occurring at a more central, cognitive level of processing. For example, if a Yankee ballplayer is perceived as more coordinated than a Royal, this cannot be readily explained by complementary chemical reactions in adjacent retinal areas.

Hering also advanced the general idea of an equilibrium state. Temperature, for example, would be felt as warm or cold depending on the relation to a physiological neutral point (Boring, 1942). This neutral point could be raised or lowered by prolonged exposure, as when tepid water is felt as cold after one steps out of a hot bath. In this example, it can be appreciated that Hering was emphasizing both the role of physiology and of context—ideas that would influence the Gestalt psychologists and psychophysics researchers.

After summarizing evidence of contrast, Wundt (1894) offered a general law of perceptual relativity for contrast: "Wherever there occurs a quantitative apprehension of sensations, whether as regards intensity or degree of quantity, the individual sensation is estimated by the relation in which it stands to other sensations of the same sense modality" (p. 119). In formulating the perceptual relativity law, Wundt drew inspiration from Weber and Fechner's psychophysical laws in which the significance of the difference between sensations depends on the *relation* of their absolute magnitudes.

The law of relativity was not restricted to sensory intensity, however. Wundt (1894) thought it was "applicable in every case where the intensity of a mental process is quantitatively apprehended and compared with that of others." Fechner (1860/1966) already had recognized the relevance of contrast for feelings of pleasure or satisfaction. According to his principle of hedonic contrast, a thing that provides pleasure gives more pleasure the more it enters into contrast with sources of lesser pleasure.

Assimilation for von Helmholtz and Wundt

Examples of assimilation are as common as those for contrast. A familiar case is the change in perceived color of a background in the direction of the color parts belonging to the foreground of a visual scene. An early experiment studied the effects of presentation of a series of preceding stimuli on judgments of succeeding stimuli. The results showed that the human judges tended to expect successive values to be close to the median value of the preceding items and to perceive new values as closer to the median than they actually were (Hollingworth, 1910). In a contemporary experiment, subjects judged a series of successive tones for loudness. A regularity in the data was that each stimulus was reported as being overly similar to the previous stimulus, "as if there is some magnetic attraction between successive trials" (Lockhead, 2002, p. 187). Offensive social examples of assimilation abound such as when Caucasians believe all Asians look alike and Asians think all Caucasians look alike.

Von Helmholtz puzzled about assimilation because, like Wundt, he drew upon English philosophers such as John Stuart Mill to understand mental content. In the so-called *mental chemistry*, any rich subjective experience was supposed to be merely a blend of impressions. How then could a simple mosaic of sensations capture assimilation? Von Helmholtz's solution was that experience and memory correct and enhance the momentary effects of stimulation. He referred to these other influences as "unconscious inference."

Wundt (1894) expanded on this idea in his *assimilation hypothesis* whereby a group of sensations aroused by the present stimulation reproduces images of previous experiences. These old images fuse with the present ones into a unity in which many properties of the former are lost, and in which the two kinds of elements, sensory and imaginal, are indistinguishable. In this way, past experience influences the integration of present stimulation, displacing it toward earlier mental elements. The reader may recognize von Helmholtz and Wundt's ideas as close relatives of the concept of priming in contemporary cognitive and social psychology (Higgins, 1996; Neely, 1991; Srull & Wyer, 1979; Wyer & Srull, 1989).

Wundt's approach relied heavily on introspection as an experimental methodology and his influence on psychology waned in the early decades of the 20th century with the rise of functionalism and behaviorism. Sensory contrast, however, continued to be an object of study within the area of sensation and perception. Considerable attention was devoted to Hering's idea of contrast as the result of complementary physiological processes at the level of peripheral sensory mechanisms. But the study of assimilation and contrast of complex cognitive and social experiences had to wait for developments in other areas of psychology.

THE GESTALTERS

The Gestalt psychologists, Wertheimer, Kohler, and Koffka, emerged during the first decades of the 20th century and represented an alternative to the mental chemistry of Wundt.[2] They rejected the mosaic view of experience as simply the sum of sensations (Dember & Bagwell, 1985).

For the Gestalters, perception and judgment depend on frame of reference and the patterning of elements. Specific sensations were considered to be less important than the relationship among them. A favorite example of the Gestalt psychologists was a melody transposed into another key. The tune is readily recognized even when notes are different because the pattern or relationship among the musical tones is preserved (Koffka, 1935, p. 612). The persistence of form with transposition was seen as a basic principle by Gestalt psychologists.

The Gestalters also emphasized how we perceive objects and arrays as well-organized wholes rather than isolated parts (Gestalt means *whole* in German). The organization of perception "was either directed toward minimizing stimulus differences so that the perceptual field becomes homogeneous [i.e., assimilation] or toward accentuating them [i.e., contrast] if the stimulus differences exceed a certain level" (Deutsch & Krauss, 1965, p. 18).

Perception was thought to be a function of innate organizational principles that describe why certain elements seem to go together. For example, according to the Gestalt law of proximity, elements near each other tend to be seen as a unit. The law of similarity states that elements similar to each other tend to be seen as a unit. The Gestaltists also thought that an array of elements is organized with respect to figure and ground. When two areas share a common boundary, the figure is the distinct shape with clearly defined edges. The ground is what is left over, forming a background. All of these aspects of perception were thought to reflect organizing principles governing brain activity. For the Gestalt psychologists, "perception is the way it is because it shares the properties of the physical system [the brain] which gives rise to it" (Dember & Bagwell, 1985, p. 272).

Like von Helmholtz and Wundt, Wertheimer, Kohler, and Koffka found many everyday examples of contrast and assimilation (e.g., Koffka, 1935; Kohler, 1929). The similarity principle was the basis for cohesive forces that organize and simplify. For example, if some of the letters in a page of ordinary print are red in color, the total shape they make (say an X) is readily apparent and the similar red letters cohere and stand out from the black letters (i.e., contrast). The same letters in black form no shape since they would cohere equally with all other black marks on the page and would not stand out (Osgood, 1953) (i.e., assimilation). Analogously, a small gray field will appear whiter when it is surrounded by a black (i.e., contrast) than by a white field because the two fields are perceived as distinct units and differences between them are accentuated. For an ambiguous element falling within the contour of a field, there is a tendency to "iron out" the differences producing uniformity with the rest of the elements (i.e., assimilation). If the ambiguous element fell outside the contour, there was a tendency to see it as different from the others (i.e., contrast). For the Gestalters, contours defined the frame of reference.

The Gestalt concept of frame of reference was related to Hering's idea about a physiological equilibrium point, but for Hering the *action* was at the peripheral level. For the Gestalters, perception of figure–ground separation seemed unlikely to be a retinal or local phenomenon (see de Weert & van Kruysbergen, 1997; Festinger, Coren, & Rivers, 1970). Hence, assimilation and contrast for more complex judgments appeared to require processing at a higher level of the central nervous system.

The Gestalt psychologists seem to us to have offered more in the way of an explanation for assimilation and contrast than had von Helmholtz or Wundt, but it relied on the assumption of certain innate organizational tendencies. This seemed plausible with respect to perceptual illusions and relatively simple cognitive stimuli, but for more complex cognitive and social stimuli, simple applications of the law of similarity and proximity seemed less likely to suffice. The Gestalt emphasis on the frame of reference is perhaps their strongest intellectual legacy, especially for social psychologists.

PSYCHOPHYSICS AND CONTEXT EFFECTS

The experimental study of sensation and perception took several directions in the first five decades of the 20th century. Some researchers focused efforts on particular sensory systems (such as vision, taste, audition) to identify the physiological structures and processes underlining basic sensory phenomena (for review see Riggs, 1985). Others who adopted the Gestalt approach searched for organizing principles that might apply across the different senses and more complex stimuli. Still others extended the psychophysical approaches pioneered by Weber and Fechner in the 19th century.

Psychophysics studies the relation between sensory responses and the antecedent physical stimuli. Typically, in standard psychophysics experimental paradigms, research participants are presented with a series of stimuli (from the same category) varying along single or multiple dimensions and are asked to make successive judgments of a quantitative nature. Although psychophysicists began their research with relatively simple stimuli, such as color, brightness, and number, developments in scale measurement encouraged study of comparative judgments of more complex stimuli (Anderson, 1981; Marks & Algom, 1998; Stevens, 1958). The research and thinking of psychophysicists about context effects is most relevant to this historical survey.

Three Psychophysical Models

Three models of psychophysical scaling and judgment, with intellectual roots in psychophysics and attitude scale construction (e.g., Thurstone & Chave, 1929), have been important in the understanding of contrast, in particular. A common premise of the three models is that judgment of a target stimulus depends on certain statistical features of the context. The differences among the models lie in the particular statistical features that are critical for the judgment process. The reader is referred to Wedell et al., chapter 2, this volume for a more detailed description and comparison of these models and to Eiser's (1990) excellent monograph on social judgment.

Adaptation-Level Theory   Helson's (1947, 1964) adaptation-level theory posits that judgments are proportional to deviations from a comparison standard. This standard, also referred to as *adaptation level* (AL), is context-sensitive, as it is conceived as the mean of the stimuli presented within a contextual set. For example, if a consumer were evaluating the price of a particular convertible automobile, he would compare it with the mean price of other convertibles with which he was familiar. The consumer's AL depends on recent stimulus history or the presence of any perceptual anchors, and determines the price that is perceived as medium. The AL marks the organism's momentary and shifting state of adaptation to all relevant inputs (in this case, other convertibles) rather than an absolute threshold value. The assumption is that the individual uses the mean from instances, or AL, to judge a relevant stimulus and this creates a different perception of the stimulus. For example, if the convertible's price exceeds the AL, it should be perceived as relatively expensive; if the price is lower than the AL, it should be evaluated as a good bargain.

Stated differently, ratings of any individual stimulus will be lower when most of the other stimuli are greater and higher when most of the stimuli have lesser values on the dimension of judgment. Contrast occurs because of movement of the AL toward the mean of contextual stimuli. For example, if low valued stimuli are presented, they pull down the AL so that subsequent target stimuli are displaced upward relative to control conditions.

Although contrast effects seem to directly follow from AL theory, it does not obviously account for assimilation. In fact, most social psychological applications of Helson's theory (e.g., Brickman & Bulman, 1977; Brickman & Campbell, 1971) describe contrast effects but rarely mention the possibility of assimilation. Helson (1971) actually argued that assimilation and contrast are not antithetical phenomena; "if there is a spread [contrast] of judgments [in some parts of the scale], there must be compression [assimilation] in other parts" (p. 8). But assimilation requires a different explanation than AL and revisions of Helson's model have been unsuccessful in accounting for assimilation (see Parducci, Perrett, & Marsh, 1969). More recent reviewers, however, note that sequential effects occur in virtually all psychophysical tasks and tend to be assimilative in nature (Marks & Algom, 1998): "That is, the response to a given stimulus on the current trial tends to be greater when the stimulus [or response] on the previous trial was greater than the current one, smaller when the stimulus [response] on the previous trial was smaller" (p. 152). To add to the debate, there also is controversy among psychophysicists about whether these sequential effects have a component of contrast (DeCarlo, 1992; Staddon, King, & Lockhead, 1980).

On one point, Helson was resolute—changes in AL produced actual perceptual shifts (e.g., Helson & Kozaki, 1968). Stevens (1958), however, argued that Helson had merely demonstrated shifts in verbal or semantic labeling. For Stevens, contextual stimuli may change the meaning and use of the labels of the rating scale, but not the actual perception of the stimulus. "Very large" means something different in the context of elephants than of robins. This idea that context only influences the interpretation and use of scale labels (i.e., response selection) continues to be important (see Biernat & Manis, chapter 3, this volume; Mussweiler, chapter 7, this volume) and cannot be fully discounted. However, contrast phenomena have been empirically demonstrated in the absence of rating scales, which do not rely on self-reports (e.g., Dijksterhuis & van Knippenberg, 1998; Stapel & Suls, 2004), and in animal studies where changes in context influenced the reinforcing value of reward (Crespi, 1942; Sarris, 2006) (see Wedell et al., chapter 2, this volume).

Volkmann's Range Theory   Volkmann (1951) proposed another model under a different set of assumptions. Unlike AL theory, his range theory assumes that judgments are based on comparisons to specific instances rather than to a summary index, such as the mean. The critical specific instances were the highest and lowest values in the contextual set. The value ascribed to a stimulus is posited to depend on its relationship to these minimum and maximum values. In this approach, contrast is produced by inclusion of a low valued contextual stimulus that lowers the subjective minimum and hence displaces judgments of targets upward.

The idea that the reference standard includes the range of the contextual set (the highest and lowest values), as well as the mean, has intuitive appeal. Evidence supporting this approach manipulates the range in sets of values while holding the mean constant (Janiszewski & Lichtenstein, 1999; Niedrich, Sharma, & Wedell, 2001). The judgment of the mean value or target stimuli should vary according to the skew of the distribution. Some evidence supports the range model (Janiszewski & Lichtenstein, 1999). However, the next model to be described performs better in accounting for the empirical evidence.

Besides the difference with AL theory about whether the mean or range is the important reference point, Volkmann (1951) also thought that changes in the context (in this case, the range) exerted their effects via shifts in the meaning of the scale labels or endpoints, that is, in response selection. According to range theory, the language that people used changes with the context, but their actual perceptions do not.

Range-Frequency Theory   According to Parducci (1963, 1984, 1995), both the endpoints of the contextual series *and* the rank of the stimulus within the series play a role. Thus, in his approach, the location of a stimulus relative to the two extremes and also the relative frequency with which various stimuli are distributed (or skew) determine the evaluation of the target stimulus. This means that judges are assumed to compare a stimulus against all of the other relevant members of the contextual set. The resulting judgment represents a compromise between the range and frequency principles. The relative weights given to the range and frequency components depend on situational factors although typically both contribute equally (Parducci & Marshall, 1961; Wedell, Parducci, & Lane, 1990). However, if judges have to retrieve values from memory, it is assumed that extreme values will be more salient and easier to retrieve from memory. Consequently, in such situations the range principle will have more influence than the frequency principle. If all relevant stimuli are present, however, the frequency effect will be larger than the range effect.

In this model, contrast is exhibited when, for example, a student is more pleased about receiving 50 points on a test when the score distribution is positively skewed and ranges from 5 to 52 points than when it is negatively skewed and ranges from 10 to 60. In experimental tests, the range-frequency model performs better than the other two models (see Wedell et al., chapter 2, this volume). Like the other models, it seems to best account for contrast. A kind of assimilation is exhibited in sequential effects, however, as noted above (e.g., Cross, 1973; Ward & Lockhead, 1971).

The range-frequency theory originally assumed that the range and frequency principles operated mainly via response selection, that is, by contextual changes in the meaning of scale labels. Recently, Parducci (1968, 1995) allows for the possibility that context may actually change the perception and encoding of the stimulus (see Wedell et al., chapter 2, this volume).

Summary

Judgmental models suggest that contextual features, such as the mean, the range, or the skew of the distribution, can help to understand contrast phenomena. Crucial experimental tests have been conducted with simple stimuli, such as tones and geometrical shapes, but the general principles have been widely applied to sources of pleasure and pain, pay satisfaction, physical attractiveness, and life satisfaction (e.g., Brickman & Campbell, 1971; Parducci, 1995; Smith, Diener, & Wedell, 1989). The psychophysical models devote most of their attention to contrast, which tends to be considered the default option because it seems more robust and explainable than assimilation (see Stapel, Koomen, & van der Pligt, 1997, and Stapel, chapter 6, this volume, for a corrective). This emphasis on contrast may change as we move into social psychology perhaps because humans seek merger or unity with other humans.

SHERIF, ASCH, AND SOCIAL JUDGMENT

Sherif's Contributions

Social Influence in Ambiguous Situations   Muzifer Sherif, who was strongly influenced by the thinking and research of the Gestalt psychologists, is probably best known for his research on social influence and interpersonal relations. The frame of reference concept was dominant in his thinking. He recognized that in vague, ambiguous, or ill-defined situations people resort to contextual standards. In a classic experiment (Sherif, 1936), subjects were exposed to a visual illusion involving the apparent movement of a pinpoint of light and asked to make estimates about how far they saw the light move. After a few initial trials, other subjects also made estimates. Sherif found that subjects' estimates tended to converge after a few trials, showing that they influenced each other although there was no explicit pressure to do so. In another variation with similar procedures, except that experimental accomplices were introduced who had been trained to make extreme estimates, subjects' judgments of movement tended to converge with those of the accomplices. In fact, even after the other subjects or accomplices left the room and the subject continued the task, the others' estimates continued to exert influence. Sherif concluded that the social environment provided a context or frame of reference for judgment of ambiguous or ill-defined stimuli. For our purposes, this experimental demonstration might be thought of as a kind of assimilation effect because the subjects' judgments were displaced toward the others' estimates.

Social Judgment Theory of Attitudes   For Sherif, the frame of reference did not stem entirely from the social environment. The person's own attitudes and emotions also could serve as a frame of reference to both categorize and discriminate objects, persons, concepts, etc. This internal frame of reference became important in the theory that Sherif developed with Hovland (Sherif & Hovland, 1961) to explain persuasion on the basis of judgmental principles.

According to their social judgment theory, people make judgments about opinion positions and persuasion communications in the same way they evaluate the heaviness of weights or any other stimulus, that is, according to AL (Sherif, Taub, & Hovland, 1958). However, in the case of attitudes, the person's own attitude serves as the AL (or anchor) and the opinions expressed by others are either displaced toward (i.e., assimilation) or away from (i.e., contrast) the person's own position. There is a hypothesized critical range of similarity around the person's own position on an issue (latitude of acceptance) such that if a source's opinion falls within this range, it is perceptually distorted to be even closer than it really is and is judged to be fair, unbiased, and true. If the source's position lies outside this range and beyond a zone of indifference (latitude of noncommitment), then the opposite tends to happen; the source's opinion is distorted so that it is perceived as laying farther away than it really is—and it is judged as unfair, biased, and probably false. These effects are supposed to be strongest when the individual is highly involved with the issue (e.g., Hovland, Harvey, & Sherif, 1957; Sherif, Sherif, & Nebergall, 1965).

This theory had an interesting implication for attitude change. Maximal attitude change is expected when the message takes a position that falls in the zone of indifference. If the message promotes a position too far from the judge's own, it will be rejected and may even produce a boomerang effect. If the message is close to the judge's initial position, he/she will assimilate it to their own position. In such cases, even if the judge moves to the new position, the attitude cannot be very large because the difference was not initially very large. As a consequence, the greatest change should occur with an intermediate discrepancy that allows for assimilation and when the distance between the judge's initial position and the message is sufficiently wide to allow for appreciable change.

This theory has intriguing predictions but has not fared very well empirically (for review see Eiser & van der Pligt, 1984). Evidence for assimilation effects is weaker and more inconsistent than for contrast in the attitude domain. This may be connected to the fact that Sherif and Hovland's (1961) theory is based on psychophysics, and those models account for contrast effects better than assimilation effects. A second problem is that the theory assumes that the perception of the opinion communication is the critical factor; that is, the judge's own position directly influences where the communication is seen on the pro–con dimension. Other theories (Eiser & Stroebe, 1972; Eiser & van der Pligt, 1984) propose that the judge's position operates indirectly through the mediation of the judge's affective reaction to the communication. In the main, empirical evidence has provided better support for this alternative theory (e.g., Judd & Harackiewicz, 1980; Lambert & Wedell, 1991).

In spite of these problems, Sherif and Hovland's (1961) theory was a significant development because it brought assimilation and contrast to the attention of mainstream social psychology and provided inspiration for later efforts. Also, the idea that the self serves as a significant anchor for social perception and judgment was an important precursor of research of Dunning, Gilovich, Krueger, and Alicke, among others (e.g., Alicke, Dunning, & Krueger, 2005).

Intergroup Relations   In his later research, Sherif introduced the concepts of assimilation and contrast into the context of intergroup relations. In the Robbers' Cave Experiment conducted at a summer camp for teenage boys, he and his colleagues (Sherif, Harvey, White, Hood, & Sherif, 1961) initially created intergroup conflict by inducing contrast between groups, and then reduced the conflict and created cooperation by inducing assimilation. In the first phase of the experiment, Sherif assigned the boys to two different bunk houses, had them create names for their group (they chose Rattlers and Eagles), and held group competitions. The result was intergroup hostility, name-calling, and attribution of extremely negative attributes to the rival group—in other words, contrast. Then Sherif et al. arranged joint cooperative activities, which required the efforts of both groups for the mutual good (e.g., repairing the water supply for the camp) to promote assimilation of the two hostile groups. Cooperation on superordinate goals was associated with a diminution of hostilities, name-calling decreased, and perceptions of the rival group became more similar to one's own group. Thus, the intergroup cooperation changed perceptions of rival group members so they came to resemble the self—in other words, assimilation.

Sherif et al.'s (1961) group interventions were multifaceted and probably worked via several psychological routes, but his demonstration of assimilation and contrast in a group setting was very influential for the social psychology of groups and for social policy (e.g., Tajfel, 1978; Tajfel & Wilkes, 1963). The basic idea still is a key premise of social identity theory and research (e.g., Turner, 1991) and for finding ways to reduce intergroup hostility and foster cooperation.

Asch's Contributions

Asch (1946, 1952), a classmate of Sherif's, was also strongly influenced by the Gestalt perspective and is probably best known for his research on conformity and person perception. His studies of impression formation stand out as a demonstrations of assimilation in social judgment and are, in many ways, the precursors of the social cognition movement.

Asch (1946) began with the Gestalt premise that an impression of a person is not merely a summation of separate characteristics. Rather the characteristics are integrated because people are viewed as unified beings. As he wrote, even if the person is many-sided and complex, we try "to bring his characteristics into relation" (Asch, 1952, p. 207). In one of his experiments, subjects were read a list of traits said to belong to a person and were instructed to form an impression and write it down. In one such experiment, two different series of traits were created:

A. intelligent–industrious–impulsive–critical–stubborn–envious
B. envious–stubborn–critical–impulsive–industrious–intelligent

The two series were identical, but Series A opened with positive qualities and ended with negative qualities. The order was reversed in Series B. Asch found that subjects hearing Series A tended to form a positive impression of the individual and, while noting he had shortcomings, they did not seem serious. In contrast, subjects exposed to Series B perceived the person as having serious difficulties. Another finding was that ambiguous qualities like impulsive and critical in the middle of the series of traits took on a positive coloring in Series A, but took a distinct negative coloring when appearing in Series B. So it appeared that the initial terms seemed to establish a direction for subjects who fitted (i.e., shifted) later characteristics to the prevailing direction. In social psychology, this became known as the *primacy effect* in impression formation, with the practical implication that initial experiences with a person may have a lasting effect. For the present purposes, the primacy effect offers clear evidence of assimilation in impression formation whereby later traits were assimilated in the impression created by the earlier traits.

In other studies of impression formation, Asch (1946) demonstrated the special role of certain kinds of traits that strongly altered the interpretation of other traits. For example, replacing the trait "warm" with "cold," while keeping all of the other traits the same, had a significant effect on the resulting impression. Asch referred to traits such as warm and cold as *central* because they had such a large impact. For Asch, the findings supported an assimilative shift in meaning depending on the context. This research became an important inspiration for subsequent research on impression formation in the 1960s and 1970s (e.g., Anderson & Jacobson, 1965; Triandis & Fishbein, 1963). Asch's methods and systematic application of Gestalt principles to social psychological phenomena laid the foundation for the development of the social cognition movement.

FESTINGER AND SOCIAL COMPARISON THEORY

Social Comparison

Inclusion here of Festinger's (1954a, 1954b) social comparison theory might seem odd because he never explicitly discussed either assimilation or contrast. Only with the advantages of hindsight can we appreciate why, four decades after he published his theory, social comparison figures so prominently in current research on assimilation and contrast (see Mussweiler, chapter 7, this volume; Stapel, chapter 6, this volume; also Mussweiler, 2003; Mussweiler & Strack, 2000; Stapel et al., 1997).

Festinger's basic premise was that people need to know what they are capable of doing and whether their opinions are correct; this is commonly referred to as the *self-evaluation motive* by contemporary social psychologists (Wood, 1989). According to Festinger, people compare with others their opinions or abilities that cannot be directly tested in the environment. This comparison is assumed to lead to pressures toward uniformity. In the realm of opinion, uniformity refers to agreement with others and indicates that one's opinion is correct. For abilities, uniformity is a sign that one is capable of doing the same things that others can do. For evaluation of both abilities and opinions, Festinger posited that the pressure toward uniformity increases with the attraction, importance, and relevance of comparison others.

Perhaps the most well-known aspect of Festinger's theory was the similarity hypothesis. The basic idea, in the case of opinions, was that finding agreement (i.e., similarity) with others makes us feel more confident in our judgment. Observing others with similar abilities allows us to know what our own possibilities for action are.

Oddly, the connection of Festinger's similarity hypothesis to Sherif and Hovland's (1961) latitudes of acceptance and rejection was overlooked at the time (McGuire, 1969). This is unfortunate because it might have led researchers to pursue connections with the psychophysical models that were then being developed. We might speculate that the common ground was not appreciated because Festinger was interested in situations when the individual was uncertain about standing and sought social consensus. In Sherif and Hovland's theory, the individual was not uncertain; in fact, one's personal opinion served as the anchor or standard to evaluate other opinion positions.

Regardless of this missed opportunity, the hypothesized pressure toward uniformity is reminiscent of assimilation. One proposition in Festinger's theory is, "When a discrepancy exists with respect to opinions or abilities, there will be tendencies to change one's own position so as to move closer to others in the group" (1954a, p. 120). A discrepancy also might be resolved by changing "others in the group to bring them closer to oneself" (p. 120). Most of Festinger's examples and the empirical evidence he cited involved mutual social influence (such as persuasion attempts). Because this is *actual* change in judgment or opinion, this is not really assimilation in the sense we have described, however.

There is a suggestion of contrast in early comparison research. In his only comparison experiment using self-evaluation as a dependent variable (Festinger, Torrey, & Willerman, 1954), one person in a group of four was made to score below the others while the other three scored about equally (control subjects). Attractiveness of the group was also manipulated with a cover story. The prediction was that if subjects were made to feel very attracted to the group (presumably creating greater pressure toward uniformity), "the more strongly would those scoring below others feel that their ability was poor and the more strongly would those scoring above others feel that their ability was good" (p. 163). The results were consistent with this pattern showing contrast. Subjects' abilities did not change because they really had no opportunity, but their self-evaluations showed contrast from the other group members.

Shortly after Festinger published social comparison theory, he moved on to the theory of cognitive dissonance. His colleague Stanley Schachter, however, demonstrated how comparison is important for the psychology of affiliation (1959) and emotional states (Schachter & Singer, 1962; Schachter & Wheeler, 1962). Neither assimilation nor contrast figured prominently in that work. Not until the publication of Latane's (1966) *Studies in Social Comparison* Supplement did social comparison again receive systematic experimental attention.

One paper in the Supplement had direct relevance to assimilation. In the original theory, Festinger had posited that opinions and abilities operate somewhat differently. People want to find agreement with others because it suggests they are correct. However, for abilities, there is a unidirectional drive upward, motivating the person to be slightly better than others (only *slightly better*, according to Festinger, because the desire to be better was counteracted by the presumed pressure toward uniformity). Festinger, however, had no direct evidence for the unidirectional drive upward.

Wheeler (1966) presented data that were consistent with unidirectional drive upward in a paradigm where people after receiving their score could choose to see the actual score of someone else of a different rank. When subjects were motivated to think they were good, the likelihood of choosing to see the score of someone ranked above them (i.e., upward comparison) was greater. More relevant, 75% of the participants who made an upward comparison felt they were more similar to the person above them in the rank order than to the person below them. Only 36% of the participants who compared downward felt more similar to the person above them. Wheeler argued that, "When an individual is highly motivated, he assumes similarity with someone who appears to be slightly superior in the ability in question. By comparing his ability with that of the slightly superior individual, the comparer is attempting to confirm the similarity he has assumed. The comparer is attempting to prove to himself that he is almost as good as the very good ones" (p. 30). Wheeler used the term "assumed similarity" rather than "assimilation," but the two terms refer to the same general phenomenon, differing in that assumed similarity occurs before a comparison, and assimilation is the result of a comparison.

Despite this evidence, assumed similarity and assimilation received little systematic empirical attention from social comparison researchers during the 1960s. The reason for this lack of interest remains unclear, but perhaps at the time contrast seemed jazzier. Also, the contrastive effects of social comparison may have been more evident with respect to practical applications and therefore more researchable. Equity theory and relative deprivation theory, both conceptual cousins of social comparison theory, are about how contrastive relative standing with a reference group induces satisfaction or dissatisfaction with personal circumstances (Adams, 1965; Pettigrew, 1967). A classic example is that African-American soldiers during the Second World War responded more favorably to army life than did Caucasian soldiers because the former perceived they had "more comparative wealth and dignity" than their civilian black counterparts living in southern towns (Stouffer, Suchman, DeVinney, Star, & Williams, 1949, p. 563). White soldiers were more dissatisfied, however, because they tended to compare with their white counterparts in civilian life, who did not have to endure the trials of military life. Independent of the juicier examples of contrast, the Zeitgeist may not have been right for assimilation. When it was substantiated and better understood by social cognition researchers two decades later, comparison research was re-examined in this new light (see below).

By the beginning of the 1970s, an experiment was published that found compelling evidence for contrast in social comparison. Morse and Gergen (1970) observed that social comparisons can be a potential source of instability in self-concept. In particular they posited that casual exposure to another person may be sufficient to produce a momentary impact on a person's concept of self. The researchers demonstrated this phenomenon by having job applicants encounter an accomplice whose personal appearance was either highly desirable (Mr. Clean) or highly undesirable (Mr. Dirty). Under the guise of collecting information about the applicants, subjects completed self-esteem scales both before and after exposure to Mr. Clean/Mr. Dirty. Morse and Gergen found that exposure to Mr. Clean produced a decrease in self-esteem and exposure to Mr. Dirty produced an increase in self-esteem. In other words, the job applicant/subjects showed demonstrable contrast effects. As the authors write, "As a result of others' characteristics appearing more desirable or less desirable than his own, a person's generalized self-estimate is displaced downward or upward" (p. 154).

The Morse and Gergen (1970) experiment had two long-term consequences. First, whereas Festinger's original theory was narrowly focused on assessments of specific abilities and opinions, Morse and Gergen recognized the relevance of social comparison to the self-concept. Second, the comparison effects found in their experiment were contrastive in nature.

THE ERAS OF ATTITUDE CHANGE, SOCIAL PERCEPTION, AND SELF-PSYCHOLOGY

Shortly after Festinger left social comparison theory, social psychology was dominated by research on attitude change. Theories emphasizing cognitive consistency, such as Festinger's theory of cognitive dissonance (1957) and the source–message–target model advanced by Hovland and his colleagues (Hovland, Janis, & Kelley, 1953), inspired enormous amounts of research from the mid-1950s into the 1970s. The concepts of assimilation and contrast were not completely ignored, because by then they were part of the social psychological canon, but they played minor roles (except in the Sherif & Hovland model), despite the creativity of some of the research efforts (see Campbell, Hunt, & Lewis, 1957; Manis, 1967).

In the 1970s (as McGuire, 1969, had predicted) social perception and attribution processes became popular. Researchers renewed their acquaintance with Asch's classic impression formation experiments and tested alternatives to the shift in meaning explanation he favored. But, as in the era of attitude change, assimilation and contrast remained interesting phenomena that were applied sporadically, but were not big news beside such things as the fundamental attribution error (Ross, 1977) or the actor/observer bias (Jones & Nisbett, 1971).

As attribution theory and research progressed in the 1970s and 1980s, connections to other theories were made. For present purposes, the most noteworthy effort was Goethals and Darley's (1977) attributional reformulation of social comparison theory. By using attribution theory to understand social comparison of opinion and ability evaluation, they refined the similarity hypothesis by showing what kinds of similar dimensions or attributes are related to performance or opinion. This related attribute approach provided clarification about the similarity hypothesis and reinvigorated research about self-evaluation via social comparison (Wheeler & Zuckerman, 1977). The attributional perspective has a key element of assimilation. Comparing with someone similar on related attributes (such as age or level of practice) can be seen as a form of assimilation: "I have the same level of practice as you, so I expect to have the same performance as you," (see the Proxy model for a recent elaboration and extension; Martin, Suls, & Wheeler, 2002; Suls, Martin, & Wheeler, 2000; Wheeler, Martin, & Suls, 1997). The comparison is made to confirm the assumed similarity of performance and, if confirmed, "All is right with the world." Unfortunately, the connection to assimilation phenomena in other areas of social psychology, cognitive psychology, and psychophysics was not fully appreciated at the time.

By the early 1980s, the seeds planted by Morse and Gergen (1970) bore fruit. Wills (1981) published a paper on downward comparison in which he proposed that people who experience a threat to self-esteem can increase subjective well-being by comparing with someone less fortunate. Although he presented no new empirical evidence, Wills presented an impressive review of studies on fear affiliation, comparison choice, scapegoating, and projection as support. Interestingly, Wills never explicitly used the word *contrast*, but the implication of his analysis was that people feel better after comparing with someone worse-off because of the contrast with the other person. This analysis also implied that upward comparisons would make people feel worse about themselves. Downward comparison theory received extra impetus with the publication of a paper showing that women with breast cancer reported feeling better after comparison with other women who were worse-off (Wood, Taylor, & Lichtman, 1985). These two developments inspired a decade of intense empirical activity, mainly of correlational descriptive studies about how distressed populations use downward comparison to repair well-being (see Buunk & Gibbons, 1997; Suls & Wills, 1991).

Another development was Tesser's (1988; Tesser & Paulhus, 1983) Self-Evaluation Maintenance Model (SEM), which contributed by equating social comparison with contrast. In his model, there are two competing processes: reflection and comparison. The first of three interdependent variables is *performance*. To the extent that performance is high, one achieves a higher self-esteem or positive affect through reflection (basking in reflected glory), and one suffers a lower self-evaluation through comparison. *Closeness* to the other person (unit relatedness; Heider, 1958) increases both reflection and comparison. Whether one reflects or compares depends upon the *relevance* of the dimension. The greater the relevance, the stronger is the tendency to compare rather than to reflect. A dimension is relevant if it is important to the individual's self-definition. In the 1988 paper, Tesser showed how individuals may try to change performance, closeness, or relevance in order to maintain a positive self-evaluation. What is notable for present purposes is that assimilation (i.e., change in self-evaluation) does not exist in Tesser's model. The comparison process always leads to contrast.

The reflection process leads to positive affect but not to increased self-evaluation *on the comparison dimension*. For example, we may bask in the reflected glory of a close friend who sings in national barbershop quartet contests only if singing at that high competitive level has no personal relevance for us (see also Cialdini et al., 1976). This point is important because sometimes researchers consider (mistakenly we think) Tesser's reflection to be just another form of assimilation. Although in writing this history a wide range of perceptual shifts have been considered as examples of assimilation (consistent with Bless et al.'s, 2003, definition), there is a reason to adopt a stricter definition of assimilation as "self-evaluative movement toward the target on the comparison dimension" in cases of self-evaluation via social comparison. To return to our example, having a friend who is a barbershop Pavarotti may make us feel good because of the bond, but should not necessarily prompt us to think we can (or should) sing outside of the shower. The difference between a comparison changing a domain-specific self-evaluation versus improving mood has real meaning with respect to the self so a narrower definition of assimilation seems needed. The parallel situation does not exist for judgments about other persons or things, so a broader definition of assimilation is sufficient for those. (We should acknowledge that not all social psychologists would agree with us; for them, both outcomes are assimilation phenomena, just different subtypes.)

Although some researchers conflated assimilation with Tesser's reflection, there is a sense in which the confusion may have had a good consequence. It represented a misunderstanding of the SEM model, but the term assimilation was reintroduced to social comparison and eventually research was published which showed that exposure to better comparison targets can increase self-evaluations.

THE ERA OF SOCIAL COGNITION

In the 1980s, social psychologists became very interested in cognitive contributions to social perceptions, judgments, and social behavior (Fiske & Taylor, 1983). Earlier research on attribution already was influenced by findings in cognitive psychology, but explicit application of cognitive psychological theories and methods to social behavior began in the era of social cognition (e.g., Hastie et al., 1980). Assimilation became a phenomenon at the forefront of many of these efforts.

Priming and Cognitive Accessibility

In the late 1970s and 1980s, E. Tory Higgins and Robert Wyer independently conducted research inspired by the *New Look* in perception movement of the 1950s and by research on experimental priming by contemporary cognitive psychologists (Meyer, & Schvaneveldt, 1971; Neely, 1976, 1991; Posner & Snyder, 1975). One of the New Look researchers, Jerome Bruner (1957), proposed that perception is a categorization process. In making this assertion, he was emphasizing that much of perception occurs at a central level of cognitive processing (rather than at the level of peripheral sense organs). Perhaps Bruner's most important idea for social cognition was that the greater the cognitive accessibility of stored category knowledge (because the person either uses the information habitually or it is made salient in the situation), the more likely a new stimulus will be recognized as a member of the accessible category. Cognitive psychologists experimentally demonstrated that increasing a category's cognitive accessibility, for example, by prior use or subliminal presentation, will increase the probability for a new, ambiguous stimulus to be interpreted consistently with the accessible category. A procedure that stimulates or activates some stored knowledge is known as *priming* (Neely, 1976, 1991).

In an early social priming experiment, Srull and Wyer (1979) had research participants perform a word comprehension task where they unscrambled four-word sequences to create three-word sentences. When unscrambled, some of these sentences described behaviors related to a trait construct—in this experiment, hostility. Srull and Wyer assumed that constructing such sentences would cognitively activate, or prime, the concept of hostility. In some experimental conditions, participants were given more sentences describing hostile behaviors than in other conditions so the effects of frequency and intensity of priming could be tested. It was assumed that the more frequent the priming, the greater the cognitive accessibility of trait hostility. Then in a supposedly unrelated experiment, participants read a passage describing a target's activities and were asked to form an impression. Some of these activities were purposely ambiguous with respect to hostility (e.g., complained to a store clerk). Then participants rated the target on several dimensions, including some that were related to hostility. Srull and Wyer found that the target's behaviors were rated as more hostile as the number of hostile sentences produced earlier increased.

The researchers had anticipated criticism that research participants may have discerned the relationship between the two experiments and believed they should make target ratings consistent with hostility. However, extensive debriefing revealed little evidence that participants were suspicious (see also Higgins, Rholes, & Jones, 1977). In any case, a replication and extension by Bargh and Pietromonaco (1982) primed constructs subliminally, that is, outside subject awareness. In this case, participants were both unaware of the association between the priming events and the second (interpretation and rating) study and of the occurrence of the priming events. Nonetheless, the strength of participants' ratings increased with the frequency of priming. In sum, whether subjects were aware or unaware of the primed category information, they were likely to assimilate new ambiguous information toward the primed category.

These results are not exceptional; an extensive body of research has demonstrated consistent effects of priming on subsequent impressions (see Higgins, 1996; for a meta-analysis see DeCoster & Claypool, 2004) and even on behavior. For example, participants primed with the concept of rudeness through sentence completions were later more rude to the experimenter. Participants who were subliminally exposed to words associated with the elderly stereotype, subsequently walked more slowly (Bargh, Chen, & Burrows, 1996). The extension to behavior seems very different from the definition of assimilation as instances when *perceptions* or *judgments* are displaced toward the context. However, social cognition researchers propose that just as priming increases the accessibility of stereotypic knowledge, it also can activate corresponding action tendencies, which are thought to follow the same laws as concepts (Carver, Ganellen, Froming, & Chambers, 1983).

Theoretical Models for Priming Effects

Three main theoretical perspectives consider how activation of one knowledge unit (e.g., a mental construct) affects the activation potential of another through priming. According to the excitation-transfer model (Higgins, Bargh, & Lombardi, 1985), using mental constructs tends to excite relevant mental representations. Priming a representation increases its excitation level and this extra excitation makes the construct easier to bring to consciousness and thereby more likely to be used in subsequent judgment.

An alternative view is Srull and Wyer's (1989) "storage bins" model that conceives of long-term memory as a set of bins containing mental constructs. To use a mental construct, its representation must first be located in the appropriate bin and then brought to awareness. Whenever a construct is taken from a bin and used, the original is left in its original location and a *copy* is placed on the top of the *stack* of representations in the bin. In subsequent situations, the individual looks through the stack in the relevant bin for a matching construct, starting with those at the top. Priming effects occur because prior exposure to a construct creates copies at the top of the relevant bins, making the construct easier to access.

These two perspectives share elements, but do make some different predictions (Higgins, 1996). For example, the storage bin model assumes a construct will remain on the top of the bin as long as other constructs in the bin are not activated. Thus, a construct will remain accessible and influence interpretation of an ambiguous stimulus regardless of the prime-to-stimulus interval if related constructs are not retrieved in the interim. The other model, however, assumes that excitation immediately starts to decay after priming so construct accessibility should decrease as the priming-to-stimulus delay increases. Although research has tried to evaluate these differential predictions, there has been no clear empirical "winner," and both models have undergone modifications to accommodate empirical findings. These extensions would take us too far afield, however (see Higgins, 1996; Smith, Stewart, & Buttram, 1992).

Both the excitation-transfer and storage bin models are referred to as *symbolic models*, in part because the strength of a construct depends on the strength of a discrete mental representation. A third, more recent approach (Conrey & Smith, in press; Smith & DeCoster, 1998) is based on connectionism (Rumelhart, McClelland, & PDP, 1986; see also the compound-cue explanation of McKoon & Ratcliff, 1992), in which representations of information are assumed to be distributed across units (i.e., neural networks). In these models, memory and knowledge for things are stored in the connections between units; concepts are actually patterns of activation over nodes. Applied to priming, a construct is accessible when its associated representation reaches a certain level of activation across the nodes. This pattern of activity (i.e., the concept) is determined partly by the strength of the external stimulus and partly by the connection strengths of the links. It is assumed that with repetitions of the pattern, the connection weights between nodes make the concept easier to reproduce in the future. Exposure to a prime makes it easier to produce the pattern of neural activity corresponding to the primed concept.

At the current time, which of the three models provides the best explanation for priming effects is unclear based on available evidence although the connectionist approach may provide the most parsimonious account (Smith & DeCoster, 1998) for effects of such factors as priming-to-stimulus interval, frequency of the prime, etc. The situation is more complex, however, when it is recognized that contrast effects also sometimes emerge in priming paradigms—the topic of the next section.

When Priming Produces Contrast

The original priming experiments found reliable evidence of assimilation, but one might question why contrast was not just as likely an outcome. Srull and Wyer (1980) speculated that priming hostility could have lead to the target's (ambiguous) behaviors to be perceived as *less* hostile—resulting in contrast, rather than assimilation. They suggested more research was needed to resolve this question.

Subsequent research (reviewed in detail in Martin, chapter 9, this volume) showed that one determining factor is how aware people are of the priming events. When constructs are primed blatantly rather than subtly, contrast is more likely to result than assimilation (Martin, 1986; Martin & Achee, 1992). Similarly, if subjects have a strong memory of a recent prime, then they are more likely to show contrast, but those who forget about the priming event exhibit assimilation (Lombardi, Higgins, & Bargh, 1985). Another factor concerns the extremity of the prime. If people are primed with extreme exemplars (e.g., Hitler, Attila the Hun), contrast effects typically result, but with moderate exemplars as primes, assimilation is more common (Herr, Sherman, & Fazio, 1983).

Two ideas have been dominant in attempts to account for these different patterns. Priming events can serve as interpretative frames (as described above) *or* as reference points or standards relative to the judged stimulus (Higgins, 1996; Srull & Wyer, 1980). The later idea is reminiscent of the psychophysics models and Sherif and Hovland's (1961) theory. When a prime (anchor) is extreme, then an ambiguous stimulus falls within the latitude of rejection and should be contrasted. If the prime is moderate or neutral, the ambiguous stimulus will fall within the latitude of acceptance and will be assimilated to the prime. Thus, a prime functions either as a standard or an interpretative frame depending on whether the prime is extreme or moderate (Interpretation Comparison Model; see Stapel, chapter 6, this volume). When a prime serves as a comparison standard or scale anchor and leads to displacement away from the context, this is referred to as *anchoring contrast* (DeCoster & Claypool, 2004; Stapel et al., 1997; Stapel, Martin, & Schwarz, 1998).

The other (not mutually exclusive) explanation focuses on the person's awareness of the priming event (Martin, 1986). With subtle priming, people are unaware the construct has been recently activated. So when the construct is elicited in the context of the ambiguous stimulus, "they are likely to infer that it is just their own spontaneous reaction to the stimulus" (Higgins, 1996, p. 150). But if the construct is blatantly primed, the person might conclude that the reaction is the result of the priming event. To counteract this perceived bias, the individual actively avoids using the primed concept so the interpretation of the stimulus is contrasted from the prime, or *correction contrast* (DeCoster & Claypool, 2004; Stapel et al., 1997).

Before moving on, Wegener and Petty's (1995) research on peoples' naïve theories about bias is relevant and should be mentioned here. These researchers observe that people have naïve beliefs about the influence of biasing information on their judgments. These beliefs, whether correct or not, influence whether they make corrections to their spontaneous judgments. As we have seen, beliefs about the effect of a blatant prime may prompt the person to make the judgment of the stimulus more different from the prime (correction contrast) (Martin, 1986). Wegener and Petty recognized that there is also another possibility. People also may believe that a prime can bias judgment to make something seem more dissimilar to the prime than it actually is (i.e., contrast). Under such circumstances, people may perform "correction assimilation." Acknowledgment that correction can go both ways, based on commonsense beliefs about biasing information, suggests there is an important role for deliberative, nonautomatic processes in understanding assimilation–contrast.

A major issue is which outcome is the default option—assimilation or contrast. Our impression from reading the empirical literature is that the priming paradigm most frequently elicits assimilation; contrast emerges more often from correction that involves awareness and deliberation (DeCoster & Claypool, 2004; Stapel et al., 1997). More will be said about default and correction as options in the next section on the inclusion/exclusion model.

In the last 15 years, the role of awareness and extremity of primes on assimilation and contrast has been studied extensively. Initial research concerned impression formation and social perception, but has been extended to social behavior and self-evaluation. Several of these research programs are reviewed in later chapters. These efforts all share the emphasis on cognitive accessibility and the importation of cognitive experimental methods to the study of assimilation and contrast in the social psychological domain.

Many social cognition researchers have tended to ignore the psychophysical models described earlier. We think this is unfortunate because the psychophysics models are every bit as cognitive as the research associated with Asch, the New Look in perception and information processing models (see Wedell et al., chapter 2, this volume; Stapel, chapter 6, this volume). This lack of contact may be the result of psychophysics and cognitive psychology having historically represented different intellectual territories and using different methodologies, as noted originally by Stapel et al. (1997). A better appreciation of their common history might bring them into closer collaboration.

The Inclusion/Exclusion Model

The inclusion/exclusion model (Schwarz & Bless, 1992) shares elements with the other social cognitive approaches, but places emphasis on the role of categorization processes. The basic premise is that assimilation occurs when the target stimulus and the contextual stimuli are assigned to the same category (i.e., inclusion); contrast occurs when they are assigned to different categories (i.e., exclusion). If any information is potentially relevant to the representation of the target, the default is inclusion, leading to assimilation. Only when features of the situation suggest that contextual information should not be used is it excluded or subtracted (similar to Martin, 1986). Thus, a relatively automatic process produces assimilation, but a more effortful correction process leads to contrast.

The model also stipulates three factors, any one of which will lead to exclusion of the contextual information and thereby result in contrast. The first factor, already mentioned, is when people think the information was made salient by an irrelevant influence and should be discounted or subtracted (e.g., Martin, 1986; Strack, Schwarz, Bless, Kübler, & Wänke, 1993).

A second factor concerns norms of conversational conduct; specifically information is excluded when its repeated use would violate norms of redundancy. This may be the case when we have already answered a specific question (e.g., pertaining to marital satisfaction) and are subsequently asked a more general question (e.g. regarding general life satisfaction). In this case, we may include the information brought to mind by the specific question to answer the general question if the two are perceived as unrelated. This inclusion would produce an assimilation effect. But if the two questions are perceived as part of the same conversational context, respondents may try to avoid redundancy by deliberately excluding information that they have already provided in the response to the specific question. This would produce a contrast effect (Schwarz, 1996; Schwarz, Strack, & Mai, 1991).

Finally, contextual information is not used when it is perceived to be unrepresentative of the target. For example, if the information represents an extreme example then it will not be considered because it is dissimilar to the target. If all three factors are present then the target is assimilated to the context.

The inclusion/exclusion model has produced a large body of empirical evidence and served as a foundation for more specialized models, for example in the area of self-evaluation (see Stapel, chapter 6, this volume). (The reader is referred to Schwarz and Bless, chapter 5, this volume, for a detailed presentation.) It is interesting that psychophysics models suggest that contrast is the more common outcome, but the inclusion/exclusion model tends to assume that assimilation is the default option. More recent approaches (see Mussweiler, chapter 7, this volume; Stapel, chapter 6, this volume) appreciate both.

SOCIAL COMPARISON REVISITED

By the 1990s, empirical evidence for assimilation provided by social cognition researchers started to influence comparison researchers. If assimilation was a common phenomenon in other areas of the social domain, such as person perception, then why should social comparison be an exception? In addition, there were reasons to begin to question some dominant assumptions of comparison researchers. An important paper by Collins (1996) noted that the popular emphasis on self-enhancement and downward comparison during the 1980s made two assumptions: "(1) the evaluative implications of comparison are intrinsic to its direction [i.e., downward comparisons increase feelings of self-regard while upward comparison decrease them]; and (2) the comparison processes involve contrasting one's abilities or attributes with those of others" (p. 159). However, some of the old empirical studies reviewed by Wills (1981) and research published afterward no longer seemed so convincing that downward comparison uniformly produced positive self-regard (e.g., Buunk, Collins, Taylor, Van Yperen, & Dakoff, 1990). Collins reviewed a variety of studies from different areas suggesting that upward comparisons need not decrease self-regard and that assimilation with upward comparison sources may actually increase self-evaluations. Specifically, if a comparer looks to an upward target and has the expectation that he or she will be similar to the target, then the comparer may find it so (see Manis, Biernat, & Nelson, 1991; Manis & Paskewitz, 1984). Collins gives the example of David who is 5′3″ and Nancy who is 5′4″ (2000, p. 163). Although Nancy is objectively taller than David, he can conclude he is about the *same height* as Nancy by perceiving the difference as very small. In this example, David changes his self-view by upward assimilation.

In Collins' review, the significance of the earlier study by Wheeler (1966) finding evidence of assumed similarity with superior performers was more clearly discerned. She also described direct evidence provided by Brown, Novick, Lord, and Richards (1992), who were actually the first to use the word *assimilation* in the social comparison literature. They found that "self-appraisals are jointly affected by another person's characteristics and our relationship to that person" (p. 725). Low self-esteem females who had the same birthday as an attractive comparison target female assimilated their own attractiveness ratings toward that target. If they did not have the same birthday, the subjects contrasted their attractiveness ratings away from her. The authors argued that this was different from Tesser's (1988) reflection process because the self-evaluation maintenance (SEM) model deals only with overtly competitive situations, and reflection occurs only when the relevance of the dimension is low for the comparer (see our earlier comments in the section "The Eras of Attitude Change, Social Perception, and Self-Psychology"). The Brown et al. procedure involved no competition and we can assume attractiveness was relevant to college-age females. The findings seem to be the result of a unit relationship (Heider, 1958) that, once established through a shared birthday, causes the characteristics of one of the entities to extend to the other entity.

Soon, more research appeared which also was interpreted as evidence for upward assimilation. Lockwood and Kunda (1997) had first- and fourth-year students read a newspaper article about an outstanding fourth-year student of matching major and gender. The student was multidimensionally outstanding, with a superb academic record and involvement in student government, sports, volunteer activities, leadership, and community involvement. In a control condi- tion, the students were not exposed to any target. The dependent variable was self-ratings on 10 adjectives relevant to general career success. For the fourth-year students, the superstar had no effect on self-ratings, but for the first-year students, those exposed to the superstar rated themselves considerably higher. A follow-up study showed that the superstar effect occurred only for first-year students with a malleable theory of intelligence, suggesting that the first-year students were looking forward to becoming as successful as the comparison target. This is interesting research in part because the attainability of the reward is made apparent, and the inspirational aspect of the target is thereby distilled.

Lockwood and Kunda's (1997) documentation of the effects of role models and superstars was a creative step. The question is whether they obtained evidence for upward assimilation, however. As we inquire elsewhere (Wheeler & Suls, in press), has assimilation occurred (i.e., my traits and abilities are currently high and similar to the target's), or has optimism been created about the possibility of having similar traits and abilities in the future, or has the participant simply been put in a good mood by hearing of the success of another person he or she is not in competition with (see also Collins' 2000 critique, pp. 162–163)? All of these outcomes are reminiscent of assimilation, broadly defined, but we wonder whether this broad definition may lump together outcomes which have different implications.

Despite these ambiguities, the larger point for this history is that, although unappreciated for decades, assimilation was recognized as a potential outcome of comparison (Suls, Martin, & Wheeler, 2002). There are two sides to social comparison—assimilation and contrast. Several chapters in this volume present research and theories about the factors that determine which outcome is exhibited in social comparison.

THE PRESENT ERA

As we have seen, contemporary research on assimilation and contrast in social psychology shows theories and methods of cognitive psychology that can facilitate the understanding of social perception, social judgment, and social behavior. Some approaches tend to emphasize the contribution of cognitive accessibility, others emphasize categorization processes, and still others borrow strongly from psychophysical models. Perspectives also differ with respect to the role of motivational and interpersonal factors and of implicit versus explicit cognitive processing.

In addition to differences in emphasis, social cognition approaches to assimilation and contrast have been extended and adapted to a variety of domains, such as self-evaluation, social perception, attitudes, prejudice, and interpersonal attraction. Extensions to new and different domains frequently necessitate the addition of special elements and the identification of boundary conditions. Nonetheless, current research on a diverse range of topics share elements, and it is not far-fetched that a more general theory of assimilation and contrast may be feasible in the future. Narrow- and medium-range theories have been dominant in social psychology for four decades. When we recall the grand theories from our "History and Systems" graduate courses, we experience a pleasant nostalgia.

LESSONS

It is said that learning about the errors of the past can help to avoid repeating them. Educating ourselves about the history of assimilation and contrast has taught us two lessons.

Lesson #1

Unlike some concepts in social psychology that were unique creations of the field (cognitive dissonance would be one prime example), assimilation and contrast originated with our colleagues in sensation and perception. For that reason alone, the social psychology of assimilation–contrast should not have been a parochial field of study. But for two decades, social comparison researchers experienced tunnel vision with respect to assimilation (Kruglanski & Mayseless, 1990; Wills & Suls, 1991). Even with the New Look in perception and a conceptual cousin, social judgment theory (Sherif & Hovland, 1961), it took too long to see that comparison had two sides—assimilation and contrast. Several of the contributors to this volume blazed that trail.

Some parochialism also can be seen among social cognition researchers. Although they have been keen on the cognitive revolution, social cognitivists have made few connections to psychophysics models. This may result from the disjuncture between methodologies: Social cognition researchers rarely employ the repeated stimulus presentations and within-subject designs popular among psychophysicists. Also, social psychologists tend to use richer, more complex stimuli, which may preclude the successive presentations employed in psychophysics. It seems unlikely, however, that these differences between the fields are insurmountable. In any case, there is good reason to try to bridge the gap. For some social cognitive researchers, assimilation is often considered the conceptual default option, but for some psychophysicists contrast is the default. This is a delicious puzzle for future researchers. The foundations for a conceptual resolution can be found in Mussweiler (chapter 7), Stapel (chapter 6), and Biernat and Manis (chapter 3) in this volume.

There also is the need to be aware of the boundary conditions of the phenomena borrowed from other fields. Although lexical priming—the direct inspiration for social priming experiments—is a replicable empirical phenomenon, its occurrence and magnitude depend on several variables. A few are the interval between the prime and the stimulus, the relationship between the prime and the stimulus (e.g., category-name and exemplar; associatively related but from different categories, e.g., rake and leaf), and whether the target is a high- versus low-frequency word (Neely, 1991). Experiments have documented that priming *can* occur across many social judgment, self-evaluative, and behavioral domains, but the robustness of the effect in the context of noisy or suboptimal conditions is unclear. There also must be conditions when perception and judgment are displaced neither toward nor away from the context.

Receptivity to new formulations is also important. As noted earlier, alternative models of priming based on distributed processing or connectionism have been proposed as alternatives to the symbolic (i.e., spreading activation) models of priming that were once dominant. New related phenomena also must be recognized. For example, a negative priming effect has been documented in cognitive psychology (Fox, 1995; May, Kane, & Hasher, 1995). This refers to impairment in responding to an item people have recently ignored. Total time to name colors in a list of Stroop words is slower if each color corresponds to the distractor immediately preceding it in the list. For example, it takes longer to respond "red" to a red stimulus printed in *green* if it is preceded by the word *red* printed in blue than it did if it was preceded by the word *yellow* printed in blue. That is, selective inhibition of distracting objects during selective attention seems to have unconscious carry-over effects. Does this mean that social perceptions can be similarly effected? If initially prompted to ignore race as a factor, will the category of race be inhibited and therefore excluded from the evaluation, resulting in contrast (see Macrae, Bodenhausen, & Milne, 1995)? Negative priming has not yet been extensively considered by social psychologists interested in assimilation and contrast (but see Glaser, chapter 10, this volume). (For other relevant phenomena from cognitive psychology, see repetition priming and anti-priming effects; Neely, VerWys, & Kahan, 1998; Marsolek, Schnyer, Deason, Ritchley, & Verfaellie, in press).

The general point is that there is a need for researchers to be keenly aware of developments in their own field as well as the ones from which they borrow. Of course, there is an irony here. Distinctive, research niches—the counterparts of the Eagles and Rattlers— in the scientific enterprise probably develop partly because of assimilation and contrast processes. Working at the edge where figure and ground can barely be discerned is precarious; at least, we suspect that is one implication of Gestalt psychology. Nonetheless, at the risk of homilizing, researchers need to try their best to resist the consequences of the very assimilation-contrast phenomena they seek to understand.

Lesson #2

In this chapter, we adopted broad definitions of assimilation and contrast—perceptions or judgments of a stimulus are displaced toward or away from the context—to permit us to review the history of several fields under a larger conceptual umbrella and to be consistent with other writers (Bless et al., 2003), including other contributors to this volume. Perceptions and judgments, which are susceptible to assimilation and contrast, come in many varieties, however, and may not all show the same effects.

One example comes from a study by Buunk and Ybema (2003), who exposed Dutch married women to a description by another married woman of her either happy or unhappy marriage. Affect was more positive following an upward comparison, but subjective evaluation of the participant's relationship was lower. Other studies also find that different kinds of outcomes move in different directions. Stapel and Koomen (2000) exposed subjects to distinct (a person exemplar; e.g., Einstein) or indistinct (a trait; e.g., intelligence) superior or inferior comparison sources. The researchers also manipulated the degree to which participants believed the comparison dimension was mutable or not. They posited that subjects would exhibit assimilation when they thought the self was mutable. Participants contrasted their intelligence from a superior target and assimilated their intelligence to the indistinct prime of intelligence when the self was mutable. When the dependent variable was mood, however, participants showed more positive mood when intelligence was primed, regardless of mutability, whereas mood was unaffected by person priming. For our purposes, this is a clear demonstration that upward assimilation of self-assessments on performance dimensions is not necessarily matched by affective responses. Earlier, we made the same observation with respect to the interpretation of Lockwood and Kunda's (1997) studies on exposure to superstars.

We do not have a comprehensive answer about why assimilation or contrast sometimes occurs for one type of outcome dimension but not for others. Models such as Mussweiler's and Biernat and Manis' posit that objective judgments are less susceptible to contrast effects than subjective scales and they have their theoretical reasons. But even among different kinds of subjective rating scales, results are heterogeneous. In some empirical cases, the differences were predicted on theory (see Stapel & Suls, 2004, Study 4), but in other instances the differences across outcomes have been glossed over or ignored.

In a recent survey of the literature on assimilation in social comparison (Wheeler & Suls, in press), we identified several kinds of outcomes measured in recent studies of assimilation and contrast: (single) attribute evaluations, global evaluative, mood, and behavior. Our advice for researchers was not to assume that all outcomes will move in the same direction and not to gloss over them if differences are indicated. In the past, some social psychological researchers have lumped outcomes together and equated assimilation with Tesser's reflection. Feeling good because one knows Mick Jagger's friend is not the same as believing one can perform before crowds in Madison Square Garden. In addition, reflection according to Tesser can only produce a positive glow; certain kinds of assimilation or contrast, however, can conceivably lead to negative mood or negative self-evaluation.

Understanding whether judgment, affect, and behavior are displaced toward or away from the context, to what degree and on what dimensions, is a challenging scientific task. The other chapters in this volume describe a variety of approaches to this challenge and document a variety of outcomes.

We do not pretend to have a solution to the "disparate outcomes problem," but we offer a suggestion for future research. Marks and Algom (1988), cognitive psychophysicists, observe that there are different stage theories of psychophysical processing and "acknowledge the possibility that context can affect processes occurring . . . in early sensory transduction, in later perceptual encoding, possible cognitive recoding and in decision response" (p. 148). Another psychophysicist, Victor Sarris (2006), suggests that context effects (such as assimilation and contrast) may represent a combination of different stage-processing effects. We are doubtful about the role of sensory transduction for the assimilation–contrast of complex social stimuli, but it cannot be entirely ruled out. In any case, different combinations of processing at the other stages are entirely plausible, as discussed by Wedell et al., chapter 2, this volume. Learning how they combine may increase our understanding of the different effects sometimes evidenced across outcomes.

CONCLUSION

Histories of psychology can be boring, but we hope this one has not been. We were initially surprised and frustrated about how challenging it was to find and connect the dots of this intellectual and empirical odyssey. All of the puzzles posed by assimilation and contrast are not solved, but perhaps your level of confusion is now more sophisticated than it was. Knowing where we started is never a bad idea, especially for phenomena that are so pervasive that they can be found in the pages of a social psychology text, an early 20th-century novel, or a recent copy of the *New York Times*.

ACKNOWLEDGMENTS

Preparation of this chapter was partly supported by National Science Foundation Grant BCS-99–10592 to Jerry Suls and by Australian Research Council grant DPO449717 to Ladd Wheeler. The authors wish to thank Renny Martin for her helpful comments on an earlier draft and Gregg Oden for his suggestions. We are also grateful to Eliot Smith and Paul Windschitl, who shared their ideas about priming and assimilation, although we ultimately decided not to follow all of their advice. No one, of course, is responsible for our errors but us.

NOTES

1. Although the term contrast is used fairly uniformly across psychological fields, assimilation has been put to various uses. Jean Piaget, a pioneer in the study of cognitive development, adapted the term from biology where it refers to the process by which the organism alters the structure of elements in the environment in order to permit their incorporation into the ongoing system (e.g., food must be chewed and broken down before it can be utilized for nutritional purposes). Piaget proposed that a similar process occurred with respect to the growth of intelligence: The person perceives new objects and concepts in terms that maximize their similarity to familiar elements so they may be incorporated into existing cognitive structures. His definition certainly shares elements with our own, but his has a distinctly functional perspective. For social, cognitive, perception, and judgment researchers, assimilation is not defined by its functions.

2. It is a little unfair to attribute this mosaic idea to Wundt, first, because he later revised his ideas to allow for emergent properties. Wundt was a prolific writer (of 53,735 pages between the years 1853 and 1920). Boring (1950) wrote of Wundt, "It was hard for a critic to riddle an argument before Wundt has changed it in a new edition" (p. 346). However, Titchner, who was Wundt's student and brought Wundt's psychology to America, described him as the proponent of the simple mosaic view and that impression tended to "stick."

REFERENCES

Adams, J. S. (1965). Inequity in social exchange. In L. Berkowitz (Ed.), *Advances in experimental social psychology* (Vol. II, pp. 267–299). New York: Academic Press.

Alicke, M., Dunning, D., & Krueger, J. (Eds.). (2005). *The self in social judgment.* New York: Psychology Press.

Anderson, N., & Jacobson, A. (1965). Effect of stimulus inconsistency and discounting instructions on personality impression formation. *Journal of Personality and Social Psychology, 4,* 531–539.

Anderson, N. H. (1981). *Foundations of information integration theory.* New York: Academic Press.

Asch, S. E. (1946). Forming impressions of personality. *Journal of Abnormal and Social Psychology, 41,* 258–290.

Asch, S. E. (1952). *Social psychology.* Englewood Cliffs, NJ: Prentice Hall.

Bargh, J. A., Chen, M., & Burrows, L. (1996). The automaticity of social behaviour: Direct effects of trait concept and stereotype activation on action. *Journal of Personality and Social Psychology, 71,* 230–244.

Bargh, J. A., & Pietromonaco, P. (1982). Automatic information processing and social perception: The influence of trait information presented outside of conscious awareness on impression formation. *Journal of Personality and Social Psychology, 43,* 437–449.

Biernat, M. (2005). *Standards and expectancies: Contrast and assimilation in judgments of self and others.* New York: Psychology Press.

Bless, H., Schwarz, N., & Wänke, M. (2003). The size of context effects in social judgment. In J. Forgas, K. D. Williams, & W. van Hippel (Eds.), *Social judgments: Implicit and explicit processes* (pp. 180–197). Cambridge, UK: Cambridge University Press.

Boring, E. G. (1942). *Sensation and perception in the history of experimental psychology.* New York: Appleton-Century.

Boring, E. G. (1950). *A history of experimental psychology* (2nd ed.). New York: Appleton-Century-Crofts.

Brickman, P., & Bulman, R. J. (1977). Pleasure and pain in social comparison. In J. Suls & R. L. Miller (Eds.), *Social comparison processes: Theoretical and empirical perspectives* (pp. 149–186). Washington, DC: Hemisphere.

Brickman, P., & Campbell, D. T. (1971). Hedonic relativism and planning the good society. In M. H. Appley (Ed.), *Adaptation-level theory: A symposium* (pp. 287–302). New York: Academic Press.

Brown, J. D., Novick, N. J., Lord, K. A., & Richards, J. M. (1992). When Gulliver travels: Social context, psychological closeness, and self-appraisals. *Journal of Personality and Social Psychology, 62,* 717–727.

Bruner, J. S. (1957). On perceptual readiness. *Psychological Review, 64,* 123–152.

Buunk, B. P., Collins, R. L., Taylor, S. E., VanYperen, N. W., & Dakof, G. A. (1990). The affective consequences of social comparison: Either direction has its ups and downs. *Journal of Personality and Social Psychology, 59,* 1238–1249.

Buunk, B. P., & Gibbons, F. X. (Eds.). (1997). *Health, coping and well-being: Perspectives from social comparison theory.* Mahwah, NJ: Lawrence Erlbaum Associates, Inc.

Buunk, B. P., & Ybema, J. F. (2003). Feeling bad, but satisfied: The effect of upward and downward comparison upon mood and marital satisfaction. *British Journal of Social Psychology, 42,* 613–628.

Campbell, D. T., Hunt, W. A., & Lewis, N. A. (1957). The effect of assimilation and contrast in judgment of clinical materials. *American Journal of Psychology, 70,* 213–217.

Carver, C. S., Ganellen, R. J., Froming, W. J., & Chambers, W. (1983). Modeling: An analysis in terms of category accessibility. *Journal of Experimental Social Psychology*, *19*, 403–421.

Cialdini, R. B., Borden, R. J., Thorne, A., Walker, M. R., Freeman, S., & Sloan, L. R. (1976). Basking in reflected glory: Three (football) studies. *Journal of Personality and Social Psychology*, *34*, 366–375.

Collins, R. L. (1996). For better or worse: The impact of upward social comparisons on self-evaluations. *Psychological Bulletin*, *119*, 51–69.

Collins, R. L. (2000). Among the better ones: Upward assimilation in social comparison. In J. Suls & L. Wheeler (Eds.), *Handbook of social comparison: Theory and research* (pp. 159–171). New York: Kluwer Academic/Plenum.

Conrey, F. R., & Smith, E. R. (in press). Attitude representation: Attitudes as patterns in a distributed, connectionist representational system. *Social Cognition*.

Crespi, L. P. (1942). Quantitative variation of incentive and performance in the white rat. *American Journal of Psychology*, *55*, 467–517.

Cross, D. V. (1973). Sequential dependencies and regression in psychophysical judgments. *Perception and Psychophysics*, *14*, 547–552.

DeCarlo, L. T. (1992). Intertrial interval and sequential effects in magnitude scaling. *Journal of Experimental Psychology: Human Perception and Performance*, *18*, 1080–1088.

DeCoster, J., & Claypool, H. M. (2004). A meta-analysis of priming effects on impression formation supporting a general model of information biases. *Personality and Social Psychology Review*, *8*, 2–27.

Dember, W. N., & Bagwell, M. (1985). A history of perception. In G. Kimble & K. Schlesinger (Eds.), *Topics in the history of psychology* (Vol. 1, pp. 261–304). Hillsdale, NJ: Lawrence Erlbaum Associates, Inc.

Deutsch, M., & Krauss, R. M. (1965). *Theories in social psychology*. New York: Basic Books.

De Weert, C. M. M., & van Kruysbergen, N. A. W. H. (1997). Assimilation: Central and peripheral effects. *Perception*, *26*, 1217–1224.

Dijksterhuis, A., & van Knippenberg, A. (1998). The relation between perception and behaviour or how to win a game of Trivial Pursuit. *Journal of Personality and Social Psychology*, *74*, 865–877.

Eiser, J. R. (1990). *Social judgment*. Pacific Grove, CA: Brooks/Cole.

Eiser, J. R., & Stroebe, W. (1972). *Categorization and social judgment*. San Diego, CA: Academic Press.

Eiser, J. R., & van der Pligt, J. (1984). Accentuation theory, polarization, and judgment of attitude statements. In J. R. Eiser (Ed.), *Attitudinal judgment* (pp. 43–63). New York: Springer-Verlag.

Fechner, G. (1966). *Elements of psychophysics* (D. W. Howe, Trans.) New York: Holt, Rinehart & Winston. (Original work published 1860)

Festinger, L. (1954a). A theory of social comparison processes. *Human Relations*, *7*, 117–140.

Festinger, L. (1954b). Motivation leading to social behavior. In M. R. Jones (Ed.), *Nebraska symposium on motivation* (pp. 191–218). Lincoln, NE: University of Nebraska Press.

Festinger, L. (1957). *A theory of cognitive dissonance*. Stanford, CA: Stanford University Press.

Festinger, L., Coren, S., & Rivers, G. (1970). The effect of attention on brightness contrast and assimilation. *American Journal of Psychology*, *83*, 189–207.

Festinger, L., Torrey, J., & Willerman, B. (1954). Self-evaluation as a function of attraction to the group. *Human Relations, 7*, 1161–1174.

Fiske, S. T., & Taylor, S. E. (1983). *Social cognition*. New York: McGraw-Hill.

Fox, E. (1995). Negative priming from ignored distractors in visual selection: A review. *Psychonomic Bulletin and Review, 2*, 145–173.

Goethals, G. R., & Darley, J. M. (1977). Social comparison theory: An attributional approach. In J. Suls & R. L. Miller (Eds.), *Social comparison processes: Theoretical and empirical perspectives* (pp. 259–278). Washington, DC: Hemisphere.

Hastie, R., Ostrom, T. M., Ebbesen, E. B., Wyer, R. S., Hamilton, D. L., & Carlston, D. E. (1980). *Person memory*. Hillsdale, NJ: Lawrence Erlbaum Associates, Inc.

Heider, F. (1958). *The psychology of interpersonal relations*. New York: Wiley.

Helson, H. (1947). Adaptation level as a frame of reference for prediction of psychophysical data. *American Journal of Psychology, 60*, 1–29.

Helson, H. (1964). *Adaptation-level theory*. New York: Harper & Row.

Helson, H. (1971). Adaptation-level theory: 1970—and after. In M. Appley (Ed.), *Adaptation-level theory: A symposium* (pp. 5–17). New York: Academic Press.

Helson, H., & Kozaki, A. (1968). Anchor effects using numerical estimates of simple dot patterns. *Perception and Psychophysics, 4*, 163–164.

Hering, E. R. (1874). Zur Lehrer vom lichtsinn. *Wein Akad Wiss Sitzbr, 69*, 85–104.

Herr, P. M., Sherman, S. J., & Fazio, R. H. (1983). On the consequences of priming: Assimilation and contrast effects. *Journal of Experimental Social Psychology, 19*, 323–340.

Higgins, E. T. (1996). Knowledge activation: Accessibility, applicability and salience. In E. T. Higgins & A. Kruglanski (Eds.), *Social psychology: Handbook of basic principles* (pp. 133–168). New York: Guilford Press.

Higgins, E. T., Bargh, J., & Lombardi, W. (1985). The nature of priming effects on categorization. *Journal of Experimental Psychology: Learning, Memory, and Cognition, 11*, 59–69.

Higgins, E. T., Rholes, W. S., & Jones, C. R. (1977). Category accessibility and impression formation, *Journal of Experimental Social Psychology, 13*, 141–154.

Hollingworth, H. L. (1910). The central tendency of judgment. *Journal of Philosophy, Psychology and Scientific Method, 7*, 461–469.

Hovland, C. I., Harvey, O. J., & Sherif, M. (1957). Assimilation and contrast effects in communication and attitude change. *Journal of Abnormal and Social Psychology, 55*, 242–252.

Hovland, C. I., Janis, I. L., & Kelley, H. H. (1953). *Communication and persuasion*. New Haven, CT: Yale University Press.

Janiszewski, C., & Lichtenstein, D. R. (1999). A range theory account of price perception. *Journal of Consumer Research, 25*, 353–368.

Jones, E. E., & Nisbett, R. E. (1971). The actor and the observer: Divergent perceptions of the cause of behavior. In E. E. Jones, D. Kanouse, H. H. Kelley, R. E. Nisbett, S. Valins, & B. Weiner (Eds.), *Attribution: Perceiving the causes of behavior* (pp. 79–94). Morristown, NJ: General Learning Press.

Judd, C. M., & Harackiewicz, J. M. (1980). Contrast effects in attitude judgment: An examination of the accentuation hypothesis. *Journal of Personality and Social Psychology, 38*, 390–398.

Koffka, K. (1935). *Principles of Gestalt psychology*. New York: Harcourt Brace.

Kohler, W. (1929). *Gestalt psychology*. New York: Liveright.

Kruglanski, A., & Mayseless, O. (1990). Classic and current social comparison research: Expanding the perspective. *Psychological Bulletin, 108*, 195–208.

Lambert, A. J., & Wedell, D. H. (1991). The self and social judgment: Effects of affective reaction and "own position" on judgments of unambiguous and ambiguous information about others. *Journal of Personality and Social Psychology, 61*, 884–897.

Latane, B. (Ed.). (1966). Studies in social comparison. *Journal of Experimental Social Psychology*, Suppl. 1.

Lockhead, G. R. (2002). Context and judgment. In *Fechner day 2001* (pp. 186–192). Leipzig, Germany: Pabst Science Publishers.

Lockwood, P., & Kunda, Z. (1997) Superstars and me: Predicting the impact of role models on the self. *Journal of Personality and Social Psychology, 73*, 91–103.

Lombardi, W. J., Higgins, E. T., & Bargh, J. A. (1987). The role of consciousness in priming effects on categorization: Assimilation versus contrast as a function of awareness of the priming task. *Personality and Social Psychology Bulletin, 13*, 411–429.

Macrae, C., Bodenhausen, G., & Milne, A. (1995). The dissection of selection in person perception: Inhibitory processes in social stereotyping. *Journal of Personality and Social Psychology, 69*, 397–407.

Manis, M. (1967). Context effects in communication. *Journal of Personality and Social Psychology, 5*, 326–334.

Manis, M., Biernat, M., & Nelson, T. F. (1991). Comparison and expectancy processes in human judgment. *Journal of Personality and Social Psychology, 61*, 203–211.

Manis, M., & Paskewitz, J. R. (1984). Judging psychopathology: Expectation and contrast. *Journal of Experimental Social Psychology, 20*, 363–381.

Marks, L. E., & Algom, D. (1998). Psychophysical scaling. In M. H. Birnbaum (Ed.), *Measurement, judgment and decision making* (pp. 81–178). San Diego, CA: Academic Press.

Marsolek, C. J., Schnyer, D., Deason R., Ritchley, M., & Verfaellie, M. (in press). Visual anti-priming: Functional evidence for superimposed visual object representation. *Cognitive, Affective and Behavioral Neuroscience*.

Martin, L. L. (1986). Set/reset: Use and disuse of concepts in impression formation. *Journal of Personality and Social Psychology, 51*, 493–504.

Martin, L. L., & Achee, J. W. (1992). Beyond accessibility: The role of processing objectives in judgment. In L. L. Martin & A. Tesser (Eds.), *The construction of social judgments* (pp. 195–216). Hillsdale, NJ: Lawrence Erlbaum Associates, Inc.

Martin, R., Suls, J., & Wheeler, L. (2002). Ability evaluation by proxy: Role of maximal performance and related attributes in social comparison. *Journal of Personality and Social Psychology: Interpersonal Relationships and Group Processes, 82*, 781–791.

May, C. P., & Kane, M., & Hasher, L. (1995). Determinants of negative priming. *Psychological Bulletin, 118*, 35–54.

McGuire, W. J. (1969). The nature of attitudes and attitude change. In G. Lindzey & E. Aronson (Eds.), *Handbook of social psychology* (2nd ed., pp. 136–314). Reading, MA: Addison-Wesley.

McKoon, G., & Ratcliff, R. (1992). Spreading activation versus compound cue accounts of priming: Mediated priming revisited. *Journal of Experimental Psychology: Learning, Memory, and Cognition, 18*, 1153–1172.

Meyer, D., & Schvaneveldt, R. W. (1971). Facilitation in recognizing pairs of words: Evidence of a dependence between retrieval operations. *Journal of Experimental Psychology, 90*, 227–234.

Morse, S., & Gergen, K. (1970). Social comparison, self-consistency and the concept of the self. *Journal of Personality and Social Psychology, 16*, 148–156.

Mussweiler, T. (2003). Comparison processes in social judgment: Mechanisms and consequences, *Psychological Review, 110*, 472–489.

Mussweiler, T., & Strack, F. (2000). The "relative self": Informational and judgmental consequences of comparative self-evaluation. *Journal of Personality and Social Psychology, 79*(1), 23–28.

Neely, J. H. (1976). Semantic priming and retrieval from lexical memory: Evidence for facilitatory and inhibitory processes. *Memory and Cognition, 4*, 648–654.

Neely, J. H. (1991). Semantic priming effects in visual word recognition: A selective review of current findings and theories. In D. Besner & G. W. Humphreys (Eds.), *Basic processes in reading: Visual word recognition* (pp. 264–336). Hillsdale, NJ: Lawrence Erlbaum Associates, Inc.

Neely, J. H., VerWys, C., & Kahan, T. A. (1998). Reading "glasses" will prime "vision," but reading a pair of "glasses" will not. *Memory and Cognition, 26*, 34–39.

New York Times (2006, February 8). The art of saying nothing, p. A-22.

Niedrich, R. W., Sharma, S., & Wedell, D. H. (2001). Reference price and price perceptions: A comparison of alternative models. *Journal of Consumer Research, 28*, 339–354.

Osgood, C. E. (1953). *Method and theory in experimental psychology*. New York: Oxford University Press.

Parducci, A. (1963). The range-frequency compromise in judgment. *Psychological Monographs, 77*(2, Whole No. 565).

Parducci, A. (1968). The relativism of absolute judgments. *Scientific American, 219*, 84–90.

Parducci, A. (1984). Value judgments toward a relational theory of happiness. In J. R. Eiser (Ed.), *Attitudinal judgment* (pp. 3–21). New York: Springer.

Parducci, A. (1995). *Happiness, pleasure and judgment: The contextual theory and its applications*. Mahwah, NJ: Lawrence Erlbaum Associates, Inc.

Parducci, A., & Marshall, L. M. (1961). Context judgments in the judgments of length. *American Journal of Psychology, 74*, 576–583.

Parducci, A., Perrett, D., & Marsh, H. (1969). Assimilation and contrast as range-frequency effects of anchors. *Journal of Experimental Psychology, 81*, 281–288.

Pettigrew, T. F. (1967). Social evaluation theory. In D. Levine (Ed.), *Nebraska symposium on motivation* (Vol. 15, pp. 241–318). Lincoln, NE: University of Nebraska Press.

Posner, M. I., & Snyder, C. R. R. (1975). Facilitation and inhibition in the processing of signals. In P. M. A. Rabbitt & S. Dornic (Eds.), *Attention and performance V*. New York: Academic Press.

Rakoff, D. (2001). *Freud: Essays*. New York: Random House.

Riggs, L. A. (1985). Sensory processes: Vision. In G. A. Kimble & K. Schlesinger (Eds.), *Topics in the history of psychology* (Vol. 1, pp. 165–219). Hillsdale, NJ: Lawrence Erlbaum Associates, Inc.

Ross, L. (1977). The intuitive psychologist and his shortcomings: Distortions in the attribution process. In L. Berkowitz (Ed.), *Advances in experimental social psychology* (Vol. 10, pp. 174–221). New York: Academic Press.

Rumelhart, D. E., McClelland, J. L. & the PDP Research Group (1986). *Parallel distributed processing, Vol. 1*. Cambridge, MA: MIT Press.

Sarris, V. (2006). *Relational psychophysics in humans and animals: A comparative-developmental approach*. London: Psychology Press.

Schachter, S. (1959). *The psychology of affiliation*. Stanford, CA: Stanford University Press.

Schachter, S., & Singer, J. E. (1962). Cognitive, social and physiological determinants of emotional state. *Psychological Review, 69*, 370–399.

Schachter, S., & Wheeler, L. (1962). Epinephrine, chlorpromazine and amusement. *Journal of Abnormal and Social Psychology, 65*, 121–128.

Schwarz, N. (1996). *Cognition and communication: Judgmental biases, research methods and the logic of conversation*. Mahwah, NJ: Lawrence Erlbaum Associates, Inc.

Schwarz, N., & Bless, H. (1992). Constructing reality and its alternatives: An inclusion/exclusion model of assimilation and contrast effects in social judgment. In L. L. Martin & A. Tesser (Eds.), *The construction of social judgments* (pp. 217–245). Hillsdale, NJ: Lawrence Erlbaum Associates, Inc.

Schwarz, N., Strack, S., & Mai, H. P. (1991). Assimilation and contrast effects in part–whole question sequences: A conversational logic analysis. *Public Opinion Quarterly, 55,* 2–23.

Sherif, C., Sherif, M., & Nebergall, R. E. (1965). *Attitude and attitude change*. Philadelphia: Saunders.

Sherif, M. (1936). *The psychology of social norms*. New York: Harper.

Sherif, M., Harvey, O. J., White, B. J., Hood, W. R., & Sherif, C. W. (1961). *Intergroup conflict and cooperation: The Robbers Cave Experiment*. Norman, OK: University of Oklahoma Book Exchange.

Sherif, M., & Hovland, C. I. (1961). *Social judgment: Assimilation and contrast effects in communication*. New Haven, CT: Yale University Press.

Sherif, M., Taub, D., & Hovland, C. I. (1958). Assimilation and contrast effects in anchoring stimuli on judgments. *Journal of Experimental Psychology, 55,* 150–155.

Smith, E. R., & DeCoster, J. (1998). Knowledge acquisition, accessibility, and use in person perception and stereotyping: Simulation with a recurrent connectionist network. *Journal of Personality and Social Psychology, 74,* 21–35.

Smith, E. R., Stewart, T. L., & Buttram, T. R. (1992). Inferring a trait from a behavior has long-term, highly specific effects. *Journal of Personality and Social Psychology, 62,* 753–759.

Smith, R. H., Diener, E., & Wedell, D. H. (1989). Intrapersonal and social comparison determinants of happiness: A range-frequency analysis. *Journal of Personality and Social Psychology, 56,* 317–325.

Srull, T. K., & Wyer, R. S. (1979). The role of category accessibility in the interpretation of information about persons: Some determinants and implications. *Journal of Personality and Social Psychology, 37,* 1660–1672.

Srull, T. K., & Wyer, R. S. (1980). Category accessibility and social perception: Some implications for the study of person memory and interpersonal judgments. *Journal of Personality and Social Psychology, 38,* 841–856.

Srull, T. R., & Wyer, R. S. (1989). Person memory and judgment. *Psychological Review, 96,* 58–83.

Staddon, J. E., King, M., & Lockhead, G. R. (1980). On the sequential effects in absolute judgment experiments. *Journal of Experimental Psychology: Human Perception and Performance, 6,* 290–301.

Stapel, D. A., & Koomen, W. (2000). Distinctiveness of others, mutability of selves: Their impact on self-evaluations. *Journal of Personality and Social Psychology, 79,* 1068–1087.

Stapel, D. A., Koomen, W., & van der Pligt (1997). Categories of category accessibility: The impact of trait versus exemplar priming on person judgments. *Journal of Experimental Social Psychology, 33,* 44–76.

Stapel, D. A., Martin, L. L., & Schwarz, N. (1998). The smell of bias: What instigates correction processes in social judgments? *Personality and Social Psychology Bulletin, 24,* 797–806.

Stapel, D. A., & Suls, J. (2004). Method matters: Effects of explicit versus implicit social comparisons on activation, behavior, and self-views. *Journal of Personality and Social Psychology, 87*(6), 860–875.

Stevens, S. S. (1958). Adaptation-level vs. the relativity of judgment. *American Journal of Psychology, 71*, 633–646.

Stouffer, S. A., Suchman, E. A., DeVinney, L. C., Star, C. A., & Williams, R. M., Jr. (1949). *The American soldier: Adjustment during army life, Vol. 1*. Princeton, NJ: Princeton University Press.

Strack, F., Schwarz, N., Bless, H., Kübler, A., & Wänke, M. (1993). Awareness of the influence as a determinant of assimilation versus contrast. *European Journal of Social Psychology, 23*, 53–62.

Suls, J., Martin, R., & Wheeler, L. (2000). Three types of opinion comparison: The triadic model. *Personality and Social Psychology Review, 4*, 219–237.

Suls, J., Martin, R., & Wheeler, L. (2002). Social comparison: Why, with whom and with what effect? *Current Directions in Psychological Science, 11*, 159–163.

Suls, J., & Wills, T. A. (Eds.). (1991). *Social comparison: Contemporary theory and research*. Hillsdale, NJ: Lawrence Erlbaum Associates, Inc.

Tajfel, H. (Ed.). (1978). *Differentiation between social groups: Studies in the social psychology of intergroup relations*. London: Academic Press.

Tajfel, H., & Wilkes, A. L. (1963). Classification and quantitative judgment. *British Journal of Psychology, 54*, 101–114.

Tesser, A. (1988). Toward a self-evaluation maintenance model of social behavior. In L. Berkowitz (Ed.), *Advances in experimental social psychology* (Vol. 21, pp 181–227). New York: Academic Press.

Tesser, A., & Paulhus, D. (1983). The definition of self: Private and public self-evaluation maintenance strategies. *Journal of Personality and Social Psychology, 44*, 672–682.

Thurstone, L., & Chave, E. J. (1929). *The measurement of attitude*. Chicago: University of Chicago Press.

Triandis, H. C., & Fishbein, M. (1963). Cognitive interaction in person perception. *Journal of Abnormal and Social Psychology, 67*, 446–453.

Turner, J. C. (1991). *Social influence*. Monterey, CA: Brooks/Cole.

Volkmann, J. (1951). Scales of judgment and their implications for social psychology. In J. H. Rohrer & M. Sherif (Eds.), *Social psychology at the crossroads* (pp. 273–294). New York: Harper.

Von Helmholtz, H. (1866). *Handbuch der physiologischen Optik*. Hamburg & Leipzig, Germany: Voss.

Ward, L. M., & Lockhead, G. R. (1971). Response system processes in absolute judgment. *Perception and Psychophysics, 9*, 73–78.

Wedell, D. H., Parducci, A., & Lane, M. (1990). Reducing the dependence of clinical judgment of immediate context: Effects of number of categories and type of anchors. *Journal of Personality and Social Psychology, 58*, 319–329.

Wegener, D. T., & Petty, R. E. (1995). Flexible correction processes in social judgment: The role of naïve theories in corrections for perceived bias. *Journal of Personality and Social Psychology, 68*, 36–51.

Wheeler, L. (1966). Motivation as a determinant of upward comparison. *Journal of Experimental Social Psychology*, Suppl. 1, 27–31.

Wheeler, L., Martin, R., & Suls, J. (1997). The proxy social comparison model for self-assessment of ability. *Personality and Social Psychology Review, 1*, 54–61.

Wheeler, L., & Suls, J. (in press). Assimilation in social comparison: Can we agree on what it is? *La Revue Internationale de Psychologie Sociale*.

Wheeler, L., & Zuckerman, M. (1977). Commentary. In J. Suls & R. L. Miller (Eds.), *Social comparison processes: Theoretical and empirical perspectives* (pp. 335–367). Washington, DC: Hemisphere.

Wills, T. A. (1981). Downward comparison principles in social psychology. *Psychological Bulletin, 90,* 245–271.

Wills, T. A., & Suls, J. (1991). Commentary: Neo-social comparison theory and beyond. In J. Suls & T. A. Wills (Eds.), *Social comparison: Contemporary theory and research* (pp. 51–78). Hillsdale, NJ: Lawrence Erlbaum Associates, Inc.

Wood, J. (1989). Theory and research concerning social comparisons of personal attributes. *Psychological Bulletin, 106,* 231–248.

Wood, J., Taylor, S. E., & Lichtman, R. (1985). Social comparison in adjustment to breast cancer. *Journal of Personality and Social Psychology, 49,* 1169–1183.

Wundt, W. (1894). *Lectures on human and animal psychology* (J. E. Creighton & E. B. Titchner, Trans.). London: Swan Sonnenschein.

2

Contrasting Models of Assimilation and Contrast

DOUGLAS H. WEDELL, SUSANNE K. HICKLIN, and
LAURA O. SMARANDESCU

The placement of value on objects, actions, events, and individuals is a persistent and continuous human endeavor. We express these values in our
everyday discourse when we say things like, "That movie was wonderful!"
Such expressions communicate the contents of our mental world through categorical terms that relate relative magnitudes along implicit dimensions. The movie
being referenced above is clearly valued more highly than movies assigned expressions such as "awful," "cheesy," or even "interesting" or "exciting." Indeed, it is
because our expressions of value typically imply ordered sets of categories that
psychologists have found it natural to collect data using category rating scales,
which formalize these gradations of value and serve as a gateway into the mental
life of the informant.

As with any measuring instrument, the issue of the validity of category ratings
can be raised. Naturally, one can argue that these public expressions of private
sentiment may be deliberately altered by the respondent, but this argument applies
to any overt measurement procedure over which one has control. On a different
front, S. S. Stevens argued against the use of rating scales because of their susceptibility to context effects (Poulton, 1979). The inclusion of contextual stimuli
often results in the rating of a target stimulus being displaced toward contextual
values (assimilation) or away from them (contrast), depending on characteristics of
the task, stimuli, and judges. Stevens' concern centered on the degree to which
assimilation and contrast effects reflect biases in translation of a true underlying
value resulting from the response elicitation procedure rather than genuine
changes in the mental representation of the target.

One empirical approach to evaluating this concern has been to examine
whether contrast and assimilation are found across different response modes.
Although the magnitude and direction of these effects are sometimes affected
by specific response characteristics, such as the subjectiveness of the scale (Biernat
& Manis, 1994; Krantz & Campbell, 1961) or number of categories (Parducci &

Wedell, 1986; Wedell & Parducci, 1988), basic context effects have proven extremely robust across response elicitation procedures. For example, context effects can be observed in physiological measures (Krupat, 1974), open-ended responses (Mellers, 1983; Simpson & Ostrom, 1976), and in the behavioral responses of animals (Crespi, 1944), implying that they often reflect more than a response or communicational bias.

Although manipulation of response mode is informative, a more enlightening approach to understanding contrast and assimilation is the specification of testable theoretical models that explicate the underlying processes. There is no shortage of such models; however, there is a need to delineate the degree to which these models make convergent or divergent predictions across different experimental manipulations. We believe that an examination of the basic constituent processes hypothesized by these models to produce contrast or assimilation will provide insight into the applicability of the models across different situations. It is important to emphasize that rather than look for a single best explanation of assimilation or contrast, we presuppose that several different processes can produce these effects. Consequently, what we examine in this chapter is how process accounts differ in their implications for the conditions producing these effects and the boundary conditions under which they operate.

OVERVIEW OF BASIC PROCESSES

Figure 2.1 presents a schematic diagram highlighting different processes operating in judgment. The boxes represent inputs and outputs while the circles represent processes. The external target is first submitted to automatic perceptual and semantic processing, which results in the establishment of a base representation. The base representation is then elaborated by memory processes and dimensional analysis to form the elaborated representation on which response selection operates to produce an overt judgment. Goals may play a key role throughout the processing of information; however, goals do not directly influence initial perceptual and semantic processes, as these are assumed to be automatic and primarily stimulus driven.[1] Although not pictured, context is assumed to be a potential influence of each of the four processes distinguished in Figure 2.1. Finally, the overt response is added to the elaborated representation as indicated by the dashed line.

A few instructive examples may clarify the distinctions being made with regard to contextual influences on processing made in Figure 2.1. The first place where context may influence processing is at initial perceptual and lexical encoding. Perceptual illusions are one example of context effects at this level. For example, when the same size circle is surrounded by larger circles, it appears smaller than when surrounded by smaller circles: the Ebbinghaus illusion. Or, if the recent context consists of words like "stream," "river," "sand," and "shore," then the term "bank" may be lexically represented as the land adjoining a river rather than a place to keep money. These kinds of low level contextual changes in the base representation undoubtedly take place, but they are generally not the locus of

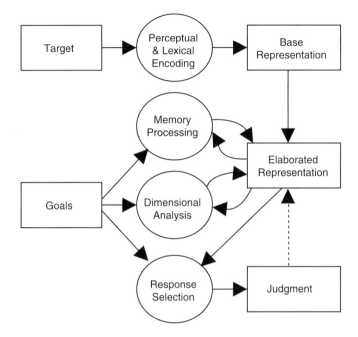

FIGURE 2.1   Basic processing model. Target information is assumed to be perceptually and lexically encoded to create a base representation. Further memory processing and dimensional analyses are used to create an elaborated representation on which response selection is based, with the overt judgment becoming a part of the elaborated representation. Goals moderate the processes determining the elaborated representation and response selection.

assimilation and contrast effects in most judgment situations of interest and will not be discussed further.

Our conceptualization then is that contrast and assimilation generally take place either at the level of the elaborated representation via memory processing or dimensional analysis, or they occur at the level of the overt judgment via response selection processes. The occurrence of these effects is likely to be moderated by goal states relevant to each of these processes. For example, if the goal is to discriminate between stimuli, then processes that lead to contrast may dominate. On the other hand, if an underlying goal is to generalize from contextual and target information, then processes that lead to assimilation may dominate.

The distinction between base and elaborated representations can be illustrated by the following example. Consider context effects on the evaluation of satisfaction with a fixed quantity of money, say $20. It is unlikely one will misperceive the $20 as $100 or $1. If one did, this effect would occur in the base representation. However, even if the base representation is fixed at $20, different evaluations are likely to occur based on elaborative processes. If the $20 is a gift from your aunt, your elaborative processing may include comparisons to gifts given to other nephews and nieces (a dimensional analysis process). If the $20 is near the bottom of this distribution of contextual comparison stimuli, then the elaborated inference is that your aunt is not particularly fond of you, which would likely lead to a reduced level of satisfaction with the $20. However, goal states may moderate the evaluation process. For example, if you are looking for reasons to support the hypothesis that your aunt favors you, you may reason that because she favors self-sufficiency, she is paying you a compliment by giving you less money than the others in your comparison set. Goals might also operate at the response selection level. For example, despite a low level of satisfaction with the gift, the communicational context of expressing your satisfaction directly to your aunt might lead you to say, "This is super!," an expression that is also added to the elaborative representation. In summary, the overt response may represent effects operating at the level of the elaborated representation or response selection, and these effects may be moderated by relevant goal states.

Accessibility of Base Representation

Note that in the $20 gift example described above, contextual effects did not occur at the level of the base representation ($20) but on the elaborated representation or on the response level. Presumably, as long as the base representation remains accessible, it may be used for context independent valuation purposes. However, studies of memory retention have demonstrated time and again that verbatim memory fades relatively quickly whereas memory for gist remains quite stable (Bransford & Franks, 1971). A consequence of the rapid forgetting of verbatim information is that even when context effects occur at the elaborated or response levels, they may have enduring consequences, for they represent the gist that remains after the verbatim information has faded. One illustration of this effect is the series of experiments by Higgins and colleagues (Higgins & Lurie, 1983; Higgins & Stangor, 1988) on the change-in-standards effect. These experiments demonstrated memory distortion of the retrieved representation a week after initial judgment was made, consistent with the idea of reconstructing the base information using the remembered judgments as gist encoding.

Another consequence of the distinction between base and elaborated representation is that the ability to ignore context may depend strongly on the type of stimuli being evaluated. For example, verbal stimuli so often used in social judgment experiments may be easier to maintain in the base representation than perceptual stimuli. Because of the rapid decay of perceptual information, reconstruction of these values from memory can show contextual effects within just a few seconds of the removal from immediate perception (Haun, Allen, & Wedell, 2005; Wedell, 1996). Thus, an important issue in gauging the impact of context is the accessibility of the base representation at the time of judgment. It is likely that in the majority of real-world social judgment situations, such as when we render a performance appraisal or an assessment of an individual's character, the information in the base representation must be reconstructed from memory and hence is susceptible to influences of the encoding and retrieval contexts.

Two Fundamental Goals: Discrimination and Generalization

In Figure 2.1, goals are assumed to affect memory processing, dimensional analysis, and response selection processes. Although several types of goals may be considered during the evaluation of a target, two fundamental types are discrimination and generalization. Note that these goals are implicit in any categorization process. Categories are most useful when they distinguish dissimilar stimuli and cluster together similar stimuli. Discrimination facilitates treating stimuli from different categories differently, whereas generalization allows one to predict behavior of a target based on that of other category members. Naturally, it follows that an emphasis on discrimination will tend to lead to contrast and an emphasis on generalization will tend to lead to assimilation (Mussweiler, 2003). Figure 2.1 suggests that the consequent assimilation and contrast may arise out of these different goals via either memory processing, dimensional analyses, or response selection processes.

At the level of memory processing, the goal to discriminate may lead to biased encoding, in which common features receive little attention and unique features become the focus of encoding (Tversky, 1977). The resulting elaborated representation should overrepresent values that differ from contextual stimuli and hence lead to contrast effects. When given the task of choosing between alternatives, the discrimination goal is naturally enhanced and leads to a tendency to weight unique features of the subject of comparison rather than the referent, resulting in contextual shifts in preference (Houston, Sherman, & Baker, 1989). These effects may occur at encoding or retrieval.

Alternatively, generalization goals may be invoked at memory encoding or retrieval and hence lead to assimilation. The generalization goal might be elicited more or less directly by designating the target as a member of a contextual group, so that missing or ambiguous target information is encoded or retrieved as consistent with contextual group information, as in false consensus effects (Marks & Miller, 1987). In addition, the nature of the task may be an important determinant of use of discrimination versus generalization goals. As noted above, choice tasks are likely to enhance discrimination processes, as one looks to select the alternative that is discriminably better than the others. On the other hand, estimation tasks may be more compatible with a generalization goal. For example, in estimating the size of a spoon, it is not particularly helpful to know that spoons are not buildings and that they are not jewelry. These contrast categories are irrelevant and cannot be used very well in generating estimates for a particular spoon. On the other hand, recalling other members of the category "eating utensils" may well help generate estimates that are relevant. Biernat and colleagues (Biernat & Manis, 1994; Biernat, Kobrynowicz, & Weber, 2003) have shown that estimates along "objective dimensions" tend to elicit assimilation whereas ratings may elicit contrast. Perhaps the difference here is in the goals evoked by estimation and rating tasks. An important goal of rating tasks may be indicating differences among stimuli (Parducci, 1995), a discrimination goal.

In addition to memory processing, goals may affect dimensional analysis. Dimensional analysis refers to the processes that use the available information to produce a value for the target along the specified attribute continuum. Much of dimensional analysis can be conceived as the judgment function, in other words, as a rule for combining information. Such rules can often be represented algebraically (Anderson, 1981), with weights representing the attention given to each piece of information and values representing degree to which the information implies a valence toward one end or the other of the attribute continuum. One common combination rule is the additive rule. To the degree that contextual information is additively combined with the target information, assimilation will typically result, as when the average of the contextual set is additively combined with the target value. Alternatively, subtraction rules are used to reveal differences, so that if contextual information is used as a baseline from which target information is subtracted, contrast will generally result.

Although additive and difference rules may be specified at the level of dimensional analysis, it may be difficult to distinguish whether they apply alternatively to memory processes rather than judgment processes. For example, a fruitful and popular way to model memory retrieval is using global vector models of memory (e.g., Hintzman, 1986; Nosofsky, 1986). In these models, the actual memory trace is never recovered but rather the retrieved memory is the result of the summed activation of memory traces relevant to the retrieval cue or probe. Because activation of memory traces is driven by similarity, the remembered stimulus value will tend to shift toward the contextual set, producing assimilation. The additive rules describing these models apply to retrieval, but they can be used to explain judgment phenomena such as the use of the availability and representativeness heuristics (Dougherty, Gettys, & Ogden, 1999). Thus it is sometimes difficult to distinguish whether the contextual shifts in value are due to an integration process applied to the stimulus information during dimensional analysis or to an additive retrieval process. Subtractive rules, which form the basis of contrast effects, are somewhat more difficult to apply to memory retrieval models, although they could represent inhibition processes rather than activation processes. Conceptually, dimensional analysis processes are distinguished from memory retrieval in that they take the existing information and use it to infer a value rather than use it to retrieve other information that changes valuation. This distinction, however, is sometimes difficult to test empirically.

The final type of processing affected by discrimination and generalization goals is response selection. An example of assimilation produced in this manner is the response matching tendency found in detection and discrimination tasks. When provided with trial to trial feedback, judges tend to match their response tendencies to the base rates of the stimuli, producing assimilation. For example, when presented with 80% small squares and 20% large squares, the judge who is unsure which square was presented will tend to use the most common contextual response, "small" in this case. Interestingly, when feedback is not given, participants tend to use a response equalization strategy that results in contrast (Parducci & Sandusky, 1965). These response effects can be modeled in terms of the location of a response criterion parameter within the usual Thurstonian or signal detection model. Alternatively, the more dynamic and process-oriented random walk or diffusion models used in cognitive psychology conceive of response bias as a biased starting point in a random walk or diffusion process in which evidence is accumulated to respond in one way or the other (Link, 1992). In such models, the response criterion parameter of signal detection models is reflected in greater prior activation or priming of one response category over the others in the response process. For example, seeing so many unhappy faces primes the response category "unhappy" so that it is more likely to be activated by presentation of a neutral face (assimilation). Once again, it can be difficult to distinguish models of assimilation and contrast occurring at response selection from dimensional analysis or memory retrieval explanations. One possibility is to examine the generality of these assimilation and contrast effects across different response modes, such as judgment, choice, matching, magnitude estimation, etc. The greater the generality, the less likely the effect is due to biases specific to a particular response mode. Another possibility exists if response bias is examined within the context of these diffusion or random walk models (Busemeyer & Townsend, 1993), which make specific predictions of how bias is related to deliberation time. In particular, these models predict that response bias effects will be greatest with short response deadlines and will be reduced or eliminated if the deliberation time is extended.

Summary of Processing Considerations

The process model of Figure 2.1 distinguishes various ways in which context can be integrated into memory processing, dimensional analysis, or response selection to produce contrast or assimilation effects. Consideration of process models of these effects is important in delimiting the conditions under which these effects will occur. Goals are assumed to be an important moderator of these effects, as goals can change how target information is encoded, retrieved, analyzed, or responded to in relation to contextual information. In the sections that follow, we use this framework to better understand different models of contrast and assimilation and potential tests of the applicability of these models.

CONTRASTING MODELS OF CONTRAST

We distinguish two general approaches to explaining contrast effects as (1) scaling models or (2) situation-specific models. Scaling models describe general principles responsible for mapping the judgment scale to the set of target and contextual stimuli, whereas situation-specific models typically posit processes that produce contrast for the specific relationships between target and context, task or setting. Scaling models are often formally developed mathematical models of judgmental principles specifying dimensional analysis, whereas situation-specific models focus more on processes that can shift the valuation of a specific stimulus in a specific context under specific task conditions. The two approaches generally lead to different methods for studying contrast effects. Scaling approaches use several target and contextual stimuli to test model predictions for patterns of responding, whereas situation-specific models focus on stimulus and task variables that moderate the effects of the contextual manipulation. In this section we first discuss scaling models and then proceed to situation-specific models.

Scaling Models of Contrast

Scaling models of contrast have often used psychophysical judgment as a foundation for model development. This is because the simple nature of the stimuli gives the experimenter a high degree of control in testing these models. Helson's (1947, 1964) adaptation-level (AL) theory was an early and highly successful model of judgment that explained basic contrast effects. According to AL theory, the organism is constantly adjusting to its changing environment by using new experiences to modify its representation of environmental categories of stimuli. Essentially, AL theory is a prototype model in which categories of stimuli are represented by a single value that stores a type of running average of the organism's relevant experiences. Helson (1964) posited three factors that determine the AL: (1) the average (or geometric average) of recent experiences (i.e., the contextual set of stimuli), (2) the relevant background stimuli (e.g., the size of the lighted screen in a size judgment task), and (3) a residual value that represents the prototype the organism has previously established. Because psychophysical stimuli, such as tones varying in intensity or squares varying in width, do not have well established residual values, the AL for such experiments should be largely determined by the experimental set of stimuli (and background features). AL theory proposes that the judgment of stimulus i in context k can be characterized as a linear function of deviations from the AL as follows:

$$J_{ik} = a + b(S_i - AL_k) \qquad (2.1)$$

where a and b are scaling constants, S_i is the context independent scale value of stimulus i, and J_{ik} may be considered the mean rating of stimulus i in context k. Contrast occurs essentially due to assimilation of the AL toward the mean of contextual stimuli. Hence, presenting low valued stimuli pulls down the AL so that subsequent target stimuli are displaced upward relative to control conditions. The basic version of the AL model presented in Equation 2.1 implies that the contextual manipulation should have a uniform effect on target stimuli, since the effect is produced by changes in a single value, the AL.

Volkmann (1951) offered an alternative explanation of contrast in his range theory based on characterizing the category described by contextual and target stimuli in terms of the two extreme values defining the range of variation for that category. The basic range model is expressed as follows:

$$R_{ik} = (S_i - S_{MIN,k})/(S_{MAX,k} - S_{MIN,k}) \qquad (2.2)$$

where $S_{MAX,k}$ and $S_{MIN,k}$ are the maximum and minimum valued stimuli evoked by the contextual set and R_{ik} is the "range" judgment of stimulus i in context k. In psychophysical experiments, the range is assumed to be strongly tied to the experimental stimulus set. Thus, contrast is produced by inclusion of a low valued contextual stimulus that lowers the subjective minimum and hence displaces judgments of targets upward. Note that range theory brings to prominence the subjective endpoints. Some support for the special significance of end stimuli can be inferred from experiments showing heightened discriminability for stimuli near endpoints along with better memory for those stimuli (Estes, Allmeyer, & Reder, 1976).

The testability of both AL and range models derives in part from their very sparse representation of the stimulus context, either defined as a moving average or defined by endpoint values. While predictions from both models provide good approximations to a variety of contextual manipulations, they have not withstood more rigorous testing (Parducci, 1965), implicating the need for a more complex representation of the context. Range-frequency (RF) theory (Parducci, 1965, 1995) assumes a representation of the stimulus context more akin to exemplar models of categorization in which multiple individual stimuli are relevant. While the range principle of the theory is identical to that of Volkmann's (1951) theory, the frequency principle introduces a new idea, namely, that stimulus value may be derived from the stimulus rank. Judgments of the stimulus based strictly on the frequency principle can be characterized by the following equation:

$$F_{ik} = (\text{Rank}_{ik} - 1)/(N_k - 1) \tag{2.3}$$

where N_k represents the maximum rank and 1 represents the minimum rank in the contextual set and F_{ik} is the "frequency" judgment of stimulus i in context k. Unlike models of Equations 2.1 and 2.2 in which judgments are linearly related to underlying scale values, the frequency principle produces nonlinear transformations based on the cumulative frequency function. Thus, for example, a bimodal contextual distribution produces a function with two inflection points. RF theory proposes that judgments are well described by a compromise between range and frequency principles as described in the following equation:

$$J_{ik} = C_{\text{MIN}} + (C_{\text{MAX}} - C_{\text{MIN}})[w R_{ik} + (1 - w)F_{ik}] \tag{2.4}$$

where R_{ik} and F_{ik} are defined in Equations 2.2 and 2.3, w is the relative weight of the range principle, C_{MAX} is the value assigned the highest response category and C_{MIN} is the value assigned the lowest response category. Numerous tests of RF theory in both social judgment and psychophysical judgment domains have demonstrated its ability to explain contrast effects and its superiority over AL and range models in psychophysical domains (Birnbaum, 1974; Parducci, 1965; Parducci & Wedell, 1986; Wedell, 1996), social domains (Smith, Diener, & Wedell, 1989; Wedell & Parducci, 1988), and applied domains (Niedrich, Sharma, & Wedell, 2001; O'Reilly, Leitch, & Wedell, 2004; Wedell, Parducci, & Lane, 1990).

Rather than going into further details of variations of these models, we concentrate in this chapter on interpreting these scaling-based contrast effects. With reference to Figure 2.1, we might ask are these effects occurring at response selection or earlier, and, if earlier, what processes are involved? AL theory was conceived by Helson as a general theory of perception and thought, not tied to the response scale. Within our framework, the AL would be retrieved and updated automatically in memory and then used during dimensional analysis so that the elaborated representation includes the deviation from the AL. Volkmann's (1951) range theory would seem to lend itself more easily to a response-based interpretation. The idea would be that, to effectively communicate variations, we need to anchor the end response categories with the relevant end stimulus values. Thus, when describing a height of 6 feet as "tall" for an adult but "short" for a building, we are communicating the relationship of the stimulus to the endpoints defining the category. It is unclear though whether these effects are operating simply on response selection or if they alter subjective impressions stored in the elaborated representation.

RF theory, like range theory, is ambiguous with respect to where in the processing system these effects may take place. The earlier formulations of the model describe these effects strictly in terms of response selection (Parducci, 1965). Hence, the frequency principle is a bias to use categories equally often and the range principle is a tendency to match the response range to the stimulus range. However, like Helson (1964), Parducci (1968) has argued that these relativistic judgments are operating to some degree at the representational level, as when he argues that RF theory predicts that greater overall happiness is tied to a negatively skewed distribution of events. This formulation of the frequency principle suggests that values are tied to relative ranks and the proportion of the range falling below the target. Thus, the theory posits that the affective reaction to receiving $20 is much more positive when the distribution of expected values is positively skewed and ranges from $3 to $22 than when it is negatively skewed and ranges from $10 to $30.

Although Parducci and Wedell (1986) found conditions under which altering the response scale altered the degree of contextual effects observed, there are several lines of research that are consistent with these effects taking place at dimensional analysis so that they are not tied simply to response selection. The most powerful evidence to this end is gleaned from experiments in which the task is changed to examine whether evaluations of differences or combinations reflect implicit RF scaling of stimuli. For example, Wedell (1996) asked participants to judge the similarity of dot patterns that varied in numerosity and were drawn from either positively or negatively skewed distributions. When the pair of dot patterns being evaluated was on the screen at the same time, there was no evidence of disordinal context effects, consistent with the idea that participants compared the context independent base representations directly. But when one of the dot patterns had to be held in memory for just a few seconds, large disordinal context effects were found that were well described by a model that assumed the RF values of the stimuli were being compared. This research then suggests that RF valuation is used to encode information into memory for additional comparison.

More generally, the finding of disordinal effects of context, such as when preferences are reversed with context, is particularly important in distinguishing between effects occurring at the level of response selection and those occurring earlier, at dimensional analysis or memory processing. This is because response selection models typically require that the ordering of magnitudes is preserved even though the relative differences in magnitudes may vary. Thus, response bias explanations are consistent with a situation in which Person A is judged moderately aggressive and Person B is judged aggressive in one context but in another context Person A is judged aggressive and Person B is judged extremely aggressive, as order is preserved. Response selection processes generally cannot account for a situation in which the context results in Person A now being judged aggressive and Person B being judged only moderately aggressive, a disordinal context effect.

In this vein, research on how values from different dimensions (such as rent and square footage of apartments) are combined shows that disordinal effects of distribution on preference are well modeled by assuming RF values along the different dimensions are combined rather than base representation values being combined (Cooke & Mellers, 1998; Mellers & Cooke, 1994). For example, Mellers and Cooke (1994) asked participants to judge the attractiveness of apartments on the basis of monthly rent and distance from campus. When the range of rent was narrow (and the range of distance was wide), the difference between a $200 apartment and a $400 apartment seemed large. In this case, a $200 apartment that was 26 minutes from campus was preferred over a $400 apartment that was 10 minutes from campus. However, when the range of rent was extended (and the range of distance was narrow), the difference between these two apartments seemed small in terms of rent. Here, demonstrating disordinal preference effects, the $400 apartment that was 10 minutes from campus was now preferred over the $200 apartment that was 26 minutes from campus.

Furthermore, modeling of attractiveness judgments has demonstrated that underlying RF processes may be partially responsible for preference reversals in choice and attractiveness judgments of alternatives that include decoys (Pettibone & Wedell, 2000; Wedell & Pettibone, 1996) and also with binary choice under different contextual sets (Simonson & Tversky, 1992; Wedell, 1998). Decoy effects in choice occur when adding a third (decoy) alternative to a choice set alters the preference ordering between the members of the other sets. For example, Wedell (1991) reported that participants preferred Car A (100 ride quality/27 miles per gallon) 69% over Car B (80 ride quality/33 miles per gallon) when the decoy alternative was Car C (100 ride quality/21 miles per gallon). However, Car B was preferred 80% over Car A when the decoy alternative was Car D (60 ride quality/ 33 miles per gallon). Note once again that this type of reversal of ordering of preferences for alternatives implies a change in the representation of the alternatives as elaborated by contextual comparison.

These demonstrations of the strong effects of implicit RF scales on subsequent comparisons imply that RF effects are not simply response based but must operate in some way on the elaborated representation. Wedell (2000) has suggested that the underlying mechanism may be that scales represent how attention is distributed across the subjective range. This interpretation is supported by demonstration of greater discriminability for reduced ranges and in areas of the range where stimuli appear most densely packed (Luce, Nosofsky, Green, & Smith, 1982; Wedell, 2000). When the range is extended, then the fixed attentional resource is distributed across a wider range of values so that the same stimulus difference is less easily discriminated. Similarly, when stimuli are packed closely within a subrange, frequency values reflect the increased attention directed toward that portion of the subrange resulting in enhanced discrimination. Because increased discrimination corresponds to decreased similarity, this mechanism is consistent with the findings of Wedell (1996). Additional research is needed to better understand the link between attention and scale values, but this interpretation allows us to better understand how the elaboration process may direct processing of stimulus values through an attentional mechanism.

Despite the evidence for implicit scaling effects operating through dimensional analysis rather than response selection, there can be no denying that there are systematic response based effects that may contribute to contrast. Baird (1997) and Haubensak (1992) have each developed theories that attempt to explain the basic RF effects in terms of sequential response strategies. In these models, the scaling effects arise from systematic sequential dependencies resulting from the manipulation of distribution. For example, one type of sequential rule would be to use a higher category than assigned to the previous stimulus in the series when the magnitude of the current stimulus is perceived to be greater, and conversely to use a lower category when the magnitude is perceived to be less. In a positively skewed distribution with a preponderance of low valued stimuli, moderate valued stimuli will be assigned higher ratings following this strategy than when they are rated within a negatively skewed distribution (with a preponderance of high valued stimuli), These models are worthy of investigation as they address sequential effects and may explain some of the variance attributed to distributional contrast. However, one clear reason to argue against these models providing a full explanation of contrast effects in scaling is that these effects occur when the same set of stimuli is rated in the same order by participants in different distributional conditions, with incidental exposure to the distribution (Parducci & Wedell, 1986; Smith et al., 1989). Thus, a complete judgment model fully explaining sequential and distributional effects has yet to be developed.

Finally, the foregoing review has emphasized the evidence supporting the idea that contrast reflects dimensional analyses processes described by range-frequency theory that alter the elaborated representation of the stimulus and can serve as input for other types of processes (such as similarity judgments). However, this does not mean that the adaptation-level characterization does not have applicability in some of these tasks. A good example of this is a study in which Wedell (1995) had participants judge which of two squares was larger than the other. Squares were either red or blue, with one set's range being shifted down relative to the other. Consistent with results using magnitude estimations, squares from the wide distribution were judged smaller than the same sized squares from the narrow distribution. Wedell manipulated the distributions of the squares from each distribution to determine if this effect could be attributed to AL effects, RF valuation within each distribution of squares, or a tendency to utilize response equalization. For example, in one condition the means or ALs of the two distributions were held constant but the proportion of responses clearly favoring each distribution differed so that context effects could be attributed to the tendency to equalize responses. In another condition, the ALs differed but the proportion of responses clearly favoring each distribution was the same so that context effects could be attributed to the tendency to evaluate each stimulus relative to the respective AL. In other conditions, ALs and response proportions favoring the distributions were held constant but stimulus ranks within the distributions were varied so that context effects could be attributed to an implicit RF valuation. The pattern of results supported attributing context effects to both AL valuation and response equalization, but not to RF valuation within distributions. This pattern of results does not overturn the large body of evidence supporting the RF over the AL model in predicting rating data, but it does suggest that different experimental paradigms may lead to different scaling processes being invoked.

Situation-Specific Models of Contrast

The scaling models described above assume that contrast is a natural consequence of the dimensional valuation process based on how the target relates to characteristics of the distribution of contextual stimuli. Alternative formulations of contrast appear to be less general and more focused on the judge's perception of specific aspects of the stimuli or task setting. Among the first theorists to proffer a situation-specific model of contrast were Sherif and Hovland (1961), who cited psycho-physical judgment data that suggested that when the target was close in value to the contextual stimulus its value tended to be assimilated rather than contrasted. They primarily applied their social judgment theory to situations in which one's own attitude served as an anchor point and evaluations of other attitudinal positions were either assimilated toward or contrasted away from one's own attitude, depending on similarity or overlap with own attitude. However, subsequent research on the effect of the self as anchor has convincingly demonstrated that these effects are primarily due to greater polarization of judgments for those with extreme attitudes rather than assimilation and contrast (Judd & Harackiewicz, 1980; Judd & Johnson, 1984; Lambert & Wedell, 1991). Polarization, according to accentuation theory (Eiser, 1990; Tajfel, 1957), implies that those with extreme attitudes tend to push values toward one end of the continuum or the other, a pattern that looks like assimilation and contrast. However, polarization is based on affective reactions to positions. When Lambert and Wedell (1991) separated effects of own attitude and affective involvement, own attitude served only to produce contrast (unless the target was ambiguous, in which case assimilation occurred).

Although the original formulation of Sherif and Hovland's (1961) model has been placed in doubt, subsequent models have demonstrated the utility of considering overlap between target and context in determining contrast versus assimilation. Herr and his colleagues (Herr, 1986; Herr, Sherman, & Fazio, 1983) varied how extreme a contextual prime was relative to the target being judged. They found that extreme primes produced contrast, but moderate primes produced assimilation. In explaining these effects, Herr (1986) argued that participants initially search for a categorical match. If the contextual prime overlaps with the target, then a match is found and the value of the contextual prime is generalized to the value of the target. When there is no match, then the retrieved extreme prime serves as a contextual anchor and typical scaling-based contrast is found.

Thus, this conception of the judgment process implies that the scaling-based contrastive process is used unless there is sufficient overlap with the prime. However, an alternative interpretation of these findings is that primes that are not remembered lead to assimilation, whereas primes that are remembered are used as standards for scaling-based contrast (Lombardi, Higgins, & Bargh, 1987). Because extreme primes are more memorable, they are likely to lead to contrast. In both of these interpretations, the situation specificity appears to relate to the occurrence of assimilation effects, whereas the contrast effects described are consistent with scaling-based contrast.

A more conceptually distinct type of contrast process from scaling-based contrast appears in models that focus on the participants' awareness of the potential biasing effects of context. These models view contrast as an effortful, corrective process that operates either at memory processing or response selection. Martin (1986) was among the first to investigate this situation using his set/reset model. Across three studies, Martin used a blatant priming task with a completion versus interruption procedure to manipulate the extent to which individuals engaged in thought perseverance. He found evidence of contrast only in the task-completion condition, but not in the task-interruption condition, even though he held constant the temporal distance between the priming task and the impression formation task. Thus, judges found it more difficult to avoid the use of the primed concepts when they continued to think about the prime (i.e., in the interrupted-task condition) than when they stopped accessing the concept at the priming task (i.e., the completed-task condition).

Martin (1986) concluded that the contrast effects observed in the completed-task conditions were likely to have resulted from participants actively inhibiting the conceptual category related to the priming task. He argued that scaling models could not easily explain the effects he observed, since participants across the interrupted-task and the completed-task conditions were exposed to the same priming stimuli and rated the same target stimulus on the same response scales. Martin also observed contrast effects on both prime-related and prime-unrelated dimensions. This finding argues against a simple effect on response selection, which would be expected to be more specific to the dimension being evaluated. Instead, it is consistent with shifts in the elaborated representation, perhaps due to biases introduced by inhibition of prime-related conceptual categories, which in turn affected the inferences generated for the target and the subsequent evaluative implications. In Martin's study, when two primed concepts were consistently favorable, participants developed a clear evaluative as well as a clear descriptive concept of the stimulus person, and contrast was observed on both the prime-related and the prime-unrelated dimensions. However, when the primed concepts were evaluatively inconsistent, a neutral general evaluative person concept was formed, and contrast was observed only on the prime-related dimensions.

An important difference between the contrast observed by Martin (1986) and scaling-based contrast is the effortfulness of the process. Scaling-based contrast appears to occur quickly, with little effort (Parducci & Wedell, 1986). However, the reset process that Martin postulated requires cognitive resources applied to suppression of the relevant conceptual category. Martin, Seta, and Crelia (1990) demonstrated the resource intensive nature of this process by showing that contrast did not occur when participants were (1) distracted, (2) given social loafing instructions, or (3) low in need for cognition.

Related to the idea of an effortful process guiding contrast are accounts that posit contrast results from a correction process. Wegener and Petty's (1995) flexible correction model suggests contrast may sometimes arise from a correction procedure in which the judge perceives potentially biasing assimilation effects and is motivated to adjust responses to the target in a direction opposite to that of the perceived bias and in an amount commensurate with the perceived amount of bias. The flexible correction model places importance on two factors: (1) motivation to correct and (2) application of naïve theories about the direction and the magnitude of bias introduced by the contextual factors. One key aspect of the flexible correction model is that it assumes that corrections are aimed at removing the perceived bias rather than the actual bias. Thus, the model suggests that correction processes may operate even when the person's belief about bias differs from the actual level of bias in the judgment setting. Unlike the set/reset model (Martin, 1986; Martin et al., 1990), which assumes that assimilative biases are default outcomes and that contrastive effects are due to effortful inhibition, the flexible correction model assumes that either assimilation or contrast can be the perceived biasing effect of a context and that either form of bias can be corrected. Using a context for which participants held a contrastive theory, Wegener and Petty found that both blatant and subtle prompts to consider possible effects of the context on target ratings led to corrections of target ratings in a direction toward (rather than away from) the context. A second way in which the flexible correction model differs from the set/reset model is that the correction appears to occur at the level of response selection. Thus, rather than inhibit a conceptual category and hence alter the elaborated representation, the judge appears to acknowledge the potential bias and simply adjust response in an opposite fashion to counteract the perceived bias.

Summary of Contrast Models

The models outlined above suggest several major distinctions that can be made concerning processes guiding contrast. Scaling-based models for the most part suggest that contrast is a natural consequence of the judgment process and requires minimal resources to produce these effects. While scaling models often include a response selection process that may account for some part of the contrast effect, they may also be formulated as occurring through dimensional analysis that alters the elaborated representation. The best evidence for scaling-based alteration of the elaborated representation is that changes in implicit scale values can be shown to affect tasks that build on these, such as multiattribute-based attractiveness evaluations, similarity evaluations, and choice (Cooke & Mellers, 1998; Mellers & Cooke, 1994; Pettibone & Wedell, 2000; Wedell, 1996, 1998; Wedell & Pettibone, 1996). For example, when considering two apartments that differ in price and location, implicit contextual comparison along each price dimension can make the relative difference in price seem large or small and thus alter which apartment is judged more attractive or chosen over the other. These implicit comparisons operate within our framework at the level of the elaborated representation through contextually dependent dimensional analysis as exemplified by range-frequency processing.

In contrast to scaling models of contrast, situation-specific models describe factors mediating when contrast will occur. One class of these models focuses on the overlap of features of target and contextual stimuli (Herr, 1986; Sherif & Hovland, 1961), with contrast occurring when stimuli are dissimilar but assimilation occurring when the target is similar to the contextual stimuli. These models are consistent with scaling-based contrast effects, but describe conditions that limit the applicability of contextual stimuli as standards of comparison. A second class of models posits that contrast may arise out of effortful expenditure of cognitive resources. Martin's (1986) set/reset model places the effortful processing at inhibition of conceptual categories, a memory process that biases the construction of the elaborated representation away from the contextual values. Wegener and Petty's (1995) flexible correction model also assumes effortful processing, but it implies the effect occurs at during response selection. Key to contrast occurring via flexible correction is that the judge is motivated to be unbiased and has a naïve theory that judgments will be biased in an assimilative direction.

CONTRASTING MODELS OF ASSIMILATION

In considering different models of assimilation, we will examine three basic experimental paradigms. The first of these we refer to as the priming paradigm, in which contextual stimuli are typically presented to judges in an unrelated task prior to the judgment of the target. The second of these we refer to as an estimation paradigm in which contextual information is presented during a task in which the judge must estimate the value of the target on some dimension. The third we will refer to as the ideal-point judgment paradigm, in which participants must evaluate stimuli on a scale that is related to the underlying dimensions of variation by a single peaked function. This last paradigm has not been explored extensively in social psychology.

Assimilation in Priming

Priming studies examine how activation from one stimulus affects the subsequent processing of another stimulus and have been used extensively in cognitive psychology to understanding effects of spreading of activation in associative networks (Collins & Loftus, 1975). In social judgment paradigms, priming generally consists of presenting traits, behaviors, or exemplars related to an evaluative concept in a task prior to the evaluation of a stimulus that is ambiguous with regard to the concept. Spreading activation models imply priming will produce assimilation, in that the semantic overlap between the prime and the target should be more likely to be activated and so evaluations of the target will be shifted toward the value of the prime. Higgins, Rholes, and Jones (1977) reported one of the first social

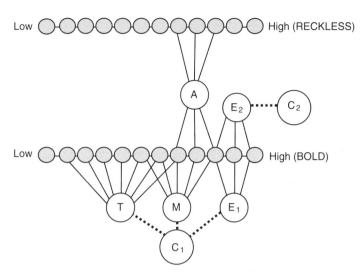

FIGURE 2.2   Diagram of conditions mitigating assimilation and contrast. Nodes indicate locations along trait dimensions "bold" and "reckless." The ambiguous (A) target has links to both. The typical target (T) has a distribution of values along one dimension, with the moderate (M) prime sharing some of these and the extreme primes (E_1 and E_2) not overlapping with T. Categories C_1 and C_2 show how highlighting categorical relevance may mediate effects.

judgment priming.studies in which participants were exposed to socially desirable traits (adventurous, self-confident, etc.) or corresponding socially undesirable traits (reckless, conceited, etc) and later asked to judge a hypothetical person based on a verbal description that was ambiguous with respect to these traits. The results clearly showed that participants were likely to use the recently activated concept to interpret the ambiguous description. The basic paradigm used by Higgins et al. is shown in the top part of Figure 2.2. The ambiguous description (A) has links both to high levels of the traits "reckless" and "bold," indicating that it can be interpreted consistently with each trait. When one trait has been recently activated, it remains in a higher state of accessibility so that the links to that trait are more likely to be accessed and used to disambiguate the stimulus within the elaborated representation. Because activation of competing concepts is assumed to be all or none, the priming of one concept gives it a head start in the race toward activation, consistent with diffusion models of category activation (Nosofsky & Palmeri, 1997).

Other researchers have developed stimuli within the priming paradigm that vary in their implications along a given trait dimension, so that the target is ambiguous with respect to its extremity along this trait dimension. For example, Srull and Wyer (1980) developed a paradigm in which participants sorted behavior reflecting hostility in an unrelated task and then rated a hypothetical target person based on a description that was ambiguous with respect to hostility. This paradigm is depicted in the lower half of Figure 2.2, with the target (T) supporting both high and low implications along the trait dimension. The activation of the high levels of the trait then make it more likely that implications consistent with high levels of the trait are accessed in memory and made part of the elaborated representation. An important aspect of their study is that they manipulated whether the prime occurred prior to the ambiguous target or after its presentation. Priming effects occurred only when the target was preceded by the prime, implying that the effects were tied to memory encoding rather than retrieval or response bias.

Herr and colleagues (Herr, 1986; Herr et al., 1983) pioneered the use of exemplars as primes. Once again, the target in those studies might be represented as having a wide dispersion of possible interpretations with respect to the trait, as in target (T). Exemplars varied in extremity, being moderate (M) or extreme (E_1) with respect to the trait. In those experiments, moderate primes produced assimilation, but extreme primes produced contrast. As depicted in Figure 2.2, moderate primes may overlap enough with the target to produce coactivation of shared values and hence increase the likelihood that these interpretations are included in the elaborated representation. The lack of overlap with the extreme prime presumably leads to an unbiased valuation of the target. However, the extreme prime is then used as a standard of comparison, producing contrast. Because spreading activation does not produce contrast, the most reasonable interpretation of the contrast effect is consistent with the proposition that the judge must remember or be aware of the extreme prime for contrast to occur (Lombardi et al., 1987; Strack, Schwarz, Bless, Kübler, & Wänke, 1993).

Other researchers have explored the priming paradigm with exemplars and traits more extensively to determine when these may lead to assimilation or contrast. Stapel and colleagues (Stapel, Koomen, & van der Pligt, 1996; Stapel, Koomen, & Velthuijsen, 1998; Stapel & Winkielman, 1998) have suggested that determining factors include context–target similarity, extremity, relevance, and distinctiveness. Note that in the experimental paradigms that these researchers investigate, the prime is often presented in the prior trial or instructional set so that it is likely to be remembered. Within this framework, the role of context–target similarity and extremity may be conceived as reflecting similar mechanisms in line with our discussion of the work of Herr and colleagues. When contextual stimuli are extreme, they likely share little overlap with the target and hence spreading-activation-based assimilation is not possible. Further, extreme stimuli are more likely to be remembered and used as a comparison standard producing contrast. These relations are captured in Figure 2.2 using the target (T), moderate prime (M), and extreme prime (E_1) representations.

Relevance is often defined as shared category membership between the target and contextual stimulus (Stapel et al., 1996, 1998; Wänke, Bless, & Igou, 2001). Stapel et al. (1998) demonstrated that contrast and assimilation and contrast effects emerge as a result of manipulations of relevance. They showed that assimilation results if the primed exemplar and the target belong to different categories (i.e., the exemplar is irrelevant), whereas contrast results when the primed exemplar and the target belong to the same category (i.e., the exemplar is relevant). In their study, judgments of the target (e.g., a new restaurant) were assimilated toward an irrelevant exemplar (e.g., a specific clothing store). On the other hand, judgments of a new restaurant were contrasted away from another restaurant. In Figure 2.2, the same category extreme exemplar (restaurant) is represented as E_1 and it is linked to the target T through a shared category (C_1). The contrast finding in this case is consistent with the use of remembered nonoverlapping exemplars as standards for comparison. The alternate-category extreme exemplar (clothing store) is represented in Figure 2.2 by E_2, which is linked to category C_2. The lack of contrast in this case would seem to be due to the contextual set being filtered by category relevance, as depicted in Figure 2.2 and consistent with research on contrast (Brown, 1953; Zellner, Rohm, Bassetti, & Parker, 2003). The occurrence of an assimilation effect for E_2, however, is somewhat more difficult to explain within our framework. If overlap is necessary for assimilation based on spreading activation, then E_2 should not lead to assimilation when it is discounted as a comparison standard. On the other hand, what may be occurring is that the irrelevant exemplar activates the trait concept, which serves to more diffusely activate values along the trait continuum (more so for high than low values). This idea is consistent with the distinctiveness notion raised by Stapel and colleagues (Stapel et al., 1996, 1998), in which exemplars have distinct boundaries and can produce contrast but traits are indistinct and therefore are likely to lead to assimilation. Further research is needed to determine the nature of assimilation involved.

Assimilation in Estimation

One type of task in which assimilation effects are often found is estimation. In estimation, one is typically attempting to assign a value to the stimulus that represents some objectively measurable aspect of the stimulus. Thus, one may estimate the size of a square by reproducing it or describing it in inches. While estimation may share similar processes with judgments of value, it also differs in that it can be viewed as having a strong memory retrieval component since its object is often to accurately reproduce one's memory for a stimulus value or event (e.g., estimating the number of countries in the UN from Africa may be conceived as a recall task in which memory is probed for the different countries from the different continents). Estimation tasks generally require individuals to describe the value of a stimulus after exposure to relevant or irrelevant stimuli. Individuals respond to this task by searching their memory and making a dimensional comparison between the target stimulus and the stimulus serving as anchor. Alternatively, when no anchor is provided, individuals may estimate the value of a stimulus by making a memory comparison with other category members.

In social judgment, contextual effects in estimation have been most thoroughly examined in the anchoring paradigm. The classic anchoring paradigm involves judges making two consecutive judgments, a comparative, and an absolute judgment, in reference to the same target. Tversky and Kahneman (1974) first asked participants to make a comparative judgment that was to assess whether the percentage of African nations in the United Nations was higher or lower than an arbitrary number serving as an anchor and found that estimates were influenced by the initial comparison in an assimilative manner. They interpreted anchoring effects as being the result of insufficient adjustment from an irrelevant value.

What is not clear from their analysis is the locus of this effect. It could occur at the response selection level, or it could occur during memory retrieval. Both interpretations are possible based on spreading activation models.

A response selection interpretation could be made along the lines of spreading activation along the response scale: Consideration of one response makes associated responses more active so that these values have a head start and thus are more likely to be selected. However, a similar argument can be made at the level of memory retrieval operating on the elaborated representation. The anchor value resides in memory so that when memory is searched for potential estimates, the retrieved value is likely to be biased toward the activated values in memory (consistent with global vector models of memory such as described by Hintzman, 1986, in which all memory traces contribute to the remembered stimulus as a function of their similarity to probe or memory cues). One difficulty in distinguishing between these interpretations is that the memory representation and responses are on the same scale. Mussweiler and Strack (2001) decoupled response-level numerical anchoring effects from semantic anchoring effects taking place at memory retrieval level by using a manipulation that included different scales with similar semantic implications. We will return to their view shortly.

Evidence favoring a response selection interpretation can be derived from sequential effects in judgment. In absolute identification tasks as well as rating tasks, the response to the current stimulus is assimilated toward the response of the prior stimulus, referred to as first order assimilation (Ward & Lockhead, 1970). According to the memory-based interpretation, the memory for the stimulus on the last trial may be confused with memory for the stimulus on the current trial, producing a distorted memory representation in line with assimilation. However, one argument against this interpretation and in favor of a response selection interpretation comes from studies in which no stimuli are presented and the participant simply guesses which stimulus is currently being presented (Wagner & Baird, 1981; Ward & Lockhead, 1971), often with the cover story that this is an ESP study and the task is to guess the next stimulus value. First order assimilation is again observed, even though there is no current stimulus to search for in memory and there is no prior stimulus to search for either. It is difficult to attribute these effects to biased memory search based on exposure to anchor stimuli, because there were no stimuli presented. Thus, the first order assimilation effects observed appear to be the result of the recent activation of a response category increasing the likelihood of using that category or similar categories on the subsequent trial.

Alternatively, evidence for memory distortion may derive from more recent conceptualizations that attribute the results observed in the standard anchoring paradigm to a mechanism of increased accessibility of anchor-consistent information (Mussweiler & Strack, 1999, 2000, 2001; Strack & Mussweiler, 1997). These accounts suggest that individuals solve the comparative task by testing the possibility that the target is equal to the anchor value on the judgmental dimension. In doing so, individuals may employ a hypothesis-consistent testing strategy and generate semantic knowledge that is consistent with the anchor. Support for this view is provided by a study in which Mussweiler and Strack (2000) asked participants to compare the average price of a German car to either a high or a low anchor value

(40,000 vs. 20,000 German Marks). Subsequent to the comparative judgment, they assessed the accessibility of the target knowledge with a lexical task. Participants made a series of lexical decisions with respect to target words associated with expensive (e.g., Mercedes, BMW) or inexpensive cars (e.g., VW). They found that response latencies for the type of words depended on the anchoring condition, judges being faster at recognizing words associated with expensive cars after a comparison with a high rather than low anchor, supporting selective accessibility.

More integrative views of anchoring suggest that anchoring consists of different processing stages that involve different mechanisms. Wilson, Houston, Etling, and Brekke (1996) suggest that numeric influences may be limited to the initial stages of determining an appropriate comparison standard, whereas semantic processes take place at later stages. Mussweiler and Strack (2001) investigated whether semantic and numeric processes influence absolute estimates in an additive manner and found that numeric influences were only limited to situations in which the semantics of anchoring could not operate. For example, they found that anchors with extremely different absolute values (e.g., 5100 m vs. 5.1 km) but with similar semantic implications (e.g., both the comparative and the absolute judgments were related to the height of the highest elevation in the Ural) produced similar estimates. In contrast, the numeric effect of anchors expressed in different measuring units was limited to situations when semantic influences could not operate because the activated semantic knowledge was held inapplicable to the judgment (i.e., the comparative judgment was concerned with the highest elevation in the Ural, and the absolute judgment with the number of languages spoken in the world). These results appear to place the memory-based interpretation on a solid footing.

Assimilation in Ideal-Point Domains

Clyde Coombs (1964) provided a useful distinction between dominance and ideal-point judgment domains. For dominance judgments, differences in ratings reflect differences in magnitudes along a dimension. For example, a person rated as "very aggressive" exhibits greater aggression than one rated as "moderately aggressive." Ideal-point domains represent preference or attractiveness evaluations, with value determined by proximity to the ideal valued stimulus. An important consequence of this analysis concerns the relationship between dominance judgments of values along a given dimension and corresponding preference judgments. Only when the ideal is located at one extreme or the other will these judgments be monotonically related to one another; otherwise, preference judgments will form a single peaked function relative to the dominance judgments. This single peaked function is the classic form of attitudinal endorsements found in the social psychology literature (Sherif & Hovland, 1961). Individual differences are reflected in different ideal-point locations so that the preference ordering of stimuli will differ for those holding different attitudes (or ideals).

The research on assimilation and contrast effects that we have reviewed has focused on dominance judgments. Even when that research has examined preference or attractiveness relations, the underlying ideal-point structure has typically been obscured so that shifts in ideal-point could not be examined. For example, Wedell (1994) demonstrated basic contrast effects in liking judgments of individuals described in terms of personality traits scaled along a liking dimension. Very different effects of context are expected for ideal-point domains in which liking or attractiveness is a function of an underlying ideal-point domain. These differences in context effects for dominance and ideal-point domains are illustrated in Figure 2.3, where the target stimuli are represented by enumerated black circles. For dominance judgments, assimilation or contrast can be represented by shifts in the rating scale along the vertical (or response) axis, as shown in the left panel of Figure 2.3. Thus, if stimuli are low in value as shown, a higher rating for Target 1 reflects a contrast effect and a lower rating for Target 1 reflects an assimilation effect. In illustrating these types of contrast effects, Wedell and Pettibone (1999) have shown that a target stimulus presented in a context of generally narrow facial features was rated as having moderately wide features, while the corresponding target stimulus in a context with generally wide facial features was rated as having moderately narrow features.

As shown in the right panel of Figure 2.3, assimilation of ideals is reflected in the rating function shifting along the horizontal axis in the direction of the values of contextual stimuli and contrast of ideals is reflected in a shift away from contextual stimuli. In the case of assimilation of ideals, Target 1 would be viewed as

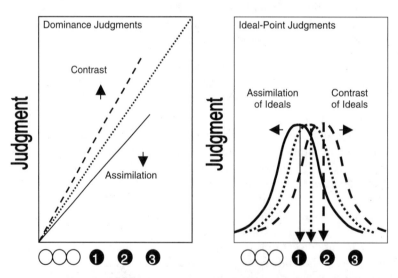

FIGURE 2.3   Illustration of contrast and assimilation. The left panel describes the situation for dominance judgments in which the inclusion of the contextual values (open circles) can lead to a displacement of responses to target stimuli (filled circles) away from the responses assigned to contextual stimuli (contrast, illustrated by the dashed line) or toward those responses (assimilation, illustrated by the solid line). The right panel describes the situation for ideal-point judgments in which inclusion of contextual stimuli may displace the ideal defining the peak of the attitude function toward contextual values (assimilation) or away from them (contrast).

more attractive than Target 2 in a context of mostly low stimulus values. However, in a context of mostly high stimulus values a reversal of preferences would occur such that Target 2 would now be rated higher than Target 1. In their study, Wedell and Pettibone (1999) showed that different ideal points are formed for contexts of faces with mostly narrow or wide features. Specifically, in the narrow context, the preferred face had narrower features than in the wide context (an assimilation of ideals). An important consequence of assimilation and contrast of ideals is that these contextual effects result in large preference reversals, and so they cannot be easily dismissed as ordinal shifts in response mapping to stimulus values. Once again, because response selection models of context effects require preserving the ordering of stimuli along the judgment dimension, the disordinal effects on preferences represented by ideal point shifts must be explained at the level of the elaborated representation through dimensional analysis or memory retrieval processes.

The typical result of contextual manipulations is that contrast on dominance domains is accompanied by assimilation of ideals on preference related judgments. For example, Riskey, Parducci, and Beauchamp (1979) manipulated the distribution of sweetness of drinks and found the most preferred drink shifted toward the mean of the contextual distribution. Wedell and Pettibone (1999) demonstrated similar assimilative shifts in ideals for ratings of the pleasantness of facial configurations in both judgment and choice. Although understudied, the assimilation of an ideal point appears robust, affecting preferences in the domains of architectural features (Baird, Cassidy, & Kurr, 1978), musical tempos (Holbrook & Anand, 1990), taste (Riskey et al., 1979), consumer products (Cooke, Janiszewski, Cunha, Nasco, & de Wilde, 2004), schematic faces (Wedell & Pettibone, 1999), and human body images (Wedell, Santoyo, & Pettibone, 2005).

One intriguing feature of these effects is that they cannot be dismissed as response bias, as they reflect disordinal shifts in the preference ordering among stimuli. In general, response biases tend to be limited to monotonic shifts of scale. What then is the mechanism for producing these effects? Essentially, two main mechanisms have been proposed. The judgment-mediated model (Cooke et al., 2004; Wedell & Pettibone, 1999) proposes that these shifts of ideals reflect underlying contrastive shifts in the dimensional scales of valuation (i.e., for the dominance judgments). Thus, for example, the ideal nose width might be one that is perceived to be moderately wide. Introducing a series of faces with narrow noses then shifts the valuation of nose widths upward (a scaling-based contrast effect) so that the width perceived as ideal or moderately wide is narrower (an assimilation of ideals). In support of this model, Wedell and Pettibone (1999) found moderate-sized correlations between contrast effects on width ratings and the assimilation of ideals on pleasantness ratings for manipulation of dimensions such as nose width or eye gap.

An alternative explanation is in terms of a memory-based mechanism. Here, the ideal for a given category of stimuli is assumed to reflect the prototypical value or average value in memory. The idea that the average of exemplars is closest to the ideal is consistent with research that finds the average of faces is more attractive than the constituent faces (Langlois & Roggman, 1990). According to the prototype-mediated model, introducing a series of faces with narrow nose widths shifts the prototype for this category toward these values so that the ideal nose becomes one that is narrower. Because the prototype-mediated model proposes that shifts of ideals arise from a different mechanism than contrastive shifts on underlying dimensions, it should be possible to dissociate these effects. Pettibone (2000) showed just such a dissociation in a study in which context was manipulated within subjects. Although both effects were obtained, their correlation typically was very low and nonsignificant. Wedell et al. (2005) have also showed this type of dissociation between ratings of width and attractiveness of body images, for at least one subgroup of their sample. Women who were dissatisfied with their own body image showed comparable contrast effects on judgments of widths of images but showed no contextual effects on the ideals, preferring the same narrow width in both positively and negatively skewed conditions. Although the judgment-mediated model may have some merit, to this point the evidence seems more supportive of different mechanisms guiding contrast on dominance ratings and assimilation of ideals.

We believe that the examination of context effects in ideal-point domains such as attitude endorsement is an important area that requires more extensive research. Thus far, these effects have been produced using perceptually based stimuli. It is an open question whether similar effects may occur for attitudes that are supported by a propositional structure (such as attitudes regarding gun control, abortion, etc.). Further investigation is needed into the conditions producing this type of assimilation of ideals. Pettibone (2000) demonstrated some limits on the generality of these effects that depended on how the contextual information was learned. On the other hand, Karpick (2004) has demonstrated that shifts in ideals occur under a wide variety of conditions, supporting the idea that the process may reflect a fairly automatic memory process.

CONCLUSIONS

In this chapter we have attempted to indicate how models of contrast and assimilation differ in terms of their conceptions of the processes involved. We believe it is useful to delineate the difference between base and elaborated representations. The base representation may provide a basis for context-independent processing, but this representation is often fragile so that the context-dependent elaborated representation will often serve as the basis for further cognitive and affective processing. We further distinguish three types of elaborations: context-influenced memory processes, context-influenced dimensional analyses, and context-influenced response processes. A key determinant of contrast versus assimilation may be the goals the judge is operating under. Many tasks emphasize discrimination of stimuli, which leads to processes that produce contrast through changes in memory processing, dimensional analysis, and response selection. Alternatively, tasks that emphasize generalization of contextual information to the target lead to processes that produce assimilation, again at these different levels. Specification of models in terms of goals and processes should lead to clearer tests of such models.

Finally, we note that an understudied area in contextual valuation is the effect of context in ideal-point domains. To date, studies show that for perceptual stimuli, preference is highly dependent on context. Because the ideal-point structure reflects basic attitude endorsement functions, it would seem imperative that more research examining the generality of these effects to typical attitudinal domains and processes should be conducted in the future.

NOTE

1. Within our framework, we maintain that goals do not play a direct role in the initial perceptual and semantic encoding of a stimulus, as these are primarily bottom-up stimulus-driven processes. Although research by Bargh and his associates (Bargh, 1990; Chartrand & Bargh, 2002) has clearly demonstrated how goals may be automatically activated and have pervasive effects on stimulus processing, we believe that these effects by and large are directed toward what we refer to as the elaborated representation through changes in attention or memory retrieval processes, or possibly directed toward response selection mechanisms. When goals do affect the initial perceptual or semantic encoding of a stimulus, we believe these effects are mediated through priming knowledge structures, and it is these knowledge structures that ultimately affect encoding. For example, Aarts, Dijksterhuis, and de Vries (2001) found that individuals who were thirsty and thus had a primed goal to drink were quicker to recognize goal-related words such as *beverage* and *quench* than were control participants. We would argue that rather than the goal directly affecting lexical access, the goal led to the activation of related semantic structures and it is the activation of these that affected lexical or perceptual encoding.

REFERENCES

Aarts, H., Dijksterhuis, A., & de Vries P. (2001). On the psychology of drinking: Being thirsty and perceptually ready. *British Journal of Psychology*, 92, 631–642.

Anderson, N. H. (1981). *Foundations of information integration theory*. New York: Academic Press.

Baird, J. C. (1997). *Sensation and judgment: Complementarity theory of psychophysics*. Mahwah, NJ: Lawrence Erlbaum Associates, Inc.

Baird, J. C., Cassidy, B., & Kurr, J. (1978). Room preference as a function of architectural features and user activities. *Journal of Applied Psychology*, 63, 719–727.

Bargh, J. A. (1990). Automotives: Preconscious determinants of social interaction. In E. T. Higgins & R. M. Sorrentino (Eds.), *Handbook of motivation and cognition: Foundations of social behavior* (Vol. 2, pp. 93–130). New York: Guilford Press.

Biernat, M., Kobrynowicz, D., & Weber, D. L. (2003). Stereotypes and shifting standards: Some paradoxical effects of cognitive load. *Journal of Applied Social Psychology*, 33, 2060–2079.

Biernat, M., & Manis, M. (1994). Shifting standards and stereotype-based judgments. *Journal of Personality and Social Psychology*, 66, 5–20.

Birnbaum, M. H. (1974). Using contextual effects to derive psychophysical scales. *Perception and Psychophysics*, 15, 89–96.

Bransford, J. D., & Franks, J. J. (1971). The abstraction of linguistic ideas. *Cognitive Psychology, 2,* 331–350.

Brown, D. R. (1953). Stimulus similarity and the anchoring of subjective scales. *American Journal of Psychology, 66,* 199–214.

Busemeyer, J. R., & Townsend, J. T. (1993). Decision field theory: A dynamic-cognitive approach to decision making in an uncertain environment. *Psychological Review, 100,* 432–459.

Chartrand, T. L., & Bargh, J. A. (2002). Nonconscious motivations: Their activation, operation and consequences. In A. Tesser, S. Diederik, & J. V. Wood (Eds.), *Self and motivation: Emerging psychological perspectives* (pp. 13–41). Washington, DC: American Psychological Association.

Collins, A. M., & Loftus, E. F. (1975). Spreading-activation theory of semantic processing. *Psychological Review, 82,* 407–428.

Cooke, A. D. J., Janiszewski, C., Cunha, M., Jr., Nasco, S. A., & de Wilde, E. (2004). Stimulus context and the formation of consumer ideals. *Journal of Consumer Research, 31,* 112–124.

Cooke, A. D. J., & Mellers, B. A. (1998). Multiattribute judgment: Attribute spacing influences single attributes. *Journal of Experimental Psychology: Human Perception and Performance, 24,* 496–504.

Coombs, C. H. (1964). *A theory of data.* New York: Wiley.

Crespi, L. P. (1944). Quantitative variation of incentive and performance in the white rat. *American Journal of Psychology, 55,* 467–520.

Dougherty, M. R. P., Gettys, C. F., & Ogden, E. E. (1999). MINERVA-DM: A memory processes model for judgments of likelihood. *Psychological Review, 106,* 180–209.

Eiser, J. R. (1990). *Social judgment.* Belmont, CA: Brooks/Cole Publishing Co.

Estes, W. K., Allmeyer, D. H., & Reder, S. M. (1976). Serial position functions for letter identification at brief and extended exposure durations. *Perception and Psychophysics, 19,* 1–15.

Haubensak, G. (1992). The consistency model: A process model for absolute judgments. *Journal of Experimental Psychology: Human Perception and Performance, 18,* 202–209.

Haun, D. B. M., Allen, G. L., & Wedell, D. H. (2005). Bias in spatial memory: A categorical endorsement. *Acta Psychologica, 118,* 149–170.

Helson, H. (1947). Adaptation-level as a frame of reference for prediction in psychophysical data. *American Journal of Psychology, 60,* 1–29.

Helson, H. (1964). *Adaptation-level theory.* New York: Harper & Row.

Herr, P. M. (1986). Consequences of priming: Judgment and behavior. *Journal of Personality and Social Psychology, 51,* 1106–1115.

Herr, P. M., Sherman, S. J., & Fazio, R. H. (1983). On the consequences of priming: Assimilation and contrast effects. *Journal of Experimental Social Psychology, 19,* 323–340.

Higgins, E. T., & Lurie, L. (1983). Context, categorization and recall: The "change-of-standard" effect. *Cognitive Psychology, 15,* 525–547.

Higgins, E. T., Rholes, W. S., & Jones, C. R. (1977). Category accessibility and impression formation. *Journal of Experimental Social Psychology, 13,* 141–154.

Higgins, E. T., & Stangor, C. (1988). A "change-of-standard" perspective on the relations among context, judgment, and memory. *Journal of Personality and Social Psychology, 54,* 181–192.

Hintzman, D. L. (1986). "Schema abstraction" in a multiple-trace memory model. *Psychological Review, 93,* 411–428.

Holbrook, M. B., & Anand, P. (1990). Effects of tempo and situational arousal on the listener's perceptual and affective responses to music. *Psychology of Music, 18,* 150–162.

Houston, D. A., Sherman, S. J., & Baker, S. M. (1989). The influence of unique features and direction of comparison on preferences, *Journal of Experimental Social Psychology, 25,* 121–141.

Judd, C. M., & Harackiewicz, J. M. (1980). Contrast effects in attitude judgment: An examination of the accentuation hypothesis. *Journal of Personality and Social Psychology, 41,* 26–36.

Judd, C. M., & Johnson, J. T. (1984). The polarizing effects of affect. In R. Eiser (Ed.), *Attitudinal judgment* (pp. 65–82). New York: Springer.

Karpick, S. M. (2004). *The role of categorical context across learning and judgment tasks.* Unpublished master's thesis, University of South Carolina.

Krantz, D. L., & Campbell, D. T. (1961). Separating perceptual and linguistic effects of context shifts upon absolute judgments. *Journal of Experimental Psychology, 62,* 35–42.

Krupat, E. (1974). Context as a determinant of perceived threat. *Journal of Personality and Social Psychology, 29,* 731–736.

Lambert, A. J., & Wedell, D. H. (1991). The self and social judgment: The effects of affective reaction and "own position" on judgments of unambiguous and ambiguous information about others. *Journal of Personality and Social Psychology, 61,* 884–897.

Langlois, K. H., & Roggman, L. A. (1990). Attractive faces are only average. *Psychological Science, 1,* 115–121.

Link, S. W. (1992). *The wave theory of difference and similarity.* Hillsdale, NJ: Lawrence Erlbaum Associates, Inc.

Lombardi, W. J., Higgins, E. T., & Bargh, J. A. (1987). The role of consciousness in priming effects on categorization: Assimilation versus contrast as a function of awareness of the priming task. *Personality and Social Psychology Bulletin, 13,* 411–429.

Luce, R. D., Nosofsky, R. M., Green, D. M., & Smith, A. F. (1982). The bow and sequential effects in absolute identification. *Perception and Psychophysics, 32,* 397–408.

Marks, G., & Miller, N. (1987). Ten years of research on the false-consensus effect: An empirical and theoretical review. *Psychological Bulletin, 102,* 72–90.

Martin L. L. (1986). Set/reset: Use and disuse of concepts in impression formation. *Journal of Personality and Social Psychology, 51,* 493–504.

Martin L. L., Seta, J. J., & Crelia, R. A. (1990). Assimilation and contrast as a function of people's willingness and ability to expend effort in forming an impression. *Journal of Personality and Social Psychology, 59,* 27–37.

Mellers, B. A. (1983). Evidence against "absolute" scaling. *Perception and Psychophysics, 33,* 523–526.

Mellers, B. A., & Cooke, A. D. J. (1994). Trade-offs depend on attribute range. *Journal of Experimental Psychology: Human Perception and Performance, 20,* 1055–1067.

Mussweiler, T. (2003). Comparison processes in social judgment: Mechanisms and consequences. *Psychological Review, 110,* 472–489.

Mussweiler, T., & Strack, F. (1999). Hypothesis consistent testing and semantic priming in the anchoring paradigm: A selective accessibility model. *Journal of Experimental Social Psychology, 35,* 136–164.

Mussweiler, T., & Strack, F. (2000). Numeric judgment under uncertainty: The role of knowledge in anchoring. *Journal of Experimental Social Psychology, 36,* 495–518.

Mussweiler, T., & Strack, F. (2001). The semantics of anchoring. *Organizational Behavior and Human Decision Processes*, *86*, 234–255.

Niedrich, R. W., Sharma, S., & Wedell, D. H. (2001). Reference price and price perceptions: A comparison of alternative models. *Journal of Consumer Research*, *28*, 339–354.

Nosofsky, R. M. (1986). Attention, similarity, and the identification-categorization relationship. *Journal of Experimental Psychology: General*, *115*, 39–57.

Nosofsky, R. M., & Palmeri, T. J. (1997). An exemplar-based random walk model of speeded classification. *Psychological Review*, *104*, 266–300.

O'Reilly, D. M., Leitch, R. A., & Wedell, D. H. (2004). The effects of immediate context on auditors judgments of loan quality. *Auditing: A Journal of Practice and Theory*, *23*, 89–105.

Parducci, A. (1965). Category judgment: A range-frequency model. *Psychological Review*, *72*, 407–418.

Parducci, A. (1968). The relativism of absolute judgments. *Scientific American*, *219*, 84–90.

Parducci, A. (1995). *Happiness, pleasure and judgment: The contextual theory and its applications*. Mahwah, NJ: Lawrence Erlbaum Associates, Inc.

Parducci, A., & Sandusky, A. (1965). Distribution and sequence effects in judgment. *Journal of Experimental Psychology*, *69*, 450–459.

Parducci, A., & Wedell, D. H. (1986). The category effect with rating scales: Number of categories, number of stimuli, and method of presentation. *Journal of Experimental Psychology: Human Perception and Performance*, *12*, 496–516.

Pettibone, J. C. (2000). *Multiple pathways for contextual recruitment in social judgment*. Unpublished doctoral dissertation, University of South Carolina.

Pettibone, J. C., & Wedell, D. H. (2000). Examining models of non-dominated decoy effects across judgment and choice. *Organizational Behavior and Human Decision Processes*, *81*, 300–328.

Poulton, E. C. (1979). Models of biases in judging sensory magnitude. *Psychological Bulletin*, *86*, 777–803.

Riskey, D. R., Parducci, A., & Beauchamp, G. K. (1979). Effects of context in judgments of sweetness and pleasantness. *Perception and Psychophysics*, *26*, 171–176.

Sherif, M., & Hovland, C. I. (1961). *Social judgment: Assimilation and contrast effects in communication and attitude change*. New Haven, CT: Yale University Press.

Simonson, I., & Tversky, A. (1992). Choice in context: Tradeoff contrast and extremeness aversion. *Journal of Marketing Research*, *29*, 281–895.

Simpson, D. D., & Ostrom, T. M. (1976). Contrast effects in impression formation. *Journal of Personality and Social Psychology*, *34*, 625–629.

Smith, R. H., Diener, E., & Wedell, D. H. (1989). Intrapersonal and social comparison determinants of happiness: A range-frequency analysis. *Journal of Personality and Social Psychology*, *56*, 317–325.

Srull, T. K., & Wyer, R. S. (1980). Category accessibility and social perception: Some implications for the study of person memory and interpersonal judgments. *Journal of Personality and Social Psychology*, *38*(6), 841–856.

Stapel, D. A., Koomen, W., & van der Pligt, J. (1996). The referents of trait inferences: The impact of trait concepts versus actor–trait links on subsequent judgments. *Journal of Personality and Social Psychology*, *70*, 437–450.

Stapel, D. A., Koomen, W., & Velthuijsen, A. S. (1998). Assimilation or contrast? Comparison relevance, distinctness, and the impact of accessible information on consumer judgments. *Journal of Consumer Psychology*, *7*, 1–24.

Stapel, D. A., & Winkielman, P. (1998). Assimilation and contrast as a function of context–target similarity, distinctness, and dimensional relevance. *Personality and Social Psychology Bulletin, 24,* 634–646.

Strack, F., & Mussweiler, T. (1997). Explaining the enigmatic anchoring effect: Mechanisms of selective accessibility. *Journal of Personality and Social Psychology, 73,* 437–446.

Strack, F., Schwarz, N., Bless, H., Kübler, A., & Wänke M. (1993). Awareness of the influence as a determinant of assimilation versus contrast. *European Journal of Social Psychology, 49,* 1460–1469.

Tajfel, H. (1957). Value and the perceptual judgment of magnitude. *Psychological Review, 64,* 192–204.

Tversky, A. (1977). Features of similarity. *Psychological Review, 84,* 327–352.

Tversky, A., & Kahneman, D. (1974). Judgment under uncertainty: Heuristics and biases. *Science, 185,* 1124–1131.

Volkmann, J. (1951). Scales of judgment and their implications for social psychology. In J. H. Roherer & M. Sherif (Eds.), *Social psychology at the crossroads* (pp. 279–294). New York: Harper & Row.

Wagner, M., & Baird, J. C. (1981). A quantitative analysis of sequential effects with numeric stimuli. *Perception and Psychophysics, 29,* 359–364.

Ward, L. M., & Lockhead, G. R. (1970). Sequential effects and memory in category judgments. *Journal of Experimental Psychology, 84,* 27–34.

Ward, L. M., & Lockhead, G. R. (1971). Response system processes in absolute judgment. *Perception and Psychophysics, 9,* 73–78.

Wänke, M., Bless, H., & Igou, E. R. (2001). Next to a star: Paling, shining, or both? Turning interexemplar contrast into interexemplar assimilation. *Personality and Social Psychology Bulletin, 27,* 14–29.

Wedell, D. H. (1991). Distinguishing among models of contextually induced preference reversals. *Journal of Experimental Psychology: Learning, Memory, and Cognition, 17,* 767–778.

Wedell, D. H. (1994). Contextual contrast in evaluative judgments: Test of pre- versus post-integration models of contrast. *Journal of Personality and Social Psychology, 66,* 1007–1019.

Wedell, D. H. (1995). Contrast effects in paired comparisons: Evidence for both stimulus and response based processes. *Journal of Experimental Psychology: Human Perception and Performance, 21,* 1158–1173.

Wedell, D. H. (1996). A constructive-associative model of the contextual dependence of unidimensional similarity. *Journal of Experimental Psychology: Human Perception and Performance, 22,* 634–661.

Wedell, D. H. (1998). Testing models of tradeoff contrast in pairwise choice. *Journal of Experimental Psychology: Human Perception and Performance, 24,* 49–65.

Wedell, D. H. (2000, November). *A range-frequency prototype model of judgment and discrimination.* Paper presented at the 41st annual meeting of the Psychonomic Society, New Orleans, LA.

Wedell, D. H., & Parducci, A. (1988). The category effect in social judgment: Experimental ratings of happiness. *Journal of Personality and Social Psychology, 55,* 341–356.

Wedell, D. H., Parducci, A., & Lane, M. (1990). Reducing the dependence of clinical judgment on the immediate context: Effects of number of categories and type of anchors. *Journal of Personality and Social Psychology, 58,* 319–329.

Wedell, D. H., & Pettibone, J. C. (1996). Using judgments to understand decoy effects in choice. *Organizational Behavior and Human Decision Processes, 67,* 326–344.

Wedell, D. H., & Pettibone, J. C. (1999). Preference and the contextual basis of ideals in judgment and choice. *Journal of Experimental Psychology: General, 128,* 346–361.

Wedell, D. H., Santoyo, E. M., & Pettibone, J. C. (2005). The thick and the thin of it: Contextual effects in body perception. *Basic and Applied Social Psychology, 27,* 213–227.

Wegener, D. T., & Petty, R. E. (1995). Flexible correction processes in social judgment: The role of naive theories in corrections for perceived bias. *Journal of Personality and Social Psychology, 68,* 36–51.

Wilson, T. D., Houston C. E., Etling, K. M., & Brekke, N. (1996). A new look at anchoring effects: Basic anchoring and its antecedents. *Journal of Experimental Psychology: General, 125*(4), 387–402.

Zellner, D. A., Rohm, E. A., Bassetti, T. L., & Parker, S. (2003). Compared to what? Effects of categorization on hedonic contrast. *Psychonomic Bulletin and Review, 10,* 468–473.

3

Stereotypes and Shifting Standards: Assimilation and Contrast in Social Judgment

MONICA BIERNAT and MELVIN MANIS

*I*n ordinary language use, words like *small* and *large* or *short* and *tall* are understood to have different meanings, depending on the object being described. For example, listeners would not be surprised to learn that a *large* cat fits comfortably in a *small* car, or that a *short* man is taller than a *tall* stack of pancakes. As noted by Kraut and Higgins (1984), how we understand the claim that "Tom is fast . . . depends on whether he is a boy or a horse" (p. 105). Key in these examples is the slippery character of adjectives; the capacity of a single description to be understood in myriad ways depending on the context or referent at hand.

This context dependence of language (and particularly of adjectival descriptors) is at the heart of a model of "shifting standards" in judgment that we have developed over the last 15 years or so. This model focuses primarily on the role of social stereotypes—beliefs about the attributes of groups—in creating the context within which subjective descriptions are interpreted. Specifically, the model suggests that beliefs that groups differ on some attribute—say, that women are less aggressive than men—lead perceivers to judge members of those groups relative to group-specific standards on that attribute. For example, a particular woman's aggressiveness will be judged relative to the (low) standards of aggression for women, whereas a particular man's aggressiveness will be judged relative to a higher standard of aggression (designed for men). The result is that the same adjectival label ("very aggressive") may mean substantially different things depending on whether a man or a woman is being so described. In this example, an act described as "very aggressive" (for a man) likely means an objectively higher level of aggression than is suggested when a woman is described as "very aggressive." Additionally, this use of shifting standards in judgment may mean that the same "objective" evidence is subjectively evaluated rather differently, depending on the sex of the actor. For example, "pushing someone" may be judged moderately aggressive in a man, but substantially more aggressive in a woman.

In this chapter, we will elaborate upon and review research evidence relevant to this shifting standards model of judgment, with a particular emphasis on what the model says about assimilation and contrast effects in judging individual members of stereotyped groups. The general perspective we advance is that social judgments may show evidence of assimilation to *or* contrast from social stereotypes, depending on the nature of the judgment at hand. Stereotyping is not strictly an assimilative phenomenon, as is commonly believed. Though it is perhaps most obvious when one judges a given woman as, say, less competent for a masculine occupation than a comparable man, stereotypes are equally operative when that same women is judged subjectively better than a man who has shown an identical level of performance. We will also review evidence that patterns of assimilation versus contrast are dependent on the *type* of standard invoked, and that behavioral responses to stereotyped group members may also show patterns of stereotype assimilation or contrast, dependent on the nature of the behavior.

Following our review of evidence relevant to the shifting standards model, we will consider some broader issues raised by our research. These include questions about the commonality of contrast effects in the research literature, the likelihood that contrast effects will emerge when judges make "objective" judgments of others, and the meaningfulness of subjective judgments, given their "fuzzy" nature.

STANDARDS AND JUDGMENT: THE SHIFTING STANDARDS MODEL

As noted above, the heart of the shifting standards model is the notion that judgments are made relative to some frame of reference, and that this frame of reference may shift for different categories or types of targets. This idea itself is not new—it is evident in a number of classic models of judgment, including Volkmann's (1951) "rubber band" model, Parducci's (1963) "range-frequency" model, and Upshaw's (1962) "variable perspective" model (see also Postman & Miller, 1945). The general idea is that when called upon to make judgments in subjective rating units (whether they be judgments of objects, people, or attitude statements), judges will fix the endpoints of the rating scale to reflect the expected distribution of targets on the judgment dimension. For example, if asked to judge the length of lines on a "very short" to "very long" scale, a 12″ line will be judged longer when the entire range of to-be-judged lines is in the 2″–12″ range than when the range is 2″–22″ (see Eiser, 1990).

The shifting standards model suggests that expectations regarding the range of to-be-evaluated targets may be provided by group stereotypes. Stereotypes include representations of the mean level of an attribute that members of a given group possess, as well as a likely range that members of the group will exhibit (Judd & Park, 1993). In this way, stereotypes serve the "endpoint setting" function described in these early judgment models, such that endpoints are set differentially for members of contrasting groups. This idea is depicted schematically in Figure 3.1. We begin with the assumption that judges hold a stereotype such as the

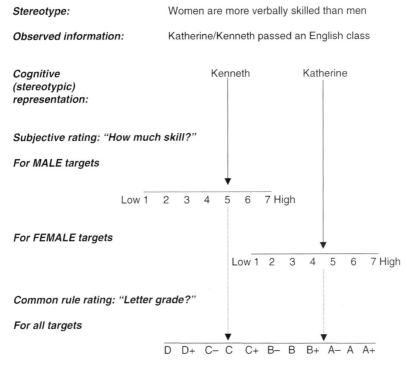

Stereotype: Women are more verbally skilled than men

Observed information: Katherine/Kenneth passed an English class

Cognitive   Kenneth   Katherine
(stereotypic)
representation:

Subjective rating: "How much skill?"

For MALE targets

Low 1   2   3   4   5   6   7 High

For FEMALE targets

Low 1   2   3   4   5   6   7 High

Common rule rating: "Letter grade?"

For all targets

D   D+   C−   C   C+   B−   B   B+   A−   A   A+

FIGURE 3.1   Schematic depiction of stereotypes influencing judgment standards and evaluations of male and female targets.

belief that women are more verbally skilled than men. In an experimental study, they might be exposed to a vignette that describes a woman or man (Katherine or Kenneth) who recently passed an English class (a piece of individuating information). Judges are then asked to rate the target person with respect to verbal skill (low to high).

The shifting standards model assumes that, initially, there is an automatic, perceptual-level *assimilative* effect in terms of the mental representation of the targets: That is, consistent with the stereotype, Katherine is assumed to be cognitively represented as more verbally skilled than Kenneth: a sort of base-rate effect (Kahneman & Tversky, 1973). The model further suggests, however, that this stereotype also contributes to the differential anchoring of subjective scales for women and men. In Figure 3.1, the expected distribution of verbal skill results in lower end-anchors for men than for women; there is also little overlap between the two distributions.[1] The result of this anchoring, and the mapping of the mental representation onto judgment, is that Kenneth is subjectively judged to be more verbally skilled than Katherine (he is rated a "5" while she is awarded a "4.5")—a *contrast* effect.

But what if we bypassed the judge's tendency to anchor subjective scales differently for female and male targets? We could do this by requiring that judgments be rendered in units that do not allow for shifts in meaning—on response scales that are "objective" or "common rule" in nature. As suggested in Figure 3.1, asking judges to estimate verbal skill by indicating what letter grade Katherine/Kenneth likely earned in the English class would force a judgment that is not open to shifts in meaning. For most people, an "A" means an "A" regardless of who earns it; that is, the scale, and the meaning associated with each rating unit, applies to all targets. As depicted in Figure 3.1, the result is that the common rule scale reveals *assimilation* to stereotypes—the cognitive representation associated with Katherine is thought to justify a higher letter grade (B+ or A–) than the C grade awarded to Kenneth.

The signature evidence that shifting standards have operated, then, is that objective or *common rule* judgment scales (like the letter grades in our example) are more likely to reveal *assimilation* to stereotypes than *subjective* scales (i.e., the subjective skill ratings). Because they invoke a within-category perspective, subjective scales may *mask* evidence of stereotyping (producing null effects) or they may show evidence of what some might call *reverse stereotyping* (contrast effects).[2]

Considerable evidence from our lab supports this common-rule/subjective difference when individual members of stereotyped groups are judged. For example, when asked to estimate the heights of photographed men and women in common-rule (feet-and-inches) or subjective scales ("short"–"tall"), common-rule judgments revealed assimilation to stereotypes whereas subjective judgments produced significant reductions of this effect (Biernat, Manis, & Nelson, 1991, Study 1). In another illustrative study, participants judged the financial success of male and female targets either in dollars earned per year or in subjective units. In this case, men were judged to earn objectively more money than women (an assimilation effect), but women were judged financially more successful than men (a contrast effect). For a woman to be labeled "moderately successful," she could earn, on average, $9000 less per year than a "moderately successful" man (Biernat et al., 1991, Study 2).

A more complex pattern suggesting the context-specific nature of stereotyping was observed in a study where a male target (Kenneth Anderson) was judged *objectively* more competent than an identically qualified female target (Katherine Anderson) for a masculine job (Executive Chief of Staff), and the female was judged objectively more competent than the male for a feminine job (Executive Secretary). However, *subjective* evaluations showed the opposite pattern—male targets were judged subjectively better secretaries than female targets, and female targets were judged subjectively better chiefs of staff than male targets (Biernat & Kobrynowicz, 1997). These latter contrast effects suggest that participants implicitly mean "*for a woman,* she'd be a pretty good chief of staff;" "*for a man,* he'd be a pretty good secretary." Standards shift. From our perspective, however, the null or contrastive effects of stereotypes that result from such shifts should not be taken at face value. By comparing subjective judgments to those made in common-rule units, or to paired-choice estimates or rank orders (who's the better leader in the group?), we know that the same judgment (e.g., "very able") may mean something different depending on the social category of the target being described (male and female in this example).

A number of other studies focusing on the assessment of individuals from contrasting gender and racial groups also support the pattern of stronger assimilative stereotyping effects in common-rule than subjective judgments (for recent reviews, see Biernat, 2003; Biernat & Thompson, 2002). Further evidence consistent with the shifting standards model comes from research demonstrating that perceivers differentially *translate* subjective judgments into common rule units based on an individual's category membership. For example, being a "good parent" is assumed to mean more objective involvement in child care activities (hours spent with a child, diapers changed, meals cooked, homework helped) if the parent is a woman than a man, and being "good at math" is presumed to indicate higher objective math grades if the student is Asian American than African American (Kobrynowicz & Biernat, 1997).

What about outside *our* laboratory, and outside the laboratory in general? One obvious domain in which evaluations matter is the world of work, where employees regularly receive performance appraisals (see Murphy & Cleveland, 1995). One central issue in the performance appraisal literature concerns how to reduce bias—including possible bias based on the target's category membership (typically, race or sex; see Martocchio & Whitener, 1992; Mobley, 1982). Interestingly, considerations of this question have often taken up the issue of *objective* versus *subjective* measures of performance—a theme with great relevance for the shifting standards model. With regard to ethnic group differences in performance appraisal, Roth, Huffcutt, and Bobko (2003) review evidence suggesting that these differences tend to be greater on *subjective* than *objective* measures. This pattern is clearly contradictory to the ideas advanced in the shifting standards model, but it *is* based on the intuitively reasonable idea that objective indicators are less open to bias than subjective indicators might be (Ford, Kraiger, & Schechtman, 1986; Rotundo & Sackett, 1999; Schmidt & Hunter, 1981).

Despite their general emphasis on the susceptibility of subjective scales to stereotyping (assimilation) in performance appraisals, in their own meta-analysis, Roth et al. (2003) generally found stronger evidence of bias on *objective* than *subjective* indicators, a pattern more consistent with that predicted by the shifting standards model. For example, for measures of job *quality*, the effect size (Whites evaluated more favorably than Blacks) was $d = .24$ for objective measures (objective indicators of work product, errors, complaints) and .20 for subjective measures (subjective ratings of quality);[3] for measures of job *quantity*, the objective effect size was $d = .32$ (e.g., number of units produced, sales volume), and the subjective effect size was $d = .09$; on measures of job *knowledge* (which included ratings [subjective] or tests [objective] of mastery of training material) the objective effect size was $d = .55$, and the subjective effect size was $d = .15$. And on measures of absenteeism, the objective effect size was $d = .23$, and the subjective effect size was $d = .13$. Several studies also indicated comparable patterns with regard to White–Hispanic differences (for job knowledge, the objective effect size was $d = .67$, and the subjective effect size was $d = .04$).

To be fair, it is important to note that Roth et al.'s (2003) meta-analysis often involved between-subject comparisons, such that a subjective effect size was calculated on a completely separate set of studies than an objective effect size (with attendant confounding based on types of jobs studied, samples, evaluators, targets, etc.). But in two within-subject studies that reported both objective and subjective measures of "job knowledge," the same pattern emerged: In a sample of medical technicians, the White–Black d was .44 for an objective test and .06 for a subjective rating, and in a sample of cartographic technicians, comparable ds were .42 and .23, respectively (Campbell, Crooks, Mahoney, & Rock, 1973). In short, judgments of real employees often indicate that evaluation standards may shift based on the target's race, and that the observed pattern is consistent with the shifting standards model predictions about the differences between objective and subjective appraisals.

TYPES OF JUDGMENT STANDARDS

All of the research we have described thus far is based on the assumption that judges have lower standards for groups stereotyped as deficient on an attribute. For example, the stereotype that men are better leaders than women means that standards or expectations are lower for judging women's leadership than men's; the stereotype that women have better verbal skills than men means that standards are lower for judging men's than women's verbal ability (see Figure 3.1). It is these lower standards that allow for contrast effects to emerge; for example, for a woman's salary (say, $45,000) to suggest greater subjective financial success than that same salary earned by a man (Biernat et al., 1991). Writing about the overly-favorable evaluations that competent African Americans may receive in academics and the workplace, law professor Stephen Carter (1993) writes, "like a flower blooming in winter, intellect is more readily noticed where it is not expected to be found" (p. 54).

However, this notion that stereotyped group members are held to lower standards may seem at odds with another sentiment described by Carter (1993): "Our parents' advice was true: We really do have to work twice as hard to be considered half as good [as Whites]" (p. 58). This statement suggests that groups stereotyped as deficient on an attribute may be held to *higher* standards than other groups, an idea also articulated in a theoretical perspective on double standards for evaluating competence (Foddy & Smithson, 1989; Foschi, 1992, 2000; Foschi & Foddy, 1988). Specifically, this perspective focuses on status characteristics—markers implying task competence—of which gender and race may be examples. These status cues implicate different standards for evaluating competence: "Those who are considered to be of lower status will have their successful performances scrutinized (since these are inconsistent with status) and then assessed by a stricter standard than similar performances by higher status actors" (Foschi, 2000, p. 25). Double standards can be evident in both quantitative terms (as when a standard for successful performance is lower for members of the high status than low status group), or in qualitative terms (as when different qualities are required from one group than another) (Foschi & Foddy, 1988). Furthermore, "the application of a more lenient standard to the higher status person ensures that more ability is assigned to him or her than to the lower status person with the same record" (Foschi, 2000, p. 26). In other words, holding lower status groups to higher standards than high status groups is conducive to *assimilation* effects.

Can both the shifting standards and "double standards" perspectives be right about how judgment standards operate? Can standards be both lower and higher for groups stereotyped as deficient on a given attribute? As a means of reconciling these perspectives, Biernat and Kobrynowicz (1997) suggested a distinction between two types of standards: (1) minimum standards—those indicating low-end expectations; the minimum qualifications necessary for a target to demonstrate that he or she may have the attribute in question (e.g., leadership skills), and (2) confirmatory (or ability) standards—those necessary for conclusively demonstrating the attribute. We predicted that when judges are asked to define *minimum standards*, these will be lower for groups stereotyped as deficient on the relevant attribute (a prediction consistent with the shifting standards model). But when asked to define *confirmatory standards*, these will be higher for those same groups (as predicted by the double standards perspective). That is, a member of a negatively stereotyped group may be held to low minimum standards (consistent with low expectations) but high confirmatory standards (consistent with requiring stronger evidence that an unexpected outcome is due to the target person's underlying ability).

To test these ideas in the context of job-related competence, Biernat and Kobrynowicz (1997) asked participants to indicate the minimum standards or the confirmatory standards they would set for a fictitious male or female job applicant (Kenneth Anderson or Katherine Anderson). When asked "how many examples [of job-relevant skills] would you require of [Kenneth/Katherine] before feeling confident that s/he meets the *minimum standard* to perform the skill?" participants indicated that Katherine could offer fewer such examples than Kenneth, who had been described in identical terms, save for his gender (Biernat & Kobrynowicz, 1997, Study 1). Similarly, in a second study that varied the race of the applicant, participants indicated that a score of 65% on a standardized ability test would meet minimum standards for the Black applicant, but a score of 71% was required for the White applicant (Study 2). These low standards for devalued groups indicate the low expectations inherent in the group stereotypes, and they set the stage for the contrast effects in judgment outlined earlier—when evaluated against a lower standard, a given "performance" looks subjectively better.

But other participants in the Biernat and Kobrynowicz (1997) studies were asked to indicate *confirmatory standards*; to indicate the evidence they would require "before feeling confident that [the applicant] has the ability to perform the skill." These judgments indicated the opposite pattern: Women were held to higher confirmatory standards than men; Black applicants to higher standards than White applicants. We suggest that these bottom-line evidentiary requirements (what does this person have to do to really show me s/he has the attribute?) set the stage for assimilation effects. Because less is expected of them, members of the group stereotyped as deficient on the attribute have to do more to prove they have the attribute. And because these confirmatory standards are higher, these individuals are less likely to meet them, and the desired attribute is less likely to be inferred (see also Bodenhausen & Wyer, 1985; Hastie, 1984; Maass, Milesi, Zabbini, & Stahlberg, 1995; Trope & Liberman, 1993, for evidence that unexpected behaviors are less likely to lead to dispositional inferences than expected behaviors).

These findings do not hold only for the inference of competence. In research examining the standards for female and male targets to "qualify" as possessing a variety of personality attributes, participants were asked to indicate either (a) "the *minimum* number of behaviors necessary to detect whether or not the target has trait X; to *give you some inkling*" that the target had the attribute, or (b) "the total number of behaviors that are necessary to *confirm* whether or not the target has trait X; to *demonstrate to you*" that the target had the attribute (Biernat, Ma, & Nario-Redmond, 2005). Participants considered either a male or female target as they made these estimates, and in separate studies they were provided with sets of 20 behaviors relevant to the traits emotional, competitive, or aggressive. The number of required behavioral examples checked was the index of the standard (minimum or confirmatory) the participant had in mind. For each trait, the group stereotyped as deficient on the attribute (men on emotionality, women on competitiveness and aggression) was held to lower *minimum* standards (e.g., fewer behaviors were required to suspect that a man might be emotional) but higher *confirmatory* standards (e.g., more behaviors required to confirm that a man is emotional) relative to the other gender group (see also Biernat & Ma, 2005; Maass, Montalcini, & Biciotti, 1998).

Again, these findings indicate that stereotypes affect the inferences we make about others—in this case, the evidentiary standards we apply to them—in either an assimilative or contrastive direction. When focused on *minimum* standards, the low expectation inherent in the stereotype means that less is required to meet the standard, and thus contrast is more likely (e.g., because it takes a relatively low score for a Black relative to White applicant to meet minimum competency standards in the work place, more Blacks can meet them). But when focused on *confirmatory* standards, the same low expectations implied by the stereotype heighten the evidence required to meet it, for essentially one is being asked to disconfirm a belief (e.g., come to the conclusion that the Black applicant is truly competent). This prompts assimilation, as members of those groups stereotyped as having the attribute will be held to lower confirmatory standards, and therefore will be more readily diagnosed as having met them.[4]

This may play out in interesting ways in the workplace, where both types of standard may apply at different points in the hiring process. For example, for many jobs, creation of a "short list" may be based on use of minimum standards: Those placed on a short list must presumably meet some minimal standard of competence. But a hiring decision may be based on the use of a confirmatory standard—decision makers want to choose the applicant they truly believe has the ability to perform the job. Based on the ideas outlined above, we suspected that if minimum standards are lower for groups stereotyped as deficient on an attribute, this should mean that Blacks and women may find it *easier* to get on the short list. At the same time, the higher confirmatory standard that drives a hiring decision may make those same individuals *less likely* to actually get the job. In two studies that simulated creation of short lists and hiring decisions, we did find that for female decision makers, and under conditions of accountability, women were more likely than men to make the short list for a masculine job, but less likely to be hired for that job (Biernat & Fuegen, 2001).

Medical decision making may be another important domain in which minimal and confirmatory standards are relevant. That is, often before *diagnosis* of an illness or condition there is a period of *suspicion* that a patient may have the condition, often marked by referral to a specialist. One interesting study examined the referral recommendations of pediatricians and family practice physicians when it came to concerns about language delay in young children (Sices, Feudtner, McLaughlin, Drotar, & Williams, 2004). Research suggests that boys develop language later than girls (Gleason & Ely, 2002); that is, the expectation (or stereotype) is that girls will be less likely to experience language delays. In the study by Sices et al. (2004), physicians read a vignette describing an 18-month-old boy or girl who was "walking well, drinking from a cup, and saying 'mama' and 'dada' (not yet specifically for each parent), and has no other words" (p. 276). (This level of expressive language development is below the 10th percentile for a 10-month-old child.) Physicians were then asked "what actions, if any" they would take in response, and referral to an audiologist was the critical dependent measure. The researchers found that the girl with a language delay was 60% more likely to be referred to audiology than a boy (a ratio of 1.57:1).

This finding seems consistent with our analysis of lower minimum standards for members of groups who are *not expected* to have an attribute. That is, pediatricians do not expect that toddler girls will have language delays, and this may translate into a low *minimum standard* for identifying girls who are experiencing language delay (higher referral rates). Although this study did not investigate what we would call confirmatory standards (i.e., did the audiologist actually diagnose a hearing problem to be treated?), several epidemiological studies have found that "mental retardation and autism spectrum disorders, which are associated with language delay and hearing loss, are actually more prevalent in boys" (Sices et al., 2004, p. 279; e.g., see Bertrand et al., 2001; Halfon & Newacheck, 1999). That is, boys are more likely to be diagnosed with disorders that are linked to language delays than girls—a finding consistent with lower *confirmatory* standards for the group *expected* to have language delays (i.e., boys).[5]

We cannot claim to have conducted a thorough search (or to have a thorough understanding) of the literature on medical diagnosis, and thus we cannot suggest with any confidence that this pattern of differential gender-based standards is common or typical. We also do not intend to claim that physician stereotypes, rather than *true* differences between presenting boys and girls, are responsible for higher rates of diagnosing autism or mental retardation in boys. But the results reported by Sices et al. (2004) are consistent with the possibility that stereotypes about language delay are manifested in lower *minimum* standards for suspecting possible language problems in girls.

Another medical study relevant to the concept of minimum standards examined the hospital records of children who were presenting to a Growth Center for short stature—that is, children who had been referred to a specialist because of concerns about their growth (Grimberg, Kutikov, & Cucchiara, 2005). Framing growth concerns in terms of gender stereotypes, we begin with the fact that boys are, on average, taller than girls. Thus, there are low expectations that boys will be short. This should translate into a *lower* minimum standard for suspecting a growth problem in boys, or a greater frequency of referral for boys than girls for concerns about growth. Indeed, Grimberg et al. (2005) found that in 1 year's worth of hospital records, boys were referred more frequently than girls (by a ratio of 1.9:1), the height deficit was greater in girls before they were first referred (i.e., it took more evidence of [normatively] poor growth before girls presented for treatment), and it took (slightly) longer for the referral to occur for girls than boys (35 vs. 24 months). Also, "the percentage of boys referred at normal height (38%) exceeded that of girls (20%)" (p. 213).

Of course, it is also possible that the greater referral rate for boys has less to do with low minimum standards based on gender and more to do with parental concerns about the negative societal consequences that short boys face (relative to short girls). For similar reasons, parents may be more concerned about girls than boys with slow language development. In the case of height, it is also the case that our analysis would hypothesize that lower minimum standards for boys are com- plemented by higher standards to *confirm* a growth problem in boys than in girls. This does not seem to be the case, as boys are more likely than girls to receive growth hormone treatment (e.g., August et al., 1996), and one experimental study found that pediatric endocrinologists recommended growth hormone treatment 1.3 times as often for hypothetical male than female case scenarios (Cuttler et al., 1996). We assume that treatment indicates a definitive diagnosis has been made, and these data therefore suggest that boys are not only referred more readily, but are more likely to be diagnosed as having growth problems requiring treatment. This pattern may suggest a limitation of our analysis—when strong motivations for diagnosis exist (as may be the case among parents concerned about the "social pressures for tall stature in men"; Grimberg et al., 2005, p. 214), both minimum and confirmatory standards may be low.

BEHAVIOR TOWARD MEMBERS OF STEREOTYPED GROUPS

We have suggested that both standards and judgment may show evidence of either assimilation or contrast with respect to group stereotypes, depending on their measurement. What about behavior? Does our behavior toward individual mem- bers of stereotyped groups sometimes show evidence of assimilation to stereo- types, and sometimes contrast? The hiring study by Biernat and Fuegen (2001) described above is suggestive of assimilation effects. That is, women were less likely than men to be "hired" for a masculine-stereotyped job (see also Davison & Burke, 2000; Heilman, 2001; Olian, Schwab, & Haberfeld, 1988). To take another example from just one employment domain, academics, national statistics indicate that women in science, technology, engineering, and mathematics are under- represented at the highest academic ranks (Nelson & Rogers, 2005; NSF, 2000), earn less than men (American Association for the Advancement of Science, 2001; Ginther, 2004; NSF, 2004), and are less likely to be promoted (NSF, 2004).

However, one can also find evidence of behavioral favorability toward members of stereotyped groups—a kind of contrast effect. In one illustrative study, Harber (1998) examined the nature of feedback White participants offered to Black versus White authors of poorly-written essays. Feedback on the essay content was more favorable when the author was thought to be Black than White (though comments on objective qualities such as grammar did not differ based on race). In an earlier study, Weitz (1972) found that vocal positivity—the warmth and admiration that were apparent when participants delivered experimental instructions to a (fictional) Black partner—was most favorable among those with the most negative attitudes toward the partner. That is, the favorable behavioral tone represented a contrast from the negative attitude (a pattern that did not hold when the fictional partner was White). And in a recent meta-analysis of studies that compared reactions (both behavioral and evaluative) to White and African American targets, Aberson and Ettlin (2004) found that under conditions that promoted egalitarianism, African Americans were favored over Whites ($d = -.34$).

There may be many moderators of behavioral assimilation versus contrast effects. Indeed, in the just-mentioned meta-analysis, Aberson and Ettlin (2004) highlighted an important moderator derived from aversive racism theory (Gaertner & Dovidio, 1986)—the normative clarity of the interracial situation. As predicted by this theory, behavioral responses favored Blacks when norms for appropriate behavior were clear or favored egalitarian responding, but Whites were favored over Blacks under conditions of norm ambiguity ($d = .21$).

In addition to these normative factors, there is increasing evidence that the character of the judge's task may importantly affect the impact of group stereotypes on behavior (Biernat, Vescio, & Manis, 1998). Specifically, we have distinguished between *zero-sum* behaviors (those involving allocation of a limited resource, such that behavior toward one individual restricts the behavioral options available toward another) and *nonzero-sum* behaviors (those involving a limitless, though often less valuable, resource). Zero-sum behaviors include decisions such as hiring, placement into positions/assignments, and allocation of money or other resources (the kinds of outcomes examined for female academics in the research cited above), whereas nonzero-sum behaviors may include nonverbals (e.g., smiles vs. frowns), or vocal or written feedback delivered toward others. One can smile at or verbally praise any number of individuals without "running out" of resources, whereas the decision to hire an individual or assign her to perform a task has a zero-sum quality.[6]

Our prediction is that zero-sum behaviors will tend to reveal assimilation to group stereotypes, whereas nonzero-sum behaviors will tend toward contrast. The main basis for this prediction lies in logic similar to what we applied to the subjective-common rule judgment distinction. Zero-sum behaviors require a *cross-category* frame of reference. For example, if an employer can hire only one person for a job, s/he must make the choice across the entire pool of male and female applicants of all racial backgrounds. This is comparable to the kind of frame of reference invoked when judgments are made on a common rule response scale (see Figure 3.1). Indeed, the judge with this frame of reference may simply compare his or her mental representation of job candidates and choose the one who seems most qualified, bypassing the subjective assessments that are depicted in Figure 3.1. And because these mental representations are likely to be influenced—perhaps automatically—by prevailing stereotypes, assimilation to stereotypes is the result. On the other hand, nonzero-sum behaviors such as provision of feedback or praise are likely made with reference to *within-category* expectations. Just as a parent may offer effusive praise to a child who reads her first sentence, Harber's (1998) White participants may have praised the bad essays written by Blacks because the quality often exceeded the judges' low expectations. The cross-category perspective invites assimilation to stereotypes; the within-category perspective is more likely to produce null effects or contrast (see Abele & Petzold, 1998).

To date, we are aware of two sets of studies that have provided explicit tests of the zero-sum/nonzero-sum distinction. In one, participants role-played being the manager of a coed softball team who had to make a variety of staffing decisions (Biernat & Vescio, 2002). From a set of 18 photos (nine male and nine female, selected from pretests that indicated equivalently perceived levels of athleticism), managers chose 13 players to be on their team, and then had to assign these players to fielding positions and a batting order (with three players benched). These were zero-sum decisions; for example, only one player could play short-stop or bat in the top of the order. Each of these decisions revealed favoritism toward the male players over the female players—assimilation to the stereotype of men as better athletes. To assess a nonzero-sum behavior, "managers" were asked to imagine that a player had hit a single, and to indicate how they would respond to this performance. We conceptualized "cheering loudly," "smiling at the player," and other responses to indicate favorable feedback compared to a "nothing in particular" response. On this index, female players evoked more favorable responses than male players—a stereotype-contrastive effect.

In the second study comparing zero-sum and nonzero-sum behaviors, male participants were placed in leadership roles and had authority over female and male subordinates (Vescio, Gervais, Snyder, & Hoover, 2005, Study 1). Assignments to valued tasks (such as being the team captain or to the first string of a team competing in an "academic challenge" contest) favored male over female subordinates. That is, zero-sum behaviors revealed a pattern of assimilation to gender stereotypes, particularly among male leaders who had been oriented (through task instructions) to avoid weaknesses in their team. At the same time, these male leaders *praised* female subordinates more than male subordinates for their work (e.g., offering such comments as "your answers during the first phase of the experiment were excellent!"). Nonzero-sum behaviors favored women over men—a contrast effect.

In sum, judgments of and behavior toward members of stereotype groups may show evidence of assimilation or contrast—indeed the standards evoked by stereotypes may be conducive to assimilation or contrast, depending on the nature of the judgment/behavior at hand. We have distinguished between judgments made in common-rule and subjective units, standards based on confirmatory and minimum evidentiary criteria, and behaviors that have a zero-sum or nonzero-sum quality. We suggest that assimilation to stereotypes will be more likely when judgments are made on common-rule scales, with reference to confirmatory standards, and when the behaviors at hand are zero-sum. Contrast effects (or null effects) will be more likely when judgments are made in subjective units, with reference to minimum standards, and when a judgment or a behavior is nonzero-sum in nature. In the work place, women and Blacks may both face difficulty in hiring but may frequently find themselves placed on more shortlists; they may receive relatively negative evaluations on common-rule scales but more favorable subjective ratings; they may be awarded fewer promotions and be assigned to fewer valuable tasks but receive more praise when they accomplish them.

BROADER ISSUES ABOUT ASSIMILATION AND CONTRAST

How Common are Contrast Effects?

We have described a number of cases in which the use of shifting standards results in contrast effects, where a target from a low-status group is evaluated more favorably than a comparable target from a high status group. For example, a woman may be described as a "better" chief of staff than a man with comparable credentials (Biernat & Kobrynowicz, 1997), women are judged more "financially successful" than men (Biernat et al., 1991), a Black law school applicant with good credentials is judged more favorably than a comparable White applicant (Linville & Jones, 1980), and a female employee is judged more agentic than a male employee (Eagly & Steffen, 1984). But a more typical judgment pattern in our research using subjective response scales is a null effect, or reduced assimilation, relative to what we find on objective scales. Furthermore, in the meta-analysis on race differences in employee evaluation described earlier, there was weak evidence of favoritism toward Whites on subjective scales (relative to objective indicators), rather than a reversal of this pattern (Roth et al., 2003). In reviewing the literature on stereotyping, Kunda and Thagard (1996) write, "There are too few demonstrations of contrast effects to permit an assessment of the question of when stereotypes will provoke contrast effects rather than the more frequently found null effects on trait ratings" (p. 294).

Though we would not characterize contrast effects as rare, we would agree that assimilation to stereotypes (especially on objective judgment scales) or null effects (especially on subjective judgment scales) is more common in our own work and the research literature more broadly. This suggests that the assimilative influence of stereotypes—the implicit reliance on base rates—is quite strong, and that the standard-shift mechanism we have posited is weaker, only occasionally suppressing assimilative forces.

But this pattern stands in contrast to a set of findings by Manis and Paskewitz (1984), which suggested that, in some cases, contrast and assimilation processes may operate at the same time, with contrast dominating. For example, in a study by Manis and Paskewitz, participants were first exposed to a series of word definitions that illustrated either high or low psychopathology (e.g., "GAMBLE: Waste money for good excitement") and were asked to indicate which definitions had been produced by schizophrenic patients. These definitions were presented to create *expectations* (stereotypes) about the kinds of patients likely to be seen later in the study, and indeed respondents assigned to the high-pathology induction expected to subsequently see more pathological definitions than those assigned to the low-pathology induction. However, when the respondents were then presented with moderately pathological test definitions, a marked contrast effect emerged; i.e., the test definitions were judged to be more pathological by those originally exposed to the nonpathological induction set (contrast), despite the fact that (a) these respondents did not expect to encounter many pathological definitions in the test series, and (b) their individual expectations were positively correlated with their subsequent judgments. In brief then, the induction phase produced "more-of-the-same" expectations that were, in turn, positively related to the respondents' judgments, a combination that would normally promote assimilation (to the induction series). But despite this assimilative pressure, overall judgments were *contrasted* from the judge's initial context experience.

In considering relevant literature for this chapter, we were drawn to a comparison between the research on stereotyping, where assimilation effects seem to prevail, and the substantial research on contextual judgment effects, including the Manis–Paskewitz findings (e.g., Helson, 1964; Parducci, 1963), where contrast seems more common. We note here that despite the many differences between these domains, they nonetheless have an important feature in common: Both literatures explore how assessments of a particular exemplar (person or stimulus) are affected by "background" considerations, such as the race of a job applicant (in the study of stereotypes), or the judge's recent experiences (in studies of judgmental context effects). Note, moreover, that in both cases probabilistic reasoning might plausibly be invoked, in that the exemplar-to-be-judged might be evaluated in the light of prior knowledge (e.g., assumptions about the target's social category in studies of stereotypes, or experience with the stimuli presented earlier in the experimental session in studies of judgmental context).

How, then, can we explain the difference between the assimilation effects that are so common in the study of stereotypes, as opposed to the contrast effects that are typical in studies inspired by Helson (1964) and others? Here are some possibilities:

1. In the context literature, experimentally created expectations (and the subjective standard shifts that follow) may dominate base rate considerations (stereotyping effects). That is, the contrastive forces that derive from the judges' activated standards appear to be very strong, and effectively hide the assimilative influences. In the study of stereotypes, on the other hand, the judge's socially-based expectations (and the assimilative influence that follows) may be more important, as beliefs about different social groups are generally long-standing and are socially reinforced on an almost daily basis.

2. The time that elapses between "induction" and assessment may also be critical, as suggested by Manis and Paskewitz (1984). That is, in many experimental studies, expectations are created by exposure to a biased set of exemplars, and judges are then immediately asked to assess a set of test targets. On the other hand, in the stereotyping literature (and in the job setting or in medical practice), base-rates (stereotypes) are established well before the judge is presented with the individual who is to be evaluated. Manis and Paskewitz proposed that the time course of the expectation and contrast paths may operate differently. Namely, they suggest that the forces promoting contrast may lose their impact more rapidly than the forces promoting assimilation. Indeed, some studies have shown that when a time delay is introduced between a "biased" induction series and the respondents' subsequent judgments, assimilation effects replaced the contrastive patterns that had initially been observed (Manis & Blake, 1963; Manis & Moore, 1978).

3. Assimilation to base rates (or expectations) is more likely than contrast when the targets generally "fit" the judges' expectation, or can be construed to do so; contrast, on the other hand, is more likely when there is a substantial discrepancy between the expectation and the target (e.g., when the target unambiguously does *not* fit). In the social psychological tradition, this idea seems mainly to derive from the classic work of Sherif and Hovland (1961), and it has subsequently received clear support in stereotyping research (e.g., see Brewer, 1988; Fiske & Neuberg, 1990; Kunda & Thagard, 1996), and in the broader literature on context effects as well (e.g., Herr, Sherman, & Fazio, 1983; Schwarz & Bless, 1992; Stapel, Koomen, and van der Pligt, 1997; Stapel & Winkielman, 1998). Research on the shifting standards model has not examined this issue, however. Instead, the bulk of our research has involved targets that might be best described as having "neutral" standing (e.g., a job application where the candidate appears to have moderate, but not extreme credentials). This may contribute to the assimilation results we have observed on common rule scales, and to the typical pattern of null effects on subjective scales.

Are Common-Rule Scales Impervious to Contrast Effects?

Examination of our model (see Figure 3.1) suggests that subjective judgments should always be moved in a contrastive direction, relative to the judge's "pure" cognitive representation, but only if the judge is led to consider the target's subjective standing relative to others in his or her group. Thus, as in Figure 3.1, ratings of Kenneth's verbal skills are likely to be enhanced by our implicit tendency to compare him to other men (who are assumed to be somewhat limited in this domain). And similarly, Katherine's verbal skills should be contrasted (underestimated) when compared with our more demanding verbal expectations for women. Suppose, however, the judge is asked to directly compare the verbal skills of Kenneth and Katherine, inviting an examination of "pure" cognitive representations. According to Figure 3.1, such a comparison should bypass the contrastive effects that derive from the judge's (shifting) subjective scales, result-ing in an assimilation effect in which Katherine is thought to be the more skillful. Regardless of the extremity of the input information and its discrepancy from the judge's expectations, our model suggests that assimilation should be observed.

However, results reported by Manis, Nelson, and Shedler (1988) indicate that contrast effects can also be observed in such circumstances, provided that there is a sufficient discrepancy between the stimuli in the induction series and those in the final judgment or "test" phase. In these experiments, judges assessed the level of psychopathology that was implied by different vocabulary definitions. The def-initions purportedly came from patients at two different hospitals: Metropolitan and Central. For some judges, Metro appeared to deal with very disturbed patients, while the patients at Central showed little evidence of psychopathology. Following an induction series which established these very different expectations for the two hospitals, judges were instructed to consider several pairs of def-initions; each pair purportedly included one definition from a Metro patient and one from a patient at Central. The judge's task was to identify the more disturbed of the two (essentially a request to compare the cognitive representations of the patients). Results indicated that if the induction definitions that established the distinction between the hospitals were sufficiently discrepant from one another (and discrepant from the moderately psychopathological test definitions), there was significant evidence of contrast in these paired-choice judgments. On the other hand, when the stereotypes established for the two hospitals were only moderately discrepant from one another (and from the test definitions), assimilation was observed.

The assimilation effect is easily explained by reference to Figure 3.1. When the definitions in the test pairs were sufficiently congruent with the stereotypes previously established for the two hospitals, the judges assumed that the def-initions that were to be compared would follow the by-then familiar pattern: Definitions from Metro would be automatically assumed to reflect a fair degree of psychopathology (like the earlier definitions from Metro), whereas those from Central would seem relatively normal. A direct comparison of these rather differ-ent cognitive representations would yield the assimilation effect that was observed. On the other hand, the contrast effects that were also observed in this study on paired-choice judgments ("Which definition suggests more disturbance—the one from Central Hospital or the one from Metro?") are a bit more puzzling. Most importantly, they do not involve the judges' subjective ratings, at least not in any obvious way. In the shifting standards model, as in other "semantic" accounts (e.g., Upshaw, 1962; Volkmann, 1951), contrast is thought to derive from shifts in the judge's frame of reference. Instead, the contrast demonstration in Manis et al. (1988) seems very similar to the kind of *sensory* adaptation described by Helson (1964)—when a hot-adapted and cold-adapted hand are simultaneously plunged into lukewarm water, that water feels colder to the "hot" hand than the "cold" hand. In the same kind of paired-choice or forced comparison judgment, moder-ate definitions seem crazier to one adapted to a low pathology hospital than a high pathology one. Can the shifting standards approach explain this finding?

Certainly the factor of standard-target discrepancy described above is relevant —contrastive effects of any sort (semantic or perceptual) may be more likely when there is a large discrepancy between what is expected and what is observed. Another possibility is that subjective assessments of the test patients (relative to other patients in their hospital) are implicitly involved, even though they are not called for by the experimenter's instructions. More particularly, the judge may assess each test definition relative to others from that same hospital. In this case, a moderately disturbed definition drawn from the more normal patient population at Central would seem relatively disturbed, while a similar definition might appear normal when implicitly compared to the various "crazies" at Metropolitan hospital. We have no evidence that this occurred of course; it seems prudent, instead, to acknowledge that the shifting standards model has its limits in accounting for judgment phenomena.

How Meaningful are Subjective Judgments?

Much of our work on the shifting standards model has suggested that subjective judgments of members of stereotyped groups cannot be taken at face value. Equivalent subjective judgments of male and female targets do not mean the targets are perceived identically (see Figure 3.1), and contrast effects do not indicate that "reverse stereotyping" has occurred. Instead, we have suggested that it is common rule judgments, along with zero-sum behavioral indicators, that provide the *best* indication of perceivers' underlying mental representations of targets.

This raises the question of whether subjective judgments (and nonzero-sum behavioral indicators) have *any* real meaning or value. That is, do they merely indicate response distortions or are they *true* reflections of judges' reactions to targets? In some ways, this question echoes the perceptual–semantic debate in the broader literature on context effects on judgment (e.g., see Eiser, 1990, for a review). Again, our research primarily suggests the "semantic" view—response-scale shifts drive the judgment patterns that emerge. At the same time, however, we recognize that judges probably do "feel" their subjective reactions in a meaningful way. For example, the manager who labels a female softball player "excellent" probably does *mean* that, at least in the within-gender context; the parent who describes the "brilliance" of her 5-year-old honestly feels the child is extraordinary. The delivery of praise to a target about whom one has low expectations may also be quite sincere. In this sense, subjective judgments and nonzero-sum behavior are "real."

Furthermore, we know from our own work that subjective judgments have predictive value—they are correlated with the delivery of nonzero-sum feedback (Biernat & Vescio, 2002). And in the broader literature, subjective judgments—often more so than objective indicators—predict important life outcomes. As a case in point, consider the finding that individuals' subjective ratings of their own health "are reasonably good predictors of longevity/death" (Nilsson et al., 1997, p. 15; see Ljungquist, Berg, & Steen, 1995). Objective health is difficult to define, and individuals' feelings about their health status are open to the kinds of standard shifts we have described here. For example, Nilsson et al. (1997) found that 35-year-olds and 80-year-olds rated themselves equally healthy; the overall correlation between age and self-reported subjective health was $r = -.06$. Nonetheless, these subjective judgments matter importantly for perhaps *the* most important dependent measure, death. In the literature on subjective well-being, it is also the case that individuals who report high global life satisfaction are less likely to become depressed (e.g., Lewinsohn, Redner, & Seeley, 1991) or to attempt suicide (Moum, 1996, cited in Diener & Biswas-Diener, 2000) than those who score low (see Diener, Suh, Lucas, & Smith, 1999, for a review of the validity of subjective well-being measures).[7]

In short, subjective judgments do clearly matter; they may reflect the reality of the moment, and their very subjectivity allows for idiosyncratic definition and weighting that appropriately capture abstract attributes such as health and life satisfaction. We would still argue, however, that in the kinds of stereotype-based judgment shifts we have discussed throughout this chapter, null effects or contrast effects that appear on subjective judgments scales may be *masking* an underlying stereotypic representation. And under most circumstances, if confronted with both their "objective" and "subjective" evaluations of targets, perceivers are likely to recognize the objective judgments as the truer of the two—the ones that *best* reflect the reality that stereotypes lead to *assimilative* representations of individual group members.

NOTES

1. This differentiation may be more extreme than is warranted by the verbal skill stereotype, but it nonetheless serves to illustrate the basic point about differential scale anchoring.

2. In our research on the shifting standards model, we have found it difficult to predict, a priori, whether subjective judgments will reveal contrastive or null effects of stereotypes. For example, will shifting standards lead perceivers to subjectively judge a particular woman *a better leader* than a comparable man, or *equally good* at leadership? As suggested by Figure 3.1, contrast should be more likely when standards (or the expected distributions) for two groups show little overlap; other research suggests that contrast should also be more likely when targets are *extreme* (Herr, 1986) or clearly violate group-based expectations (Bettencourt, Dill, Greathouse, Charlton, & Mulholland, 1997). However, the difficulty of assessing standards with a precision that captures mean, range, endpoint anchors, and distribution overlap has meant that we typically frame our predictions regarding subjective judgments in terms of *reduced assimilation* (relative to findings on common rule scales) rather than contrast effects. From our perspective, it is this relative difference in judgment patterns between subjective and common rule scales that is critical to the shifting standards model.

3. The effect size *d* indicates the mean difference between groups (in this case, the difference between Blacks and Whites) divided by the pooled standard deviation of the two groups. By convention, an effect size of $d = .2$ is considered small, $d = .5$ is considered medium, and $d = .8$ is considered large (see Cohen, 1988).

4. Interestingly, although we frame the pattern of differential confirmatory standards in terms of bias, it is also generally consistent with Bayesian reasoning. According

to Bayes' rule, when the available case information is not fully compelling (e.g., when one has some, though not definitive, behavioral evidence that a target has attribute X), it may be wise to take base rate information into account to inform the judgment—i.e., to consider group stereotypes as a basis of judgment (Bar-Hillel, 1980; Funder, 1995; Kahneman & Tversky, 1973). Unfortunately, such a "rational" strategy will normally serve to perpetuate stereotypes and social stratification.

5. Of course, these higher rates for boys may simply reflect reality, rather than the biasing impact of physicians' expectations.

6. Although these examples suggest that zero-sum behaviors are more valuable or important than nonzero-sum behaviors, this need not be the case. One can envision, for example, a situation in which the pleasant versus unpleasant interaction style of an individual creates significant advantages versus problems for the other interaction partner (Rosenthal, 2002).

7. With regard to subjective well-being and shifting standards, it is also the case that most people report positive feelings most of the time (Andrews, 1991; Diener & Diener, 1996), and that factors such as income or health are only modestly predictive of how satisfied or happy one is with one's life (e.g., Diener & Seligman, 2004).

REFERENCES

Abele, A. E., & Petzold, P. (1998). Pragmatic use of categorical information in impression formation. *Journal of Personality and Social Psychology, 75*(2), 347–358.

Aberson, C. L., & Ettlin, T. E. (2004). The aversive racism paradigm and responses favoring African Americans: Meta-analytic evidence of two types of favoritism. *Social Justice Research, 17*(1), 25–46.

American Association for the Advancement of Science. (2001). *General contentment masks gender gap in first AAAS salary and job survey.* Retrieved September 15, 2006, from http://www.sciencemag.org/cgi/reprint/294/5541/396.pdf

Andrews, F. M. (1991). Stability and change in levels and structure of subjective well-being: USA 1972 and 1988. *Social Indicators Research, 25*(1), 1–30.

August, G. P., Lippe, B. M., Blethen, S. L., Rosenfeld, R. G., Seelig, S. A., Johanson, A. J., et al. (1996). Growth hormone treatment in the United States: Demographic and diagnostic features of 2331 children. In National Cooperative Growth Study (NCGS) Advisory Group (Ed.), *Growth hormone: Science, research and the NCGS: 10 years of research* (pp. 179–183). Califon, NJ: Gardiner-Caldwell SynerMed.

Bar Hillel, M. (1980). The base-rate fallacy in probability judgments. *Acta Psychologica, 44*(3), 211–233.

Bertrand, J., Mars, A., Boyle, C., Bove, F., Yeargin-Allsopp, M., & Decoufle, P. (2001). Prevalence of autism in a United States population: The Brick Township, New Jersey, investigation. *Pediatrics, 108*, 1151–1161.

Bettencourt, B. A., Dill, K. E., Greathouse, S. A., Charlton, K., & Mulholland, A. (1997). Evaluations of ingroup and outgroup members: The role of category-based expectancy violation. *Journal of Experimental Social Psychology, 33*, 244–275

Biernat, M. (2003). Toward a broader view of social stereotyping. *The American Psychologist, 58*(12), 1019–1027.

Biernat, M., & Fuegen, K. (2001). Shifting standards and the evaluation of competence: Complexity in gender-based judgment and decision making. *Journal of Social Issues, 57*(4), 707–724.

Biernat, M., & Kobrynowicz, D. (1997). Gender- and race-based standards of competence: Lower minimum standards but higher ability standards for devalued groups. *Journal of Personality and Social Psychology, 72*(3), 544–557.

Biernat, M., & Ma, J. E. (2005). Stereotypes and the confirmability of trait concepts. *Personality and Social Psychology Bulletin, 31*(4), 483–495.

Biernat, M., Ma, J. E., & Nario-Redmond, M. R. (2005). *The role of stereotypes and judgment standards in trait diagnosis.* Unpublished manuscript, University of Kansas.

Biernat, M., Manis, M., & Nelson, T. F. (1991). Stereotypes and standards of judgment. *Journal of Personality and Social Psychology, 60*(4), 485–499.

Biernat, M., & Thompson, E. R. (2002). Shifting standards and contextual variation in stereotyping. In W. Stroebe & M. Hewstone (Eds.), *European review of social psychology* (Vol. 12, pp. 103–137). London: Wiley.

Biernat, M., & Vescio, T. K. (2002). She swings, she hits, she's great, she's benched: Implications of gender-based shifting standards for judgment and behavior. *Personality and Social Psychology Bulletin, 28*(1), 66–77.

Biernat, M., Vescio, T. K., & Manis, M. (1998). Judging and behaving toward members of stereotyped groups: A shifting standards perspective. In C. Sedikides, J. Schopler, & C. Insko (Eds.), *Intergroup cognition and intergroup behavior* (pp. 151–175). Mahwah, NJ: Lawrence Erlbaum Associates, Inc.

Bodenhausen, G. V., & Wyer, R. S. (1985). Effects of stereotypes in decision making and information-processing strategies. *Journal of Personality and Social Psychology, 48,* 267–282.

Brewer, M. B. (1988). A dual process model of impression formation. In T. K. Srull & R. S. Wyer, Jr. (Eds.), *Advances in social cognition* (Vol. 1, pp. 1–36). Hillsdale, NJ: Lawrence Erlbaum Associates, Inc.

Campbell, J. T., Crooks, L. A., Mahoney, M. H., & Rock, D. A. (1973). *An investigation of sources of bias in the prediction of job performance: A six-year study* (Final Project Rep. No. PR–73–37). Princeton, NJ: Educational Testing Services.

Carter, S. L. (1993). *Reflections of an affirmative action baby.* New York: Basic Books.

Cohen, J. (1988). *Statistical power analysis for the behavioral sciences.* Hillsdale, NJ: Lawrence Erlbaum Associates, Inc.

Cuttler, L., Silvers, J. B., Singh, J., Marrero, U., Finkelstein, B., Tannin, G., et al. (1996). Short stature and growth hormone therapy: A national study of physician recommendation patterns. *Journal of the American Medical Association, 276,* 531–537.

Davison, H. K., & Burke, M. J. (2000). Sex discrimination in simulated employment contexts: A meta-analytic investigation. *Journal of Vocational Behavior, 56*(2), 225–248.

Diener, E., & Biswas-Diener, R. (2000). New directions in subjective well-being research: The cutting edge. *Indian Journal of Clinical Psychology, 27,* 21–33.

Diener, E., & Diener, C. (1996). Most people are happy. *Psychological Science, 7*(3), 181–185.

Diener, E., & Seligman, M. E. P. (2004). Beyond money: Toward an economy of well-being. *Psychological Science in the Public Interest, 5,* 1–31.

Diener, E., Suh, E. M., Lucas, R. E., & Smith, H. L. (1999). Subjective well-being: Three decades of progress. *Psychological Bulletin, 125*(2), 276–302.

Eagly, A. H., & Steffen, V. J. (1984). Gender stereotypes stem from the distribution of women and men into social roles. *Journal of Personality and Social Psychology, 46*(4), 735–754.

Eiser, J. (1990). *Social judgment*. Pacific Grove, CA: Brooks/Cole.

Fiske, S. T., & Neuberg, S. L. (1990). A continuum of impression formation, from category-based to individuating processes: Influences of information and motivation on attention and interpretation. In M. Zanna (Ed.), *Advances in experimental social psychology* (Vol. 23, pp. 1–74). New York: Academic Press.

Foddy, M., & Smithson, M. (1989). Fuzzy sets and double standards: Modeling the process of ability inference. In J. Berger, M. Zelditch, & B. Anderson (Eds.), *Sociological theories in progress: New formulations* (pp. 73–99). Newbury Park, CA: Sage.

Ford, J., Kraiger, K., & Schechtman, S. L. (1986). Study of race effects in objective indices and subjective evaluations of performance: A meta-analysis of performance criteria. *Psychological Bulletin, 99*(3), 330–337.

Foschi, M. (1992). Gender and double standards for competence. In C. L. Ridgeway (Ed.), *Gender, interaction, and inequality* (pp. 181–207). New York: Springer-Verlag.

Foschi, M. (2000). Double standards for competence: Theory and research. *Annual Review of Sociology, 26,* 21–42.

Foschi, M., & Foddy, M. (1988). Standards, performances, and the formation of self–other expectations. In M. Foschi & M. Webster, Jr. (Eds.), *Status generalization: New theory and research* (pp. 248–260). Stanford, CA: Stanford University Press.

Funder, D. C. (1995). Stereotypes, base rates, and the fundamental attribution mistake: A content-based approach to judgmental accuracy. In Y.-T. Lee, L. J. Jussim, & C. R. McCauley (Eds.), *Stereotype accuracy: Toward appreciating group differences* (pp. 141–156). Washington, DC: American Psychological Association.

Gaertner, S. L., & Dovidio, J. F. (1986). The aversive form of racism. In J. F. Dovidio & S. L. Gaertner (Eds.), *Prejudice, discrimination, and racism* (pp. 61–89). Orlando, FL: Academic Press.

Ginther, D. K. (2004). Why women earn less: Economic explanations for the gender salary gap in science. *AWIS Magazine, 33,* 21–26.

Gleason, J., & Ely, R. (2002). Gender differences in language development. In A. McGillicudy-DeLisi & R. DeLisi (Eds.), *Biology, society, and behavior: The development of sex differences in cognition* (pp. 127–154). Westport, CT: Ablex.

Grimberg, A., Kutikov, J. K., & Cucchiara, A. J. (2005). Sex differences in patients referred for evaluation of poor growth. *Journal of Pediatrics, 146,* 212–216.

Halfon, N., & Newacheck, P. W. (1999). Prevalence and impact of parent-reported disabling mental health conditions among US children. *Journal of the American Academy of Child and Adolescent Psychiatry, 38,* 600–609.

Harber, K. D. (1998). Feedback to minorities: Evidence of a positive bias. *Journal of Personality and Social Psychology, 74*(3), 622–628.

Hastie, R. (1984). Causes and effects of causal attribution. *Journal of Personality and Social Psychology, 46*(1), 44–56.

Heilman, M. E. (2001). Description and prescription: How gender stereotypes prevent women's ascent up the organizational ladder. *Journal of Social Issues, 57*(4), 657–674.

Helson, H. (1964). *Adaptation-level theory*. Oxford, UK: Harper & Row.

Herr, P. M. (1986). Consequences of priming: Judgment and behavior. *Journal of Personality and Social Psychology, 51,* 1106–1115.

Herr, P. M., Sherman, S. J., & Fazio, R. H. (1983). On the consequences of priming: Assimilation and contrast effects. *Journal of Experimental Social Psychology, 19,* 323–340.

Judd, C. M., & Park, B. (1993). Definition and assessment of accuracy in social stereotypes. *Psychological Review, 100*(1), 109–128.

Kahneman, D., & Tversky, A. (1973). On the psychology of prediction. *Psychological Review, 80*, 225–251.

Kobrynowicz, D., & Biernat, M. (1997). Decoding subjective evaluations: How stereotypes provide shifting standards. *Journal of Experimental Social Psychology, 33*(6), 579–601.

Kraut, R. E., & Higgins, E. T. (1984). Communication and social cognition. In R. S. Wyer & T. K. Srull (Eds.), *Handbook of social cognition* (Vol. 3, pp. 87–127). Hillsdale, NJ: Lawrence Erlbaum Associates, Inc.

Kunda, Z., & Thagard, P. (1996). Forming impressions from stereotypes, traits, and behaviors: A parallel-constraint-satisfaction theory. *Psychological Review, 103*(2), 284–308.

Lewinsohn, P. M., Redner, J. E., & Seeley, J. R. (1991). The relationship between life satisfaction and psychosocial variables: New perspectives. In M. Argyle & F. Strack (Eds.), *Subjective well being: An interdisciplinary perspective* (pp. 141–169). Elmsford, NY: Pergamon Press.

Linville, P. W., & Jones, E. E. (1980). Polarized appraisals of out-group members. *Journal of Personality and Social Psychology, 38*(5), 689–703.

Ljungquist, B., Berg, S., & Steen, B. (1995). Prediction of survival in 70-year-olds. *Archives of Gerontology and Geriatrics, 20*(3), 295–307.

Maass, A., Milesi, A., Zabbini, S., & Stahlberg, D. (1995). Linguistic intergroup bias: Differential expectancies or in-group protection? *Journal of Personality and Social Psychology, 68*(1), 116–126.

Maass, A., Montalcini, F., & Biciotti, E. (1998). On the (dis-)confirmability of stereotypic attributes. *European Journal of Social Psychology, 28*, 383–402.

Manis, M., Biernat, M., & Nelson, T. F. (1991). Comparison and expectancy processes in human judgment. *Journal of Personality and Social Psychology, 61*(2), 203–211.

Manis, M., & Blake, J. B. (1963). Interpretation of persuasive messages as a function of prior immunization. *Journal of Abnormal and Social Psychology, 66*, 225–230.

Manis, M., & Moore, J. C. (1978). Summarizing controversial messages: Retroactive effects due to subsequent information. *Social Psychology, 41*(1), 62–68.

Manis, M., Nelson, T. F., & Shedler, J. (1988). Stereotypes and social judgment: Extremity, assimilation, and contrast. *Journal of Personality and Social Psychology, 55*, 28–36.

Manis, M., & Paskewitz, J. R. (1984). Judging psychopathology: Expectation and contrast. *Journal of Experimental Social Psychology, 20*(4), 363–381.

Martocchio, J. J., & Whitener, E. M. (1992). Fairness in personnel selection: A meta-analysis and policy implications. *Human Relations, 45*(5), 489–506.

Mobley, W. H. (1982). Supervisor and employee race and sex effects on performance appraisals: A field study of adverse impact and generalizability. *Academy of Management Journal, 25*(3), 598–606.

Murphy, K. R., & Cleveland, J. N. (1995). *Understanding performance appraisal: Social, organizational, and goal-based perspectives.* Thousand Oaks, CA: Sage.

National Science Foundation (NSF). (2000). *Women, minorities, and persons with disabilities in sciences and engineering: 2000* (Rep. No. 00–327). Arlington, VA: Author.

National Science Foundation (NSF), Division of Science Resources Statistics (2004). *Gender differences in the careers of academic scientists and engineers* (Rep. No. 04–323). Arlington, VA: Author.

Nelson, D. J., & Rogers, D. C. (2005). *A national analysis of diversity in science and engineering faculties at research universities.* Retrieved September 15, 2006, from http:/cheminfo.chem.ou.edu/~djn/diversity/briefings/Diversity%20Report%20 Final.pdf

Nilsson, L. G., Backman, L., Erngrund, K., Nyberg, L., Adolfsson, R., Bucht, G., et al. (1997). The Betula prospective cohort study: Memory, health, and aging. *Aging, Neuropsychology, and Cognition, 4*(1), 1–32.

Olian, J. D., Schwab, D. P., & Haberfeld, Y. (1988). The impact of applicant gender compared to qualifications on hiring recommendations: A meta-analysis of experimental studies. *Organizational Behavior and Human Decision Processes, 41*(2), 180–195.

Parducci, A. (1963). Range-frequency compromise in judgment. *Psychological Monographs, 77*(Whole No. 565), 1–29.

Postman, L., & Miller, G. A. (1945). Anchoring of temporal judgments. *American Journal of Psychology, 58*, 43–53.

Rosenthal, R. (2002). Covert communication in classrooms, clinics, court rooms, and cubicles. *The American Psychologist, 57*, 839–849.

Roth, P. L., Huffcutt, A. I., & Bobko, P. (2003). Ethnic group differences in measures of job performance: A new meta-analysis. *Journal of Applied Psychology, 88*(4), 694–706.

Rotundo, M., & Sackett, P. R. (1999). Effect of rater race on conclusions regarding differential prediction in cognitive ability tests. *Journal of Applied Psychology, 84*(5), 815–822.

Schmidt, F. L., & Hunter, J. E. (1981). Employment testing: Old theories and new research findings. *The American Psychologist, 36*(10), 1128–1137.

Schwarz, N., & Bless, H. (1992). Constructing reality and its alternatives: An inclusion/exclusion model of assimilation and contrast effects in social judgment. In L. L. Martin & A. Tesser (Eds.), *The construction of social judgments* (pp. 217–245). Hillsdale, NJ: Lawrence Erlbaum Associates, Inc.

Sices, L., Feudtner, C., McLaughlin, J., Drotar, D., & Williams, M. (2004). How do primary care physicians manage children with possible developmental delays? A national survey with an experimental design. *Pediatrics, 113*, 274–282.

Stapel, D. A., Koomen, W., & van der Pligt, J. (1997). Categories of category accessibility: The impact of trait concept versus exemplar priming on person judgments. *Journal of Experimental Social Psychology, 33*(1), 47–76.

Stapel, D. A., & Winkielman, P. (1998). Assimilation and contrast as a function of context–target similarity, distinctness, and dimensional relevance. *Personality and Social Psychology Bulletin, 24*(6), 634–646.

Trope, Y., & Liberman, A. (1993). The use of trait conceptions to identify other people's behavior and to draw inferences about their personalities. *Personality and Social Psychology Bulletin, 19*(5), 553–562.

Upshaw, H. S. (1962). Own attitude as an anchor in equal-appearing intervals. *Journal of Abnormal and Social Psychology, 64*, 85–96.

Vescio, T. K., Gervais, S. J., Snyder, M., & Hoover, A. (2005). Power and the creation of patronizing environments: The stereotype-based behaviors of the powerful and their effects on female performance in masculine domains. *Journal of Personality and Social Psychology, 88*(4), 658–672.

Volkmann, J. (1951). Scales of judgment and their implications for social psychology. In J. H. Rohrer & M. Sherif (Eds.), *Social psychology at the crossroads* (pp. 273–294). New York: Harper.

Weitz, S. (1972). Attitude, voice, and behavior: A repressed affect model of interracial interaction. *Journal of Personality and Social Psychology, 24*, 14–21.

4

Assimilation and Contrast Effects of Affect on Judgment

FRANÇOIS RIC and PAULA M. NIEDENTHAL

*I*n recent years a growing number of studies have emphasized the role of affect (i.e., emotions and mood) in judgmental outcomes (e.g., Bower, 1981; Damasio, 1994; Johnson & Tversky 1983; Niedenthal, Halberstadt, & Setterlund, 1997). For instance, research on mood-congruent judgment has demonstrated that evaluations of other people may be assimilated to the tonality of one's affective state. Compared with individuals in a neutral nonmanipulated affective state, sad or angry people evaluate other people or objects more negatively. In contrast, being happy makes people evaluate other people as well as objects more positively.

In this chapter, we review and discuss empirical and theoretical work that addresses these assimilation but also contrast effects of affect on social judgment.[1] We begin the chapter with a discussion of "direct" assimilation and contrast effects of affect on judgment that are demonstrated in mood-(in)congruent judgments. These effects are said to be *direct* because the judgment is thought to be assimilated, and sometimes contrasted, with a direct reference to the affect experienced by the judge. We then turn our attention to studies suggesting that these "direct" effects are sometimes fundamentally modified when other information relevant for the judgment, as for instance the target's category membership or other related constructs, are provided. In such conditions, affect moderates individuals' reliance on constructs conceptually unrelated to their current affective state (e.g., stereotypes), yielding what we refer to as *"indirect effects"* of affect on judgment. Although we acknowledge that assimilation and contrast effects of affect may be due to several processes, we will argue that the findings from research on direct and indirect effects of affect may be integrated on the basis of recent extensions of informational theories of affect (Bless, Clore, et al., 1996; Clore et al., 2001; Schwarz, 1990).

In the second part of the chapter, we address the question of whether assimilation and contrast effects of affect are specifically due to affective state or, alternatively, to a more general kind of conceptual priming. Given the importance of the valence dimension in affect, we first consider whether the effects of affect should be conceptualized as evaluative priming effects. Then we address the role of affective feelings and of affective concepts in the production of assimilation and contrast effects. In line with the theoretical position endorsed in the first part of the chapter, we argue that the effects of affect can be reduced neither to evaluative nor to conceptual priming. In contrast, we highlight the role of dimensions other than valence and propose a discrete affective states level of analysis. Finally, we emphasize the role of affective feelings in the production of these effects.

MOOD-(IN)CONGRUENCE EFFECTS: DIRECT ASSIMILATION AND CONTRAST EFFECTS OF AFFECT

Assimilation Effects

Numerous studies have documented individuals' tendency to make judgments congruent with their current affective state (see, for review, Clore, Schwarz, & Conway, 1994; Forgas, 1995; Niedenthal, Krauth-Gruber, & Ric, 2006). It is now widely believed that experiencing positive, compared to negative, affect leads people to express more positive judgments of other people (e.g., Forgas & Bower, 1987; Gouaux, 1971; Innes-Ker & Niedenthal, 2002), of their present life (e.g., Schwarz & Clore, 1983), of themselves (Sedikides, 1995), and of the future (e.g., Johnson, & Tversky, 1983). In other words, it is widely accepted that people's current affective state influences their judgment in an *assimilative* manner. Two main accounts have been proposed for these findings: the mood priming and the affect-as-information models.

Mood Congruency as Priming   In an extension of associative network models of memory (e.g., Collins & Loftus, 1975), Bower (1981) proposed that a restricted number of basic emotions (e.g., sadness, happiness, anger, fear, disgust) are represented in memory as specific nodes or informational units. These units represent behavioral and physiological expressions of emotions. They are also linked to representations of eliciting events and verbal labels associated with each emotion. When a unit of information is excited, activation automatically spreads throughout the network and potentiates associated units. For instance, feeling happy activates the happiness unit of information and, through spreading activation, other concepts that are related to happiness. Therefore, material associated with happiness becomes highly accessible and is more likely to guide attention (e.g., Niedenthal et al., 1997), and to be integrated in subsequent judgments.

Affect-as-Information   According to the second account, the affect-as-information model (Schwarz & Clore, 1983), assimilation effects are due to the individuals' use of their affect as an indicator of their attitude toward an object (or person). When evaluating their attitude toward an attitude object, individuals may rely on a "how do I feel about it?" heuristic. Relying on such a heuristic should lead people in a positive affective state to infer that they *like* the target, whereas people in a negative affective state should infer that they *do not like* the target object or person. According to the model, such a heuristic is used only when one's affective state is thought to be a reliable indicator of one's attitude toward the object. If people do not think that their affective state has been induced by the attitude object but by another factor unrelated to attitude object (e.g., the weather, a gift, or an emotional film sequence), they are able to discount the effects of affect in making the judgment.

Consistent with this account, Schwarz and Clore (1983) found that life satisfaction was reported to be higher if the respondent was questioned on a sunny rather than a rainy day. This effect was interpreted as due to the influence of the (positive) weather on individuals' affective state. However, when the participants' attention was drawn to the irrelevant source of their affective state (i.e., the experimenter asked about the weather in the participants' city), life satisfaction judgments were no longer influenced by the participants' affective state (by the weather). In other words, the participants attributed their mood to the weather and discounted it as useful for making the life satisfaction judgment.

Contrast Effects

The findings by Schwarz and Clore (1983) suggest that individuals are able to partial out the influence of affect on judgments when they realize that their current affective state is an irrelevant basis for judgment. Other studies have found contrast effects of affect on judgment, that is *mood-incongruent* judgment (e.g., Abele & Petzold, 1999; Berkowitz & Troccoli, 1990; DeSteno, Petty, Wegener, & Rucker, 2000; Isbell & Wyer, 1999; Ottati & Isbell, 1996; Strack, Schwarz, & Gschneidinger, 1985). The literature suggests that these contrast effects can be due to two different types of processes: correction processes of unwanted influence (e.g., Berkowitz & Troccoli, 1990; Ottati & Isbell, 1996; Wegener & Petty, 1997) and standard comparison processes (e.g., Abele & Petzold, 1999; Strack et al., 1985).

Correction Processes   Contrast effects were not originally predicted by mood congruence-models. Thus, researchers have attempted to extend these models in order to provide an explanation of contrast effects (e.g., Ottati & Isbell, 1996). Three distinct correction processes have been proposed, with only two predicting contrast effects of mood in judgment.

First, the already mentioned *discounting process* consists of not taking into account one's affective state as a source of information and to focus on information relevant to the judgment (Schwarz & Clore, 1983). The two other correction processes are especially likely to occur when individuals' (irrelevant) affective state is closely intertwined with judgment-relevant information. In such conditions, individuals may correct their evaluations using a *subtraction process* (Martin, 1986; Schwarz & Bless, 1992). That is, they may partial out, or subtract, the hypothesized influence of their affective state in the judgment. Individuals may also *adjust* their judgment in a way that is opposite to the hypothesized influence of their affective state (Wegener & Petty, 1997). Because an accurate evaluation of the impact of the affect on one's judgment is difficult, subtraction and adjustment processes are likely to be inaccurate and thus to result in *attenuation* (i.e., a persistent although reduced assimilation effect) or in *overcorrection* effects (i.e., a contrast effect), depending upon the strength of the corrective processes people engage in.

Empirical evidence suggests that correction occurs only when several conditions hold. First, as we have already seen, in order to correct their judgment, individuals have to recognize the irrelevance of their affective state for the judgment at hand (e.g., Schwarz & Clore, 1983; Isbell & Wyer, 1999). For instance, if individuals are reminded just before they begin a task that they had been previously exposed to a sad movie excerpt as part of an "unrelated" study, they become aware of the potential biasing impact of the film (their affective state) and attempt to correct it (DeSteno et al., 2000; Neumann, Seibt, & Strack, 2001). Second, correction is more likely when individuals are motivated to formulate unbiased judgments (Isbell & Wyer, 1999). And finally, because correction is cognitively costly, individuals must be able to process information efficiently to successfully correct their judgment (e.g., Ottati & Isbell, 1996; Wegener & Petty, 1997). In the absence of processing resources, noncorrected assimilation effects are more likely (Berkowitz & Troccoli, 1990; DeSteno et al., 2000; Ottati & Isbell, 1996). In addition to these conditions, an overestimation of the impact of affect on judgment is necessary for the people to produce contrast effects.

Standard Comparison Processes   Affect can also make salient a standard of comparison against which the target stimulus is evaluated (e.g., Abele & Petzold, 1999; Schwarz & Bless, 1992). For instance, remembering a sad event from the past can lead people to evaluate their current life satisfaction as higher (i.e., same category effect; Strack et al., 1985). This contrast effect is due to the comparison of the target (e.g., one's current life) with an extreme standard activated in the emotion induction phase (e.g., a particularly sad event). Thus, a same contrast effect could be observed in person judgment if affect was induced by a procedure that involves exposure to a particularly negative or positive type of individual (e.g., an essay about a child abuser or about someone who dedicated her life to helping others, respectively). Moreover, because this contrast effect depends on the similarities between the judgment dimension and the affect eliciting event, it is possible to obtain, in the very same situation, both a contrast effect on a judgment dimension that is closely related to the affect induction procedure and an assimilation effect on another less closely related dimension (Abele & Petzold, 1999; Schwarz, Strack, Kommer, & Wagner, 1987).

These effects only require a change in perspective; they do not require either high motivation or the availability of cognitive resources. Research by Stapel, Koomen, and Ruys (2002) is illustrative of such processes. Stapel and colleagues found that participants subliminally primed with happy faces for 30 ms evaluated an ambiguous face as expressing more happiness than participants previously primed with sad faces. However, when the presentation of the primes was extended, although still subliminal (100 ms), a contrast effect appeared, that is the ambiguous face was evaluated as expressing more sadness when participants were previously exposed to happy faces. These intriguing effects may be best under-stood in reference to the setting of a comparison standard. Stapel and colleagues argued that affective information is detected at a very early processing stage. At this stage (30 ms presentation), affective information is diffuse and undedicated (i.e., without an object; Murphy & Zajonc, 1993). As a result, the affective informa-tion is used to interpret the ambiguous stimulus, and assimilation occurs. As exposure duration increases, specific nonaffective features of the primed stimuli are nonconsciously detected and the affective connotation becomes thus attached to the primed stimulus. In such conditions, individuals are likely to evaluate an ambiguous stimulus of the same category (e.g., a face) compared with the primed stimulus. As a result, contrast is likely.

BEYOND MOOD-CONGRUENCE EFFECTS: INDIRECT ASSIMILATION AND CONTRAST EFFECTS

The research findings reviewed so far suggest that people's judgments about other individuals are often influenced by their own affect in either an assimilative or contrastive way. Now, we turn our attention to other results indicating that affect influences people's reliance on highly accessible information such as, for instance, stereotypes in person judgment research (e.g., Bodenhausen, Kramer, & Süsser, 1994), or peripheral cues (e.g., source attractiveness, source credibility) in persua-sion research. Such findings can be thought of as limitations to the assimilation and contrast effects described in the first part of this chapter. These results suggest indeed that assimilation and contrast can be modified, disappear, or even reversed when other judgment-relevant information, such as the category membership of the target in a person perception paradigm, is activated. In the following paragraphs we will first present the findings observed in this research area and then we will attempt to reconcile these findings with those described in the mood-(in)congruence literature.

Evidence of Assimilation and Contrast to the Activated Category Due to Affect

Early research on intergroup relations as well as commonsense has frequently associated prejudice and stereotyping with negative affect (e.g., Dollar, Miller, Doob, Mowrer, & Sears, 1939; Islam & Hewstone, 1993; Wilder & Shapiro, 1989). In contrast with such a view, more recent research has found that happiness increases reliance on stereotypes in person judgment (e.g., Abele, Gendolla, & Petzold, 1998; Bless, Schwarz, & Wieland, 1996; Bodenhausen, Kramer, & Süsser, 1994; Krauth-Gruber & Ric, 2000), whereas sadness causes people to correct their judgment with regard to a stereotype, sometimes leading to contrast effects when judgments are overcorrected (Lambert, Khan, Lickel, & Fricke, 1997).

   These processes were observed in a study by Krauth-Gruber and Ric (2000). Participants induced to feel either happy, sad, or in a nonmanipulated affective state condition completed a guilt judgment task. In this task, they received a case

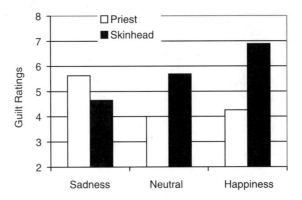

FIGURE 4.1 Effects of induced affective states on guilt judgment (from Krauth-Gruber & Ric, 2000).

description of a physical aggression.[2] The suspect was either a member of a group stereotypically associated with the offence (i.e., a *skinhead*) or a member of a group counterstereotypically associated with the offence (i.e., a *priest*). Happy participants relied more on stereotypes rendering their guilt judgment than sad participants (see Figure 4.1). Clearly, these results are inconsistent with the mood-congruence effects presented in the first part of this chapter since they indicate that a member of a negative category will be evaluated more negatively by happy people than by sad people.

Theoretical Accounts

These effects are not easily explained by the theoretical explanations of mood-(in)congruence effects. This has led researchers to propose other accounts of affect on judgment that can be regrouped in two main theoretical perspectives: the hedonic and the informational approaches.[3]

The Hedonic Model   According to the *hedonic model* (e.g., Isen, 1987; Wegener, Petty, & Smith, 1995) the findings just summarized can be accounted for by a change in processing strategy that is triggered by affect-regulation processes. That is, they suggest that in general individuals are motivated to maintain their positive or to repair their negative affective state. Sad individuals are therefore more likely to engage themselves deeply in any (distracting) task at hand, because such an activity would provide an opportunity to change their affective state. Thus, in most situations, sad individuals tend to process information carefully and rely little on heuristics (such as stereotypes) when formulating judgments. In contrast, when in happy states individuals are reluctant to engage in new (and potentially distracting) tasks unless either the task is believed to have potential positive consequences or unless they believe that not engaging in the task will result in negative consequences. Therefore, happy individuals are likely to rely on heuristics that provide them with a sufficient answer with minimal cognitive investment.

In sum, this approach suggests that happiness (or any either pleasant state) leads to the assimilation of judgment to the most salient relevant piece of information, that is heuristic information (e.g., stereotypes). Sadness (or any given unpleasant state), on the other hand, leads individuals to consider the relevant information at hand, which results in minimal assimilation to an available heuristic cue in most situations. One implication of this account is that sadness should lead people not to take into account the target's category membership when evaluating a target person. Thus, sadness is more likely to cause an absence of use of the target's category rather than overcorrection or contrast effects.

Informational Accounts   The informational approaches are extensions of the affect-as-information model (Schwarz & Clore, 1983). These models (e.g., Bless, Schwarz, & Wieland, 1996; Clore et al., 2001; Schwarz, 1990) share the basic assumption that feelings inform the individual about the state of the environment. A positive state signals that the environment is safe. Consequently, when in positive states, individuals can make judgments by relying on general knowledge structures, or pre-existing concepts and expectations, and devote extra resources to other tasks (Bless, Clore et al., 1996; Bless, Schwarz, & Wieland, 1996). In contrast, a negative affect signals to the individual that the environment is problematic. When in negative states, reliance on general knowledge structures may have negative consequences, and so careful attention to new (judgment-related) information should occur (Bless, Schwarz, & Wieland, 1996).

Recently, Clore et al. (2001) have extended this perspective by suggesting that the influence of affect on knowledge application is not restricted to general knowledge structures, but applies to the content of one's mind, that is, to any information that is highly accessible. Stereotypes—like other general knowledge structures—are activated very early and automatically in encounters with other individuals (e.g., Devine, 1989). Therefore, the content of stereotypes quickly becomes highly accessible during the formation of an impression or the expression of a judgment about a target person. As a result, in such situations affect indicates to the individuals whether they can rely on the activated stereotypes because stereotype-related information is accessible. However, the same rule could apply to any other information than stereotypes (e.g., specific individual features of the target) if this information was made accessible.

Bless and Fiedler (1995) conducted a study that is particularly illustrative of this point. These researchers induced participants to feel happy or sad before they completed a task in which they had to indicate with a button press whether certain attributes (behavior and traits) presented sequentially on a computer screen described a target person. In one half of the trials, behaviors (e.g., "attack someone") were primed by a related trait (e.g., "aggressive") presented one or two trials beforehand. In the other half of the trials, the traits and the behaviors referred to different social dimensions. Latencies indicated that happy participants responded faster than sad participants for the primed behaviors, whereas no difference between these groups was found for unprimed behaviors. Therefore, these results suggest that a positive affective state such as happiness increases priming effects and should thus lead to assimilation to the primed construct, whereas sadness decreases priming effects and is thus more likely to interfere with the application of highly accessible thoughts.

Consistent with the informational view, research has further revealed that the effects of affect on stereotype use are moderated by the same factors as mood congruency effects. They can disappear (i.e., a discounting effect; Sinclair, Mark, & Clore, 1994) or even be reversed (i.e., a contrast effect; Wyer, Clore, & Isbell, 1999) when individuals think that the informative function of their feelings has to be questioned, for instance by making individuals aware of the irrelevant source of their affective state.

In sum, in contrast to the hedonic approach, the informational approach may account relatively easily for both direct and indirect effects of affect on judgment. Indeed, according to the informational approach affect could inform individuals both about how they feel about the target person and also about whether the accessible information should be used as a basis for judgment. Whether people use their feelings to either directly evaluate the target or to evaluate the content of their thoughts is not clearly specified in the models. However, it may depend on individuals' attentional focus at the time of judgment, as well as on the applicability of their affective reactions or current thoughts for the judgment. For instance sometimes affect is of no use for the judgment (e.g., "How large is the figure in this picture?"). In other cases, it can be that no accessible information other than affect is unambiguous and relevant for the judgment. Thus, in such a case, individuals will be likely to use their affective state as a basis of judgment (as long as the state is in some way relevant to the judgment, see the preceding point). This is typically the case in impression formation studies in which people are provided with ambiguous and/or weak individuating information. When relevant information is accessible (e.g., a stereotype that is relevant for the judgment has been activated), one's affective state should be used to evaluate its relevance.

EVALUATIVE OR CONCEPTUAL PRIMING?

In the preceding discussion, we reviewed research illustrative of the variety of the assimilation and contrast effects of affect and have argued that these effects are more easily accounted by the informational view. However, it could still be argued that the summarized effects are in no way specific to affect and that they are due to more general conceptual priming processes. For example, it could be objected that some of the assimilation (spreading activation network; Bower, 1981) and all of the contrast processes (Martin, Seta, & Crelia, 1990; Schwarz & Bless, 1992, Wegener & Petty, 1997) are merely due to semantic priming of emotion concepts and that affective processes per se are irrelevant to the observed assimilation and contrast effects. If it were the case that the processes described in the first part of the chapter were imputable to conceptual priming, it would have important consequences. For instance, the numerous explanatory theories that attribute a central role of affect in cognition would be no longer useful.

In the next section we discuss these points in the light of relevant data. We will treat this question in two different phases. First, we will argue that the assimilation effects of affect on judgment cannot be attributed solely to the activation of the evaluative dimension of affect, thus to evaluative priming processes. Then, we will discuss the role of affective concepts and of affective feelings in the production of these effects.

A Potential Role of Evaluative Priming

Valence is a central dimension of affect (e.g., Russel, 1980; Smith & Ellsworth, 1985) and most of the theories concerning the role of affect in cognition emphasize this dimension. As has been clear from our discussion, both hedonic and informational models of the influence of affect on judgment rely heavily on the valence dimension of affect. The (un)pleasantness of the affective experience for the hedonic account, as well as its valence for the informational view, is considered the proximal cause of assimilation effects.

One possibility, then, is that the effects of affect on judgment reflect the priming of the evaluative dimension, which is necessarily associated with affect induction. Results by Stapel and Koomen (2000) provide support for such a possibility. In two parallel studies, Stapel and Koomen either primed evaluative concepts (i.e., good vs. bad) or induced participants' affective state (i.e., positive vs. negative) before the participants completed an impression formation task. The studies revealed parallel assimilative effects of evaluative priming and of affect. That is, participants either primed with positive information or induced to feel a positive affect evaluated the target more positively than participants primed with negative information or induced to feel a negative affect, respectively. Importantly, evaluative priming had no impact on affective measures, suggesting that the effects of evaluative priming are unlikely to be due to affect induced by the priming procedure. Therefore, this research indicates that evaluative priming (i.e., priming of evaluative concepts) produces effects similar to the induction of affective feelings.

However, this does not mean that all the effects of affect are due to their valence dimension. The findings by Stapel and Koomen (2000) seem to imply that as long as the required judgment includes a strong evaluative component, affect may produce effects similar to those produced by evaluative priming. This is not totally surprising again if we consider that the valence is one of the central features of affect. However, this is not to say that the effects of affect can be reduced to evaluative priming. In many areas other than judgment, research has already shown that the effects of affect were frequently better predicted in terms of discrete affective states than in terms of general valence. Studies have shown, for example, that perception (Niedenthal et al., 1997), categorization of affective stimuli (Niedenthal, Halberstadt, & Innes-Ker, 1999), as well as response to emotion eliciting events (Frijda, Kuipers, & ter Schure, 1989), appear more clearly determined by the discrete emotions evoked by these stimuli (or events) than by their general valence. As an example, Niedenthal et al. (1997) demonstrated that being induced to feel an affective state (e.g., sadness) facilitates the processing of words associated with this state (i.e., sad words) in a lexical decision task. However, this induction does not facilitate the processing of words related to another affective state of the same valence (e.g., anger). These categorical effects were found for both participants experiencing a negative (i.e., sad) and a positive (i.e., happy) affect (who processed words related to happiness with greater efficiency, but not words related to love). Therefore, it appears that valence is neither the only nor the main determinant of the influences of affect on information processing.

More directly relevant for our purpose, related findings were obtained in the judgment domain. For instance, DeSteno and colleagues (2000) induced sadness or anger in the participants and then asked them to evaluate the likelihood of a series of events. The events were either related to sadness (e.g., "Of the 60,000 orphans in Romania, how many are malnourished due to food shortages?") or to anger (e.g., "Of the 2,000,000 people in the US who will buy a used car this year, how many will intentionally be sold a 'lemon' by a dishonest car dealer?"). Findings showed that participants gave higher estimates to events congruent with their current affect than to events incongruent with their state, even though all of the events were negative in valence (see related results, Lerner & Keltner, 2001; Tiedens & Linton, 2001). Thus, in the present case, assimilation in judgment occurred at the discrete affective state instead of at the valence level.

Similar findings have been obtained in the stereotyping domain. For instance, anger increases assimilation to the activated stereotypes, whereas sadness decreases it and can even lead to contrast effects with regard to the activated stereotype (Bodenhausen, Sheppard, & Kramer, 1994; Lambert et al., 1997). Similarly, disgust has been found to increase assimilation to stereotypes in comparison with fear (Tiedens & Linton, 2001). Tiedens and Linton (2001; see also Lerner & Keltner, 2001) proposed that the main determinant of these effects is the degree of certainty/uncertainty, and not the valence, associated with the state. For instance, anger, disgust, and happiness are associated with appraisals of certainty about the emotional event, whereas fear and to some extent sadness are associated with feelings of uncertainty about what will happen (e.g., Smith & Ellsworth, 1985). As a result, angry, disgusted, and happy individuals should be more certain about what would happen and thus should rely on superficial cues whereas fearful and sad individuals should pay attention to details and process information carefully.

These studies may have important implications for the understanding of processes underlying assimilation (and to a lesser extent contrast) effects of affect. First, they suggest that these effects cannot always be explained in terms of the general valence of the induced affect. Affect may, in special cases, influence evaluative judgments the same way as does evaluative priming (Stapel & Koomen, 2000) because the valence dimension determines very general evaluative judgments (e.g., general likeability). However, if the judgment is related to a categorical emotion (e.g., anger, sadness, or fear), or if the judgment requires a response related to another affect on a dimension of importance (e.g., certainty, controllability; Smith & Ellsworth, 1985), the general valence dimension is no longer of importance.

Second, this analysis also suggests that theoretical explanations of the influence of affect on judgments that emphasize (or only rely on) the valence of affect are not appropriate accounts. This is typically the case for the hedonic approach, which would have trouble accounting for these findings. This does not mean that a focus on valence in judgment is untenable, only that its explanatory power is limited to a restricted set of conditions.

To some extent, the informational view also strongly emphasizes the valence dimension of affect. Information concerning one's attitude toward the target (Schwarz & Clore, 1983), the state of the environment (Schwarz, 1990), or the appropriateness of one's thoughts (Clore et al., 2001), is held to be primarily conveyed by valence. For instance, a negative affect indicates to individuals that they do not like the target, that the environment is problematic, or that their current thoughts are inappropriate. However, this perspective can be easily extended by suggesting that affect provides more specific information about the state of the environment as well as about the means to deal with it (see DeSteno et al., 2000, for a related idea). For instance, it is possible that anger informs the organism that it is blocked in the attainment of a desired goal and that the activity must be directed toward the fast removal of the obstacle, which is likely to take the form of an aggressive behavior (Frijda et al., 1989). Transposed in the judgment domain, being angry could thus lead people to express negative evaluations of other objects and persons, but also to rely on superficial cues (e.g., the target's category) that allow for a speedy response. In contrast, fear informs the organism of a threat and that the activity should be directed toward figuring out a way to escape and to find a safe place.

Affective Concept Versus Affective Feelings: Are the Effects of Affect a Special Kind of Semantic Priming?

We have argued that the effects of affect on judgment could not be accounted in terms of evaluative priming and that the valence of affective states is not the only and sometimes not the most important determinant of its influence. It is, however, still possible that the dimensions of importance can be activated in the absence of an induced affect. In other words, it remains possible that these effects are not due to feelings per se, but to knowledge about (discrete) affects, that is "affective concepts."

Recent research by Innes-Ker and Niedenthal (2002), which bears directly on this issue, reports some evidence against such a possibility. In one of their studies, half of the participants were induced to feel happy, sad, or a neutral state by watching films. The remaining participants were primed with happy or sad emotion concepts or neutral ideas by asking them to unscramble a series of four words presented in a scrambled order to form a sentence. Participants subsequently read a text presenting a series of behaviors performed by a hypothetical target person. Then they evaluated the target's affect as well as aspects related to the situation in which the target finds herself (e.g., the novel she was reading; the contentment of her cat) on scales related to sadness versus happiness/contentment. As shown in Figure 4.2, participants in the sad feelings condition judged the target and aspects of the target's situation as sadder than did happy feeling participants, with neutral participants falling in between. However, the

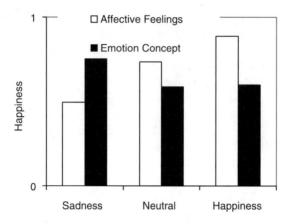

FIGURE 4.2   Mean ratings of happiness, contentment, and pleasantness of targets as a function of induced affective states and activation of emotion concepts (from Innes-Ker & Niedenthal, 2002).

activation of emotion concept of sadness and happiness did not affect the judgments. Therefore, it can be concluded from this study that affect, but not the activation of affective concept, is a necessary condition for the occurrence of assimilation effects of affect.

These findings may be reconciled with those of Stapel and Koomen (2000) described earlier by considering that the judgments used in the Innes-Ker and Niedenthal's (2002) study *were not* evaluative in nature but more directly related to the pleasantness or unpleasantness of the situation, that is, to affective feelings. And, even though people's evaluations are frequently inferred from their affective feelings (Clore et al., 2001; Schwarz, 1990; Schwarz & Clore, 1983), the reverse is probably less likely since evaluations can be attributed to a number of factors other than their affective state (e.g., the specific features of the target person). Thus, it is probable that individuals engage in specific processes when answering questions about their as well as other's feelings. For instance, they may rely on what they thought would be their feelings in the same situation, recruit episodic memories, and eventually partially simulate their reactions in such a situation (Niedenthal, Ric, & Krauth-Gruber, 2002; Robinson & Clore, 2002). For such judgments, affective feelings are probably considered as the (only) relevant source of information (Wyer et al., 1999). Information provided by the activation of the emotion concepts would not be applicable. Therefore, according to this position the assimilative effects of affect on judgment are not totally attributable to the evaluative priming or to the activation of affective concepts, at least for what concerns feeling-related judgments.

A study by Ric (2004) suggests that this reasoning may not be restricted to feeling-related judgment but extend to general evaluative judgments. In his study, participants were primed outside of awareness with words related to sadness, to happiness, or with words unrelated to either happiness or sadness (control condition). Then, they completed a guilt judgment task similar to the one used by

Krauth-Gruber and Ric (2000) and described earlier. Results indicated that the effects of affect were not replicated when only affective concepts were primed. In contrast, participants primed with sad words relied *more* on stereotypes than those primed with happy words (see also Ric, Leygue, & Adam, 2004). Moreover, these effects were found to be independent of those of affect. Participants' self-reports of affect (self-report of happiness and sadness) were not affected by the primes. They, however, significantly predicted stereotype use, although in the direction opposed to the effect of the primes, and hence in the direction predicted by traditional models. For instance, when the suspect was a skinhead, self-reported happiness was positively correlated with guilt judgment, whereas the sign of the correlation was negative when the suspect was a priest.

Several explanations may be offered for these results, though a detailed discussion of them is beyond the scope of this chapter. However, it remains that these results, compared with those obtained in studies by Krauth-Gruber and Ric (2000) in which affect was induced, suggest that the mere activation of affective concept is not sufficient for the occurrence of assimilation and contrast effects of affect on judgment. Even though the priming of affective concepts may produce assimilation effects on evaluative judgments (Stapel & Koomen, 2000), the assimilation effects observed on affective judgments (Innes-Ker & Niedenthal, 2002) as well as effects of assimilation and contrast to the activated category (Ric, 2004) are not attributable to affective concepts but require that people feel the affective state.

CONCLUSION

In this chapter we reviewed research showing that individuals' affect can exert assimilation and contrast effects on judgments. Taken together, the extant findings show that the specific effects of affect on judgment are rich and varied, probably reflecting the adaptive value of affect (e.g., Cosmides & Tooby, 2000; Smith & Kirby, 2000). A definitive statement about how affect influences judgment is still a matter of debate. We have, however, suggested that most of the findings reviewed in this chapter could be seen as consistent with an extended version of the mood-as-information model according to which affect would not only inform the organism of the valence of the situation (Bless, Clore et al., 1996; Clore et al., 2001; Schwarz, 1990) but also of more specific dimensions (e.g., controllability, certainty, adapted actions) of the situation as well as of the related possibilities of action. It will be left to further research to provide empirical tests of these hypotheses.

Finally, it may be tempting to equate the effects of affect to a (special) kind of either evaluative or conceptual priming. Nevertheless, a look at relevant data indicates that they do not provide evidence for such accounts. To the contrary, the present review suggests that affective states have specific effects and that these effects are not only due to their valence. This is not to say that evaluative priming and affect could not have similar effects in specific conditions. They should have similar effects when the judgment requires a strong purely evaluative answer (e.g., "How likeable is this person?"). However, only affect (neither affective nor evaluative concepts) should have an impact on judgments that require imagining the inner feelings of the target person (e.g., "is this person happy?"; Innes-Ker & Niedenthal, 2002). Concerning the effects of affect on assimilation and contrast to the activated category, there is no evidence that the priming of emotion concepts can produce effects similar to those of affect, suggesting that affective feeling has to be felt to produce assimilation or contrast to the accessible information (e.g., stereotypes). Such findings speak in favor of the specificity of some of the assimilation and contrast effects due to affect. As a result, they also highlight the diversity of the processes underlying assimilation and contrast effects in social perception and judgment to which this book is devoted.

NOTES

1. For the sake of comparability and brevity we mainly restrict the scope of our discussion to the domain of person perception and judgment even though we believe that our analysis also applies to other judgment areas.
2. The proportion of incriminating information was manipulated in this experiment. However, for ease of presentation and for comparability with other studies presented later in this chapter, we consider only the ambiguous information condition in which the case description contained the same proportion of evidence implying the suspect's guilt and implying his innocence.
3. Due to space limitations, we will not discuss differences between theoretical accounts within a perspective unless they are directly relevant to our purpose.

REFERENCES

Abele, A., Gendolla, G. H., & Petzold, P. (1998). Positive mood and in-group-out-group differentiation in a minimal group setting. *Personality and Social Psychology Bulletin, 24*, 1343–1357.

Abele, A., & Petzold, P. (1999). Satisfaction judgments in positive and negative moods: Effects of concurrent assimilation and contrast producing processes. *Personality and Social Psychology Bulletin, 25*, 883–895.

Berkowitz, L., & Troccoli, B.T. (1990). Feelings, direction of attention, and expressed evaluations of others. *Cognition and Emotion, 4*, 305–325.

Bless, H., Clore, G. L., Schwarz, N., Golisano, V., Rabe, C., & Wölk, M. (1996). Mood and the use of scripts: Does a happy mood really lead to mindlessness? *Journal of Personality and Social Psychology, 71*, 665–679.

Bless, H., & Fiedler, K. (1995). Affective states and the influence of activated general knowledge. *Personality and Social Psychology Bulletin, 21*, 766–778.

Bless, H., Schwarz, N., & Wieland, R. (1996). Mood and the impact of category membership and individuating information. *European Journal of Social Psychology, 26*, 935–959.

Bodenhausen, G. V., Kramer, G. P., & Süsser, K. (1994). Happiness and stereotypic thinking in social judgment. *Journal of Personality and Social Psychology, 66*, 621–632.

Bodenhausen, G. V., Sheppard, L. A., & Kramer, G. P. (1994). Negative affect and social judgment: The differential impact of anger and sadness. *European Journal of Social Psychology, 24*, 45–62.

Bower, G. H. (1981). Mood and memory. *The American Psychologist, 36*, 129–148.

Clore, G. L., Schwarz, N., & Conway, M. (1994). Affective causes and consequences of social information processing. In R. S. Wyer & T. K. Srull (Eds.), *Handbook of social cognition* (2nd ed., pp. 323–418). Hillsdale, NJ: Lawrence Erlbaum Associates, Inc.

Clore, G. L., Wyer, R. S., Dienes, B., Gasper, K., Gohm, C., & Isbell, L. (2001). Affective feelings as feedback: Some cognitive consequences. In L. L. Martin & G. L. Clore (Eds.), *Theories of mood and cognition: A user's guidebook* (pp. 27–62). Mahwah, NJ: Lawrence Erlbaum Associates, Inc.

Collins, A. M., & Loftus, E. F. A. (1975). A spreading-activation theory of semantic processing. *Psychological Review, 82*, 407–428.

Cosmides, L., & Tooby, J. (2000). Evolutionary psychology and emotions. In M. L. Lewis & J. M. Haviland-Jones (Eds.), *Handbook of emotions* (pp. 91–115). New York: Guilford Press.

Damasio, A. R. (1994). *Descartes' error: Emotion, reason, and the human brain*. New York: Grosset/Putnam.

DeSteno, D., Petty, R. E., Wegener, D. T., & Rucker, D. D. (2000). Beyond valence in the perception of likelihood: The role of emotion specificity. *Journal of Personality and Social Psychology, 78*, 397–416.

Devine, P. G. (1989). Stereotypes and prejudice: Their automatic and controlled components. *Journal of Personality and Social Psychology, 56*, 5–18.

Dollar, J., Miller, N. E., Doob, L. W., Mowrer, O. H., & Sears, R. R. (1939). *Frustration and aggression*. New Haven, CT: Yale University Press.

Forgas, J. P. (1995). Mood and judgment: The affect infusion model (AIM). *Psychological Review, 117*, 39–66.

Forgas, J. P., & Bower, G. H. (1987). Mood effects on person perception judgments. *Journal of Personality and Social Psychology, 53*, 53–60.

Frijda, N. H., Kuipers, P., & ter Schure, E. (1989). Relations among emotion, appraisal, and emotional action readiness. *Journal of Personality and Social Psychology, 57*, 212–228.

Gouaux, C. (1971). Induced affective states and interpersonal attraction. *Journal of Personality and Social Psychology, 20*, 37–43.

Innes-Ker, Å., & Niedenthal, P. M. (2002). Emotion concepts and emotional states in social judgment and categorization. *Journal of Personality and Social Psychology, 83*, 804–816.

Isbell, L. M., & Wyer, R. S. (1999). Correcting for mood-induced bias in the evaluation of political candidates: The roles of intrinsic and extrinsic motivation. *Personality and Social Psychology Bulletin, 25*, 237–249.

Isen, A. M. (1987). Positive affect, cognitive processes, and social behaviour. In L. Berkowitz (Ed.), *Advances in experimental social psychology* (Vol. 20, pp. 203–253). New York: Academic Press.

Islam, M. R., & Hewstone, M. (1993). Dimensions of contact as predictors of intergroup anxiety, perceived out-group variability, and out-group attitude: An integrative model. *Personality and Social Psychology Bulletin, 19*, 700–710.

Johnson, E. J., & Tversky, A. (1983). Affect, generalization, and the perception of risk. *Journal of Personality and Social Psychology, 45*, 20–31.

Krauth-Gruber, S., & Ric, F. (2000). Affect and stereotypic thinking: A test of the mood-and-general-knowledge model. *Personality and Social Psychology Bulletin, 26*, 1587–1597.

Lambert, A. J., Khan, S. R., Lickel, B. A., & Fricke, K. (1997). Mood and the correction of positive versus negative stereotypes. *Journal of Personality and Social Psychology*, 72, 1002–1016.

Lerner, J. S., & Keltner, D. (2001). Fear, anger, and risk. *Journal of Personality and Social Psychology*, 81, 146–159.

Martin, L. L. (1986). Set/reset: Use and disuse of concepts in impression formation. *Journal of Personality and Social Psychology*, 51, 493–504.

Martin, L. L., Seta, J. J., & Crelia, R. A. (1990). Assimilation and contrast as a function of people's willingness and ability to expend effort in forming an impression. *Journal of Personality and Social Psychology*, 59, 27–37.

Murphy, S. T., & Zajonc, R. B. (1993). Affect, cognition, and awareness: Affective priming with suboptimal and optimal stimulus. *Journal of Personality and Social Psychology*, 64, 723–739.

Neumann, R., Seibt, B., & Strack, F. (2001). The influence of mood on the intensity of emotional responses: Disentangling feeling and knowing. *Cognition and Emotion*, 15, 725–747.

Niedenthal, P. M., Halberstadt, J. B., & Innes-Ker, A. H. (1999). Emotional response categorization. *Psychological Review*, 106, 337–361.

Niedenthal, P. M., Halberstadt, J. B., & Setterlund, M. B. (1997). Being happy and seeing "happy": Emotional state mediates visual word recognition. *Cognition and Emotion*, 11, 403–432.

Niedenthal, P. M., Krauth-Gruber, S., & Ric, F. (2006). *The psychology of emotion: Interpersonal, experiential, and cognitive approaches*. New York: Psychology Press.

Niedenthal, P. M., Ric, F., & Krauth-Gruber, S. (2002). Explaining emotion congruence and its absence in terms of perceptual simulation. *Psychological Inquiry*, 13, 80–83.

Ottati, V. C., & Isbell, L. M. (1996). Effects of mood during exposure to target information on subsequently reported judgments: An on-line model of misattribution and correction. *Journal of Personality and Social Psychology*, 71, 39–53.

Ric, F. (2004). Effects of the activation of affective information on stereotyping: When sadness increases stereotype use. *Personality and Social Psychology Bulletin*, 30, 1310–1321.

Ric, F., Leygue, C., & Adam, C. (2004). Activation of affective information and stereotyping: Does the salience of affective information matter? *Current Psychology of Cognition*, 22, 497–517.

Robinson, M. D., & Clore, G. L. (2002). Belief and feeling: Evidence for an accessibility model. *Psychological Bulletin*, 128, 934–960.

Russel, J. A. (1980). A circumplex model of affect. *Journal of Personality and Social Psychology*, 39, 1161–1178.

Schwarz, N. (1990). Feelings as information: Informational and motivational functions of affective states. In R. M. Sorrentino & E. T. Higgins (Eds.), *Handbook of motivation and cognition: Foundation of social behavior* (Vol. 2, pp. 527–561). New York: Guilford Press.

Schwarz, N., & Bless, H. (1992). Constructing reality and its alternatives: An inclusion/exclusion model of assimilation and contrast effects in social judgment. In L. L. Martin & A. Tesser (Eds.), *The construction of social judgments* (pp. 217–245). Hillsdale, NJ: Lawrence Erlbaum Associates, Inc.

Schwarz, N., & Clore, G.L. (1983). Mood, misattribution, and judgments of well-being: Informative and directive functions of affective states. *Journal of Personality and Social Psychology*, 45, 513–523.

Schwarz, N., Strack, F., Kommer, D., & Wagner, D. (1987). Soccer, rooms, and the quality of your life: Mood effects on judgments of satisfaction with life in general and with specific domains. *European Journal of Social Psychology, 17*, 69–79.

Sedikides, C. (1995). Central and peripheral self-conceptions are differently influenced by mood: Tests of the differential sensitivity hypothesis. *Journal of Personality and Social Psychology, 69*, 759–777.

Sinclair, R. C., Mark, M. M., & Clore, G. L. (1994). Mood-related persuasion depends on (mis)attributions. *Social Cognition, 12*, 309–326.

Smith, C. A., & Ellsworth, P. C. (1985). Patterns of cognitive appraisals in emotion. *Journal of Personality and Social Psychology, 48*, 813–838.

Smith, C. A., & Kirby, L. D. (2000). Consequences require antecedents: Toward a process model of emotion elicitation. In J. P. Forgas (Ed.), *Feeling and thinking: The role of affect in social cognition* (pp. 83–106). Cambridge, UK: Cambridge University Press.

Stapel, D. A., & Koomen, W. (2000). How far do we go beyond the information given? The impact of knowledge activation on interpretation and inference. *Journal of Personality and Social Psychology, 78*, 19–37.

Stapel, D. A., Koomen, W., & Ruys, K. I. (2002). The effects of diffuse and distinct affect, *Journal of Personality and Social Psychology, 83*, 60–74.

Strack, F., Schwarz, N., & Gschneidinger, E. (1985). Happiness and reminiscing: The role of time perspective, affect, and mode of thinking. *Journal of Personality and Social Psychology, 49*, 1460–1469.

Tiedens, L. Z., & Linton, S. (2001). Judgment under emotional certainty and uncertainty: The effects of specific emotions on information processing. *Journal of Personality and Social Psychology, 81*, 973–988.

Wegener, D. T., & Petty, R. E. (1997). The flexible correction model: The role of naïve theories of bias in bias correction. In M. P. Zanna (Ed.), *Advances in experimental social psychology* (Vol. 29, pp. 141–208). San Diego, CA: Academic Press.

Wegener, D. T., Petty, R. E., & Smith, S. M. (1995). Positive mood can increase or decrease message scrutiny: The hedonic contingency view of mood and message processing. *Journal of Personality and Social Psychology, 69*, 5–15.

Wilder, D. A., & Shapiro, P. N. (1989). Role of competition-induced anxiety in limiting the beneficial impact of positive behavior by an out-group member. *Journal of Personality and Social Psychology, 56*, 60–69.

Wyer, R. S., Clore, G. L., & Isbell, L. (1999). Affect and information processing. In M. P. Zanna (Ed.), *Advances in experimental social psychology* (Vol. 31, pp. 3–78). Mahwah, NJ: Lawrence Erlbaum Associates, Inc.

Section II

Social Cognitive Perspectives

5

Mental Construal Processes: The Inclusion/Exclusion Model

NORBERT SCHWARZ and HERBERT BLESS

*T*he terms assimilation and contrast describe the direction of contextual influences on evaluative judgment. Researchers speak of "assimilation" or "carry-over" effects whenever judgments are positively correlated with the valence of the context information, that is, when positive contextual information results in a more positive evaluation or negative contextual information results in a more negative evaluation. Conversely, they speak of "contrast" or "backfire" effects whenever judgments are negatively correlated with the valence of the context information, that is, when positive contextual information results in a more negative evaluation or negative contextual information results in a more positive evaluation. The sources of these effects are as varied as the sources of information that can serve as input into evaluative judgment.

At the most general level, evaluative judgments can be based on declarative as well as experiential information. First, judges may form a mental representation of the target (i.e., object of judgment) based on specific descriptive features and may compare it to some standard to arrive at an evaluation (e.g., Schwarz & Bless, 1992a). Second, they may rely on target-related metacognitive experiences as a source of information, e.g., how easy or difficult it was to recall target features or to process a target description (e.g., Schwarz, Bless et al., 1991; for a review see Schwarz, 2004). Third, judges may use their apparent affective reaction to the target as a source of information, without necessarily considering specific descriptive features of the target (e.g., Schwarz & Clore, 1983; for reviews see Pham, 2004; Schwarz & Clore, 1996). Finally, any of these sources of information may be perceived as exerting an undue influence and judges may attempt to correct for this influence (e.g., Strack & Hannover, 1996; Wilson & Brekke, 1994). To do so, they may draw on another source of information to form a judgment. If none is available, they may merely adjust their evaluation to compensate for the perceived bias. All of these routes to judgment can give rise to assimilation and contrast effects, reflecting that these terms serve as "catch-all" concepts that merely describe the direction of an observed contextual influence.

This chapter addresses feature-based judgments and explores the mental construal processes involved in forming representations of the target and standard. It highlights that the same piece of information can result in assimilation as well as contrast effects, depending on how it is used. We begin with a discussion of mental construal processes. Subsequently we address the variables that determine whether a given piece of information is used in constructing the target, giving rise to assimilation effects, or in constructing the standard, giving rise to contrast effects. Throughout, our discussion follows the logic of our inclusion/exclusion model (IEM; Schwarz & Bless, 1992a), which has fared well over the decade since its original presentation. We conclude with a discussion of the implications of construal processes for three applied issues, namely asymmetries in public opinion and the dynamics of stereotype change and brand extensions.

MENTAL CONSTRUAL PRINCIPLES

Any feature-based evaluative judgment requires a representation of the target (i.e., the object of judgment), as well as a representation of some standard against which the target is evaluated. We assume that both representations are constructed on the spot, based on the subset of potentially applicable information that is most accessible at the time of judgment. As has been observed in numerous studies, people rarely retrieve all information that may be relevant to a judgment but truncate the search process as soon as "enough" information has come to mind to form a judgment with sufficient subjective certainty (for reviews see Bodenhausen & Wyer, 1987; Higgins, 1996). This accessibility principle implies that the chronically or temporarily most accessible information exerts a disproportionate influence. Moreover, the use of highly accessible information is accompanied by a metacognitive experience of fluent processing, which lends additional credibility and weight to the information (Schwarz, 2004).

How chronically or temporarily accessible information influences the judgment depends on how it is used (Schwarz & Bless, 1992a). First, a given target is evaluated more positively the more positive features its representation includes, and more negatively the more negative features its representation includes. This effect is more pronounced the more extreme the evaluative implications of these features are. Accordingly, any contextual influence that affects the construal of the target gives rise to assimilation effects. Second, a given target is evaluated more negatively when it is compared to a positive rather than negative standard or rated relative to a positive rather than negative scale anchor. Accordingly, any contextual influence that affects the construal of the standard or scale anchor gives rise to contrast effects. These mental construal principles are central to the IEM (Schwarz & Bless, 1992a) and a close reading of the contributions to the present volume will show that most variables known to influence the emergence of assimilation and contrast effects can be conceptualized in terms of their influence on the representations formed of the target and standard or scale anchor.

It is worth noting that the role of experiential information can also be conceptualized in these construal terms. First, when relevant features are easy to

INCLUSION/EXCLUSION **121**

bring to mind, the experienced ease of recall suggests that there are many of them, consistent with Tversky and Kahneman's (1973) availability heuristic. Accordingly, the resulting representation is more positive when positive features are easy rather than difficult to bring to mind (for reviews see Schwarz, 1998; Schwarz, Bless, Wänke, & Winkielman, 2003). This increases the size of assimilation effects when the features bear on the representation of the target, but increases the size of contrast effects when they bear on the representation of the standard. Experienced difficulty of recall exerts the opposite influence. Second, people may draw on their apparent affective reaction to the target as a basis of judgment, essentially asking themselves, "How do I feel about this?" (for a review see Schwarz & Clore, 1996). In doing so, they may misread pre-existing moods (e.g., Schwarz & Clore, 1983), affective responses to contextual information (e.g., Winkielman, Zajonc, & Schwarz, 1997), or the positive affect resulting from processing fluency (e.g., Reber, Winkielman, & Schwarz, 1998) as their response to the target. This apparent affective response to the target may either be used in lieu of a more feature-based representation or may be considered an additional relevant feature, depending on feature accessibility and the judge's processing motivation. In either case, the apparent affective response results in assimilation effects, here in the form of affect-congruent judgments (e.g., Schwarz & Clore, 1983). The influence of experiential information is eliminated when the informational value of the recall experience or affective reaction is undermined through (mis)attribution manipulations, thus rendering the experience irrelevant to the target at hand.

ASSIMILATION EFFECTS

Whenever contextual variables bring information to mind that is included in the representation formed of the target, they give rise to assimilation effects. However, contextual variables can do so in a number of different ways.

First, as numerous priming experiments have shown, ambiguous information is interpreted in terms of the most accessible applicable concepts, resulting in more positive target representations when positive rather than negative concepts come to mind (e.g., Higgins, Rholes, & Jones, 1977; Srull & Wyer, 1979; for a review see Higgins, 1996). This conceptual priming process is at the heart of the interpretation component of Stapel and colleagues' (chapter 6, this volume; Stapel & Koomen, 1998, 2001) interpretation-comparison model. Going beyond classic conceptual priming effects, Stapel and Koomen's research illustrates that a range of contextual variables, including specific exemplars, can serve interpretive functions when an interpretation mindset is experimentally induced (e.g., Stapel & Koomen, 2001).

Second, contextual variables may bring features to mind that may otherwise not be considered. When these features are included in the representation of the target, they result in more positive or negative target representations, depending on the valence of the included features. For example, Schwarz, Strack, and Mai (1991; see also Strack, Martin, & Schwarz, 1988) asked survey respondents to report their marital satisfaction and their general life satisfaction in different question orders. When the general life satisfaction question preceded the marital satisfaction question, the answers correlated $r = .32$. Reversing the question order, however, increased the correlation to $r = .67$. This reflects that the marital satisfaction question brought marriage-related information to mind, which was included in the temporary representation that respondents formed of the target "my life." Accordingly, happily married respondents reported higher, and unhappily married respondents reported lower, general life satisfaction in the marriage–life than in the life–marriage order. Similarly, thinking about a politician who was involved in a scandal (say, Richard Nixon) decreases the perceived trustworthiness of politicians in general (Schwarz & Bless, 1992b). In theoretical terms, the accessible exemplar (Nixon) is included in the representation formed of the target (politicians), resulting in an assimilation effect.

Third, contextual variables may influence the categorization of the target. Assigning the target to a category results in the inclusion of category-consistent features in the representation of the target. Accordingly, the resulting target representation is more positive when the target is assigned to a positive rather than negative category. As observed in numerous stereotyping studies, the extent to which the representation also includes individuating information about the specific target depends on the perceiver's processing motivation and capacity (cf. Fiske & Neuberg, 1990). As addressed later, categorization processes are influenced by perceived fit, that is, the overlap between features of the target and features of the category and related variables. However, different categorizations can also be elicited through questions that invite different category assignments, even when motivation, capacity, and fit are held constant (e.g., Bless, Schwarz, Bodenhausen & Thiel, 2001; Bless & Wänke, 2000; Stapel & Schwarz, 1998).

The assumption that assimilation effects are a function of the information that is included in the representation of the target also specifies the key determinants of the *size of assimilation effects*. One determinant is the extremity of the contextual information that is included in the representation of the target (Schwarz & Bless, 1992a). Not surprisingly, including extremely negative information results in a more negative judgment than including only mildly negative information. A second, and theoretically more interesting, set of determinants derives from the set size principle of models of information integration (for reviews see Anderson, 1981; Wyer, 1974). On the one hand, the size of assimilation effects increases with the amount of contextual information added to the representation of the target. For example, the trustworthiness of politicians as a group should be evaluated less favorably when three scandal-ridden politicians are brought to mind than when only one is rendered accessible. On the other hand, the influence of a given piece of accessible information decreases with the amount and extremity of other information that is included in the representation of the target. For example, in the above marital satisfaction study (Schwarz, Strack, & Mai, 1991), the correlation of marital satisfaction and life satisfaction dropped from $r = .67$ to $r = .43$ when questions about three different life domains (job, leisure time, and marriage) preceded the general life satisfaction question, thus bringing a more diverse range of relevant information to mind. Similarly, Bless, Igou, Wänke, and Schwarz (2000) found that bringing a scandal-ridden politician to mind had less influence on judgments of the trustworthiness of politicians in general, the more other, trustworthy politicians were rendered accessible. Extending these findings to a natural context, Simmons, Bickart, and Lynch (1993) observed in an election study that the influence of earlier questions on subsequent political judgments decreased as the election neared, presumably because an increasing amount of relevant information became chronically accessible over the course of the campaign. Bless, Schwarz, and Wänke (2003) provide a more detailed discussion of the size of context effects.

In sum, assimilation effects arise when contextual information is used to form a representation of the target. The size of assimilation effects follows the set size principle of information integration models (e.g., Anderson, 1981). On the one hand, assimilation effects increase with the amount and extremity of the included contextual information. On the other hand, the impact of a given piece of contextual information decreases with the amount of other information included in the representation of the target.

CONTRAST EFFECTS

Whereas assimilation effects are a function of the representation formed of the target, contrast effects are a function of the representation of the standard or scale anchor. Whenever the evaluative implications of positive (negative) temporarily accessible information are more extreme than the evaluative implications of chronically accessible information used in constructing a standard, they result in a more extreme positive (negative) standard. Application of this standard elicits contrast effects on all judgments to which it may be relevant. Hence, judgments are less positive the more positive the standard is and less negative the more negative the standard is.

As an example, consider the impact of political scandals on assessments of the trustworthiness of politicians. As already noted, thinking about a scandal-ridden politician, say Richard Nixon, decreases trust in politicians in general, reflecting that the exemplar can be included in the representation formed of the political class (i.e., a superordinate category), resulting in an assimilation effect. If the trustworthiness question pertains to a specific politician, however, say Bill Clinton, the primed exemplar cannot be included in the representation formed of the target—after all, Bill Clinton is not Richard Nixon (i.e., lateral categories are mutually exclusive). In this case, Nixon may be used in constructing a standard of comparison, relative to which Clinton seems very trustworthy. An experiment with German exemplars confirmed these predictions (Schwarz & Bless, 1992b): Thinking about a politician who was involved in a scandal decreased the trustworthiness of politicians in general, but increased the trustworthiness of all specific exemplars assessed. Hence, the *same* information can result in assimilation as well as contrast effects, depending on whether it is used in forming a representation of the target or of the standard.

As discussed in the next section, numerous different variables can influence whether information is used in constructing a representation of the target or of the standard. It is the diversity of these variables, rather than the diversity of the underlying processes, that results in the richness of empirical research into assimilation and contrast effects.

The *size of contrast effects* follows the same logic as the size of assimilation effects, except that the rules of the set size principle now apply to the representation formed of the standard (see Bless et al., 2003). First, the extremity of the standard is a function of the amount and extremity of the information used in forming a representation of the standard. Hence, the more extreme the contextual information used in constructing a standard, the larger the contrast effect. Second, the impact of a given piece of contextual information decreases with the amount and extremity of other information that enters the construction of the standard. For example, thinking of a scandal-ridden politician increases the perceived trustworthiness of other politicians, as discussed above (Schwarz & Bless, 1992b). However, when additional politicians, who were not involved in the scandal, are brought to mind, the resulting standard of comparison is less extreme. Judged against this less negative standard, other politicians are now evaluated less positively. Hence, Bless and colleagues (2000) observed that individual politicians were perceived as more trustworthy after participants thought about a single scandal-ridden politician (an extremely negative standard) than after they thought about a mix of a scandal-ridden politician and several moderately trustworthy ones (a moderate standard).

In sum, contrast effects arise when contextual information is used in forming a representation of the standard. The size of contrast effects again follows the set size principle of information integration models (e.g., Anderson, 1981). On the one hand, contrast effects increase with the amount and extremity of the contextual information used in constructing a standard. On the other hand, the impact of a given piece of contextual information decreases with the amount of other information included in the representation of the standard (see Bless et al., 2003, for a more detailed discussion).

A NOTE ON SUBTRACTION PROCESSES

The above assumptions capture the bulk of assimilation and contrast effects, as usually understood. However, the logic of mental construal entails two additional possibilities that give rise to conditions under which judgments may shift toward (assimilation), or away from (contrast), the evaluative implications of contextual information. To date, these possibilities have received little empirical attention.

First, judgments may sometimes shift away from the implications of temporarily accessible information *without* involving a change in standards. This is the case when a contextual variable (a) draws attention to a chronically accessible positive (negative) feature of the target *and* (b) elicits the exclusion of this feature from the representation of the target, thus resulting in a target representation that is less positive (negative). Suppose, for example, that a political party has a highly respected politician, who figures prominently in citizens' representation of his party and contributes favorably to its evaluation. If citizens were induced to exclude this politician from the mental representation of his party, the party would be evaluated more negatively. Empirically, this is the case. For example, Bless and Schwarz (1998) asked German participants a knowledge question that (a) brought a highly respected German politician to mind and (b) reminded them that this politician holds an office that "prevents him from participating in party politics." As expected, this manipulation resulted in less favorable evaluations of this politician's party, *without* affecting evaluations of other parties. This indicates that the manipulation only affected the representation formed of the target party, but not the representation formed of the standard, which would result in contrast effects that generalize across applicable targets (as observed in Schwarz & Bless, 1992b).

We refer to this possibility as a *subtraction-based contrast effect*. On theoretical grounds, we assume that such effects are rare. They require (a) that a positive (negative) feature is chronically accessible and (b) attention is drawn to it through a contextual influence. Moreover, this influence (c) needs to elicit the exclusion of this feature from the representation of the target, without (d) eliciting its inclusion in the representation of the standard. These conditions were met in the above experiment. Presumably, reminding participants that this politician's office puts him above the fray of party politics not only prompted his exclusion from the representation of his own party, but also rendered him irrelevant as a standard for evaluating any other party.

As a second possibility, judgments can shift toward the evaluative implications of contextual information without requiring a change in the representation of the target. Suppose, for example, that citizens' representation of the standard against which they evaluate politicians includes a highly accessible villain, say Richard Nixon. If a contextual variable (a) brought Nixon to mind *and* (b) elicited his exclusion from the representation of the standard, it would result in a more positive standard. Any politician evaluated against this more positive standard would now appear more negative. Such a *subtraction-based assimilation effect* would merely require a change in the standard, without an accompanying change in the representation of the target. This possibility awaits systematic investigation.

SUMMARY

In sum, the IEM (Schwarz & Bless, 1992a) traces the emergence of assimilation and contrast effects to changes in the mental representations formed of the target and standard. Information that is included in the representation formed of the target results in assimilation effects. Information that is included in the representation formed of the standard results in comparison-based contrast effects, provided that the resulting extremity of the standard differs from the target representation. Comparison-based contrast effects generalize across all targets to which the standard is applicable. Finally, information that is merely excluded from the representation of the target, and not used in forming a representation of the standard, results in subtraction-based contrast effects, which are limited to the specific target. Conversely, information that is merely excluded from the representation of the standard, and not used in forming a representation of the target, results in subtraction-based assimilation effects. Subtraction-based assimilation effects generalize to all targets to which the standard is applied. Throughout, the size of assimilation and contrast effects can be predicted on the basis of a set size principle. Next, we address the variables that determine whether a given piece of information is used in constructing a representation of the target or a representation of the standard.

DETERMINANTS OF INFORMATION USE

A plethora of different variables has been shown to elicit assimilation or contrast effects. The IEM conceptualizes their operation in terms of their influence on information use: Do they increase the likelihood that a given piece of information is used in forming a representation of the target? Or do they increase the likelihood that a given piece of information is used in forming a representation of the standard? The operation of these variables can be organized by assuming that perceivers tacitly ask themselves three questions, which serve as filters that channel information use. These filters determine if the information is used to form a representation of the target, resulting in an assimilation effect, or a representation of the standard, resulting in a contrast effect.

Why Does It Come to Mind?

Some of the information that comes to mind may be clearly irrelevant to the judgment and needs no further consideration. Information that may potentially be relevant to the judgment needs to pass a first filter: "Am I only thinking of this information because it was brought to mind due to some irrelevant influence?" If so, the accessible information is not used in forming a representation of the target. For example, in conceptual priming experiments, highly accessible concepts are not used in forming a representation of the target when participants are aware of the potential influence of the priming episode (e.g., Lombardi, Higgins, & Bargh, 1987; Martin, 1986; Strack, Schwarz, Bless, Kübler, & Wänke, 1993). Awareness of an irrelevant influence is more likely when the contextual information is externally presented (e.g., by an experimenter), rather than generated by participants themselves (e.g., Mussweiler & Neumann, 2000).

The (seemingly) self-generated nature of one's own thoughts is one of the reasons why information brought to mind by preceding questions in a survey interview is more likely to pass the first filter than information brought to mind by other contextual variables. Moreover, survey respondents usually assume that adjacent questions are substantively related, unless indicated otherwise (Schwarz, 1996). In combination, this renders it unlikely that the thoughts elicited by preceding questions are seen as exerting an undue influence under regular interview or questionnaire conditions. At the other extreme, most priming experiments explicitly present the priming and judgment tasks as unrelated. This increases the likelihood that the "why-does-it-come-to-mind?" filter is applied when a possible influence is perceived. Many natural priming episodes, like exposure to television news, fall in between these extremes.

Finally, it is worth noting that experiential information is similarly filtered with respect to why one has this experience at this point in time. If variables likely to affect experiential information are perceived as exerting an undue influence, the informational value of the experience is undermined. Under these conditions, the experiential information is not used and judges turn to other inputs, if available (e.g., Schwarz & Clore, 1983, with regard to affect; Schwarz, Bless et al., 1991, with regard to ease of recall).

Does It Bear on the Target?

When the information passes this first test, the second filter is: "Does this information represent a feature of the target?"

Concept Priming   The answer to this question is always positive when the contextual influence is due to concept priming, unless participants are aware of the potential influence of the priming episode (e.g., Martin, 1986; Strack et al., 1993). This reflects that highly accessible concepts influence the encoding of the target information itself, resulting in different perceptions of ambiguous target behaviors (e.g., Higgins et al., 1977; Srull & Wyer, 1979). Interpretation-based assimilation effects (see Stapel et al., chapter 6, this volume) are therefore likely to be robust. Not surprisingly, these effects are not obtained when participants are implicitly or explicitly instructed to engage in a comparison process, thus inducing them to use the primed information in constructing a representation of the standard rather than the target (e.g., Stapel & Koomen, 2001).

Most contextual information, however, requires a decision on how it should be used. This decision is driven by the numerous variables known to influence the categorization in general, as a few examples may illustrate.

Category Structure   As already noted, thinking of a scandal-ridden German politician decreased the trustworthiness of German politicians in general, but increased the trustworthiness of every individual politician evaluated (Schwarz & Bless, 1992b). This reflects that the target category "German politicians" is super-ordinate to the context information (a specific scandal-ridden politician) and hence invites the inclusion of the subordinate scandalous exemplar. In contrast, other specific politicians are lateral target categories, which are mutually exclusive. As a result, exemplar priming elicits assimilation effects on judgments of super-ordinate targets, but contrast effects on judgments of lateral targets, as has been observed across a wide range of different tasks (e.g., Bless et al., 2000; Schwarz & Bless, 1992b; Stapel & Schwarz, 1998; Wänke, Bless, & Igou, 2001; Wänke, Bless, & Schwarz, 1998).

As Stapel and Koomen (2001) illustrated, however, the trait concepts brought to mind by exemplars can be used in interpreting target information when the perceiver is in an interpretative mindset. In this case, the interpretive effects of concept priming can override the comparison effects imposed by a lateral category structure. Theoretically, this should be most likely when the target description is ambiguous, consistent with standard concept priming results (e.g., Higgins et al., 1977).

Category Boundaries

Not surprisingly, categorization decisions are strongly influenced by salient category boundaries. For example, Strack, Schwarz, and Gschneidinger (1985) asked participants to recall a positive or negative life event that happened either recently or several years ago. Recent events resulted in an assimilation effect on later judgments of current life satisfaction, whereas distant events resulted in a contrast effect. This reflects that recent events could be included in the representation of the target category "my life now," whereas the distant events could not, and hence served as a standard of comparison. In follow-up experiments (reviewed in Schwarz & Strack, 1999), freshmen were asked during their first month at college to recall a positive or negative life event that happened "during the last two years." Replicating the earlier findings, these recent events resulted in assimilation effects on current life satisfaction. Other freshmen were given the same task, except for a small addition to the instructions: They were asked to recall a positive or negative event that happened "during the last two years, that is, before you came to the university." This addition emphasized a category boundary that invited them to chunk the stream of life into their high school time and college time. Under this condition, a contrast effect emerged, indicating that it is not temporal distance per se, but the categorization of the accessible event that drives assimilation and contrast.

Conversely, imposing a shared categorization can blur the otherwise perceived category boundaries. For example, Seta, Martin, and Capehart (1979) observed assimilation effects in attractiveness ratings of two target persons when both were assigned to the same category (college major), but contrast effects when they were not. Similarly, Brown, Novick, Lord, and Richards (1992) obtained assimilation effects on self-evaluations when participants shared a birthday with the comparison other, but contrast effects otherwise. In a particularly interesting variation on this theme, Stapel and Koomen (2005) showed that cooperation gives rise to assimilation effects on self-evaluations, whereas competition gives rise to contrast effects. Presumably, cooperation imposes a shared categorization ("we"), much as shared majors or birthdays can do.

Feature Overlap

Another general determinant of categorization is feature overlap: A given stimulus is more likely to be assigned to a given category, the more it shares category features. For example, Herr, Sherman, and Fazio (1983; see also Herr, 1986) observed assimilation effects when a target stimulus was rated in the context of moderate stimuli, but contrast effects when it was rated in the context of extreme stimuli. They concluded that "to the extent that a comparison of features of the activated category and the target stimulus results in matching or overlap, a judgment of category membership should occur" (Herr, 1986, p. 1107), eliciting an assimilation effect. If the overlap is insufficient, on the other hand, thus constituting an exclusion relationship, "the priming exemplars serve as standards of comparison" (p. 1107), resulting in a contrast effect.

Similarly, Mussweiler, Rüter, and Epstude (2004; Mussweiler, 2003) observed that a search for similarities between the self and a comparison person elicited assimilation effects on self-evaluations, consistent with the high feature overlap resulting from a similarity search. Conversely, a search for dissimilarities elicited contrast effects, consistent with the perception of low feature overlap. Note that these differential search foci are likely to simultaneously affect the representations formed of the target and of the standard, which gives additional power to the effect. By definition, similarities are features that are shared by the self and other and can hence enter into both representations. Including similarities in the representation of the self results in assimilation, while their simultaneous inclusion in the representation of the other results in a standard that is similar to the self, thus also attenuating any contrast that may otherwise be observed. Dissimilarities, on the other hand, imply that some feature X applies to the self, whereas some feature non-X applies to the other. Including feature X in the self again elicits assimilation toward X. However, including feature non-X in the representation of the other results in a standard that is dissimilar to the self with regard to X, further enhancing the judgment that the self is high on X.

Findings of this type converge on the conclusion that "distinct" information (low feature overlap) elicits contrast effects, whereas "nondistinct" information (high feature overlap) elicits assimilation effects, as Stapel and colleagues observed in numerous experiments (e.g., Stapel & Koomen, 2000; Stapel & Winkielman, 1998; see Stapel, chapter 6, this volume for a review).

Category Heterogeneity and Mutability   Categories differ in heterogeneity. People assume, for example, that the members of a natural category (e.g., birds) are more similar to one another than the members of an artifactual composite category (e.g., things in a house). Not surprisingly, the perceived internal homogeneity or heterogeneity of a category constrains the range of information that can be included in the category representation. Ceteris paribus, a given piece of information is therefore more likely to result in assimilation effects in judgments of heterogeneous target categories, but to result in contrast effects in judgments of homogeneous target categories. Similarly, target categories that are perceived as highly mutable allow for the inclusion of a more varied set of information than less mutable target categories, giving rise to assimilation effects in the former, and contrast effects in the latter case (e.g., Stapel & Koomen, 2001).

In a related vein, Lambert and Wyer (1990) demonstrated that exemplars that fell within perceivers' range of beliefs resulted in assimilation effects, whereas contrast effects emerged when exemplars fell outside perceivers' range of beliefs.

Direct Manipulations   In many of the preceding examples, categorization was driven by characteristics of the target category and the context information. This renders it difficult to determine with certainty that the observed effects are due to categorization per se, rather than to some other characteristic of the information. To avoid this ambiguity, we often relied on direct categorization manipulations in tests of the IEM. As already seen, this can be achieved by asking knowledge questions that invite the inclusion or exclusion of an exemplar from the superordinate category (e.g., Bless & Schwarz, 1998; Stapel & Schwarz, 1998) or the assignment of several targets to the same or different categories (e.g., Wänke, Bless, & Schwarz, 1999).

In a related approach, Bless and Wänke (2000) presented all participants with the same list of moderately typical TV shows, thus keeping the features of the exemplar and category constant. To manipulate participants' perceptions of the shows' typicality, participants were asked to select two shows that they considered either (a) "typically favorable," (b) "atypically favorable," (c) "typically unfavorable," or (d) "atypically unfavorable." Classifying a show as "typically" favorable or unfavorable evoked its inclusion in the superordinate category, resulting in assimilation effects on ratings of TV shows in general. Conversely, classifying a show as "atypically" favorable or unfavorable evoked its exclusion from the superordinate category, resulting in contrast effects on ratings of TV shows in general. Similarly, Bodenhausen, Schwarz, Bless, and Wänke (1995) demonstrated that the impact of highly successful African Americans (e.g., Michael Jordan) on judgments of perceived discrimination was moderated by knowledge questions that invited the inclusion or exclusion of the primed exemplar from the superordinate category. Such findings highlight that differential categorization can drive the emergence of assimilation and contrast effects even under conditions of otherwise identical target and context information.

Presentation and Judgment Order
In addition, categorization decisions can also be a function of more fortuitous aspects of the experimental procedures used, such as the order in which stimuli are presented or judgments are assessed. For example, Wedell, Parducci, and Geiselman (1987) asked participants to rate the attractiveness of faces that were either presented successively or in pairs. When the faces were presented successively, the same face was rated more favorably when presented in the context of less attractive faces, reflecting a contrast effect. When the faces were presented in pairs, however, the same face was rated less favorably when presented simultaneously with a less attractive face, reflecting an assimilation effect. The authors traced this assimilation effect "to a failure to separate the individual stimulus from other stimuli that are simultaneously present" (Wedell et al., 1987, p. 231). Apparently, the use of a successive or simultaneous presentation format influenced the categorization of the stimuli, mediating the emergence of assimilation and contrast effects.

Similarly, Martin and Seta (1983) observed the emergence of assimilation and contrast effects in an experiment that followed Byrne's (1971) similarity-attraction paradigm. Their participants received descriptions of two target persons and learned that one person shared their attitudes on three out of six issues, whereas the other shared their attitudes on all six issues. Participants rated the attractiveness of the targets either sequentially, after having read the respective individual description, or simultaneously, after having read both descriptions. As usual, target persons who agreed on all issues were rated as more attractive than target persons who agreed only on half of the issues. More important, this difference was more pronounced under sequential than under simultaneous rating conditions. This again indicates that sequential ratings foster contrast between targets, whereas simultaneous ratings foster assimilation, as observed by Wedell et al. (1987).

Summary   As our selective review illustrates, *any* variable that influences the categorization of information can determine whether a given piece of information is included in the representation of the target or in the representation of the standard. This suggests a crucial role for numerous variables that have so far received little attention in assimilation and contrast research. For example, several studies indicate that individuals form broader categories, and include less typical exemplars, when in a happy rather than sad mood (e.g., Bless, Hamilton, & Mackie, 1992; Isen, Daubman, & Gorgolione, 1987; Sinclair & Mark, 1992; for a review see Schwarz, 2002; Schwarz & Clore, 1996). This suggests that assimilation effects should be more likely when perceivers are happy rather than sad. Similarly, cultural research indicates that individuals with an independent self-construal are likely to focus on focal objects, whereas individuals with an interdependent self-construal are likely to integrate the object in its context (for reviews see Nisbett, 2003; Oyserman, Sorensen, Cha, & Schwarz, 2006). Hence, assimilation effects should be more likely for individuals with an interdependent self-construal and contrast effects for individuals with an independent self-construal (for suggestive evidence see Hannover, Kühnen, & Birkner, 2000). These possibilities await systematic testing.

Conversational Norms

The third and final filter pertains to the norms of conversational conduct that govern information use in conversations: "Is it conversationally appropriate to use this information?" Conversational norms prohibit redundancy and invite speakers to provide information that is new to the recipient, rather than to reiterate information that the recipient already has (Grice, 1975; for reviews see Schwarz, 1994, 1996). Hence, highly accessible information is not used when it violates this conversational norm, again resulting in contrast effects.

For example, recall the previously reviewed marital satisfaction study, where life satisfaction and marital satisfaction correlated $r = .32$ in the life–marriage order, but $r = .67$ in the marriage–life order (Schwarz, Strack, & Mai, 1991; see also Haddock & Carrick, 1999; Strack et al., 1988). As discussed earlier, this assimilation effect reflects that the preceding marital satisfaction question brought marriage-related information to mind, which respondents used in forming a representation of their lives in general. In another condition, both questions were explicitly placed in the same conversational context, thus evoking the norm of nonredundancy. This was accomplished by a joint lead-in to both that read, "Now we would like to learn about two areas of life that may be important for people's overall well-being: happiness with marriage and happiness with life in general." Subsequently, both happiness questions were asked in the marriage–life order. With this lead-in, the correlation dropped from the previously obtained $r = .67$ to $r = .18$, indicating that respondents deliberately disregarded information that they had already provided in response to the marital satisfaction question when making a subsequent general life satisfaction judgment, despite its high accessibility in memory. Presumably, they interpreted the general question as if it referred to aspects of their life that they had not yet reported on. Supporting this interpretation, a condition in which the general question was reworded in this way resulted in a nearly identical correlation of $r = .20$.

Paralleling these differences in correlation, respondents who were induced to disregard their marriage in evaluating their life-as-a-whole reported higher life satisfaction when they were unhappily married, and lower life satisfaction when they were happily married, than respondents who were not induced to exclude this information. Thus, contrast effects were obtained when conversational norms elicited the exclusion of the primed information from the representation formed of one's life, despite its obvious substantive relevance to this judgment.

Cultural Differences Subsequent research showed first evidence for cultural differences in the emergence of assimilation and contrast effects. In general, interdependent cultures value more indirect forms of communication, which require a higher amount of "reading between the lines," based on close attention to the conversational context. If so, interdependent individuals may be more sensitive to the potential redundancy of their answers to related questions than independent individuals. Empirically, this is the case. In a conceptual replication of the Schwarz, Strack, and Mai (1991) study, Haberstroh, Oyserman, Schwarz, Kühnen, and Ji (2002) asked German and Chinese students to report on their general life satisfaction as well as their academic satisfaction. Both questions were presented without a joint lead-in to explore if chronically interdependent Chinese are more sensitive to conversational context than chronically independent Germans (for evidence on these chronic differences see Oyserman, Coon, & Kemmelmeier, 2002). Replicating earlier results, the answers of German students correlated $r = .53$ in the life–academic order, and this correlation increased to $r = .78$ in the academic–life order, indicating an assimilation effect. The answers of the Chinese students showed a nearly identical correlation of $r = .50$ in the life–academic order, yet this correlation dropped to $r = .36$ in the academic–life order, indicating a contrast effect. Subsequent experiments with German participants (Haberstroh et al., 2002) tested the causal role of independence/interdependence through priming procedures, resulting in parallel effects.

In combination, these findings indicate that cultural differences in conversational conduct can give rise to cultural differences in the emergence of assimilation and contrast effects. Theoretically, the same holds true for any other cultural difference that may affect information use, as discussed in the context of cultural differences in categorization strategies.

Putting It Together

We reviewed three "filters" that capture the major determinants of information use. The first filter checks whether the information may have come to mind for an irrelevant reason; the second filter tests if the information represents features of the target; and the final filter addresses whether use of the information is conversationally appropriate. Information that passes all three tests is included in the representation formed of the target and results in assimilation effects. Information that fails any one of these filters is excluded from the representation formed of the target, but may be used in forming a representation of the standard, resulting in contrast effects.

Attention and Capacity   Application of these filters requires attention and cognitive capacity, suggesting that assimilation effects are more likely than contrast effects under conditions of low cognitive resources. However, different filter variables are likely to be differentially susceptible to attention and capacity constraints.

Suppose, for example, that a contextual influence brings an exemplar to mind and the judgment requires evaluation of another exemplar. Given that lateral categories are mutually exclusive, no elaborate categorization decisions need to be made and contrast is likely even under low attention conditions. In fact, contrast effects have been observed even when the primed exemplar is presented subliminally and the judgment is to be made fast (Winkielman, Coleman, & Schwarz, 1994). At the other end of the continuum, noticing the potential redundancy of one's answers to related questions in the absence of strong conversational cues requires close attention to the conversational common ground. As seen above, contrast effects are more likely under these conditions when chronic or temporary interdependence fosters attention to the common ground (Haberstroh et al., 2002), and limited cognitive capacity would presumably disrupt this process. Similarly, noticing an undue influence and correcting for it requires cognitive resources and the otherwise resulting contrast effects are eliminated under low resource conditions (e.g., Martin & Achee, 1992; Meyers-Levy & Tybout, 1997). Other categorization relevant variables fall in between these extremes and the systematic exploration of attention and capacity issues provides a promising avenue for future research.

Information Use, Not the Information Itself, is Crucial   As our review of the IEM indicates, the model assigns the crucial role to how contextual information is *used*, rather than to the characteristics of the information itself. As discussed above, characteristics of the contextual information can be powerful determinants of information use. However, even when we hold all features constant, the *same* information can give rise to assimilation *and* contrast effects, depending on how it is used. The most compelling evidence for this implication of the IEM is provided by experiments that manipulated the categorization of accessible information directly, without involving changes in the presented features (e.g., Bless & Schwarz, 1998; Bless et al., 2001; Bless & Wänke, 2000; Stapel & Schwarz, 1998; Wänke et al., 1999). Hence, any approach that focuses primarily on characteristics of the target or context information results in overly localized explanations of limited explanatory power. More important, the effects predicted by these approaches can be easily overridden by other variables that affect information use, like direct manipulations of how the information is categorized. From the perspective of the IEM, the diversity of the variables that can elicit assimilation or contrast does not reflect a diversity of the underlying processes. Instead, the operation of the variables can be parsimoniously conceptualized by identifying their influence on information use, that is, whether a given piece of information is used in constructing a mental representation of the target or of the standard against which the target is evaluated.

APPLIED IMPLICATIONS: PERCEPTIONS OF EXEMPLARS AND GROUPS

In addition to providing an integrative conceptualization of the processes underlying the emergence of assimilation and contrast effects, the theoretical assumptions of the IEM bear on core issues of substantive interest to social psychologists. In this final section, we address tradeoffs in the perception of exemplars (e.g., persons or products) and their superordinate category (e.g., social group or brand) that have been observed across a wide range of content domains. As will become apparent, what is favorable for evaluations of the exemplar is usually unfavorable for evaluations of the exemplar's group, and vice versa, giving rise to a natural tension in interests.

Public Opinion

As already noted, accessible exemplars can be included in the representations formed of their groups, a superordinate category. However, they cannot be included in representations formed of other exemplars, reflecting that lateral categories are mutually exclusive. Accordingly, exemplars elicit assimilation effects on judgments of their groups, but contrast effects on judgments of their peers (with exceptions discussed in the section on category structure).

These diverging effects give rise to diverging interests between individuals and their groups. For example, in the domain of public opinion, individual politicians suffer from the accessibility of a respected star, but benefit from the accessibility of a suspected crook. Conversely, the political class as a whole, and the exemplar's party, benefit from respected stars, but suffer from suspected crooks (e.g., Bless et al., 2000; Schwarz & Bless, 1992b; Stapel & Schwarz, 1998). Similarly, the high accessibility of Martin Luther King, Jr. during Martin Luther King Day celebrations in the United States improves perceptions of African Americans as a group, but hurts perceptions of individual African-American leaders (Konrath & Schwarz, 2005).

The same process is at the heart of numerous asymmetries in public opinion. For example, Americans distrust congress in general, but trust their own representative (e.g., Erikson, Luttbeg, & Tedin, 1988) and support capital punishment in general, but are less likely to apply it in any specific case (e.g., Ellsworth & Gross, 1994). Moreover, members of minority groups consistently report severe discrimination against their group, yet also report that their own personal experiences were more benign. These asymmetries are to be expected when we assume that some extreme instances of dishonesty, crime, and discrimination are chronically accessible and likely to come to mind when a relevant question is asked. When the question pertains to the general class, these instances are included in the representation formed, resulting in assimilation effects; when the question pertains to other instances, they serve as standards of comparison and result in contrast effects. Accordingly, common asymmetries in public opinion do not reflect the use of different information but the diverging effects of using the same information.

Stereotype Change

Social psychologists have long assumed that exposure to favorable members of a negatively stereotyped group will elicit stereotype change through inclusion of the exemplar in the representation formed of the group (for a review see Rothbart, 2001). Presumably, this would benefit the group as well as its members. The IEM offers a less optimistic prediction, highlighting differential interests of the group and its most favorable members. On the one hand, inclusion of a positive exemplar in the representation of a negatively stereotyped group does indeed improve the perception of the group. On the other hand, however, it imposes the negative attributes of the group on the perception of the exemplar, resulting in less favorable evaluations of the exemplar. In short, the assimilation effect elicited by inclusion of the exemplar in the group works both ways, which benefits a negative group, but hurts a positive exemplar (e.g., Bless et al., 2001). Conversely, excluding a favorable exemplar from the representation of the group increases the negativity of the group stereotype, but benefits the perception of the exemplar, which is now evaluated against the standard of the group (e.g., Bless et al., 2001). Again, contrast works both ways, here hurting the group but benefiting the exemplar.

In combination, these findings highlight that stereotype change involves tradeoffs between the exemplar and the group: What is good for the group is bad for the exemplar, and vice versa. Unfortunately, we cannot improve the perception of one entity without hurting the perception of the other.

Brand and Product Line Extensions

The same principles apply in the nonsocial domain, as an example from marketing research may illustrate. Marketers often introduce new products as an extension of an existing respected brand, hoping that the positive brand evaluation would "transfer" to the new product. This "transfer" is best conceptualized as an assimilation effect and successful extensions are assumed to require a high feature overlap between the brand and the extension (e.g., Aaker & Keller, 1990; Boush et al., 1987). However, from the perspective of the IEM, feature overlap is only one of many variables that determine the emergence of assimilation effects and the IEM draws attention to opportunities as well as risks in brand extension.

First, while marketers cannot easily change the actual features of the brand or extension, they can apply a number of other strategies to influence the categorization process to facilitate assimilation effects. For example, superficial similarities in product names have been found to facilitate assimilation (Wänke et al., 1998) and questions that evoke different categorizations can override the impact of actual features (Wänke et al., 1999).

Second, marketers often assume that the worst case scenario is a simple failure of the intended transfer—the brand does not help the product. However, the IEM suggests a worse case: A positive brand may not only fail to help the new product, but may actually hurt the new product by giving rise to a contrast effect. This is to be expected when the positive brand serves as a standard of comparison, relative to which the new product is evaluated less positively than it would be evaluated without the brand association. Wänke and colleagues (1998) showed that superficial dissimilarities, like a product name that does not match the naming tradition of the brand, are sufficient to elicit such backfire effects.

Finally, our discussion of the differential impact of context information on the evaluation of superordinate and lateral categories draws attention to an even worse case: The new product may hurt all other products of the brand. For example, a new and better product may serve as a highly positive standard of comparison, relative to which all other products of the brand are evaluated less positively (see Wänke et al., 2001, for an example), paralleling the interexemplar contrast effects discussed earlier. At the same time, the new product will have a favorable impact on the evaluation of the brand as a whole, given that the brand as a superordinate category invites its inclusion. Which of these two alternative effects drives a consumer's choice will depend on the choice situation. For example, when a consumer considers one of the older products of the brand in isolation, the positive impact of the new product on the brand as a whole may transfer to the old product, making it more attractive. But when the old and new products are considered in combination, the new product will hurt the attractiveness of the previous one. The IEM specifies the processes underlying these exemplar–category assimilation and exemplar–exemplar contrast effects and identifies numerous variables that can be used to manage them.

CONCLUDING REMARKS

As our review indicates, the inclusion/exclusion model provides a parsimonious account of the emergence and size of assimilation and contrast effects. First, representations of targets and standards are constructed on the basis of accessible information. Second, information used to form a representation of the target results in assimilation effects, whereas information used to form a representation of the standard results in contrast effects. Third, the size of both effects can be predicted by applying the set size principle to the respective representation.

To many readers, this summary may seem at odds with the enormous complexity of the empirical results that have been accumulated in decades of research (for a comprehensive review see Biernat, 2005). From our perspective, this complexity merely reflects that a myriad of different variables can influence whether information is used in constructing a representation of the target or of the standard. It is the diversity of these variables, rather than the diversity of the underlying processes, that results in the complexity of empirical research into assimilation and contrast effects.

ACKNOWLEDGMENTS

We thank Marcus Maringer, Daphna Oyserman, and Diederik Stapel for helpful comments on an earlier draft and the Deutsche Forschungsgemeinschaft for support of much of the reported research.

REFERENCES

Aaker, D. A., & Keller, K. L. (1990). Consumer evaluations of brand extensions. *Journal of Marketing, 54*(1), 27–41.

Anderson, N. H. (1981). *The foundations of information integration theory.* New York: Academic Press.

Biernat, M. (2005). *Standards and expectancies.* New York: Psychology Press.

Bless, H., Hamilton, D. L., & Mackie, D. M. (1992). Mood effects on the organization of person information. *European Journal of Social Psychology, 22,* 497–509.

Bless, H., Igou, E. R., Schwarz, N., & Wänke, M. (2000). Reducing context effects by adding context information: The direction and size of context effects in political judgment. *Personality and Social Psychology Bulletin, 26,* 1036–1045.

Bless, H., & Schwarz, N. (1998). Context effects in political judgment: Assimilation and contrast as a function of categorization processes. *European Journal of Social Psychology, 28,* 159–172.

Bless, H., Schwarz, N., Bodenhausen, G. V., & Thiel, L. (2001). Personalized versus generalized benefits of stereotype disconfirmation: Tradeoffs in the evaluation of atypical exemplars and their social groups. *Journal of Experimental Social Psychology, 37,* 386–397.

Bless, H., Schwarz, N., & Wänke, M. (2003). The size of context effects in social judgment. In J. P. Forgas, K. D. Williams, & W. von Hippel (Eds.), *Social judgments: Implicit and explicit processes* (pp. 180–197). Cambridge, UK: Cambridge University Press.

Bless, H., & Wänke, M. (2000). Can the same information be typical and atypical? How perceived typicality moderates assimilation and contrast in evaluative judgments. *Personality and Social Psychology Bulletin, 26,* 306–314.

Bodenhausen, G. V., Schwarz, N., Bless, H., & Wänke, M. (1995). Effects of atypical exemplars on racial beliefs: Enlightened racism or generalized appraisal? *Journal of Experimental Social Psychology, 31,* 48–63.

Bodenhausen, G. V., & Wyer, R. S. (1987). Social cognition and social reality: Information acquisition and use in the laboratory and the real world. In H. J. Hippler, N. Schwarz, & S. Sudman (Eds.), *Social information processing and survey methodology* (pp. 6–41). New York: Springer-Verlag.

Boush, D., Shipp, S., Loken, B., Gencturk, E. Corckett, S., Kennedy, E., et al. (1987). Affect generalization to similar and dissimilar brand extensions. *Psychology and Marketing, 4,* 225–237.

Brown, J. D., Novick, N. J., Lord, K. A., & Richards, J. M. (1992). When Gulliver travels: Social context, psychological closeness, and self-appraisals. *Journal of Personality and Social Psychology, 62,* 717–727.

Byrne, D. (1971). *The attraction paradigm*. New York: Academic Press.

Ellsworth, P. C., & Gross, S. R. (1994). Hardening of the attitudes: Americans' views on the death penalty. *Journal of Social Issues, 50*, 19–52.

Erikson, R. S., Luttbeg, N. R., & Tedin, K.T. (1988). *American public opinion* (3rd ed.). New York: Macmillan.

Fiske, S. T., & Neuberg, S. L. (1990). A continuum of impression formation from category-based to individuating processing: Influences of information and motivation on attention and interpretation. *Advances in Experimental Social Psychology, 23*, 1–74.

Grice, H. P. (1975). Logic and conversation. In P. Cole & J. L. Morgan (Eds.), *Syntax and semantics: Vol. 3. Speech acts* (pp. 41–58). New York: Academic Press.

Haberstroh, S., Oyserman, D., Schwarz, N., Kühnen, U., & Ji, L. (2002). Is the inter-dependent self more sensitive to question context than the independent self? Self-construal and the observation of conversational norms. *Journal of Experimental Social Psychology, 38*, 323–329.

Haddock, G., & Carrick, R. (1999). "The Queen Mother and I": Assimilation, contrast, and attitudes toward social groups. *European Journal of Social Psychology, 29*, 123–129.

Hannover, B., Kühnen, U., & Birkner, N. (2000). Interdependent and independent self-knowledge as a determinant of assimilation versus contrast in contextual priming. *Zeitschrift für Sozialpsychologie, 31*, 44–56.

Herr, P. M. (1986). Consequences of priming: Judgment and behavior. *Journal of Personality and Social Psychology, 51*, 1106–1115.

Herr, P. M., Sherman, S. J., & Fazio, R. H. (1983). On the consequences of priming: Assimilation and contrast effects. *Journal of Experimental Social Psychology, 19*, 323–340.

Higgins, E. T. (1996). Knowledge activation: Accessibility, applicability, and salience. In E. T. Higgins & A. W. Kruglanski (Eds.), *Social psychology: Handbook of basic principles* (pp. 133–168). New York: Guilford Press.

Higgins, E. T., Rholes, W. S., & Jones, C. R. (1977). Category accessibility and impression formation. *Journal of Experimental Social Psychology, 13*, 141–154.

Isen, A. M., Daubman, K. A., & Gorgoglione, J. M. (1987). The influence of positive affect on cognitive organization: Implications for education. In R. E. Snow & M. J. Farr (Eds.), *Aptitude, learning and instruction* (Vol. 3, pp. 143–162). Hillsdale, NJ: Lawrence Erlbaum Associates, Inc.

Konrath, S., & Schwarz, N. (2005, January). *MLK Day and attitude change: Liking the group more but specific exemplars less*. Paper presented at the Society for Personality and Social Psychology, New Orleans, LA.

Lambert, A. J., & Wyer, R. S. (1990). Stereotypes and social judgment: The effects of typicality and group heterogeneity. *Journal of Personality and Social Psychology, 59*, 676–691.

Lombardi, W. J., Higgins, E. T., & Bargh, J. A. (1987). The role of consciousness in priming effects on categorization: Assimilation and contrast as a function of awareness of the priming task. *Personality and Social Psychology Bulletin, 13*, 411–429.

Martin, L. L. (1986). Set/reset: Use and disuse of concepts in impression formation. *Journal of Personality and Social Psychology, 51*, 493–504.

Martin, L. L., & Achee, J. W. (1992). Beyond accessibility: The role of processing objectives in judgment. In L. L. Martin & A. Tesser (eds), *The construction of social judgments* (pp. 195–216). Hillsdale, NJ: Erlbaum.

Martin, L. L., & Seta, J. J. (1983). Perceptions of unity and distinctiveness as determinants of attraction. *Journal of Personality and Social Psychology, 44*, 755–764.

Meyers-Levy, J., & Tybout, A. M. (1997). Context effects at encoding and judgment in consumption settings: The role of cognitive resources. *Journal of Consumer Research, 24*, 1–14.

Mussweiler, T. (2003). Comparison processes in social judgment: Mechanisms and consequences. *Psychological Review, 110*, 472–489.

Mussweiler, T., & Neumann, R. (2000). Sources of mental contamination: Comparing the effects of selfgenerated versus externally provided primes. *Journal of Experimental Social Psychology, 36*, 194–206.

Mussweiler, T., Rüter, K., & Epstude, K. (2004). The ups and downs of social comparison: Mechanisms of assimilation and contrast. *Journal of Personality and Social Psychology, 87*, 832–844.

Nisbett, R. E. (2003). *The geography of thought: How Asians and Westerners think differently and why*. New York: Free Press.

Oyserman, D., Coon, H., & Kemmelmeier, M. (2002). Rethinking individualism and collectivism: Evaluation of theoretical assumptions and meta-analyses. *Psychological Bulletin, 128*, 3–73.

Oyserman, D., Sorensen, N., Cha, O., & Schwarz, N. (2006). *Thinking about "me" or "us" in East and West: Priming independence and interdependence influences Stroop performance*. Unpublished manuscript, University of Michigan.

Pham, M. T. (2004). The logic of feeling. *Journal of Consumer Psychology, 14*, 360–369.

Reber, R., Winkielman, P., & Schwarz, N. (1998). Effects of perceptual fluency on affective judgments. *Psychological Science, 9*, 45–48.

Rothbart, M. (2001). Category dynamics and the modification of outgroup stereotypes. In R. Brown & S. Gaertner (Eds.), *Blackwell handbook of social psychology: Intergroup processes* (pp. 45–64). Oxford, UK: Blackwell.

Schwarz, N. (1994). Judgment in a social context: Biases, shortcomings, and the logic of conversation. *Advances in Experimental Social Psychology, 26*, 123–162.

Schwarz, N. (1996). *Cognition and communication: Judgmental biases, research methods, and the logic of conversation*. Hillsdale, NJ: Lawrence Erlbaum Associates, Inc.

Schwarz, N. (1998). Accessible content and accessibility experiences: The interplay of declarative and experiential information in judgment. *Personality and Social Psychology Review, 2*, 87–99.

Schwarz, N. (2002). Situated cognition and the wisdom of feelings: Cognitive tuning. In L. Feldman Barrett & P. Salovey (Eds.), *The wisdom in feelings* (pp. 144–166). New York: Guilford Press.

Schwarz, N. (2004). Meta-cognitive experiences in consumer judgment and decision making. *Journal of Consumer Psychology, 14*, 332–348.

Schwarz, N., & Bless, H. (1992a). Constructing reality and its alternatives: Assimilation and contrast effects in social judgment. In L. L. Martin & A. Tesser (Eds.), *The construction of social judgments* (pp. 217–245). Hillsdale, NJ: Lawrence Erlbaum Associates, Inc.

Schwarz, N., & Bless, H. (1992b). Scandals and the public's trust in politicians: Assimilation and contrast effects. *Personality and Social Psychology Bulletin, 18*, 574–579.

Schwarz, N., Bless, H., Strack, F., Klumpp, G., Rittenauer-Schatka, H., & Simons, A. (1991). Ease of retrieval as information: Another look at the availability heuristic. *Journal of Personality and Social Psychology, 61*, 195–202.

Schwarz, N., Bless, H., Wänke, M., & Winkielman, P. (2003). Accessibility revisited. In G. V. Bodenhausen & A. J. Lambert (Eeds.), *Foundations of social cognition: A*

Festschrift in honor of Robert S. Wyer, Jr. (pp. 51–77). Mahwah, NJ: Lawrence Erlbaum Associates, Inc.

Schwarz, N., & Clore, G.L. (1983). Mood, misattribution, and judgments of well-being: Informative and directive functions of affective states. *Journal of Personality and Social Psychology*, 45, 513–523.

Schwarz, N., & Clore, G. L. (1996). Feelings and phenomenal experiences. In E. T. Higgins & A. Kruglanski (Eds.), *Social psychology: Handbook of basic principles* (pp. 433–465). New York: Guilford Press.

Schwarz, N., & Strack, F. (1999). Reports of subjective well-being: Judgmental processes and their methodological implications. In D. Kahneman, E. Diener, & N. Schwarz (Eds.), *Well-being: The foundations of hedonic psychology* (pp. 61–84). New York: Russell-Sage.

Schwarz, N., Strack, F., & Mai, H. P. (1991). Assimilation and contrast effects in part–whole question sequences: A conversational logic analysis. *Public Opinion Quarterly*, 55, 3–23.

Seta, J. J., Martin, L. L., & Capehart, G. (1979). Effects of contrast and assimilation on the attitude similarity–attraction relationship. *Journal of Personality and Social Psychology*, 37, 462–467.

Simmons, C. J., Bickart, B. A., & Lynch, J. G. (1993). Capturing and creating public opinion in survey research. *Journal of Consumer Research*, 20, 316–329.

Sinclair, R. C., & Mark, M. M. (1992). The influence of mood state on judgment and action: Effects on persuasion, categorization, social justice, person perception, and judgmental accuracy. In L. L. Martin & A. Tesser (Eds.), *The construction of social judgment* (pp. 165–193). Hillsdale, NJ: Lawrence Erlbaum Associates, Inc.

Srull, T. K., & Wyer, R. S. (1979). The role of category accessibility in the interpretation of information about persons. *Journal of Personality and Social Psychology*, 38, 841–856.

Stapel, D. A., & Koomen, W. (1998). Interpretation versus reference framing: Assimilation and contrast effects in the organizational domain. *Organizational Behavior and Human Decision Processes*, 76, 132–148.

Stapel, D. A., & Koomen, W. (2000). Distinctness of others, mutability of selves: Their impact on selfevaluations. *Journal of Personality and Social Psychology*, 79, 1068–1087.

Stapel, D. A., & Koomen, W. (2001). The impact of interpretation versus comparison mindsets on knowledge accessibility effects. *Journal of Experimental Social Psychology*, 37, 134–149.

Stapel, D. A., & Koomen, W. (2005). Competition, cooperation, and the effects of others on me. *Journal of Personality and Social Psychology*, 88, 1029–1038.

Stapel, D. A., & Schwarz, N. (1998). The Republican who did not want to become President: An inclusion/exclusion analysis of Colin Powell's impact on evaluations of the Republican Party and Bob Dole. *Personality and Social Psychology Bulletin*, 24, 690–698.

Stapel, D. A., & Winkielman, P. (1998). Assimilation and contrast as a function of context–target similarity, distinctness, and dimensional relevance. *Personality and Social Psychology Bulletin*, 24, 634–646.

Strack, F., & Hannover, B. (1996). Awareness of influence as a precondition for implementing correctional goals. In P. M. Gollwitzer & J. A. Bargh (Eds.), *The psychology of action: Linking cognition and motivation to behavior* (pp. 579–596). New York: Guilford Press.

Strack, F., Martin, L. L., & Schwarz, N. (1988). Priming and communication: The social determinants of information use in judgments of life-satisfaction. *European Journal of Social Psychology, 18*, 429–442.

Strack, F., Schwarz, N., Bless, H., Kübler, A., & Wänke, M. (1993). Awareness of the influence as a determinant of assimilation versus contrast. *European Journal of Social Psychology, 23*, 53–62.

Strack, F., Schwarz, N., & Gschneidinger, E. (1985). Happiness and reminiscing: The role of time perspective, mood, and mode of thinking. *Journal of Personality and Social Psychology, 49*, 1460–1469.

Tversky, A., & Kahneman, D. (1973). Availability: A heuristic for judging frequency and probability. *Cognitive Psychology, 5*, 207–232.

Wänke, M., Bless, H., & Igou, E. R. (2001). Next to a star: Paling, shining, or both? Turning inter-exemplar contrast into inter-exemplar assimilation. *Personality and Social Psychology, 27*, 14–29.

Wänke, M., Bless, H., & Schwarz, N. (1998). Contrast and assimilation in product line extensions: Context is not destiny. *Journal of Consumer Psychology, 7*, 299–322.

Wänke, M., Bless, H., & Schwarz, N. (1999). Lobster, wine, and cigarettes: Ad hoc categories and the emergence of context effects. *Marketing Bulletin, 10*, 52–56.

Wedell, D. H., Parducci, A., & Geiselman, E. R., (1987). A formal analysis of ratings of physical attractiveness: Successive contrast and simultaneous assimilation. *Journal of Experimental Social Psychology, 23*, 230–249.

Wilson, T. D., & Brekke, N. (1994). Mental contamination and mental correction: Unwanted influences on judgments and evaluations. *Psychological Bulletin, 116*, 117–142.

Winkielman, P., Coleman, J., & Schwarz, N. (1994, July). *Contrast and assimilation effects in subliminal priming: The role of category width*. Washington, DC: American Psychological Society.

Winkielman, P., Zajonc, R. B., & Schwarz, N. (1997). Subliminal affective priming resists attributional interventions. *Cognition and Emotion, 11*, 433–465.

Wyer, R. S. (1974). *Cognitive organization and change: An information processing approach*. New York: Wiley.

6

In the Mind of the Beholder: The Interpretation Comparison Model of Accessibility Effects

DIEDERIK A. STAPEL

Was Audrey Hepburn a good actress? Is your colleague a friendly person? Was John F. Kennedy a successful President? Is the book you are reading worth its money? Was the Iraq War a just war? Are you intelligent? The correct answer to each of these questions is of course "Well, it depends." There are no absolute criteria for judging the quality of someone's acting, the goodness of a person's character, the successfulness of a Presidency, the value of a collection of writings, the morality of an international conflict, or one's mental dexterity. Although people prefer to think that what they see is what is really there, their impressions of the world and its inhabitants are typically subjective interpretations rather than correct apprehensions of it. One of the major lessons modern as well as classic social psychology have taught us is what people see depends on *who* they are and *where* they are. Social perception is a function of personality–situation interactions. That is, whereas person A thinks Hepburn was a "superb" actress, person B mainly remembers her irritating mannerisms. And similarly, whereas in situation X (during dinner at home) a colleague's stories about his love life may be perceived as revealing and interesting, in situation Y (during lunch at work) the same anecdotes are more likely to be perceived as inappropriate and embarrassing. Thus, although people may believe that funniness is a property of the clown and beauty is in the object, more often than not such impressions reside mainly *in the eye of the beholder* rather than in the features of the stimulus (Bruner, 1957; Stapel & Koomen, 2005c).

THE MIND OF THE BEHOLDER

When it concerns the study of the mental underpinnings of social behavior, an important question is thus what—besides the properties of the stimulus—

determines the content of the *eye of the beholder*. Yes, social perception is subject-ive, but what determines the specific content of subjectivity? As noted above, *who* and *where* the beholder is determine what he or she perceives. Unfortunately, however, such a focus is not very helpful when it concerns the psychological mechanisms underlying the making of subjectivity. There are simply too many personalities, motives, and expectancies, attitudes, stereotypes, and prejudices to effectively and elegantly determine *who* people are. And similarly, there are sim-ply too many types of situations, contexts, locations, or positions to effectively and elegantly determine *where* people are.

Social cognition research has shown that the concept of *cognitive accessibility* provides a more proximal and therefore more promising route to answering the question of what determines the making of subjectivity, the content of the eye of the beholder. Thus, whether Hepburn's acting is interpreted as superb or manner-ist, whether a colleague's intimate revelations are evaluated as interesting or embarrassing, is perhaps best explained in term of what is cognitively accessible, or put differently, *what is in the mind of the beholder*. That is, the cognitive accessibility construct answers the question of what (besides the properties of the stimulus) determines the content of the eye of the perceiver by focusing on what is on *top* of the perceiver's mind. When a stimulus can be perceived in a variety of ways, then the information that is cognitively *most* accessible will "capture" the stimulus and guide the way in which it is perceived (Bruner, 1957). "Cognitive accessibility" refers to the ease or speed that given knowledge is used to interpret or evaluate a target stimulus under varying conditions. Thus, the cognitive accessi-bility concept bypasses the "what is weighed most heavily" problem of the classic "who × where" or "person × situation" approach to understanding social behavior as follows: Personality and situation features are important determinants of per-ception. However, whether or not specific personality and situation features will affect perception depends on the relative cognitive accessibility of these features. Features that are cognitively more accessible are more likely to affect perception than features that are cognitively less accessible. Thus, the main determinant of the contents of subjectivity is cognitive accessibility.

Perhaps the most prominent and well-known demonstrations of the import-ance of cognitive accessibility for the contents of social perception are so-called *trait priming* studies (e.g., Higgins, Rholes, & Jones, 1977; Srull & Wyer, 1979). These studies show that the encoding of behavior is guided by which trait concepts are accessible at the time of impression formation. For example, Srull and Wyer (1979) used a "priming" task to increase the accessibility of the concepts *hostile* versus *kind*. After this task, participants were asked to give their impression of a description of "Donald," who behaved in an ambiguously hostile manner. Donald was rated in more negative terms following the priming of hostility, and more positively following the priming of kindness.

Importantly, a number of studies have now shown that conscious awareness of the primed information is not necessary for cognitively accessible information to produce effects. To give an example, Bargh and Pietromonaco (1982) found that participants who were exposed subliminally to hostile-relevant stimuli rated Srull and Wyer's Donald as more hostile than did nonprimed participants (see also

Devine, 1989; Erdley & D'Agostino, 1987; Neuberg, 1988; Stapel & Koomen, 2005a, 2005b).

THE IMPORTANCE OF WHAT IS IN ONE'S MIND: THE POLITICS OF ACCESSIBILITY EFFECTS

Although there have been a myriad of experimental laboratory studies showing the importance of cognitive accessibility for the understanding of social psychological phenomena, the importance of cognitive accessibility for the way people perceive and interpret the social world is nicely illustrated when looking at how the shaping of cognitive accessibility is used as a strategic tool in political communication (see Stapel & Marx, in press; Stapel & Spears, 1995, 1996b).

Politicians, journalists, and propagandists often try to shape the public's understanding of new events (e.g., the Iraq War) by making certain possible interpretations more accessible than others ("Iraq is Bush's Vietnam" vs. "Saddam Hussein is a modern-day Adolf Hitler"; see Stapel & Marx, in press; Stapel & Spears, 1995, 1996b). Gilovich (1981) was among the first to provide experimental evidence for subtle influence of cognitive accessibility in political reasoning. In one of his studies, political science majors were asked to render judgments about the wisdom of American intervention in a hypothetical conflict. As they did so, however, the relative accessibility of two familiar and evocative scenarios from 20th-century history was subtly manipulated. Embedded in the information about the conflict were irrelevant phrases designed to highlight the similarities in the hypothetical crisis to either the war against Nazi Germany or that against North Vietnam. For example, the political science majors were either told that minorities were fleeing the democratic country via boxcars on freight trains or via small boats; the impending invasion was referred to as a Blitzkrieg or a Quickstrike; the current US president was from the state of New York (as was F. D. Roosevelt) or from Texas (as was L. B. Johnson). Did these irrelevant but highly accessible references to previous international references influence judgments about what should be done about the crisis? They did. Gilovich found that the students for whom "Nazi Germany" cues were made accessible were more likely to recommend US military intervention than those for whom "Vietnam" was made relatively accessible. This finding suggests the influential role of momentarily activated irrelevant category labels on persons' impressions of political events and actions. It shows that people's responses to the actions of particular individuals may often be shaped by analogies and other cognitive categories that are in turn triggered, without awareness, by cues and associations that we would recognize to be logically irrelevant and probably would actively resist if we were aware of the connection being made (see also Stapel & Marx, in press).

In real life, the denotative and the connotative qualities of cognitively accessible knowledge are used by journalists, politicians, and propagandists to shape the public's image of politicians and their policies. Public relations consultants and politicians have long recognized the denotative and connotative power of labels that shape public perception. When, after the first televised presidential debate, a journalist likened Kennedy to "a fictional hero—something like a shy young sheriff" and said Nixon looked like "the railroad lawyer who signs leases that are not in the interests of the folks in the little town," these labels clearly were employed to shape the public image of the debaters, and not without success (see Patterson, 1994).

Labeling a "fresh" political scandal in a way that explicitly refers to the Watergate scandal (e.g., Irangate, Iraqgate, Lewinskigate, Whitewatergate, Enrongate) is probably one of the most typical ways in which people attempt to shape the meaning of new political events. Of course, it is expected that the public will infer from the Watergate analogy that the scope of the recent scandal is enormous and that the new scandal should be treated as such. Consequently, the cognitive accessibility of this "prime" may change the image of and the trust in the politicians involved in the new scandal dramatically.

As these examples of the use of labels, past events, and analogies suggest, in real life the strategic use of cognitive accessibility effects may shape the way people make sense of the world they live in. Whether the Iraq War is seen as "a guerrilla war, just like Vietnam" or as "something completely different—Vietnam was then, this is now" is essential for the public's opinion about this war and may thus affect international political decision making (see Stapel & Marx, in press). In other words, accessibility matters. But what exactly determines the impact of accessible knowledge?

NATURAL ASSIMILATION EFFECTS AND THE COGNITIVIST BIAS

The above review of cognitive accessibility effects on social perception suggests that relative accessibility is an important determinant of what specific person and situation features are likely to guide social perception and behavior on a given occasion. Thus, cognitive accessibility shapes and colors the eyes of the social perceiver. It is important to note, however, that the relevant *social cognition* literature suggests that it does so mainly in an assimilative fashion. That is, social cognition research has documented abundant evidence for the notion that accessible knowledge is likely to result in *assimilation* effects (impressions shift toward the activated knowledge). Recent views of the impact of attitudes, expectancies, stereotypes, motivations, and goals on the interpretation of social stimuli all come to the same, general conclusion: Accessible knowledge guides the interpretation of the social world and thus mainly produces assimilation effects (e.g., Bargh & Ferguson, 2001; DeCoster & Claypool, 2004).

This abundance of assimilation effects in studies of knowledge accessibility effects has led some authors to conclude that assimilation is the "basic effect of recent and frequent activation" (Higgins, 1989, p. 78), that assimilation is the most natural, automatic accessibility effect (see Ford & Thompson, 2000; Markman & McMullen, 2003; Martin, 1986; Schwarz & Bless, 1992).

Granted, the *social cognition* literature is abundant with studies demonstrating how (supraliminal or subliminal) priming leads to assimilation. However, the conclusion that the *natural* or *default* accessibility effect is assimilation lacks a solid empirical basis and is thus unwarranted. After all, in the *social judgment* and *social comparison* literatures there is abundant evidence that *contrast* effects (impressions shift away from the activated knowledge) may occur as spontaneously and efficiently as assimilation effects, suggesting that perhaps both assimilation and contrast effects may be natural or default.

To give an example of automatic contrast effects, in a study of accessibility effects on emotion judgments, Stapel, Koomen, and Ruys (2002) showed that participants who were subliminally primed with a happy face subsequently rated a neutral facial expression as relatively sad, whereas participants who were subliminally primed with a sad face subsequently rated the neutral face as relatively happy. Similarly, but now in the domain of automatic behavior priming, Dijksterhuis and colleagues (1998) showed that participants who were primed with the Dutch queen mother (who, at the time of the study was very old and very slow) walked away faster from the room where the priming experiment had taken place than subjects in a control group. And finally, Gordijn and Stapel (in press) showed that Dutch university students who were exposed to a very intelligent student at a rivaling university compared and contrasted and thus did worse on a general knowledge task (a game of trivial pursuit) than students who were exposed to a very dumb student from the other university.

Given that automatic contrast effects are relatively ubiquitous, why then do so many reviews of accessibility research (e.g., Bargh & Ferguson, 2001; DeCoster & Claypool, 2004; Ford & Thompson, 2000), bestselling social psychology textbooks (e.g., Aronson, Wilson, & Akert, 2004; Bless, Fiedler, & Strack, 2004; Kunda, 1999), as well as recent empirical journal articles reporting accessibility effects (e.g., Chartrand & Bargh, 1999), suggest that assimilation is the natural, automatic outcome of accessibility process?

I think that the answer to this question can be found in what could be called the "cognitivist" bias of modern, mainstream social psychology (see also Stapel & Koomen, 2001b). Most modern studies of accessibility effects in social psychology looked at the impact of priming manipulations from a predominantly "cognitive" perspective. And, as Mervis and Rosch (1981) argued, one of the basic tenets of the cognitive or information processing perspective in modern psychology is the belief that categorization is fundamental to cognition. As an offspring of cognitive psychology, "cognitivist" social psychology has emphasized the question of how social knowledge may affect social categorization processes. Social cognition research has excelled in demonstrating how different kinds of accessible cognitive structures (e.g., traits, attitudes, expectancies, stereotypes, emotions) may guide the *interpretation* of target stimuli. Given that the interpretation of a stimulus involves the *integration* of stimulus material with cognitively accessible knowledge, this "filling in" process is *by definition* assimilative. Hence, I argue, a cognitive approach to the study of accessibility effects is—*because of its metatheoretical* perspective (an interest in categorization processes)—destined to find interpretative assimilation rather than other effects (see also Stapel & Koomen, 2001b).

THE POSSIBILITY OF NATURAL CONTRAST EFFECTS

I would like to argue that for a complete understanding of the full array of possible accessibility effects, social cognition researchers need to take off their biasing and narrowing, cognitivist "categorization glasses" and entertain the possibility that accessible knowledge can do more than "fill in" the gaps when the world is ambiguous and open to interpretation. Unfortunately, because of the success of the social cognition movement in general and priming and accessibility research in particular, studies that have looked at the impact of accessible knowledge on processes other than interpretation have been largely neglected in theorizing about the consequences of accessibility for judgment and behavior. Specifically, studies that demonstrate the comparative rather than the interpretative nature of social perception and focus on the use of accessible knowledge as a *comparison standard* rather than an *interpretation frame* are seldom cited in social psychological reviews of accessibility effects (see Aronson et al., 2004; Bargh & Ferguson, 2001; Ford & Thompson, 2000; Kunda, 1999).

To put it differently, it could be argued that the social cognition approach to accessibility effects has typically focused on how accessible knowledge may affect the representation of the target stimulus *at the expense* of an interest on how such knowledge may affect the representation of the reference frame, the comparison standard that is used to place targets in context. This focus on target rather than standard representations is unfortunate because it leaves out (at least) half of the story.

Just like one needs peanut butter and jelly to make a peanut butter and jelly sandwich, one needs a reference frame as well as a target stimulus to make a judgment. That is, when perceiving some target stimulus one needs to construe a cognitive representation of what is perceived. Less obvious, perhaps, is the notion that one also needs some reference frame to put the target stimulus in context. However, people mainly know what things are by relating their attributes to those of other stimuli. Thus, the "absolute" statement *Marcella is happy* already suggests that Marcella is happier than *others* (or that Marcella is happier than she usually is) and is thus essentially comparative (Eiser, 1990; Festinger, 1954; Mussweiler, 2003; Schwarz & Bless, 1992; Tajfel, 1959).

This comparative perspective on judgment construction implies that most, if not all, perception consists of at least two core ingredients, a target (e.g., *Marcella*) and a standard (e.g., *others*). How these two ingredients are perceived and cognitively represented thus provides important input for the impression formation process (see Schwarz & Bless, 1992).

As extensively reviewed in the paragraphs above, social cognition research has demonstrated how cognitively accessible information may affect the interpretation and categorization of all kinds of *target* objects. Similarly, it could be argued that social comparison and social judgment research could be seen as mainly investigating whether and how "primed" information may serve as a *standard* of comparison or a frame of reference during impression formation (Stapel & Koomen, 2006).

The first studies of how "primed" information may act as a comparison standard in judgments of a target stimulus were conducted by researchers interested in psychophysical phenomena. Consider, for example, a task requiring subjects to identify the intensity of a number of auditory tones, which vary in their degree of loudness. Whether a tone will be classified as "very loud" depends, among other things, on the other tones being judged in the experimental session. In the context of several relatively quiet tones, a medium range tone will be judged as louder than it would be in the context of several relatively quiet tones. This type of influence was termed *comparison contrast* because it shows how judgments are contrasted away from the values in the surrounding context to which the target can be compared (see e.g., Beebe-Center, 1929).

The use of accessible information as a comparison standard has probably led to the most dramatic and vivid contrast effects in the domain of social comparison research. Social comparison research investigates how the perception of others may affect the people's self-views and behaviors (Festinger, 1954). A number of experiments have shown that people's self-perceptions are often contrasted away from upward (better) or downward (worse) comparison others. This type of comparison contrast is probably best illustrated by a well-known study of Morse and Gergen (1970). These investigators led subjects to believe that they were interviewing for a position as a research assistant. Subjects were asked to wait for the alleged interview in the company of another applicant—a confederate. In the "Mr. Clean" condition, the confederate was impeccably well-mannered and professional in all respects; in the "Mr. Dirty" condition, the confederate was disheveled and slovenly. Compared with earlier appraisals of the self, the self-esteem of subjects waiting with the undesirable confederate rose; the reverse was true for those who waited with the desirable confederate.

Stapel and Blanton (2004) showed that the Morse–Gergen type of effect may occur spontaneously and completely automatically. Neither conscious awareness of the comparison other, nor an explicit self-evaluative judgment task is needed for such contrastive social comparison effects to occur. Specifically, Stapel and Blanton showed that comparison contrast may occur even when the primed information is flashed too quickly to be detected by conscious awareness: Subliminal priming of extreme comparison standards led to automatic contrast effects on an unobtrusive, implicit self-evaluation measure, people's signature size: Unconscious exposure to Einstein led to a relatively small signature (decreased self-evaluation), whereas unconscious exposure to a clown lead to a relatively large signature (increased self-evaluation; see for similar results Mussweiler, Rüter, & Epstude, 2004).

FROM PARADIGMATIC CLOSE-MINDEDNESS TO COMPREHENSIVE INTEGRATION

Interestingly, whereas there is a tendency in social cognition research to assume that assimilation is the basic effect in all types of accessibility-driven judgments, students of the use of accessible information as a reference frame in comparison processes have argued that contrast is probably the most natural effect. For example, Herr, Sherman, and Fazio (1983, p. 325) write that "the predominant context effect in the social judgment literature is the contrast effect. It has often been noted that the judgment of a given target stimulus is inversely related to the values of the stimuli that accompany it."

As I argued when discussing social cognition's obsession with natural assimilation effects, social judgment and comparison researchers' obsession with natural contrast effects is probably best explained by pointing to the metatheoretical interests of these perspectives. Whereas social cognition research is primarily concerned with issues of categorization and interpretation, the social comparison and judgment approaches primarily focus on the comparative nature of all sorts of social judgments. This focus on comparison may have led to the design of experimental paradigms that instigated contrastive comparison processes rather than the assimilative interpretation processes that seem to be the logical outcomes of the experiments designed by social cognition researchers. In other words, the theoretical perspective behind social cognition research on the one hand and social comparison and judgment research on the other hand may have created different empirical phenomena, that is "natural assimilation" and "natural contrast" respectively (see further Stapel & Koomen, 2001b).

On one level this observation may come across as somewhat cynical and pessimistic and may remind the attentive reader of the deconstructionist musings of postmodern theorists ("Theories shape results, methods mold findings;" "One always finds what one is looking for"). On another level, however, the observation that different research literatures have looked at different *uses* (interpretation vs. comparison) of accessible information and that these different uses are associated with specific *effects* (assimilation vs. contrast) of such information on judgment and behavior suggests that one important determinant of the impact of accessible information on people's lives is *how* this information is *used*. That is, when one is in search of a practical, psychological theory of accessibility effects, of assimilation and contrast effects—which we are—the observation that interpretation processes (as studied in social cognition research) typically lead to assimilation, whereas comparison processes (as studied in social judgment and comparison research) more easily result in contrast effects, suggests that the world of assimilation and contrast effects could be modeled by positing an Interpretation Comparison Model (ICM) of accessibility effects (see Stapel & Blanton, 2004; Stapel & Koomen, 2000, 2001a, 2001b, 2001c, 2005c; Stapel et al., 2002; Stapel & Suls, 2004).

THE INTERPRETATION COMPARISON MODEL

The Interpretation Comparison Model (ICM) of accessibility effects postulates a direct relation between the *consequences* of accessible knowledge and the way this knowledge is *used* during the comparison process. Specifically, following earlier work on knowledge accessibility effects (e.g., Manis & Paskewitz, 1984; Philippot, Schwarz, Carrera, de Vries, & van Yperen, 1991; Schwarz & Bless, 1992), the ICM posits that accessible knowledge can instigate two different processes with possibly opposing effects. On the one hand, accessible knowledge may be used as an interpretation frame that gives meaning to and makes sense of stimuli—a "pull" toward assimilation. On the other hand, accessible knowledge may be used as a comparison standard against which target information is evaluated—a "pull" toward contrast.

But what determines whether the pull toward interpretation and assimilation or comparison and contrast wins out in any given situation? What determines whether accessibility effects are driven mainly by social cognitive processes that typically result in assimilation or by social comparative processes that may result in contrast? The past decade's research has identified several determinants of whether—in a particular comparison situation—the interpretative or the comparative pull of accessible information is stronger.

Distinctness

The first empirical tests of the ICM were inspired by the observation that the social cognition and social judgment literatures not only differ in what is thought to be the default, natural accessibility effect (assimilation and contrast, respectively), but also in the *type of stimuli* that were used to study accessibility effects (Stapel, Koomen, & van der Pligt, 1996, 1997). Specifically, whereas in social cognition research priming *trait* categories (e.g., "hostile" vs. "friendly") led to assimilation in subsequent person judgment (e.g., Srull & Wyer, 1979), in social judgment research priming *person exemplars* of these categories (e.g., "Adolph Hitler" vs. "Shirley Temple") led to contrast (e.g., Herr, 1986).

Based on the metatheoretical focus guiding social cognition versus social judgment research (interpretation vs. comparison), Stapel et al. (1996, 1997) postulated that, whereas primed trait concepts (e.g., "hostility") are more likely to be used in the encoding of ambiguous information, primed person exemplars—if sufficiently extreme (e.g., "Hitler")—will predominantly be used as a comparison standard against which the evaluation of target persons is contrasted. But what, then, is the difference between trait concepts and person exemplars that will trigger interpretation versus comparison processes, respectively? What is the crucial difference between trait and exemplar priming that may explain their opposite effects? To answer this question, we (Stapel et al., 1996, 1997), introduced the construct of *distinctness*.

The distinctness notion refers to the idea that when abstract trait concepts such as *lust, hostility,* or *beauty* are primed, these concepts will be perceived as less distinct than when specific prototypes and/or cultural icons that exemplify these categories are activated (e.g., *Marilyn Monroe, Adolf Hitler, Cindy Crawford*). Such person exemplars constitute distinct and separate entities with relatively clear object boundaries and are therefore more likely to be used as comparison standards. An abstract trait concept or attribute with no clear object boundaries lacks the distinctness to be used as a comparison standard and thus is used as interpretation rather than reference: As Murphy and Zajonc (1993) put it, diffuse information is more likely than distinct information to "spill over" and "fill in" the gaps in vague target information.

In the past decade, several studies have tested the notion that diffuse trait priming is more likely to result in assimilation, whereas distinct person exemplar priming is likely to result in contrast. For example, Stapel et al. (1997) found that priming *friendly* versus *hostile* resulted in assimilation in judgments of a target person, whereas priming *Mandela* versus *Stalin* resulted in contrast. Similarly, Stapel and Blanton (2004) showed that priming the words *smart* versus *dumb* resulted in assimilation on self-evaluative ratings, whereas priming *Einstein* versus *Clown* led to contrast effects. What is more, these effects have been found on judgments as well as on unobtrusive behavioral measures, such as performance on a general knowledge test (Trivial Pursuit). Similar effects have been found using walking speed, lexical decision tasks, coloring, and puzzle tasks as dependent measures (see Gordijn & Stapel, in press; Spears, Gordijn, Stapel, & Dijksterhuis, 2004; Stapel & Suls, 2004).

In general, the notion that trait priming yields assimilation and exemplar priming yields contrast has now been shown in the domain of attribution (Stapel & Spears, 1995), stereotyping (Stapel & Koomen, 1998b), and expectancy (Stapel & Schwarz, 1998a), and in more applied settings such as responses to advertising (Stapel, Koomen, & Velthuijsen, 1998), political judgments (Stapel & Schwarz, 1998b; Stapel & Spears, 1996a, 1996b), and issues relevant for organizational decision making (Stapel & Koomen, 1998a). Thus, the notion that distinctness may determine the *direction* of knowledge accessibility effects is well-established. The question remains, however, whether we can establish that these assimilation effects are due to interpretation, whereas the contrast effects are due to comparison—as the ICM posits.

Ambiguity, Timing, and Extremity

Ambiguity   First, there are several studies that demonstrate the impact of the *ambiguity* of the target stimulus on accessibility effects. These studies demonstrate that diffuse accessible knowledge produces assimilation effects when the target is ambiguous but not when it is unambiguous. For example, Stapel et al. (1997) showed that trait priming results in assimilative interpretation effects for ambiguous targets (e.g., participants rate a person description that could be interpreted as more or less hostile). No such assimilation effects emerge when the target stimulus is unambiguous and thus needs no interpretative efforts (e.g., participants rate one of their friends; see also Philippot et al., 1991). Similarly, in the domain of social comparison research, Stapel and Koomen (2000) showed that when the behavior of a comparison target activates diffuse trait information ("rich") rather than a distinct actor–trait link ("Stanley is rich"), self-evaluation is likely to show an assimilation effect ("I am rich"). However, such assimilative interpretation effects are only likely for participants whose self-concept is mutable or unclear, such that there is room for "filling in the gaps." No interpretative assimilation effects occurred when the self is viewed as clear and immutable (see also Pelham & Wachsmuth, 1995; Stapel & Marx, 2006; Stapel & Suls, 2004).

Timing   Second, in a number of studies it has been demonstrated that the *time* at which priming stimuli are presented is essential in the case of diffuse concept priming but inconsequential in the case of distinct exemplar priming. For example, in an experiment in which the effects of trait concept priming and person exemplar priming were compared, Stapel et al. (1996) manipulated whether these priming stimuli were presented *before* participants were exposed to an ambiguous target description or *after* they had read and encoded this description. The findings showed that, whereas trait concept priming resulted in assimilation effects only when these concepts were primed *before* an ambiguous target was encoded, extreme person exemplar priming resulted in contrast independent of whether these exemplars were primed *before* or *after* encoding.

Thus, consistent with the logic of the ICM, whereas diffuse trait priming results in assimilation only when there is something to be interpreted, distinct exemplar priming results in contrast, independent of whether interpretation has already taken place (see further, Koomen, Stapel, Jansen, & In 't Veld, 1998; Maringer, Stapel, & Otten, 2006; Stapel & Koomen, 1997; Stapel & Winkielman, 1998).

Extremity   Third, the hypothesis that different effects (assimilation vs. contrast) of different types of knowledge accessibility (diffuse vs. distinct primes) are the consequence of different types of processing (interpretation vs. comparison) is corroborated by the fact that *extremity* manipulations have opposite impact on distinct versus diffuse priming effects (Haefner & Stapel, 2006; Stapel et al., 1997). In social comparison and judgment research, extremity (or the distributional norm) of accessible knowledge is considered an important determinant of whether assimilation or contrast occurs. That is, social comparison and judgment researchers may posit that contrast is the default effect of accessible information, *given* that such information is relatively extreme.

The notion that extremity is a moderator of assimilation and contrast in social judgments is probably best illustrated in Sherif and Hovland's (1961) theory of attitudinal judgment. One of the key assertions of that theory is the assumption that attitude statements (e.g. "I like Ike") can be ordered along an evaluative continuum. Specifically, the location of people's preferred attitude position determines how they judge attitude statements. When a single statement or position advocated in a message is relatively close to a person's attitude, assimilation occurs (an accentuation of similarities). When an attitude statement advocates a position that is relatively discrepant with a person's attitude, contrast occurs (an accentuation of dissimilarities). Herr (1986) imported these principles of attitudinal judgment to the domain of person perception and argued that when accessible information is extreme, contrast is more likely to follow, whereas assimilation is relatively likely to occur when activated information is moderate (see also Manis, Nelson, & Shedler, 1988; Parducci & Wedell, 1990). More recently, Mussweiler (2003) has presented a new, more systematic and cognitively-grounded analysis of comparison processes in which the importance of extremity (and accentuation of similarities versus dissimilarities) for the occurrence of assimilative and contrastive comparison effects also plays a central role.

Whereas studies of comparative judgment processes suggest that increasing the extremity of exemplar primes may lead to a *switch* in accessibility effects from assimilation to contrast effects (e.g., Herr, 1986; Manis et al., 1988; Parducci &

Wedell, 1990; Sherif & Hovland, 1961), trait priming studies suggest that increasing the extremity of priming stimuli *strengthens* rather than reverses assimilation effects (Moskowitz & Skurnik, 1999; Skowronski, Carlston, & Isham, 1993; Stapel & Koomen, 1997).

Thus, another way in which the ICM may be tested and the distinction between the interpretative effects of trait priming and the comparative effects of exemplar priming may be demonstrated is by showing the opposing impact of extremity manipulations on person exemplar versus trait concept priming. This was done in a study by Stapel et al. (1997). As Table 6.1 shows, the findings of this study clearly indicate that when judging an ambiguous person stimulus (friendly/hostile Donald) extreme person exemplar primes ("Hitler" vs. "Mandela") result in contrast, whereas moderate person exemplar primes ("Napoleon" vs. "Robin Hood") result in assimilation. However, increasing the extremity of trait concept priming *strengthens* interpretation effects. Priming moderately extreme trait concepts ("unfriendly" vs. "considerate") leads to assimilation and priming extreme trait concepts ("cruel" vs. "sweet") leads to even stronger assimilation.

Interpretation Comparison Mindsets

The above discussion of the impact of ambiguity, timing, and extremity manipulations on diffuse trait priming versus distinct exemplar priming provides strong backing for the idea that the assimilative effects that are typically obtained after trait priming may be understood as the result of interpretation processes, whereas the contrastive effects that are typically obtained after exemplar priming may be understood as the result of comparison processes. Thus, this type of evidence indirectly supports the notion that the way accessibility information is used during impression formation is an important determinant of the direction of accessibility effects.

TABLE 6.1 Mean ratings (*SD*) of Ambiguous Friendly/Hostile Donald as a Function of Prime Type (Trait Concept, Person Exemplar), Prime Valence (Friendly, Hostile), and Prime Extremity (Moderate, Extreme) (from Stapel et al., 1997)

	Prime type			
	Trait concept		**Person exemplar**	
Prime valence	**Friendly**	**Hostile**	**Friendly**	**Hostile**
Prime extremity				
Moderate	4.35	3.99	4.73	3.62
	(0.88)	(0.88)	(0.98)	(0.84)
Extreme	4.66	3.59	3.73	4.64
	(0.98)	(1.27)	(1.18)	(1.18)

Note: Scale range is from 1 to 9. Higher scores indicate more positive ratings.

More *direct* support for the Interpretation Comparison Model is provided by studies reported in Stapel and Koomen's (2001a, 2001c, 2005a) work on the impact of "mindset priming" on the occurrence of assimilation versus contrast effects. Inspired by the work on automatic goal activation of Bargh (1997) that suggests that goals are represented in memory in the same way that constructs, attitudes, and stereotypes are, Stapel and Koomen argued that similar rules should apply for the activation of goals or mindsets. Stapel and Koomen (2001a, 2001c, 2005a) primed participants via a "language" test with words like "interpretation" versus "comparison" and thus activated the associated mindsets. Results of *trait priming-person judgment* (e.g., prime "friendly" or "hostile" before judging ambiguous person target) and exemplar priming-person judgment (e.g., prime "Mandela" or "Hitler" before judging ambiguous person target) experiments (Stapel & Koomen, 2001c) as well as comparison other priming-self evaluation (e.g., prime "Einstein" or "Clown" before making self-evaluations) experiments (Stapel & Koomen, 2001a, 2005a) performed after this mindset activation showed a strong mindset activation effect. As the ICM predicts, interpretation mindset priming resulted in assimilation, while comparison mindset priming resulted in contrast. Interestingly, the mindset manipulation was so strong that it overruled the "classic" assimilative trait priming and contrastive exemplar priming effects.

Some Cautionary Notes

Interpretation leads to assimilation, comparison results in contrast—that is the simple and straightforward mantra of the Interpretation Comparison Model of accessibility effects. It is important to note, however, that of course the social world and people's mental representation of it do not fit such a naïve, simplified view on the determinants of assimilative versus contrastive accessibility effects. A number of extra assumptions, a number of cautionary "only ifs," are needed to make the ICM useful as an explanatory tool for making sense of accessibility effects.

First, as noted before, it is important to remember that *interpretative* accessibility effects will only occur when there is something to be *interpreted*, that is, when the target stimulus is *ambiguous* rather than unambiguous (see Stapel et al., 1997).

Second, one needs to know that of course not all types of (diffuse) accessible information may yield interpretation effects. As a myriad of diffuse trait priming studies have shown, in order to exert interpretation effects, accessible information has to be *applicable* to interpretation of the target (see Higgins, 1996). Thus, when one is trying to form an impression of behavior that can be interpreted as persistent or stubborn (e.g., "She never changes her mind"), the accessibility of inapplicable constructs (e.g., "adventurous" vs. "reckless") will exert no interpretation effect, whereas the accessibility of applicable constructs ("persistent" vs. "stubborn") may yield assimilative interpretation effects (see Higgins et al., 1977; Stapel & Koomen, 2005a, 2005b).

Third, it is important to note that interpretation and comparison processes outlined by the ICM are thought to result in the associated assimilation and contrast effects only when people are not *aware* of their biasing, contaminating influence. As a number of studies have pointed out, when people are aware that a reliance on accessible information is inappropriate and that this may create a bias in their judgment, they are likely to instigate correction-for-bias processes. Depending on the ability and motivation to debias judgments, such correction processes may result in null or reverse priming effects (see Martin, 1986; Schwarz & Bless, 1992; Stapel, Koomen, & Zeelenberg, 1998; Stapel, Martin, & Schwarz, 1998; Strack, 1992; Wegener & Petty, 1995).

Fourth, and perhaps most important, it is important to know that when comparison processes are stronger than interpretation processes, this does not necessarily mean that contrast will result. As we noted above, for comparison to result in contrast, the primed information needs to be sufficiently extreme. Moderate primes, even when they are "distinct," typically result in assimilation (see Herr, 1986; Stapel et al., 1997). However, extremity and distinctness are not always enough to lead to contrast effects. When there is no categorical overlap between primes and targets, when there is no prime–target similarity, comparison and thus contrast is unlikely to result. As the age-old adage that "one should not compare apples and oranges" suggests, objects that belong to the same category more readily invite comparison processes than objects that belong to dissimilar categories (see Festinger, 1954; Manis, Biernat, & Nelson, 1991; Mussweiler, 2003).

In an empirical test of this similarity criterion, Stapel et al. (1997) asked respondents to form an impression of an ambiguous target stimulus, friendly or hostile Donald. Before they were exposed to the description of Donald, respondents were primed with names of animal exemplars or person exemplars. Half of the participants were primed with names of either extremely hostile or friendly *persons* ("Dracula," "Mandela"). The other half of the participants was exposed to names of either extremely hostile or friendly *animals* ("Shark," "Bunny"). As predicted, contrast was found in the person priming conditions, but assimilation was found in the animal priming conditions. Because of their categorical dissimilarity, the animal names could not act as a relevant comparison standard for judgments of friendly or hostile Donald. However, because of the traits they activated (Shark = hostile, Bunny = friendly), they guided the interpretation of Donald's behavior.

Stapel and Koomen (1997) found a similar effect when comparing friendly–hostile person versus brand names of friendly fabric softeners (e.g., Woolite) and hostile abrasives and bleaches (e.g., Glorix). Stapel and Schwinghammer (2004) demonstrated the importance of the similarity criterion in a study in which they found that psychology students felt less intelligent when they had just read a newspaper story about a smart fellow *psychology student* than when exposed to a stupid fellow student. However, when the (same) story was about a "smart" versus a "stupid" *fox*, assimilation occurred (see also Stapel & Winkielman, 1998).

Together, these findings indicate that exposure to rather extreme and distinct exemplar primes may result in assimilation as well as in contrast effects. Which of these effects emerges importantly depends on the perceived categorical similarity between these exemplars and the target stimulus.

Summary

In conclusion then, although the empirical support for the ICM seems to be strong, it is important to note that interpretation-driven accessibility effects do not always lead to assimilation and comparison-driven accessibility effects do not always lead to contrast. First and perhaps foremost it is important to remember that any spontaneous accessibility effect (albeit interpretation- or comparison-driven) can only emerge when people are not aware of the contaminating influence of what is cognitively accessible. When people think their judgments or actions may be biased, correction rather than interpretation or comparison processes are likely to become the main determinant of accessibility effects.

When people are unaware of possible bias, the ICM posits that the impact of primed information will depend mainly on the way this information is used, thus on the goal it serves. When the main goal is comprehension, categorization, or sense making, accessible information that is applicable to the target stimulus may be used as an interpretation frame and result in assimilation. When the main goal is comparison and evaluation, accessible information is used as a comparison standard and contrast is more likely, especially when the information is extreme rather than moderate. These interpretation and comparison goals may be triggered in different ways. Specific situations, context, or instructions may implicitly or explicitly activate an interpretative or a comparative mindset and thus the associated processing style.

Relatively central in tests and applications of the ICM has been the notion that specific types of accessible information instigate different types of "use." As is evidenced by a large number of experimental studies, distinct primes ("Tom is nice") are more likely to instigate comparison processes, whereas diffuse primes ("nice") are more likely to instigate interpretation processes.

CONCLUSION: A MODEL FOR ALL SEASONS

What is on the top of our mind determines what we see and what we do. Because of this accessibility research is central to the study of social behavior. Perhaps, however, from the pallid and nitty-gritty demonstrations of how different types of cognitive accessibility yield different effects one concludes that all this is much ado about nothing. After all, who cares whether Donald is hostile or adventurous? Such a conclusion would not only be unfortunate, but also wrong. Accessibility effects guide people's perceptions, evaluations, and behaviors in important and dramatic ways. As the current chapter shows, accessibility effects may not only affect how one perceives and evaluates other people, but also how one views oneself as well as how one behaves and acts. Accessibility may affect who one is and what one does: smart or dumb, pretty or ugly, happy or sad, friendly or hostile.

The Interpretation Comparison Model (ICM) attempts to give a comprehensive perspective on the effects of accessible knowledge by focusing on the way such knowledge is used during impression formation. The ICM postulates that— given that people are not aware of the influence of such information—using accessible information as an interpretation frame is more likely to result in assimilation, whereas using such information as a reference frame is more likely to result in contrast—given that the primed information is sufficiently extreme and that there is prime–target similarity.

The integrative nature of the ICM is perhaps best illustrated by pointing out that the ICM finds its basis in and is heavily inspired by two (now classic) models of assimilation and contrast, the Manis–Paskewitz (1984) model of expectation and contrast effects and the Schwarz–Bless (1992) inclusion/exclusion model of assimilation and contrast effects.[1] The ICM is in some ways similar to Manis and Paskewitz's (1984) model of "expectation and contrast." The Manis–Paskewitz model also suggests that assimilative and contrastive influences may derive from exposure to the same exemplars. Similar to the present conceptualization, the Manis–Paskewitz model recognizes that the cognitively accessible exemplar information may simultaneously affect target impressions in two ways: (1) by providing a basis for comparison when we have to judge the target (contrast) and (2) by guiding the interpretation and categorization of the target (assimilation). Importantly, the ICM model extends the Manis–Paskewitz model by providing insight into the factors that may influence the relative strength of the assimilative and contrastive influences of category exemplar priming: When sufficiently extreme and categorically similar to the target, the contrastive effects of exemplars are likely to predominate their assimilative effects. Target-dissimilar exemplars, however, are likely to play the role only of interpretation frame and result in assimilation.

The ICM is also consistent with Schwarz and Bless' (1992) inclusion/exclusion model of assimilation and contrast effects (see also Wyer & Srull, 1989). The Schwarz–Bless model predicts assimilation when a primed construct is "included" in the target and contrast when the primed information is "excluded" from the target. Although research testing the inclusion/exclusion model has not focused specifically on the processes (interpretation vs. comparison) underlying assimilation and contrast effects, in inclusion/exclusion terminology the present perspective suggests that the Schwarz–Bless model can be extended as follows: Broader and less distinct priming stimuli that lack categorical target similarity (such as trait concepts or animal primes in person perception tasks) are likely to be "included" in and assimilated to an ambiguous target. Likewise, narrow and distinct priming stimuli that do possess target similarity (such as person exemplars in person perception tasks) are more likely to be "excluded" from and may be contrasted to such targets. But most importantly, the ICM suggests that comparative exclusion or contrast effects do not necessarily need more effort than interpretative inclusion or assimilation effects, as the Schwarz–Bless model assumes. The studies of subliminal priming effects on unobtrusive, implicit measures that have been discussed in this chapter attest to the idea that *both* assimilation and contrast can occur without effort or intention.

As these descriptions of the Manis–Paskewitz and Schwarz–Bless models suggest, the ICM was not designed to be an alternative to other explanations of accessibility effects, such as *comparison* theories that have explained the occurrence of assimilation and contrast in terms of the perceived extremity or (dis)similarity between objects (e.g., Eiser, 1990; Herr, 1986; Mussweiler, 2003; Sherif & Hovland, 1961) or *priming* theories that have explained the occurrence of assimilation and contrast in terms of level of awareness or the perceived appropriateness of the accessible information (e.g., DeCoster & Claypool, 2004; Ford & Thompson, 2000; Markman & McMullen, 2003; Martin, 1986; Strack, 1992; Schwarz & Bless, 1992).

Rather, the ICM is an attempt to be a model for all seasons. Its main purpose is to provide an integrative perspective on previous knowledge accessibility studies. The ICM tries to amalgamate the divergent findings from the social comparison, judgment, and cognition paradigms—where comparison and priming effects are studied—by pointing to the differences in the *stimuli* used within these paradigms (diffuse vs. distinct) and by postulating that these stimuli affect different *components* of the impression formation process (interpretation vs. comparison).

Interestingly, although the ICM started out as a review of accessibility effects in the social cognition, comparison, and judgment literatures, specifying the model generated several new hypotheses. Studies investigating the impact of activated mindsets, the ambiguity of target stimuli, the timing, extremity, and target-similarity of priming stimuli, as well as tests of the notion that both interpretation and comparison are spontaneous processes that can be instigated by subliminally presented priming information, were all consequences rather than antecedents of the ICM. Let us hope the future has new tests and applications of the ICM in store. And let us hope that such tests ultimately lead to its falsification. After all, as a famous supermodel once lamented, "in the end, all models grow old, lose their appeal, and then they die."

ACKNOWLEDGMENTS

The author thanks Willem Koomen for everything. The research and writing were supported by a "Pionier" grant from the Dutch Science Foundation (Nederlandse Organisatie voor Wetenschappelijk Onderzoek).

NOTE

1. The notion that the ICM is intellectually indebted by these models is not too surprising when one considers that many of the theoretical details and specifics of the ICM were formulated when I visited the University of Michigan and was advised by both Schwarz and Manis.

REFERENCES

Aronson, E., Wilson, T. D., & Akert, R. M. (2004). *Social psychology* (5th ed.). Garden City, NJ: Prentice Hall.

Bargh, J. A. (1997). The automaticity of everyday life. In R. S. Wyer (Ed.), *Advances in social cognition* (Vol. 10, pp. 1–61). Mahwah, NJ: Lawrence Erlbaum Associates, Inc.

Bargh, J. A., & Ferguson, M. J. (2001). Beyond behaviorism: On the automaticity of higher mental processes. *Psychological Bulletin, 126*, 925–945.

Bargh, J. A., & Pietromonaco, P. (1982). Automatic information processing and social perception: The influence of trait information presented outside of conscious awareness on impression formation. *Journal of Personality and Social Psychology, 43*, 437–449.

Beebe-Center, J. G. (1929). The law of affective equilibrium. *American Journal of Psychology, 41*, 54–69.

Bless, H., Fiedler, K., & Strack, F. (2004). *Social cognition: How individuals construct social reality*. Hove, UK: Psychology Press.

Bruner, J. S. (1957). On perceptual readiness. *Psychological Review, 64*, 123–152.

Chartrand, T. L., & Bargh, J. A. (1999). The chameleon effect: The perception–behavior link and social interaction. *Journal of Personality and Social Psychology, 76*, 893–910.

DeCoster, J., & Claypool, H. M. (2004). A meta-analysis of priming effects on impression formation supporting a general model of informational biases. *Personality and Social Psychology Review, 8*, 2–27.

Devine, P. G. (1989). Stereotypes and prejudice. Their automatic and controlled components. *Journal of Personality and Social Psychology, 56*, 5–18.

Dijksterhuis, A., Spears, R., Postmes, T., Stapel, D. A., Koomen, W., van Knippenberg, A., & Scheepers, D. (1998). Seeing one thing and doing another: Contrast effects in automatic behavior. *Journal of Personality and Social Psychology, 75*, 862–871.

Eiser, J. R. (1990). *Social judgment*. Milton Keynes, UK: Open University.

Erdley, C. A., & D'Agostino, P. R. (1988). Cognitive and affective components of automatic priming effects. *Journal of Personality and Social Psychology, 54*, 741–747.

Festinger, L. (1954). A theory of social comparison processes. *Human Relations, 7*, 117–140.

Ford, T. E., & Thompson, E. P. (2000). Preconscious and postconscious processes underlying construct accessibility effects: An extended search model. *Personality and Social Psychology Review, 4*, 317–336.

Gilovich, T. (1981). Seeing the past in the present: The effect of associations to familiar events on judgments and decisions. *Journal of Personality and Social Psychology, 40*, 797–808.

Gordijn, E. H., & Stapel, D. A. (in press). Behavioral effects of automatic interpersonal versus intergroup social comparison. *British Journal of Social Psychology*.

Haefner, M., & Stapel, D. A. (2006). When beauty stops shining: Priming and comparison effects of role models in advertising. *Manuscript submitted for publication*.

Herr, P. M. (1986). Consequences of priming: Judgment and behavior. *Journal of Personality and Social Psychology, 51*, 1106–1115.

Herr, P. M., Sherman, S. J., & Fazio, R. H. (1983). On the consequences of priming: Assimilation and contrast effects. *Journal of Experimental Social Psychology, 19*, 323–340.

Higgins, E. T. (1989). Knowledge accessibility and activation: Subjectivity and suffering from unconscious sources. In J. S. Uleman & J. A. Bargh (Eds.), *Unintended thought* (pp. 75–152). New York: Guilford Press.

Higgins, E. T. (1996). Knowledge activation: Accessibility, applicability, and salience. In E. T. Higgins & A. W. Kruglanski (Eds.), *Social psychology: Handbook of basic principles* (pp. 133–168). New York: Guilford Press.

Higgins, E. T., Rholes, W. S., & Jones, C. R. (1977). Category accessibility and impression formation. *Journal of Experimental Social Psychology, 13*, 141–154.

Koomen, W., Stapel, D. A., Jansen, S. S., In 't Veld, K. H. R. (1998). Priming and timing: A test of two perspectives. *European Journal of Social Psychology, 28*, 681–686.

Kunda, Z. (1999). *Social cognition*. Cambridge, MA: MIT Press.

Manis, M., Biernat, M., & Nelson, T. F. (1991). Comparison and expectancy processes in human judgment. *Journal of Personality and Social Psychology, 61*, 203–211.

Manis, M., Nelson, T. F., & Shedler, J. (1988). Stereotypes and social judgment: Extremity, assimilation, and contrast. *Journal of Personality and Social Psychology, 55*, 28–36

Manis, M., & Paskewitz, J. (1984). Judging psychopathology: Expectation and contrast. *Journal of Personality and Social Psychology, 20*, 363–381.

Maringer, M., Stapel, D. A., & Otten, S. (2006). The question determines the answer: Affective information effects on judgments of likeability and judgments of happiness. *Manuscript submitted for publication*.

Markman, K. D., & McMullen, M. N. (2003). A reflection and evaluation model of comparative thinking. *Personality and Social Psychology Review, 7*, 244–267.

Martin, L. L. (1986). Set/reset: Use and disuse of concepts in impression formation. *Journal of Personality and Social Psychology, 51*, 493–504.

Mervis, C. B., & Rosch, E. (1981). Categorization of natural objects. *Annual Review of Psychology, 32*, 89–115.

Morse, S., & Gergen, K. J. (1970). Social comparison, self-constancy, and the concept of the self. *Journal of Personality and Social Psychology, 16*, 148–156.

Moskowitz, G. B., & Skurnik, I. W. (1999). Contrast effects as determined by the type of prime: Trait versus exemplar primes initiate processing strategies that differ in how accessible constructs are used. *Journal of Personality and Social Psychology, 76*, 911–927.

Murphy, S. T., & Zajonc, R. B. (1993). Affect, cognition, and awareness: Affective priming with optimal and suboptimal stimulus exposures. *Journal of Personality and Social Psychology, 64*, 723–739.

Mussweiler, T. (2003). Comparison processes in social judgment: Mechanisms and consequences. *Psychological Review, 110*, 472–489.

Mussweiler, T., Rüter, K., & Epstude, K. (2004). The man who wasn't there: Subliminal social standards influence self-evaluation. *Journal of Experimental Social Psychology, 40*, 689–696.

Neuberg, S. L. (1988). Behavioral implications of information presented outside of conscious awareness: The effect of subliminal presentation of trait information on behavior in the Prisoner's Dilemma Game. *Social Cognition, 6*, 207–230.

Parducci, A., & Wedell, D. (1990). The context of evaluative judgments: Psychophysics and beyond. In H. H. Geissler (Ed.), *Psychological explorations of mental structures* (pp. 94–103). Göttingen, Germany: Hogrefe & Huber.

Patterson, T. E. (1994). *Out of order*. New York: Vintage.

Pelham, B. W., & Wachsmuth, J. O. (1995). The waxing and waning of the social self: Assimilation and contrast in social comparison. *Journal of Personality and Social Psychology, 69*, 825–838.

Philippot, P., Schwarz, N., Carrera, P., de Vries, N., & van Yperen, N. W. (1991). Differential effects of priming at the encoding and judgment stage. *European Journal of Social Psychology, 21*, 293–302.

Schwarz, N., & Bless, H. (1992). Constructing reality and its alternatives: An inclusion/exclusion model of assimilation and contrast effects in social judgment. In L. L. Martin & A. Tesser (Eds.), *The construction of social judgments* (pp. 217–245). Hillsdale, NJ: Lawrence Erlbaum Associates, Inc.

Sherif, M., & Hovland, C. I. (1961). *Social judgment, assimilation, and contrast effects in communication and attitude change.* New Haven, CT/London: Yale University Press.

Skowronski, J. J., Carlston, D. E., & Isham, J. T. (1993). Implicit versus explicit impression formation: The differing effects of overt labeling and covert priming on memory and impressions. *Journal of Experimental Social Psychology, 29*, 17–41.

Spears, R., Gordijn, E., Stapel, D. A., & Dijksterhuis, A. P. (2004). Reaction in action: Intergroup contrast in automatic behavior. *Personality and Social Psychology Bulletin, 30*, 605–616.

Srull, T. K., & Wyer, R. S. (1979). The role of category accessibility in the interpretation of information about persons: Some determinants and implications. *Journal of Personality and Social Psychology, 37*, 1660–1672.

Stapel, D. A., & Blanton, H. (2004). From seeing to being: Subliminal social comparisons affect implicit and explicit self evaluations. *Journal of Personality and Social Psychology, 87*, 468–481.

Stapel, D. A., & Koomen, W. (1997). Using primed exemplars during impression formation: Interpretation or comparison? *European Journal of Social Psychology, 27*, 357–367.

Stapel, D. A., & Koomen, W. (1998a). Interpretation versus reference framing: Assimilation and contrast effects in the organizational domain. *Organizational Behavior and Human Decision Making Processes, 76*, 132–148.

Stapel, D. A., & Koomen, W. (1998b). When stereotype activation results in (counter)stereotypical judgments: Priming stereotype-relevant traits and exemplars. *Journal of Experimental Social Psychology, 34*, 136–163.

Stapel, D. A., & Koomen, W. (2000). Distinctness of others and malleability of selves: Their impact on social comparison effects. *Journal of Personality and Social Psychology, 79*, 1068–1087.

Stapel, D. A., & Koomen, W. (2001a). Let's not forget the past when we go to the future: On our knowledge of knowledge accessibility effects. In G. Moskowitz (Ed.), *Cognitive social psychology* (pp. 229–246). Mahwah, NJ: Lawrence Erlbaum Associates, Inc.

Stapel, D. A., & Koomen, W. (2001b). I, we, and the effects of others on me: How self-construal moderates social comparison effects. *Journal of Personality and Social Psychology, 80*, 766–781.

Stapel, D. A., & Koomen, W. (2001c). The impact of interpretation versus comparison goals on knowledge accessibility effects. *Journal of Experimental Social Psychology, 37*, 134–149.

Stapel, D. A., & Koomen, W. (2005a). Competition, cooperation, and the effects of others on me. *Journal of Personality and Social Psychology, 88*, 1029–1038.

Stapel, D. A., & Koomen, W. (2005b). Multiple ambiguity and an impression formation focus make inapplicable primes useful. *Social Cognition, 4*, 324–335.

Stapel, D. A., & Koomen, W. (2005c). When less is more: The consequences of affective primacy for subliminal priming effects. *Personality and Social Psychology Bulletin, 31*, 1286–1295.

Stapel, D. A., & Koomen, W. (2006). The flexible unconscious: Investigating the judgmental impact of varieties of unaware perception. *Journal of Experimental Social Psychology, 42*, 112–119.

Stapel, D. A., Koomen, W., & Ruys, K. (2002). The effects of diffuse and distinct affect. *Journal of Personality and Social Psychology, 83*, 60–74.

Stapel, D. A., Koomen, W., & van der Pligt, J. (1996). The referents of trait inferences: The impact of trait concepts versus actor–trait links on subsequent judgments. *Journal of Personality and Social Psychology*, 70, 437–450.

Stapel, D. A., Koomen, W., & van der Pligt (1997). Categories of category accessibility: The impact of trait versus exemplar priming on person judgments. *Journal of Experimental Social Psychology*, 33, 44–76.

Stapel, D. A., Koomen, W., & Velthuijsen, A. S. (1998). Assimilation or contrast? Comparison relevance, distinctness, and the impact of accessible information on consumer judgments. *Journal of Consumer Psychology*, 7, 1–24.

Stapel, D. A., & Koomen, W., & Zeelenberg, M. (1998). The impact of accuracy motivation on interpretation, comparison, and correction processes: Accuracy motivation × knowledge accessibility effects. *Journal of Personality and Social Psychology*, 74, 878–893.

Stapel, D. A., Martin, L. L., & Schwarz, N. (1998). The smell of bias: What instigates correction processes in social judgments? *Personality and Social Psychology Bulletin*, 24, 797–806.

Stapel, D. A., & Marx, D. M. (2006). Hardly thinking about others: On target closeness and cognitive busyness in social comparison effects. *Journal of Experimental Social Psychology*, 42, 397–405.

Stapel, D. A., & Marx, D. M. (in press). Making sense of war: Using the Interpretation Comparison Model to understand the Iraq conflict. *European Journal of Social Psychology*.

Stapel, D. A., & Schwarz, N. (1998a). Similarities and differences between trait concept and expectancy priming: What matters is whether the target stimulus is ambiguous or mixed. *Journal of Experimental Social Psychology*, 34, 227–245.

Stapel, D. A., & Schwarz, N. (1998b). The Republican who did not want to become President: An inclusion/exclusion analysis of Colin Powell's impact on evaluations of the Republican party and Bob Dole. *Personality and Social Psychology Bulletin*, 24, 690–699.

Stapel, D. A., & Schwinghammer, S. A. (2004). Defensive social comparison and the constraints of reality. *Social Cognition*, 22, 147–167.

Stapel, D. A., & Spears, R. (1995). Reflected or deflected glory? The impact of analogies on the perception of politicians and their policies. *Politics, Groups and the Individual*, 5, 21–30.

Stapel, D. A., & Spears, R. (1996a). Event accessibility and context effects in causal inference: Judgment of a different order. *Personality and Social Psychology Bulletin*, 22, 979–992.

Stapel, D. A., & Spears, R. (1996b). Guilty by disassociation (and innocent by association): The impact of relevant and irrelevant analogies on political judgments. *Political Behavior*, 18, 289–310.

Stapel, D. A., & Suls, J. (2004). Method matters: Effects of implicit versus explicit social comparisons on activation, behavior, and self-views. *Journal of Personality and Social Psychology*, 87, 860–875.

Stapel, D. A., & Winkielman, P. (1998). Assimilation and contrast as a function of context–target similarity, distinctness, and dimensional relevance. *Personality and Social Psychology Bulletin*, 24, 634–646.

Strack, F. (1992). The different routes to social judgments: Experiential versus informational strategies. In L. L. Martin & A. Tesser (Eds.), *The construction of social judgments* (pp. 249–276). Hillsdale, NJ: Lawrence Erlbaum Associates, Inc.

Tajfel, H. (1959). Quantitative judgment in social perception. *British Journal of Psychology*, 50, 16–29.

Wegener, D. T., & Petty, R. E. (1995). Flexible correction processes in social judgment: The role of naive theories in corrections for perceived bias. *Journal of Personality and Social Psychology, 68*, 36–51.

Wyer, R. S., & Srull, T. K. (1989). *Memory and social cognition in its social context*. Hillsdale, NJ: Lawrence Erlbaum Associates, Inc.

7

Assimilation and Contrast as Comparison Effects: A Selective Accessibility Model

THOMAS MUSSWEILER

*H*uman information processing does not take place in an isolated ether. Rather, the judgments we make, the feelings we experience, and the behaviors we engage in are situated in a rich psychological context, which includes context stimuli that are immediately present, remembered, or constructed on the spot. Much of the research in psychology over the past 50 or so years has examined how this psychological context shapes our judgments, feelings, and behaviors. This research has described two general context effects: assimilation and contrast. Our judgments, feelings, and behaviors may either be displaced toward (assimilation) or away from (contrast) context stimuli.

Over the decades, abundant demonstrations of both types of context effects have accumulated. Sometimes judgments, feelings, and behaviors are assimilated toward the psychological context; at other times they are contrasted away from this context. Evidence demonstrating assimilative and contrastive context effects is particularly plentiful in the realm of human judgment. Here, contrast is apparent in the fact that a target person may be judged to be less hostile in the context of extremely hostile others (e.g., Adolf Hitler) than in the context of extremely peaceful others (e.g., the Pope; Herr, 1986) or that the self may be judged to be less competent in the context of a competent other than in the context of an incompetent other (Morse & Gergen, 1970). Assimilation, on the other hand, is apparent in the fact that the same target quantity (e.g., length of the Mississippi river) may be judged to be longer in the context of a high rather than a low numeric standard (Tversky & Kahneman, 1974) and that the self may be judged to be more competent in the context of a competent rather than an incompetent other (e.g., Brewer & Weber, 1994; Pelham & Wachsmuth, 1995; Suls, Martin, & Wheeler, 2002).

Similar context effects have also been demonstrated for affective reactions. Research on emotional contagion (Hatfield, Cacioppo, & Rapson, 1992), for example, has demonstrated that sometimes our feelings are assimilated toward those of a comparison other (Neumann & Strack, 2000), so that we feel better in the context of a happy rather than a sad context person. At other times, however, our feelings are contrasted away from a comparison other, so that we feel worse in the context of a happy rather than a sad person (Englis, Vaughan, & Lanzetta, 1981). Finally, recent research on automatic behavior effects has demonstrated that our behaviors may also be assimilated toward or contrasted away from contextual information (Bargh, Chen, & Burrows, 1996; Chartrand & Bargh, 1999; Dijksterhuis et al., 1998). This evidence demonstrates that the psychological context many influence judgment, feelings, and behavior in an assimilative or a contrastive manner.

A COMPARISON PERSPECTIVE ON CONTEXT EFFECTS

How can these diverging context effects be explained? Why do our judgments, feelings, and behaviors depend on the contexts in which they arise? Why are our judgmental, affective, and behavioral reactions toward the very same target stimulus so strikingly different depending on their context? What are the psychological mechanisms that underlie these diverging context effects?

One possible answer to these questions emphasizes the role of comparison processes. In fact, there are ample conceptual and empirical reasons to believe that comparison processes critically contribute to context effects in judgment, affect, and behavior. A salient context can only influence reactions toward a target, if a relation between context and target is established (Brown, 1953). This necessity equally applies to judgments, feelings, and behaviors. In order to influence target judgments, for example, the hostility of a set of comparison others (Herr, 1986) has to be related to the target in some way. Similarly, in order to influence one's own feelings, the affective state of a target other (Neumann & Strack, 2000) somehow has to be related to the self. And, by the same token, in order to influence one's behavior, the actual (Chartrand & Bargh, 1999) or imagined (Dijksterhuis et al., 1998) behavior of others somehow has to be related to the self. Comparison processes are a primary way to establish such relations. In this respect, comparisons may be the crucial mechanism in forming the essential link between the psychological context on the one hand, and judgments, feelings, and behaviors on the other.

This possibility is further supported by a host of findings emphasizing how naturally and spontaneously comparisons arise in social information processing. Whenever information is perceived, processed, or evaluated—it seems—this information is compared to a salient context, norm, or standard. Even the mere perception of a physical object involves a comparison with a pertinent standard (Helson, 1964). The perceived size of a target circle, for example, critically depends on whether the target is surrounded by a set of large or small circles, as is evident in the classic Ebbinghaus illusion (Coren & Enns, 1993). Similarly, the perceived weight of a target object depends on whether it is presented with a set of heavy or light objects (Brown, 1953). The proclivity to engage in comparisons is so much part and parcel of human information processing that even stimuli that are not consciously perceived because they are presented subliminally are compared to a pertinent standard (Dehaene et al., 1998). This tendency toward comparative information processing is remarkably robust. For one, comparisons are engaged even if they are not explicitly asked for. When processing information about another person, for example, people spontaneously compare this person to themselves (Dunning & Hayes, 1996). Similarly, when processing information about themselves, people spontaneously compare themselves to another person (Festinger, 1954; Mussweiler & Rüter, 2003). Recent evidence suggests that this tendency to make spontaneous comparisons when processing information about a given target goes so far that people even use comparison standards that— phenomenologically—are not even there, because they were presented subliminally (Mussweiler & Englich, 2005; Mussweiler, Rüter, & Epstude, 2004a). In addition, the leaning toward comparative processing is so robust that comparisons are even engaged with standards that—from a normative perspective—are unlikely to provide useful information about the target. In one study demonstrating this robustness (Gilbert, Giesler, & Morris, 1995), for example, participants compared their own performance in a task to a salient other, even if this person clearly constituted an inappropriate standard (Goethals & Darley, 1977) because he had received additional training in the critical ability.

Taken together, this body of evidence suggests that comparisons are naturally and spontaneously involved whenever context information is processed. Together with the above-mentioned theoretical arguments that emphasize the potential role of comparisons in assimilative and contrastive context effects, this empirical evidence suggests that comparison processes may be the driving force behind context effects on judgment, affect, and behavior. Comparisons are a primary way to relate context stimuli to the target stimulus, which is a logical necessity for context effects to occur in the first place. Furthermore, comparisons are spontaneously engaged whenever context information is processed. Given their logical necessity and spontaneous engagement, it seems natural to examine to what extent comparison processes can be used to explain assimilative and contrastive context effects in general. Comparisons can lead to assimilation as well as contrast (e.g., Brewer & Weber, 1994; Pelham & Wachsmuth, 1995), so that they may well be the psychological mechanism that produces assimilative and contrastive context effects. To understand how comparisons contribute to assimilative and contrastive context effects, one has to take a closer look at the psychological mechanisms that underlie comparisons.

COMPARISON PROCESSES: SIMILARITY AND DISSIMILARITY TESTING

More specifically, to understand how comparisons contribute to assimilation and contrast one has to examine their informational underpinnings (Mussweiler, 2001a, 2001b, 2003; Mussweiler & Strack, 2000a, 2000b). Starting from this general assumption, we have developed and tested a selective accessibility model of comparison consequences (for an overview, see Mussweiler, 2003) that integrates basic principles of social cognition research.

The Selective Accessibility Mechanism

To make a comparison between a given target and a salient standard, judges have to obtain relevant information about target and standard. This specific knowledge is best obtained by an active search for information, which often takes the form of a hypothesis-testing process in which judges relate their stored knowledge regarding the target to the judgmental task at hand (Trope & Liberman, 1996). Such hypothesis-testing processes are often selective in that they focus on one single hypothesis that is then evaluated against a specific criterion (Sanbonmatsu, Posavac, Kardes, & Mantel, 1998; see also Klayman & Ha, 1987; Trope & Lieberman, 1996). Rather than engaging in an exhaustive comparative test of all plausible hypotheses, judges often limit themselves to the test of a single focal hypothesis. This is also likely to be the case for hypothesis-testing processes during comparison.

In the case of comparative information processing, two hypotheses can be distinguished. Judges can either test the possibility that the target is similar to the standard or they can test the possibility that the target is dissimilar from the standard. Which of these hypotheses is tested depends on the overall perceived similarity of the target and the standard. As an initial step in the selective accessibility mechanism, judges engage in a quick assessment of target and standard (Smith, Shoben, & Rips, 1974) in which they briefly consider a small number of salient features (e.g., category membership, salient characteristics) to determine whether both are generally similar or dissimilar. The outcome of this screening is a broad assessment of similarity. Although such an assessment is by itself too general to be used as the basis for target evaluation, it is sufficient to determine the specific nature of the hypothesis that is then tested. The hypothesis-testing mechanism thus focuses on the possibility that is suggested by the initial holistic assessment. If this assessment indicates that the target is generally similar to the standard, judges will engage in a process of similarity testing and test the hypothesis that the target is similar to the standard. If the initial assessment indicates that the target is dissimilar from the standard, however, judges will engage in a process of dissimilarity testing and test the hypothesis that the target is dissimilar from the standard.

The literature on hypothesis testing further suggests that once a hypothesis is selected, it is often tested by focusing on hypothesis-consistent evidence (Klayman & Ha, 1987; Snyder & Swann, 1978; Trope & Bassok, 1982; Trope & Lieberman, 1996). Applied to the case of hypothesis testing in comparative information processing, this suggests that judges selectively generate information that is consistent with the focal hypothesis of the comparison. If judges test the hypothesis that the target is similar to the standard, for example, they will do so by selectively searching for standard-consistent target knowledge—evidence indicating that the target's standing on the judgmental dimension is indeed similar to that of the standard. By the same token, if judges test the hypothesis that the target is dissimilar from the standard, they do so by selectively searching for standard-inconsistent target knowledge—evidence indicating that the target's standing differs from that of the standard. This selectivity in the acquisition of judgment-relevant knowledge about the target has clear informational consequences. The mechanism of similarity testing selectively increases the accessibility of standard-consistent target knowledge, whereas dissimilarity testing selectively increases the accessibility of standard-inconsistent target knowledge. This selective accessibility effect constitutes the core informational consequence of comparison (see Figure 7.1).

To the extent that the target knowledge that became accessible during the comparison forms the basis for subsequent judgments, feelings, and behaviors, these psychological reactions will reflect the implications of this knowledge. If standard-consistent target knowledge forms the basis, then judgment, feelings, and behavior are assimilated toward the standard. If standard-inconsistent knowledge forms the basis, then judgment, feelings, and behavior are contrasted away from the standard.

Supporting Evidence in Judgment, Feelings, and Behavior

From this perspective, whether judges engage in the alternative comparison processes of similarity or dissimilarity testing critically determines comparison consequences. The informational focus that judges take during the comparison—whether they focus on similarities or differences—determines whether their psychological reactions are assimilated toward or contrasted away from the standard.

Direct support for the critical effect that judges' informational focus on similarities versus differences has on the direction of comparison consequences stems from a series of studies that manipulated participants' informational focus during a comparison. In the first of these studies, I directly manipulated participants'

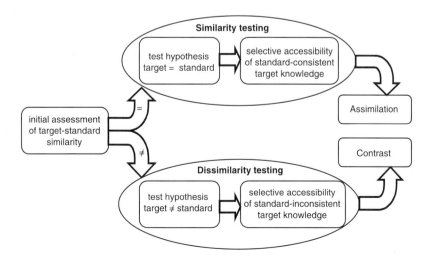

FIGURE 7.1   The selective accessibility mechanism (from Mussweiler, 2003).

informational comparison focus and examined how this manipulation influenced judgmental comparison consequences (Mussweiler, 2001a). To do so, I used a procedural priming task (for an overview, see Smith, 1994)—a task in which participants' tendency to rely on a particular processing style is strengthened by engaging them in this type of processing in a preceding unrelated task. More specifically, I induced participants to focus either on similarities or on differences, via a picture comparison task. Participants were given sketches of two scenes and were asked to either list all the similarities or all the differences they could find for the two pictures. Doing so sets participants' minds on either of these two alternative processing styles, so that they apply the same informational focus to a subsequent comparison task. Participants who focused on similarities between the two pictures also focus on similarities between target and standard in a subsequent comparison that is otherwise unrelated to the picture comparison task. In the context of this study, participants were asked to engage in a social comparison, in which they compared themselves with a social standard who was either high or low on the critical dimension of adjustment to college (Mussweiler, 2001a). Subsequent to this comparison, participants evaluated their own adjustment to college. Consistent with a selective accessibility perspective on comparison consequences, self-evaluations critically depended on whether participants were induced to focus on similarities or differences (see Figure 7.2). Judges who were primed to focus on similarities and to thus engage in similarity testing assimilated self-evaluations toward the standard. These judges evaluated their own adjustment to college to be better after a comparison with a high rather than a low standard. Judges who were primed to focus on differences and to thus engage in dissimilarity testing, on the other hand, contrasted self-evaluations away from the standard. These judges evaluated their own adjustment to college to be worse after a comparison with a high rather than a low standard.

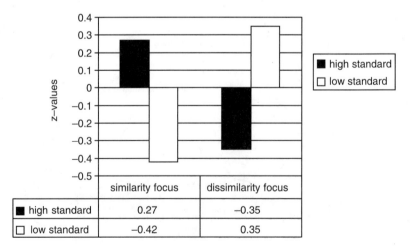

FIGURE 7.2 Self-evaluations of adjustment to college after comparison with a high versus low standard by similarity versus dissimilarity focus (from Mussweiler, 2001a).

More recently, similar judgmental consequences of a focus on similarities versus differences were demonstrated for sequential performance judgments in sports (Damisch, Mussweiler, & Plessner, 2006). In this series of studies, a focus on similarities versus differences was again directly induced via the picture comparison task. Results demonstrated that judgments about the athletic performance of a target athlete are assimilated toward the performance of the preceding athlete under conditions that foster similarity testing, and contrasted away from the preceding performance under conditions that foster dissimilarity testing. These findings demonstrate that whether judgments are assimilated toward or contrasted away from a context stimulus depends on whether judges focus on similarities or differences between context and target.

Extending this initial work on judgmental comparison consequences, more recent evidence shows similar effects in the realm of affect and behavior. Epstude and Mussweiler (2006), for example, demonstrated that whether participants' affective state was assimilated toward or contrasted away from a comparison other depended on a focus on similarities versus differences, which was induced using Mussweiler's (2001a) picture comparison task. Participants who were primed on similarity testing felt better after exposure to a series of pictures of faces with an emotionally positive expression than after exposure to faces with an emotionally negative expression. This is an assimilation effect. For participants who were primed on dissimilarity testing, however, the reverse pattern occurred, which corresponds to a contrast effect. In much the same way, behavioral context effects also depend on whether participants are induced to focus on similarities or differences. Specifically, it has been demonstrated that participants who are induced to focus on similarities assimilate their behavior toward a set of context stimuli, whereas participants who are induced to focus on differences contrast their behavior away from the exact same stimuli (Haddock, Macrae, & Fleck, 2002). More specifically, judges who focused on similarities among a set of supermodels behaved unintelligently. That is, they assimilated their behavior toward the behavior that is stereotypically associated with supermodels (an assimilation effect). Judges who focused on differences between the models, however, behaved more intelligently and thus contrasted their behavior away from the context stimuli. Taken together, these findings demonstrate that how a given context influences judgment, affect, and behavior critically depends on whether judges focus on similarities or differences. This is consistent with the assumption that similarity and dissimilarity testing are crucial mechanisms that underlie assimilation and contrast effects.

Furthermore, recent evidence (Mussweiler, Rüter, & Epstude, 2004b) demonstrates that assimilative and contrastive comparison consequences are often accompanied by traces of the two alternative selective accessibility mechanisms of similarity and dissimilarity testing. In one study, for example, participants who were asked to evaluate their own athletic abilities were confronted with either moderate or extreme comparison standards of athletic ability. For example, participants were either confronted with the moderately low standard Bill Clinton or with the extremely low standard Pope John Paul. They then evaluated a number of core athletic abilities, such as the number of sit-ups they can perform and the time they need to run 100 meters. Consistent with evidence in the social judgment literature (Herr, 1986), participants assimilated their self-evaluations to the moderate standards and contrasted them away from the extreme standards. Subsequent to these assimilative and contrastive comparisons, we assessed participants' focus on similarities versus dissimilarities. To do so, we used a picture comparison task, similar to the one I had previously applied to *induce* a focus on similarities versus differences (Mussweiler, 2001a), to *assess* these alternative informational foci. Specifically, participants were asked to compare two pictures that were unrelated to the preceding social comparison and to indicate how similar these pictures are. If assimilation is indeed produced by an informational focus on similarities and contrast results from a focus on dissimilarities, then these respective foci should carry over to the picture comparison. Participants who assimilated self-evaluations toward the moderate standards because they selectively focused on similarities to these standards should also focus on similarities between the two pictures; participants who contrasted self-evaluations away from extreme standards because they selectively focused on dissimilarities should also focus on dissimilarities between the two pictures. Consistent with these expectations, our results demonstrate that participants rated both pictures to be more similar after comparing themselves with a moderate rather than an extreme social comparison standard (see Figure 7.3). That is, judgmental assimilation was accompanied by a general informational focus on similarities, whereas judgmental contrast was accompanied by a general focus on differences.

In examining how a different moderator influences the emergence of judgmental assimilation and contrast, Stapel and Koomen (2005) provide a conceptual replication of this finding. These researchers demonstrated that judges tend to assimilate self-judgments toward a social standard if they are in a cooperative context. In a competitive context, however, judges tend to contrast self-judgments

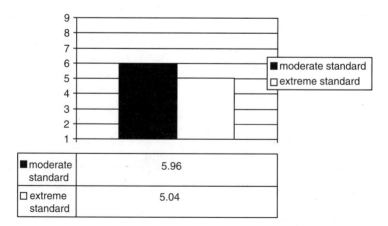

FIGURE 7.3 Similarity focus (judgments of similarity in picture comparison task) subsequent to social comparison with a moderate (assimilation) versus extreme (contrast) standard (Mussweiler et al., 2004a).

away from a social comparison standard. Using our picture comparison task (Mussweiler, 2001a; Mussweiler et al., 2004b), Stapel and Koomen demonstrate that the cooperative contexts in which assimilation occurred are accompanied by a similarity focus, whereas the competitive contexts are accompanied by a difference focus.

Taken together, these findings demonstrate that the alternative informational foci on similarities versus dissimilarities are closely associated with assimilative and contrastive context effects on judgment, affect, and behavior. Inducing participants to focus on similarities versus differences determines whether they assimilate their judgments, feelings, and behaviors toward context stimuli or whether they contrast away from the context. Vice versa, assimilating toward the context induces participants to focus on similarities, whereas contrasting away from the context induces them to focus on differences. This intimate link between assimilation versus contrast on the one hand, and similarity versus dissimilarity focus on the other, suggests that assimilative and contrastive context effects are produced by the two alternative selective accessibility mechanisms of similarity and dissimilarity testing.

This conclusion is further supported by research examining what specific target knowledge is activated in the case of assimilation versus contrast to context stimuli. From a selective accessibility perspective, assimilation versus contrast is ultimately produced by differences in the accessibility of target knowledge. Specifically, similarity testing increases the accessibility of knowledge indicating that target and standard are similar on the critical dimension. Dissimilarity testing, however, selectively increases the accessibility of knowledge, which indicates that target and standard are dissimilar on the critical dimension. Consistent with this assumption, recent evidence demonstrates that conditions that lead to assimilation versus contrast influence the accessibility of target knowledge in diverging ways. One of these studies (Mussweiler & Bodenhausen, 2002) made use of the fact that in the context of spontaneous social comparison, assimilation is more likely to occur if the self and the standard belong to the same social category, whereas dissimilarity testing is more likely if both belong to different categories. If these divergent judgmental consequences are indeed produced by the selective accessibility mechanisms of similarity and dissimilarity testing, then social comparisons with intracategorical versus extracategorcial standards should render divergent sets of standard-consistent versus standard-inconsistent self-knowledge accessible. This was indeed the case. In a variant of a lexical decision task (Dijksterhuis et al., 1998)—a task assessing the accessibility of a critical concept by examining how fast participants are in responding to words that are or are not associated with this concept—standard-consistent self-knowledge was more accessible after a spontaneous comparison with an ingroup member than after a comparison with an outgroup member.

Using standard extremity as a moderator for assimilation versus contrast, this finding was conceptually replicated by Smeesters and Mandel (2006). These researchers built on previous studies demonstrating that exposure to moderate context stimuli leads to judgmental assimilation, whereas exposure to extreme stimuli leads to contrast (Herr, 1986; Mussweiler et al., 2004a, 2004b). If these divergent consequences are also produced by the selective accessibility mechanisms of similarity and dissimilarity testing, then exposure to moderate versus extreme standards should again render divergent sets of standard-consistent versus standard-inconsistent self-knowledge accessible. In fact, this is what Smeesters and Mandel demonstrate. Exposure to moderately thin versus heavy models renders standard-consistent self-knowledge accessible, whereas exposure to extremely thin versus heavy models renders standard-inconsistent self-knowledge accessible. For the realm of judgmental assimilation and contrast, these studies demonstrate that standard-consistent knowledge is more accessible in assimilative situations, whereas standard-inconsistent knowledge was more accessible in contrastive situations.

Similar evidence has been gathered for affective and behavioral assimilation and contrast. For example, using an emotional contagion paradigm—a paradigm in which the affective state of an observed person spontaneously transfers to the observer—Epstude and Mussweiler (2006) demonstrate that in situations that promote affective assimilation, standard-consistent self-knowledge is more accessible. In situations that promote affective contrast, however, standard-inconsistent knowledge is particularly accessible. In much the same way, situations that lead to behavioral contrast also appear to involve a selective increase in the accessibility of standard-inconsistent knowledge. For example, exposing participants to an extremely intelligent standard like Albert Einstein not only leads to behavioral contrast so that participants behave less intelligently. It also renders self-knowledge indicating low intelligence accessible (Dijksterhuis et al., 1998). In a lexical decision task that assessed the specific accessibility of self-related knowledge, judges who had been exposed to Albert Einstein responded faster to words associated with low intelligence (e.g., stupid, dumb). Thus, judgmental, affective, and behavioral assimilation versus contrast appear to be accompanied by a selective increase in the accessibility of standard-consistent versus standard-inconsistent target knowledge.

In summary, the described body of evidence is consistent with the notion that assimilation and contrast in judgment, affect, and behavior are produced by the two alternative selective accessibility mechanisms of similarity and dissimilarity testing. Inducing judges to focus on similarities leads to assimilation in judgment, affect, and behavior, whereas inducing judges to focus on differences leads to contrast. Furthermore, assimilation is accompanied by a generalized focus on similarities, whereas contrast is accompanied by a focus on differences. Finally, in situations that promote assimilation, standard-consistent target knowledge is particularly accessible, whereas in situations that promote contrast, standard-inconsistent knowledge is accessible. These findings demonstrate that assimilation is closely associated with a focus on similarities and accessibility of standard-consistent knowledge, whereas contrast is closely associated with a focus on differences and accessibility of standard-inconsistent knowledge. The selective accessibility mechanisms of similarity and dissimilarity testing may thus well be the psychological mechanisms that underlie assimilation and contrast effects in a variety of domains.

The Ubiquity of the Selective Accessibility Mechanism

Assimilation and contrast can be obtained under different conditions. One particularly salient differentiation involves the spontaneity in the use of context information. Sometimes judges are explicitly induced to use salient context information; at other times, they use this information spontaneously, without being explicitly asked to do so. Does this difference in the antecedents of context use influence the direction of the resulting effect or its underlying mechanisms? From a selective accessibility perspective, context effects result from a comparison between the target and salient context information. As a consequence, the question about potential differences between explicit and spontaneous use of context information translates into a question about potential differences between explicit and spontaneous comparisons.

On theoretical grounds there seems little reason to assume that either the underlying mechanisms or the consequences of explicit versus implicit comparisons differ. This is primarily the case because the spontaneous versus explicit comparison distinction pertains to an early processing stage in which it is determined whether context information is to be used at all. The subsequent processing stage in which context knowledge is related to the target, however, is the critical one at which the selective accessibility mechanisms of similarity and dissimilarity testing operate and that is thus ultimately responsible for assimilation and contrast. Whether a given context is explicitly provided or whether it is spontaneously used is extraneous to the subsequent process of relating the context to the standard. Whatever the source of a context, judges have to relate its features to those of the target to carry out a comparison. There is no a priori reason to believe that this comparison takes different forms depending on the source of the context. Keeping this distinction between different processing stages in mind, selective accessibility is thus likely to play a role no matter whether a context is explicitly provided or spontaneously selected.

Consistent with this reasoning the previously described empirical support for the selective accessibility mechanism actually stems from paradigms which have examined explicit as well as spontaneous comparisons. In some studies (Mussweiler & Strack, 2000a) participants were explicitly asked to compare a given target to a context standard. In other studies (e.g., Damisch et al., 2006; Mussweiler & Bodenhausen, 2002; Smeesters & Mandel, 2006) they were simply asked to judge a piece of context information before the critical target judgment without asking for or implying a comparison. In still other studies, participants were subliminally exposed to context information while forming a target judgment (Mussweiler & Englich, 2005; Mussweiler et al., 2004a). In all of these cases, the resulting effects of context information as well as the psychological mechanisms that produced them were exactly the same. No matter whether judges were explicitly asked to compare their athletic abilities to those of Bill Clinton (Mussweiler & Strack, 2000a) or whether they were subliminally presented with his name while thinking about their athletic abilities (Mussweiler et al., 2004a), they assimilated self-evaluations toward him. Similarly, no matter whether judges were explicitly asked to compare the average price of a midsize car to a numeric standard (Mussweiler & Strack, 2000c), or whether this standard was subliminally presented while thinking about car prices (Mussweiler & Englich, 2005), the accessibility of standard-consistent knowledge was selectively increased. These findings clearly show that explicit and spontaneous comparisons typically involve the same mechanisms and lead to the same effects.

This is also demonstrated by a recent set of studies that examined assimilation and contrast as consequences of exposure to moderate versus extreme context information, as well as the psychological mechanisms that underlie these effects (Smeesters & Mandel, 2006). In these studies, participants were exposed to ads that involved models who were moderate versus extremely thin versus heavy. Participants first rated the quality of these ads on some peripheral dimensions. Then they either evaluated their own physical appearance, or worked on a task that assessed the accessibility of self-knowledge that indicates thinness versus heaviness. In this paradigm, participants were thus neither explicitly asked to use the given context information (i.e., the models) nor were they instructed to compare these models to themselves in any way. Nevertheless, the results that were obtained in this spontaneous comparison paradigm again perfectly matched onto previous findings on the judgmental consequences of explicit comparisons with moderate and extreme standards (Mussweiler et al., 2004a; Mussweiler & Strack, 2000a). Furthermore, the demonstrated selective accessibility effect in the activation of self-knowledge was also perfectly in line with selective accessibility effects that result for explicit comparisons (e.g., Mussweiler & Strack, 2000a). Taken together, these findings from a variety of different paradigms suggest that explicit and spontaneous comparisons typically involve the same psychological mechanisms and yield the same consequences.

One recent set of studies suggests that under specific conditions, however, an explicit comparison instruction may alter the nature of the comparison mechanism that would naturally occur. Specifically, it has been demonstrated that explicitly asking participants to compare themselves to a maximally extreme standard (e.g., Albert Einstein for intelligence) may induce them to focus more on similarities to this standard (Stapel & Suls, 2004). As is true for other inductions of a similarity focus (e.g., Häfner, 2004; Mussweiler, 2001a, 2001b; Mussweiler et al., 2004a), this fosters tendencies to assimilate even to extreme standards. It is important to note, however, that this possibility is not unique to explicit instructions that induce a similarity focus. Subtle influences can induce judges to focus on similarities even to extreme standards and consequently assimilate toward them in much the same way. For example, exposing participants to ads with extremely athletic models leads them to evaluate themselves as more athletic if the ad heading includes words that are associated with similarity (e.g., "same body—same feeling") so that participants are subtly induced to engage in similarity testing (Häfner, 2004).

In summary, the bulk of evidence clearly suggests that explicit and spontaneous comparisons typically involve the same psychological mechanisms and lead to the same effects. Depending on whether a focus on similarities or differences is induced, explicit and spontaneous comparisons can both lead to assimilation or contrast. Thus, it does not appear to matter whether judges are explicitly asked to consider a specific context or whether they do so spontaneously. The resulting context effects are typically the same. Furthermore, in both situations, these context effects appear to be produced by the two alternative selective accessibility mechanisms of similarity and dissimilarity testing.

RELATION TO OTHER MODELS OF ASSIMILATION AND CONTRAST

On a general level, the selective accessibility framework is related to alternative social cognition perspectives on assimilation and contrast effects in a number of ways. This is the case, because in keeping with its sibling models, the selective accessibility model takes an informational perspective on assimilation and contrast. To understand how a given context influences judgments, feelings, and behavior, these models assume one has to examine the informational underpinnings of these psychological reactions. Such an informational approach is derived from the basic tenets of social cognition research (Higgins, 1996; Wyer & Srull, 1989).

In examining the relation between these different perspectives on assimilation and contrast, it is important to keep in mind a basic distinction between different processing stages that these different models primarily focus on. The selective accessibility mechanism focuses on the process of generating target knowledge in the light of and in comparison to accessible context knowledge. Other social cognition models of assimilation and contrast effects, on the other hand, focus on the use of accessible context knowledge in the process of forming a target evaluation. Whereas the selective accessibility framework is primarily concerned with mechanisms of knowledge activation, alternative social cognition models are primarily concerned with knowledge use. Clearly, to some extent both processing stages will work in tandem. Once a particular set of target knowledge has become accessible via the selective accessibility mechanism, the basic principles that underlie the effects of accessible knowledge (e.g., applicability; Higgins, Rholes, & Jones, 1977) also operate on this accessible knowledge.

This focus on different processing stages may stem from a primary interest in different types of knowledge. Whereas the selective accessibility model deals with knowledge that pertains directly to the target itself, alternative models have mostly focused on the use of context knowledge that does not directly pertain to the target itself. Although such context knowledge (e.g., knowledge about a comparison other) may be relevant for evaluations of the critical target (e.g., the self), it does not directly pertain to this target. Our research demonstrates that the primary determinant of assimilation and contrast effects is the specific target knowledge (e.g., self-related knowledge) that is generated in comparison to accessible context knowledge (e.g., a social comparison standard) rather than this context knowledge itself. This is, for example, apparent in the fact that in the context of comparative evaluation, judgmental consequences of exposure to a salient standard do not generalize to judgmental targets to which context knowledge would be applicable but which were not directly involved in the comparison process. For example, comparing oneself to a given performance standard only influences judgments about one's own ability, not the ability of another person (Mussweiler & Strack, 2000c). Notably, this is the case although the given context knowledge is equally applicable to the self and the other judgmental target. Furthermore, it has been demonstrated that it is the changes in the accessibility of specific target knowledge rather than more generally applicable knowledge that correspond most closely to assimilative and contrastive context effects on judgment, affect, and behavior (e.g., Dijksterhuis et al., 1998; Epstude & Mussweiler, 2006; Mussweiler & Bodenhausen, 2002; Mussweiler & Strack, 2000a; Smeesters & Mandel, 2006). These findings suggest that the changes in the accessibility of target knowledge which are conceptualized in the selective accessibility mechanism may be the primary determinant of assimilative and contrastive context effects.

To amplify these distinctions, I will discuss similarities and differences between the selective accessibility model and the major social cognition perspectives on assimilation and contrast. In doing so, I will follow the differentiation between categorization models (e.g., Herr, 1986; Schwarz & Bless, 1992), processing stage models (e.g., Philippot, Schwarz, Carrera, de Vries, & van Yperen, 1991; Stapel, Koomen, & van der Pligt, 1997), and correction models (e.g., Martin, 1986; Strack, 1992; Wegener & Petty, 1997) of assimilation and contrast effects that was proposed by Ford and Thompson (2000).

Categorization Models

The basic tenet of categorization models of assimilation and contrast (e.g., Herr, 1986; Schwarz & Bless, 1992) is that the way in which accessible context knowledge influences target evaluations critically depends on how this knowledge is categorized relative to the target. In their inclusion/exclusion model, for example, Schwarz and Bless (1992) propose that target evaluations are assimilated toward accessible knowledge if this knowledge is included in the target category. If accessible knowledge is excluded from the target category, however, contrast is likely to result. As is true for other fundamental processes of forming a target evaluation on the basis of accessible knowledge, the inclusion/exclusion mechanism can in principle also operate on the target knowledge that was rendered accessible via the selective accessibility processes of similarity and dissimilarity testing. Because this knowledge pertains directly to the judgmental target itself, however, it will typically be included in the judgment-relevant target representation. Exclusion is thus rarely likely to play a role for selective accessibility. As a consequence, target evaluations will typically be consistent with the implications of the target knowledge that was rendered accessible via the selective accessibility mechanism.

On a more general level, the basic assumption that the judgmental effects of accessible context knowledge principally depend on how this knowledge is categorized is also of central importance for an understanding of the selective accessibility mechanisms of similarity and dissimilarity testing. Similarity testing is more likely to occur if the target and the standard are ascribed to the same category, whereas dissimilarity testing is more likely to be engaged if they belong to different categories. The mechanisms that are responsible for the development of assimilation in knowledge use thus appear to have similar effects on knowledge activation. Many of the factors that have been found to determine whether context information will be included or excluded in the target category, such as feature overlap (Herr, Sherman, & Fazio, 1983) and category width (for a detailed discussion, see Schwarz & Bless, 1992), are thus also likely to influence whether judges engage in similarity or dissimilarity testing. At the same time, similarity/dissimilarity testing and inclusion/exclusion are clearly distinct processes because both are concerned with different processing stages (knowledge activation vs. use) and focus on different types of knowledge (specific target knowledge vs. general context knowledge).

Correction Models

The basic assumption of correction models (e.g., Martin, 1986; Strack, 1992; Wilson & Brekke, 1994; Wegener & Petty, 1997) is that how accessible knowledge influences target judgments depends on whether judges perceive this knowledge as biasing their judgment and whether they attempt to correct for this bias. If accessible knowledge is not seen as a biasing or contaminating factor, it will be used as a basis for the judgment so that evaluations are consistent with the implications of this knowledge. If, however, judges perceive their judgments to be contaminated by accessible knowledge, they will attempt to counteract this influence by either trying to ignore this knowledge ("resetting"; Martin, 1986) or by adjusting their evaluation in a way that compensates for the perceived bias (Strack, 1992; Wegener & Petty, 1997). In this case, target judgments will typically be inconsistent with the implications of accessible knowledge or go in the direction opposite to the perceived bias. Such correction mechanisms play a minor role in selective accessibility mechanisms. Because the critical knowledge that is rendered accessible via the selective accessibility mechanism directly pertains to the target itself and was self-generated by the judges, it is unlikely to be seen as contaminated (Mussweiler & Neumann, 2000; Mussweiler & Strack, 1999). As a result, judges will typically not engage in corrective attempts, so that judgments, feelings, and behaviors are by default consistent with the implications of accessible knowledge.

Processing Stage Models

Processing stage models, as a third perspective on assimilative and contrastive effects of accessible knowledge (e.g., Philippot et al., 1991; Stapel & Koomen, 2001; Stapel et al., 1997) assume that whether target evaluations are assimilated toward or contrasted away from accessible context knowledge depends on the processing stage at which this knowledge exerts an influence. If accessible knowledge is used to interpret target information in the encoding stage, then assimilation will result. If accessible knowledge is used as a reference point in the judgment stage (a process labeled "comparison"), however, then contrast is more likely to occur. From this perspective, the net judgmental effect that accessible knowledge has on target evaluations depends on whether conditions that promote or hinder the interpretation and reference point mechanisms are in place. For accessible knowledge to have an assimilative effect on the interpretation of target information, for example, this information has to be ambiguous. Unambiguous target information requires no interpretation, so that the mechanism that leads to assimilation is incapacitated (Stapel et al., 1997). For accessible knowledge to be used as a reference point, on the other hand, it has to be distinct (Brown, 1953; Helson, 1964) and relevant for target evaluation (Stapel et al., 1997). Assimilation is thus most likely to be the net effect of accessible knowledge if the target information is ambiguous and accessible knowledge is indistinct and irrelevant. Contrast, on the other hand, is most likely to result if target information is unambiguous and accessible knowledge is distinct and relevant.

The contrastive reference point mechanism that operates at the judgment stage also plays a crucial role in determining the judgmental effects of selective accessibility by determining the net judgmental outcome on subjective judgment scales (Mussweiler & Strack, 2000a; see Mussweiler, 2003, for a more detailed discussion). The assimilative interpretation mechanism, on the other hand, is quite distinct from the selective accessibility mechanism. For one, it specifies the process of applying accessible context knowledge to given target knowledge rather than of searching and activating novel target knowledge. Furthermore, the interpretation mechanism is assumed to have solely assimilative effects, whereas selective accessibility can produce assimilation or contrast, depending on whether similarity or dissimilarity testing are engaged. Finally, target ambiguity plays less of a role in the selective accessibility mechanism. Although an ambiguous target may allow for more flexibility in the hypothesis-testing mechanism of selective accessibility, similarity and dissimilarity testing can also be engaged for unambiguous targets. In principle, however, the interpretation mechanism could well operate in addition to mechanisms of selective accessibility. Just as the interpretation of given target knowledge is influenced by accessible context knowledge, this may also be the case for the interpretation of the target knowledge that was generated through a selective accessibility mechanism. To the extent that some of the knowledge participants seek and activate is ambiguous, accessible context knowledge may well unfold its interpretive effects. As is apparent from this discussion, the selective accessibility mechanism is both distinct from and related to alternative models of assimilation and contrast.

ASSIMILATION AND CONTRAST AS COMPARISON EFFECTS

In the present chapter, I have proposed that comparison processes critically contribute to assimilation and contrast effects in judgment, affect, and behavior. Abundant evidence demonstrates that comparisons are spontaneously engaged whenever people process information. In fact, comparisons appear to occur so naturally that they are even engaged with standards that are clearly irrelevant (Gilbert et al., 1995; Tversky & Kahneman, 1974) or—at least phenomenologically—not even there (Mussweiler et al., 2004a). Given this apparently inescapable leaning toward comparative information processing, it seems natural to assume that the context information that produces assimilation and contrast is spontaneously used for comparison. From this perspective, comparison processes are at the core of assimilative as well as contrastive context effects.

The assumption that comparisons may be responsible for assimilative as well as contrastive context effects is somewhat in conflict with previous accounts of the direction of comparison effects. Oftentimes, it is assumed that comparison leads to contrast (e.g., Schwarz & Bless, 1992; Stapel et al., 1997). In fact, the terms comparison and contrast are often used interchangeably. The present perspective, however, suggests that comparisons may lead to assimilation as well as contrast. The evidence I have presented clearly demonstrates that a comparison does not inevitably lead to either of these directionally opposing effects. Whether a comparison leads to assimilation or contrast depends on which type of comparison process is engaged. Similarity testing leads to assimilation, whereas dissimilarity testing leads to contrast. As a consequence, any factor that induces judges to focus on similarities between target and context information fosters assimilative context effects. By the same token, any factor that induces judges to focus on differences fosters contrast. Thus, a broader perspective on comparison processes seems to be in place. Comparison consequences appear to be more variable than is often assumed.

Notably, this is the case for explicit as well as spontaneous comparisons. It has been claimed that "implicit comparisons typically lead to contrast, whereas explicit comparisons may lead to assimilation or contrast" (Stapel & Suls, 2004, p. 873). Clearly, this assumption is inconsistent with abundant evidence demonstrating that, just as explicit comparisons, spontaneous (i.e., implicit) comparisons can lead to assimilation as well as contrast (e.g., Mussweiler & Bodenhausen, 2002; Mussweiler et al., 2004a, 2004b; Smeesters & Mandel, 2006; Wilson, Houston, Etling, & Brekke, 1996). No matter whether judges are explicitly asked to compare a target to salient context information, or whether they use this information spontaneously, can comparisons lead to assimilation and contrast? In fact, recent research clearly shows that the same factors that lead to assimilation and contrast in explicit comparisons determine the direction of spontaneous comparison effects in an identical way (e.g., Mussweiler et al., 2004a; Smeesters & Mandel, 2006). Whether a comparison leads to assimilation or contrast thus depends on the type of comparison process that is engaged (i.e., similarity or dissimilarity testing), not on whether the comparison is explicitly asked for or spontaneously evoked.

The fact that comparisons can lead to assimilation as well as contrast emphasizes that, in order to truly understand the nature of context effects in judgment, affect, and behavior, one has to distinguish between the resulting effect and the psychological process that produced it. "Comparison contrast" is just as likely to occur as "comparison assimilation." Keeping this in mind allows for the examination of the role that comparison processes play in both types of context effects. Such a comparison perspective on assimilation and contrast not only provides for a parsimonious account of context effects in judgment, affect, and behavior; it also builds on one of the fundamental properties of the human psyche, namely the essential relativity of social information processing.

ACKNOWLEDGMENTS

Our research described in this chapter was supported by a grant from the German Research Foundation (DFG). We would like to thank the members of the Würzburg Social Cognition Group for stimulating discussions of this work.

REFERENCES

Bargh, J. A., Chen, M., & Burrows, L. (1996). Automaticity of social behavior: Direct effects of trait construct and stereotype activation on action. *Journal of Personality and Social Psychology, 71,* 230–244.

Brewer, M. B., & Weber, J. G. (1994). Self-evaluation effects of interpersonal versus intergroup social comparison. *Journal of Personality and Social Psychology, 66,* 268–275.

Brown, D. R. (1953). Stimulus-similarity and the anchoring of subjective scales. *American Journal of Psychology, 66,* 199–214.

Chartrand, T. L., & Bargh, J. A. (1999). The Chameleon effect: The perception–behavior link and social interaction. *Journal of Personality and Social Psychology, 76,* 893–910.

Coren, S., & Enns, J. T. (1993). Size contrast as a function of conceptual similarity between test and inducers. *Perception and Psychophysics, 54,* 579–588.

Damisch, L., Mussweiler, T., & Plessner, H. (2006). Olympic medals as fruits of comparison? Assimilation and contrast in sequential performance judgments. *Journal of Experimental Psychology: Applied, 12,* 166–178.

Dehaene, S., Naccache, L., Le Clec'H, G., Koechlin, E., Mueller, M., Dehaene-Lambertz, G., et al. (1998, October 8). Imaging unconscious semantic priming. *Nature, 395,* 597–600.

Dijksterhuis, A., Spears, R., Postmes, T., Stapel, D. A., Koomen, W., van Knippenberg, A., & Scheepers, D. (1998). Seeing one thing and doing another: Contrast effects in automatic behavior. *Journal of Personality and Social Psychology, 75,* 862–871.

Dunning, D., & Hayes, A. F. (1996). Evidence of egocentric comparison in social judgment. *Journal of Personality and Social Psychology, 71,* 213–229.

Englis, B. G., Vaughan, K. B., & Lanzetta (1981). Conditioning a counter-empathetical emotional response. *Journal of Experimental Social Psychology, 18,* 375–391.

Epstude, K., & Mussweiler, T. (2006). What you get is what you see? Comparisons influence the social induction of affect. *Manuscript submitted for publication.*

Festinger, L. (1954). A theory of social comparison processes. *Human Relations, 7,* 117–140.

Ford, T. E., & Thompson, E. P. (2000). Preconscious and postconscious processes underlying construct accessibility effects: An extended search model. *Personality and Social Psychology Review, 4,* 317–336.

Gilbert, D. T., Giesler, R. B., & Morris, K. A. (1995). When comparisons arise. *Journal of Personality and Social Psychology, 69,* 227–236.

Goethals, G. R., & Darley, J. M. (1977). Social comparison theory: An attributional approach. In J. M. Suls & R. L. Miller (Eds.), *Social comparison processes: Theoretical and empirical perspectives* (pp. 259–278). Washington, DC: Hemisphere.

Haddock, G., Macrae, C. N., & Fleck, S. (2002). Syrian science and smart supermodels: On the when and how of perception-behavior effects. *Social Cognition, 20,* 469–479.

Hatfield, E., Cacioppo, J. T., & Rapson, R. L. (1992). *Emotional contagion*. New York: Cambridge University Press.

Häfner, M. (2004). How dissimilar others may still resemble the self: Assimilation and contrast after social comparison. *Journal of Consumer Psychology, 14*, 187–196.

Helson, H. (1964). *Adaptation level theory: An experimental and systematic approach to behavior*. New York: Harper.

Herr, P. M. (1986). Consequences of priming: Judgment and behavior. *Journal of Personality and Social Psychology, 51*, 1106–1115.

Herr, P. M., Sherman, S. J., & Fazio, R. H. (1983). On the consequences of priming: Assimilation and contrast effects. *Journal of Experimental Social Psychology, 19*, 323–340.

Higgins, E. T. (1996). Knowledge activation: Accessibility, applicability, and salience. In E. T. Higgins & A. W. Kruglanski (Eds.), *Social psychology: Handbook of basic principles* (pp. 133–168). New York: Guilford Press.

Higgins, E. T., Rholes, W. S., & Jones, C. R. (1977). Category accessibility and impression formation. *Journal of Experimental Social Psychology, 13*, 141–154.

Klayman, J., & Ha, Y.-W. (1987). Confirmation, disconfirmation, and information in hypotheses testing. *Psychological Review, 94*, 211–228.

Martin, L. L. (1986). Set/reset: Use and disuse of concepts in impression formation. *Journal of Personality and Social Psychology, 51*, 493–504.

Morse, S., & Gergen, K. J. (1970). Social comparison, self-consistency, and the concept of self. *Journal of Personality and Social Psychology, 16*(1), 148–156.

Mussweiler, T. (2001a). "Seek and ye shall find": Antecedents of assimilation and contrast in social comparison. *European Journal of Social Psychology, 31*, 499–509.

Mussweiler, T. (2001b). Focus of comparison as a determinant of assimilation versus contrast in social comparison. *Personality and Social Psychology Bulletin, 27*, 38–47.

Mussweiler, T. (2003). Comparison processes in social judgment: Mechanisms and consequences. *Psychological Review, 110*, 472–489.

Mussweiler, T., & Bodenhausen, G. (2002). I know you are but what am I? Self-evaluative consequences of judging ingroup and outgroup members. *Journal of Personality and Social Psychology, 82*, 19–32.

Mussweiler, T., & Englich, B. (2005). Subliminal anchoring: Judgmental consequences and underlying mechanisms. *Organizational Behavior and Human Decision Processes, 98*, 133–143.

Mussweiler, T., & Neumann, R. (2000). Sources of mental contamination: Comparing the effects of self-generated versus externally-provided primes. *Journal of Experimental Social Psychology, 36*, 194–206.

Mussweiler, T., & Rüter, K. (2003). What friends are for! The use of routine standards in social comparison. *Journal of Personality and Social Psychology, 85*, 467–481.

Mussweiler, T., Rüter, K., & Epstude, K. (2004a). The man who wasn't there: Subliminal social comparison standards influence self-evaluation. *Journal of Experimental Social Psychology, 40*, 689–696.

Mussweiler, T., Rüter, K., & Epstude, K. (2004b). The ups and downs of social comparison: Mechanisms of assimilation and contrast. *Journal of Personality and Social Psychology, 87*, 832–844.

Mussweiler, T., & Strack, F. (1999). Hypothesis-consistent testing and semantic priming in the anchoring paradigm: A selective accessibility model. *Journal of Experimental Social Psychology, 35*, 136–164.

Mussweiler, T., & Strack, F. (2000a). The "relative self": Informational and judgmental consequences of comparative self-evaluation. *Journal of Personality and Social Psychology*, 79, 23–38.

Mussweiler, T., & Strack, F. (2000b). Consequences of social comparison: Selective accessibility, assimilation, and contrast. In J. Suls & L. Wheeler (Eds.), *Handbook of social comparison: Theory and research* (pp. 253–270). New York: Plenum.

Mussweiler, T., & Strack, F. (2000c). The use of category and exemplar knowledge in the solution of anchoring tasks. *Journal of Personality and Social Psychology*, 78, 1038–1052.

Neumann, R., & Strack, F. (2000). "Mood contagion": The automatic transfer of mood between persons. *Journal of Personality and Social Psychology*, 79, 211–223.

Pelham, B. W., & Wachsmuth, J. O. (1995). The waxing and waning of the social self: Assimilation and contrast in social comparison. *Journal of Personality and Social Psychology*, 69(5), 825–838.

Philippot, P., Schwarz, N., Carrera, P., de Vries, N., & van Yperen, N. W. (1991). Differential effects of priming at the encoding and judgment stage. *European Journal of Social Psychology*, 21, 293–302.

Sanbonmatsu, D. M., Posavac, S. S., Kardes, F. R., & Mantel, S. P. (1998). Selective hypothesis testing. *Psychonomic Bulletin and Review*, 5, 197–220.

Schwarz, N., & Bless, H. (1992). Constructing reality and its alternatives: An inclusion/exclusion model of assimilation and contrast effects in social judgment. In H. Martin & A. Tesser (Eds.), *The construction of social judgment* (pp. 217–245). Hillsdale, NJ: Lawrence Erlbaum Associates, Inc.

Smeesters, D., & Mandel, N. (2006). Positive and negative media effects on the self. *Journal of Consumer Research*, 32, 576–582.

Smith, E. E., Shoben, E. J., & Rips, L. J. (1974). Structure and process in semantic memory: A featural model for semantic decisions. *Psychological Review*, 81, 214–241.

Smith, E. R. (1994). Procedural knowledge and processing strategies in social cognition. In R. S. Wyer & T. K. Srull (Eds.), *Handbook of social cognition* (2nd ed., Vol. 1, pp. 99–152). Hillsdale, NJ: Lawrence Erlbaum Associates, Inc.

Snyder, M., & Swann, W. B. (1978). Hypothesis-testing processes in social interaction. *Journal of Personality and Social Psychology*, 36, 1202–1212.

Stapel, D., & Koomen, W. (2001). Let's not forget the past when we go to the future: On our knowledge of knowledge accessibility effects. In G. Moswoitz (Ed.), *Cognitive social psychology: The Princeton symposium on the legacy and future of social cognition* (pp. 229–246). Mahwah, NJ: Lawrence Erlbaum Associates, Inc.

Stapel, D., & Koomen, W. (2005). Competition, cooperation and the effects of others on me. *Journal of Personality and Social Psychology*, 88, 1029–1038.

Stapel, D., Koomen, W., & van der Pligt, J. (1997). Categories of category accessibility: The impact of trait versus exemplar priming on person judgments. *Journal of Experimental Social Psychology*, 33, 44–76.

Stapel, D., & Suls, J. (2004). Method matters: Effects of explicit versus implicit social comparisons on activation, behaviour and self-views. *Journal of Personality and Social Psychology*, 87, 860–875.

Strack, F. (1992). The different routes to social judgments: Experiential versus informational strategies. In L. L. Martin & A. Tesser (Eds.), *The construction of social judgment* (pp. 249–275). Hillsdale, NJ: Lawrence Erlbaum Associates, Inc.

Suls, J., Martin, R., &. Wheeler, L. (2002). Social comparison: Why, with whom, and with what effect? *Current Directions in Psychological Science*, 11, 159–163.

Trope, Y., & Bassok, M. (1982). Confirmatory and diagnostic strategies in social information gathering. *Journal of Personality and Social Psychology*, 43, 22–34.

Trope, Y., & Liberman, A. (1996). Social hypothesis testing: Cognitive and motivational factors. In E. T. Higgins & A. W. Kruglanski (Eds.), *Social psychology: Handbook of basic principles* (pp. 239–270). New York: Guilford Press.

Tversky, A., & Kahneman, D. (1974). Judgment under uncertainty: Heuristics and biases. *Science, 185*, 1124–1130.

Wegener, D. T., & Petty, R. E. (1997). The flexible correction model: The role of naive theories of bias in bias correction. In M. P. Zanna (Ed.), *Advances in experimental social psychology* (Vol. 29, pp. 141–208). San Diego, CA: Academic Press.

Wilson, T. D., & Brekke, N. (1994). Mental contamination and mental correction: Unwanted influences on judgments and evaluations. *Psychological Bulletin, 116*, 117–142.

Wilson, T. D., Houston, C., Etling, K. M., & Brekke, N. (1996). A new look at anchoring effects: Basic anchoring and its antecedents. *Journal of Experimental Psychology: General, 4*, 387–402.

Wyer, R. S., & Srull, T. K. (1989). *Memory and cognition in its social context*. Hillsdale, NJ: Lawrence Erlbaum Associates, Inc.

8

Assimilation and Contrast in Counterfactual Thinking and Other Mental Simulation-Based Comparison Processes

KEITH D. MARKMAN, JENNIFER J. RATCLIFF,
NOBUKO MIZOGUCHI, RONALD A. ELIZAGA, and
MATTHEW N. McMULLEN

*I*n the film *It's a Wonderful Life* (1946), George Bailey (played by James Stewart) is feeling suicidal after misplacing an $8,000 loan. To save him, Clarence, his guardian angel, gives him an opportunity to see how his prosperous town of Bedford Falls would have turned out if he had never been born. George learns that if he had not been born, his wife Mary would have instead become a bitter old maid, and Bedford Falls would have become run-down because the family-owned Bailey Loan Company would have gone out of business. Realizing that he meant so much to a great many people, George decides not to throw his life away.

Although it is rare for individuals to be provided with the opportunity to see what would have happened if a different decision had been made or, more dramatically, if they had never lived at all, it is nevertheless very common for people to reflect upon selves that could be, would be, could have been, and should have been.

Thinking about and comparing oneself to standards, be they real or imagined, evokes a powerful array of emotions and impacts the nature of self-evaluations. Some of these responses are *contrastive* in nature, in that they are displaced away from a comparison standard, whereas others are *assimilative* in nature, in that they are pulled toward a comparison standard. The goal of this chapter is to examine when and how *mental simulation*—the consideration of alternatives to present reality—produces emotional responses that reflect either contrast or assimilation. We will begin by examining the comparison domain that is most commonly associated with mental simulation—counterfactual thinking—after which we will broaden our focus by considering how mental simulation may play a pivotal role in determining assimilative and contrastive responses to other types of comparisons. Finally, we will advance a model of mental simulation-based comparison processes and situate it within the context of other currently prevailing comparison models.

CONTRAST EFFECTS IN COUNTERFACTUAL THINKING

Since the publication of Kahneman and Tversky's (1982) seminal chapter on the simulation heuristic, the vast majority of research on counterfactual thinking has focused on the contrastive nature of cognitive and emotional responses to counterfactuals. Norm theory (Kahneman & Miller, 1986), the guiding theoretical formulation for the bulk of social psychological research on counterfactual thinking (Roese & Olson, 1995), focuses on the perceived discrepancy between an outcome and a judgmental (i.e., counterfactual) standard. Thus, for instance, the comparison between a student's B on an exam and the A that the student would have liked to attain elicits disappointment. The innovation of norm theory over previous social judgment formulations (e.g., Helson's, 1964, adaptation level theory; Thibaut & Kelley's, 1959, comparison level theory) was the assertion that judgmental standards, or norms, may be constructed online in response to specific outcomes. Although norms are constructed, in part, from beliefs and expectancies derived from past experience, the particular character of each norm is, as Roese and Olson (1995) describe it, "reconstructed uniquely in light of a specific outcome" (p. 7). According to norm theory, abnormal outcomes are those that evoke norms that differ from the outcome and are, thus, counterfactual in nature. When mutable or changeable aspects of events (e.g., magnitude of effort, voluntary actions, or decisions) precede an outcome, it becomes easy to imagine how the outcome could have been different, and thus the outcome will be perceived as abnormal. On the other hand, when more immutable and less changeable aspects of events (e.g., abilities, physical laws) precede an outcome, it becomes more difficult to imagine how the outcome could have been different, and thus the outcome will be perceived as normal.

Contrastive Effects on Judgments

Counterfactual thinking has been shown to have implications for a variety of social judgments, including expressions of sympathy and blame. For instance, Miller and McFarland (1986) found that thinking about how a victim's misfortune could easily have been avoided made the outcome seem more poignant, thereby causing people to feel more sympathy for the victim and recommend a higher level of monetary compensation. In kind, Davis, Lehman, Silver, Wortman, and Ellard (1996) found that the more that victims of spinal cord injuries believed they could have avoided their accident, the more they blamed themselves for having caused the accident.

Counterfactual thinking also influences judgments of causality (e.g., Cheng & Novick, 1990; Hilton & Slugoski, 1986; Lipe, 1991). For instance, Wells and Gavanski (1989) hypothesized that an event will be judged as having caused an outcome if the alternative event that most readily comes to mind successfully undoes that outcome. In one of their experiments, a woman was described as having died from an allergic reaction to a meal ordered by her boss. When the boss was described as having considered ordering another meal without the allergic ingredient, his causal role in her death was judged to be greater than when the alternative meal was also described as having had the allergic ingredient.

Contrastive Effects on Affect

Regret is a negative emotion that derives from imagining how one's present situation would have or could have been better (for a review, see Connolly & Zeelenberg, 2002), and Kahneman and Miller (1986) suggested that emotions such as regret and disappointment derive from counterfactual inferences. Moreover, such "counterfactual emotions" may be differentiated on the basis of the types of antecedents that are mutated. For instance, Niedenthal, Tangney, and Gavanski (1994) showed that the experience of shame relies upon counterfactual inferences that mutate characterological aspects of the self (e.g., "If only I were a more honest person . . ."), whereas guilt is engendered by counterfactual inferences that mutate one's behavior (e.g., "If only I had listened to her more closely . . .").

Upward and Downward Counterfactual Thinking
Researchers (e.g., Markman, Gavanski, Sherman, & McMullen, 1993; McMullen, Markman, & Gavanski, 1995; Roese, 1994) have also classified counterfactuals on the basis of their direction of comparison. Borrowing a theoretical distinction drawn in the social comparison literature between upward and downward comparisons (e.g., Collins, 1996; Taylor, Buunk, & Aspinwall, 1990; Wood, 1989), researchers classified counterfactuals into those that construct imagined alternatives that are evaluatively better than reality (i.e., *upward* counterfactuals) and those that are evaluatively worse than reality (i.e., *downward* counterfactuals).

To empirically demonstrate contrastive emotional responses following the generation of upward and downward counterfactuals, Markman et al. (1993) employed a computer-simulated blackjack game that examined the spontaneous generation of counterfactuals within the context of two factors—outcome valence and event repeatability. Negative and repeatable outcomes evoked a greater tendency to engage in upward than downward counterfactual thinking and, in turn, upward counterfactuals heightened feelings of dissatisfaction (see also McMullen et al., 1995). In addition, Roese (1994) induced participants to consider either upward or downward counterfactuals about a recent life event. Those who generated upward counterfactuals subsequently reported more negative affect than those who generated downward counterfactuals.

Medvec and her colleagues have provided particularly compelling demonstrations of counterfactual contrast. In observations of Olympic athletes, Medvec, Madey, and Gilovich (1995) found that silver medalists actually experienced less satisfaction with their achievement than did bronze medallists, presumably because the former were focused on not having won the gold medal (i.e., an upward counterfactual), whereas the latter were focused on the possibility of not having won a medal at all (i.e., a downward counterfactual). Similarly, Medvec and

Savitsky (1997) found more negative affect expressed by students who nearly attained a cutoff point (i.e., a grade of 89%), than by students who just barely attained a cutoff point (i.e., a grade of 87%). According to Medvec et al., proximity to category boundaries draws attention to counterfactual outcomes, thereby eliciting contrastive effects on subsequent affective responses (see also Mellers, Schwartz, Ho, & Ritov, 1997)

Affective Assimilation   Up to this point, a survey of the counterfactual thinking literature would indicate that affective contrast is the norm: Upward counterfactuals always produce negative affect, whereas downward counterfactuals always produce positive affect. Recently, however, this assumption has been strongly challenged (e.g., Markman & Tetlock, 2000; McMullen, 1997; McMullen & Markman, 2000, 2002). To illustrate, consider the case of flight attendant Kim Stroka, who claimed that she was too distraught to return to work after her co-worker died on United Airlines Flight 93, which was hijacked after taking off from Newark Liberty International Airport en route to San Francisco on September 11, 2001. Stroka had apparently traded shifts with her co-worker and, thus, would have died instead of her colleague if she had worked her normal shift. Claiming that she was having difficulty eating and sleeping and that she was being treated by a psychologist for posttraumatic stress disorder, Stroka applied for medical and disability payments but was turned down by the state appellate court. According to the court, Stroka was not entitled to the award because, "nothing happened while she was working which led to her current condition" (Associated Press Online, 2003).

Clearly, Kim Stroka is reflecting on a downward counterfactual. She did not die, but she can easily imagine how she could have died—indeed, she *would* have died. Just as clearly, however, generating this downward counterfactual has not made her feel any better. Instead, her consideration of the downward counterfactual world engenders feelings of sadness, guilt, and fear. The Stroka case helps us make the more general point that although contrast-based affective reactions to counterfactuals are common, they are hardly the rule. Rather, Stroka's downward counterfactual is assimilative in nature, in that her affective experience has been pulled toward the counterfactual standard. In the next section, we will discuss the important aspects of a model that attempts to explain how the very same counterfactual can engender dramatically different affective reactions. According to the model, assimilative versus contrastive responses to upward and downward comparisons are mediated by *simulation mode*—the extent to which one is engaging in *reflective* versus *evaluative* processing.

THE REFLECTION AND EVALUATION MODEL OF COMPARATIVE THINKING

Inclusion/Exclusion

In an effort to define a coherent set of principles that explain when assimilation and contrast effects occur in social comparison, Stapel and Koomen (2000, 2001;

see also Blanton, 2001) suggested that comparison is more likely to lead to assimilation when this information is "included in," or perceived as part of one's self-construal, whereas contrast is more likely when such inclusion processes do not occur (Gardner, Gabriel, & Hochschild, 2002; Schwarz & Bless, 1992). Thus, contextual features such as closeness/low relevance (Tesser, 1988), controllability (Major, Testa, & Bylsma, 1991), attainability (Lockwood & Kunda, 1997), and similarity (Brown, Novick, Lord, & Richards, 1992), all produce assimilation effects because they encourage the inclusion of social comparison information in self-construals. Conversely, Stapel and Koomen suggest that comparison information is more likely to be excluded from the self to the extent that the information is perceived to be distinct and the self is perceived to be immutable, with contrast effects being the likely result.

The inclusion/exclusion mechanism can also be used to understand how assimilation and contrast effects arise in temporal and counterfactual comparisons. Regarding the former, Strack, Schwarz, and Gschneidinger (1985) found that recalling long-past events elicited a contrast effect on judgments of well-being, and recalling very recent events elicited an assimilation effect. Schwarz and Bless (1992) later argued that long-past events are excluded from one's construal of *my life now*, and thus exert contrast effects on judgments of one's present standing, whereas recent events are included in one's construal of *my life now* and, thus, exert assimilation effects. Likewise, McMullen (1997) suggested that the inclusion of information about the counterfactual standard in self-construals should produce assimilation effects (e.g., "To think . . . I could have been on that plane"), whereas the exclusion of such information should produce contrast effects (e.g., "If I had been on that plane [but I was not], I would have been killed").

Reflective and Evaluative Modes of Mental Simulation

The Reflection and Evaluation Model (REM) of comparative thinking (Markman & McMullen, 2003, 2005) was developed in order to provide an organizing framework for understanding how assimilation and contrast effects arise following counterfactual, social, and temporal comparisons. At the heart of the model is the assertion that two psychologically distinct modes of mental simulation operate during comparative thinking. The first of these modes is *reflection*, an experiential ("as if") mode of thinking whereby one vividly simulates that information about the comparison standard is true of, or is part of, oneself or one's present standing. The second of these modes is *evaluation*, whereby the outcome of a mental simulation run is used as a reference point against which to evaluate oneself or one's present standing.

Figure 8.1 depicts the interaction between simulation direction and simulation mode. To illustrate with a counterfactual thinking example, consider the student who receives a B on an exam but realizes that an A was easily attainable with some additional studying. In the case of upward evaluation (UE), the student switches attention between the outcome (a grade of B) and the counterfactual standard (a grade of A). According to the REM, such attentional switching ("I got a B . . . I could have gotten an A but instead I got a B") involves using the standard as a reference point and thereby instigates evaluative processing. In the case of upward reflection (UR), however, the student's attention is focused mainly on the counterfactual itself. Focusing on the counterfactual instigates reflective processing whereby the student considers the implications of the counterfactual and temporarily experiences the counterfactual as if it were real ("What if I had actually gotten an A?"). In a sense, the student is "transported" into the counterfactual world (Green & Brock, 2000; Kahneman, 1995). Likewise, consider the case of a driver who pulls away from the curb without carefully checking rear and side-view mirrors, and subsequently slams on the brakes as a large truck whizzes by. In the case of downward evaluation (DE), the driver switches attention between the counterfactual standard (being hit by the truck) and the outcome (not being hit by the truck), thereby instigating evaluative processing ("I was fortunate to not have been hit by that truck"). In the case of downward reflection (DR), however, the driver's attention is mainly focused on the counterfactual itself, thereby instigating reflective processing ("I nearly got hit by that truck") (see Figure 8.1).

Accessibility Mechanism

Reflective and evaluative processing of counterfactuals yield predictable affective reactions and, according to the model, this is accomplished through an accessibility mechanism. Recent work by Mussweiler and his associates (e.g., Mussweiler, 2003; Mussweiler, Rüter, & Epstude, 2004; Mussweiler & Strack, 2000) within the social comparison domain suggests that comparative self-evaluation produces two informational consequences. First, comparing oneself to a given standard increases the accessibility of standard-consistent knowledge about the self. Thus, upward comparisons render knowledge indicating a high standard of the self more accessible, whereas downward comparisons render knowledge indicating a low standard of the self more accessible. Secondly, comparative self-evaluation provides a reference point against which the implications of this knowledge can be evaluated.

In a similar vein, counterfactual comparisons can also yield two informational consequences. First, making counterfactual comparisons should enhance the

Mode

Direction	Reflection	Evaluation
Upward	"I almost got an A"	"I got a B...I failed to get an A"
Downward	"I nearly got hit by that truck"	"I was fortunate to not have been hit by that truck"

FIGURE 8.1   The interaction between simulation direction and mode.

accessibility of cognitions about the self that are evaluatively consistent with the counterfactual standard. In turn, affect should be derived from thoughts about the standard that implicate the self, thereby yielding affective assimilation (Schwarz & Clore, 1983; Strack et al., 1985). To illustrate, consider an individual who learns that the aircraft she had originally planned to take had crashed with everyone on board killed. Simulating the counterfactual possibility, "I could have been on that plane" (DR), renders standard-consistent cognitions about the self more accessible (e.g., "I could be dead," "I would never have been able to see my family again," "I would never have been able to accomplish what I wanted to in life"), and reflecting on these accessible cognitions produces counterfactual-congruent (in this case, negative) affect. On the other hand, employing the counterfactual as a standard against which to evaluate reality (DE) produces positive affect via a contrast effect: "I'm lucky to be alive." Notably, then, the relationship between simulation mode and the accessibility mechanism is of critical importance: Reflective and evaluative modes of mental simulation both activate and enhance the operation of the accessibility mechanism. The more vivid the simulation (cf. Strack et al., 1985), and the easier it is to engage in the simulation (Sherman, Cialdini, Schwartzman, & Reynolds, 1985), the greater will be the accessibility of self-implicating cognitions and, thus, the stronger will be the emotional experience derived from engaging in the comparison.

More generally, the notion that the very same counterfactual can produce both assimilative and contrastive reactions has intriguing implications for affective experience, as it may be that the mixed emotions (Larsen, McGraw, and Cacioppo, 2001) that are often felt after events such as switching from the doomed plane flight are the result of reflective and evaluative modes of mental simulation operating in parallel (cf. Biernat & Manis, 1994; Biernat, Manis, & Kobrynowicz, 1997; Mussweiler, 2003; see also Markman & McMullen, 2003, for a more detailed discussion of this issue). In this way, one may feel fortunate to be alive, yet deeply troubled by thoughts of what might have been.

INCLUSION/ EXCLUSION FEATURES

This section examines contextual features that promote inclusion and exclusion and thereby instigate reflection and evaluation. The variables described in this section are not meant to be an exhaustive list of all potential features. Rather, we have chosen several variables to focus on that offer suggestive evidence of the operation of reflective and evaluative modes of mental simulation.

Attentional Focus

The most straightforward inclusion/exclusion feature we have identified is attentional focus. According to the REM, focusing attention solely on the comparison standard itself should encourage inclusion of the counterfactual standard in self-construals, thereby instigating reflective processing that produces assimilation effects, whereas focusing attention on the explicit comparison between one's present standing and the comparison standard should encourage the exclusion of the counterfactual standard from self-construals, thereby instigating evaluative processing that produces contrast effects.

Empirical Evidence McMullen (1997, Study 1) instructed participants to recall a somewhat negative event in their own lives and imagine how the event could have turned out better or worse than it actually did. In order to manipulate simulation mode, participants in the reflection condition were then instructed to "vividly imagine what might have happened instead," whereas those in the evaluation condition were instructed to "evaluate what happened in comparison to what could have happened." Participants in both conditions then described their thoughts in writing and reported their mood. Content analyses performed on the written responses indicated that participants in the evaluation condition did indeed show more evidence of evaluative comparison in their responses, whereas those in the reflection condition showed more evidence of reflective experiencing. Furthermore, participants in the reflection condition reported more positive affect after making upward counterfactuals and negative affect after making downward counterfactuals (assimilation), whereas in the evaluation condition participants reported more negative affect after making upward counterfactuals and positive affect after making downward counterfactuals (contrast).

These results indicate that contrast is neither the only nor necessarily the most likely consequence of counterfactual thinking. That prior research had reported a preponderance of contrast effects was probably due to the nature of the scenarios employed. In previous research, participants read about an individual who experienced a particularly striking negative outcome and were then made aware that the outcome could have been avoided if the normal routine had been followed. In such a situation, what is salient is not the counterfactual, but the factual event, and thus attention is likely focused upon it. The critical point, however, is that salient occurrences such as violations of expectancies and changes in the status quo may occur in either the factual *or* the counterfactual world, and where they occur determines attentional focus. Consider, then, the distinction between "he *could have been killed* but was not" versus "he *was killed* but it could have been avoided." In the former, attention is focused upon what could have happened, and thus assimilation is more likely, whereas in the latter, attention is focused upon what actually happened, and thus contrast is more likely.

Temporal Perspective

The previously described studies by Medvec and her colleagues that demonstrated affective contrast in response to close-call counterfactuals focused exclusively on *final* outcomes—Medvec and Savitsky (1997) examined students' perceptions of their final semester grades, and Medvec et al. (1995) examined reactions to medals awarded to athletes after the competition was over. Yet, relatively few of the outcomes people experience in their lives are actually final. Rather, students receive individual grades throughout the semester, and athletes spend a great deal of time training in preparation for final events. From the perspective of the

REM, close upward counterfactuals following repeatable outcomes suggest that better possibilities are easily attainable (e.g., "I almost did it; I will do it next time"), whereas close downward counterfactuals suggest a vulnerability to worse possibilities (e.g., "I nearly failed; I could fail next time").

McMullen and Markman (2002) hypothesized that reflective thinking would more likely be elicited by the presence of clear future possibilities, as when a student has received feedback on a midterm exam and is thinking about future exams, whereas evaluative thinking would be more likely when future possibilities are absent, as when a student has received a final grade in a course, or when an athlete has competed in the final event of a competition. In their study, participants read descriptions of a basketball game from the perspective of a fan of one of the two teams. Participants either read an account of the first half of the basketball game (*future outcome* condition) or the second half of the game (*final outcome* condition), after which they reported their affect regarding the outcome of the game. Affective contrast effects were obtained in the *final outcome* condition: Being a fan of the losing team felt better if the second half was a blowout (15-point difference) compared to a close game (1-point difference), and being a fan of the winning team felt better if the second half was close compared to a blowout. On the other hand, however, the *future outcome* condition yielded an affective assimilation effect: At halftime, fans of the team that was down by 1 point actually felt *better* than fans of the team that was up by 1 point.

Feedback Dynamics

Recent work conducted in our lab (Markman, Elizaga, Ratcliff, & McMullen, in press) has explored a variable termed "feedback dynamics." At times, individuals receive outcome feedback in a vacuum. For instance, a student may receive an "89" on an exam without having previously received grades on any of the other exams in that course. This feedback experience is "static" in the sense that it does not occur within the context of other feedback experiences. Alternatively, a student may receive an "89" on an exam in a course after having received outcome feedback on two previous exams (e.g., an "85" and an "87"). This feedback experience is "dynamic" in the sense that it *is* preceded by a prior series of outcomes that may provide additional context for evaluating the most recent feedback (cf. Roese & Olson, 1995). In this case, the experience of receiving three increasingly higher scores may imbue one with a sense of "momentum"—that one is on a trajectory toward receiving higher exam scores in the future.

According to Kahneman and Varey (1990), propensities "indicate advance toward the focal outcome, or regression away from it" (p. 1105), and it is this perception of dynamic and accelerating movement toward a win or loss that may trigger counterfactuals such as, "We almost won," or "We nearly blew it" (see also Hsee, Salovey, & Abelson, 1994). According to the REM, to the extent that individuals perceive themselves to be on a trajectory toward either a desired or undesired end-state, assimilation should occur as a direct consequence of reflection (via inclusion of the comparison standard). Thus, comparisons to an upward counterfactual outcome should elicit positive affect and cognitions, whereas comparisons to a downward counterfactual outcome should elicit negative affect and cognitions. On the other hand, outcomes that are perceived as static should evoke contrast as a direct consequence of evaluation (via exclusion of the comparison standard). Thus, upward counterfactuals should elicit negative affect and cognitions, whereas downward counterfactuals should elicit positive affect and cognitions.

Recent work on stereotyping and social comparison (e.g., Biernat & Manis, 1994; Biernat et al., 1997; Mussweiler & Strack, 2000) has noted distinctions between making judgments along either subjective or objective response scales. These studies suggest that subjective scales can produce contrast effects if judges use salient standards to anchor the response scale. Objective scales, conversely, sometimes produce assimilation effects if the underlying response scale requires no interpretation by the judge. In such cases, judgments may be based on the implications of accessible self-knowledge (Mussweiler & Strack, 2000). Markman et al. (in press) hypothesized that feedback dynamics would affect the processing of counterfactuals such that dynamic feedback would evoke reflection upon the counterfactual, whereas static feedback would evoke evaluation of the counterfactual in light of the actual outcome, and that these effects would be moderated by judgment type—whether the judgment in question was made along a subjective versus objective response scale.

Empirical Evidence   Participants in the Markman et al. (in press) study engaged in an analogy-solving task that purported to be a measure of verbal intelligence. After learning that they needed to attain a particular target score in order to be eligible for a prize, participants completed the task and experienced one of four types of feedback. Participants in the upward condition learned that they just barely missed the target score, whereas those in the downward condition learned that they just barely attained the target score. Furthermore, participants in the static condition received this feedback in the absence of any prior feedback, whereas participants in the dynamic condition received this feedback after having received feedback on five previous occasions that conformed to either an ascending (upward) or descending (downward) pattern. After receiving feedback, participants were instructed to write down any "if only" or "what if" thoughts that came to mind about their performance. Finally, participants provided perceptions of their own levels of verbal intelligence on both a subjective ("How verbally intelligent do you take yourself to be?") and objective ("If you were given 30 analogies to solve like the ones you just completed, how many could you correctly answer in 15 minutes?") measure (Mussweiler & Strack, 2000).

Based on the results of social judgment studies that have indicated that objective measures can sometimes elicit assimilation effects (e.g., Mussweiler & Strack, 2000), a main effect of counterfactual direction was predicted—upward counterfactuals should elicit higher self-perceptions of verbal intelligence than should downward counterfactuals. In turn, although social judgment work has indicated that subjective measures will sometimes elicit contrast effects, other findings have indicated that counterfactuals generated following outcomes that convey a sense of trajectory will tend to elicit assimilation effects (Kahneman & Varey, 1990;

Markman & Tetlock, 2000). For instance, employing a computer simulation in which monthly stock investment outcomes were slowly revealed in a manner that evoked perceptions of "nearly winning" and "nearly losing," Markman and Tetlock (2000) observed abundant evidence for assimilation effects and little evidence for contrast effects. On subjective ratings, then, it was predicted that the dynamic conditions should elicit assimilative judgments (i.e., higher ratings in the upward relative to the downward conditions), whereas the static conditions should elicit contrastive judgments (i.e., lower ratings in the upward relative to the downward conditions).

The results conformed to predictions. First, the objective measure yielded the predicted direction main effect—participants in the upward conditions predicted that they would answer more items correctly than did those in the downward conditions.

The subjective measure, on the other hand, yielded the predicted Direction × Feedback dynamic interaction. Whereas participants in the upward/dynamic condition perceived themselves as being higher in verbal intelligence than did those in the downward/dynamic condition, participants in the upward/static condition perceived themselves as being lower in verbal intelligence than did those in the downward/static condition (see Figure 8.2).

Dissociations Between Affect and Expectations   One of the more intriguing findings in the Markman et al. (in press) study concerns the assimilative effect of comparison direction on expectations regarding future performance (i.e., the objective measure). Building on this result, we speculate that even in

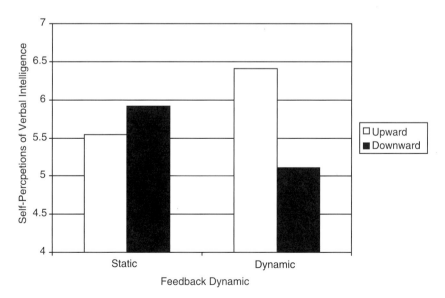

FIGURE 8.2   Self-perceptions of verbal intelligence as a function of direction and feedback dynamics.

cases where counterfactuals elicit affective contrast, the set of expectations regarding future performance and outcomes that also derive from the counterfactual (cf. Roese, 1997) may nevertheless assimilate to the standard. Essentially, counterfactual generation may *change the standard* by which future performance and outcomes are evaluated (cf. Biernat, 2003). Thus, although upward counterfactual thinking (e.g., "I got a B . . . if only I had gotten an A") may engender negative affect via contrast, the standard, simultaneously, may also be raised—via cognitive assimilation, the individual has become a potential A student. Similarly, although downward counterfactual thinking (e.g., "At least I didn't get a C") may engender positive affect via contrast, the standard may also be lowered—the individual has become a C student who was lucky to have obtained a B.

Anecdotally, we have made note of the generation of these types of counterfactual comparisons in television and newspaper media during discussions of the recent Abu Ghraib prison scandal involving American soldiers accused of torturing Iraqi prisoners. Some commentators have noted that although the torture that occurred at Abu Ghraib was certainly heinous, the prisoners who were tortured there would nevertheless have had it much worse if (former Iraqi president) Saddam Hussein had imprisoned them instead. This type of (downward) comparison has the odd effect of both mitigating the perceived cruelty of the American soldiers' actions (via affective contrast), while at the same time lowering the standards by which the United States and its allies are expected to behave toward prisoners of war in the future (via cognitive assimilation). Research is presently under way to examine possible dissociative effects of counterfactual generation on affect and expectations.

MENTAL SIMULATION-BASED COMPARISON PROCESSES

REM Versus SAM

Mussweiler (2003; Mussweiler et al., 2004; Mussweiler & Strack, 2000) has advanced a theoretical framework that specifies how assimilation and contrast effects arise in comparisons. According to the Selective Accessibility Model (SAM), testing the hypothesis "I am similar to the standard" heightens the accessibility of standard-consistent knowledge such that self-evaluations will be assimilated toward the standard. Conversely, testing the hypothesis "I am different from the standard" heightens the accessibility of standard-inconsistent knowledge such that self-evaluations will be contrasted away from the standard.

Although empirical evidence for the SAM has been garnered within the domain of social comparisons, Mussweiler (2003) has also suggested that the similarity-testing mechanism should account for assimilation and contrast effects in all types of comparisons. However, although similarity testing may indeed account for some social comparison phenomena, we believe that this mechanism is substantially less useful for explaining how assimilation and contrast effects arise in counterfactual thinking. To illustrate, consider the student who just misses receiving a final grade of "A" in a class by a tenth of a percentage point. If the similarity-testing mechanism were applied, then the student would presumably arrive at the conclusion that her 89.4 was very similar to the 89.5 that she could have received and thus given her an A for the semester. According to the SAM, testing for similarity in this case should engender assimilation, thereby leading the student to feel good about her 89.4. Our intuitions, however, suggest that the very opposite would occur. The student would probably feel quite frustrated, bemoaning the fact that she "just missed" getting an A. In fact, we would argue that the similarity of the real grade to the imagined grade has actually played a role in giving rise to the student's feelings of frustration (i.e., via affective contrast).

In our view, similarity testing has a difficult time accounting for both the assimilative *and* contrastive consequences of close-call counterfactuals; by definition, closeness evokes counterfactual thinking by virtue of the proximity (i.e., similarity) of the actual outcome to the counterfactual standard. Although similarity may play a critical role in the *activation* of counterfactual thinking (Roese & Olson, 1995, 1997), other contextual features, such as attentional focus, temporal perspective, or feedback dynamics, may be more crucial determinants of whether the reaction to any given counterfactual will be assimilative versus contrastive in nature, as such variables instigate reflective and evaluative processing. Moreover, the results of the Markman et al. (in press) analogy-solving study provide empirical support for the notion that reflective and evaluative modes of mental simulation directly influence the elicitation of assimilation and contrast effects. The key distinction between the SAM and the REM, then, centers on the mechanism that each model specifies to be underlying assimilation and contrast effects. Whereas the SAM champions similarity testing as the critical underlying mechanism, the REM focuses instead on the role of mental simulation.

We further question the generality of the similarity-testing mechanism because some social comparison phenomena are not easily amenable to a similarity-as-mediator account. A particularly illustrative example is Lockwood and Kunda's (1997) work on role models. In Study 2, these researchers exposed first-year and fourth-year accounting students to a description of a spectacular graduating student who had majored in accounting. Lockwood and Kunda reasoned that because the achievements of the graduating superstar would seem attainable to first-year students whose university careers still lay ahead and for whom any level of accomplishment would seem within reach, these students would be inspired by comparisons to the star and thus evaluate themselves more positively relative to a no-target control group. Conversely, because the achievements of the superstar would seem unattainable to fourth-year students for whom it was already too late to achieve a similar level of success, it was predicted that these students would be discouraged by comparisons with the star and thus evaluate themselves more negatively relative to a control group. The data conformed to predictions. Moreover and, importantly, *subsequent* to providing their self-evaluations, participants rated the extent to which the star was relevant to them for the purpose of comparison. The results revealed that fourth-year students rated the target as less relevant than did the first-year students.

Based, in part, on these relevance ratings, Mussweiler (2003) asserted that the similarity-testing mechanism accounts for Lockwood and Kunda's (1997) effects. Thus, assimilation was engendered by similarity testing (i.e., first-year students believed that the star was a relevant comparison target), whereas contrast was engendered by dissimilarity testing (i.e., fourth-year students did not believe that the star was a relevant comparison target). Arguably, however, the relevance ratings did not reflect participants' *initial* perceptions of similarity to the target. Rather, because the relevance ratings were made *after* participants had already evaluated themselves, it is likely that these ratings were reflective of a *defensive* reaction to the deflating comparison. Simply put, we find it implausible that fourth-year students could have perceived themselves to be less similar to the superstar than did first-year students and would argue instead that they perceived themselves to be as similar, if not more similar, than did the first-year students. If this were the case, then a similarity-testing mechanism would have predicted assimilation, and not contrast, for fourth-year students. From our perspective, alternatively, the deflating consequences of comparison to the superstar derived from initial perceptions of similarity to the target ("I am at the same stage of my career as this student"), coupled with subsequent perceptions of unattainability ("I cannot see myself succeeding at the level of this student"). According to Lockwood and Kunda, attainability

> illustrates the wonderful heights of accomplishment one can hope to achieve, encourages and motivates one to strive for this now all the more palpable success, indicates particular goals to aim for along the way, points to the road one should follow to achieve them, and makes one feel more competent and capable of such achievement. (p. 93)

Attainability, then, clearly involves some form of mental simulation. Moreover, we argue that it was the ease of engaging in mental simulation (Sherman et al., 1985), as opposed to similarity testing, that accounted for the obtained effects; perceptions of attainability encouraged inclusion and instigated reflective processing among first-year students, thereby eliciting assimilation effects, whereas perceptions of unattainability encouraged exclusion and instigated evaluative processing among fourth-year students, thereby eliciting contrast effects.

As a final illustration, consider Nike's "Be Like Mike" (i.e., NBA former player Michael Jordan) advertising campaign from a few years ago. Following the logic of similarity testing, most people should conclude that they are dissimilar to Jordan, thereby engendering contrast. However, the observation that children and adults alike pretend that they are "being like Mike" when they get on the basketball court indicates clearly that this is not what is happening. Instead, we argue that it is the act of reflecting on *what it would be like* to experience the success of Michael Jordan that enhances the accessibility of standard-consistent thoughts about the self—it is hardly necessary to test for similarity between the self and Michael Jordan in order to produce assimilation. In fact, testing the hypothesis that one is similar to Michael Jordan would simply highlight how dissimilar one is to him. Thus, the reflection process provides a better account of the "Be Like Mike" effect than does the similarity-testing mechanism.

Directive and Projective Social Comparisons   We believe that it is useful to draw a distinction between two types of social comparisons—*directive* and *projective*—that are primarily distinguishable by the specific mechanism that accounts for the assimilative versus contrastive consequences of each comparison type. Directive comparisons serve to diagnose one's present standing and abilities (Festinger, 1954) and can be further subdivided into global directive comparisons that require the matching of shared and unique features across multiple dimensions (e.g., "How much am I like him?"—see Hodges, Bruininks, & Ivy, 2002; Holyoak & Gordon, 1983; Tversky, 1977). Specific directive comparisons test for similarity along one dimension (e.g., "How intelligent am I in comparison to him?"). Such comparisons are fairly static, do not typically involve mental simulation processes, and exert only modest effects on emotional and motivational responses. In contrast, projective comparisons also serve a diagnostic function, but they do so through a process of mental simulation (e.g., "Could I ever be as good as her?," "What would it be like to be him for a day?") that heightens emotional responses and motivational concerns. The consequences of projective comparisons involving imagined alternatives to reality (e.g., Karniol & Ross, 1996; Klinger, 1990; Markman et al., 1993), past selves (e.g., Suls, Marco, & Tobin, 1991; Wilson & Ross, 2000, 2001), possible selves (e.g., Markus & Nurius, 1986; Oettingen, 1996; Taylor & Pham, 1996), positive and negative role models (e.g., Evans, 2003; Lockwood, Jordan, & Kunda, 2002; Marx, Stapel, & Muller, 2005), and a proxy's related attributes (e.g., Martin, Suls, & Wheeler, 2002) are all driven, at least to some degree, by mental simulation processes of one form or another. Overall, we speculate that the assimilative versus contrastive consequences of directive social comparisons are more likely mediated by similarity testing, whereas the consequences of projective social comparisons are more likely mediated by the extent to which reflective versus evaluative processing has been instigated.

Ease of Simulation as a Determinant of Responses to Projective Social Comparisons

An important direction for future work will be to examine the role of ease of simulation as a determinant of assimilative and contrastive responses to projective social comparisons. The role of simulation ease has been implicated in other types of social judgments. For instance, Sherman et al. (1985) found that the imaginability of a set of disease symptoms increased participants' ratings of the likelihood that they might contract the disease (see also Anderson, 1983; Carroll, 1978; Ross, Lepper, Strack, & Steinmetz, 1977). Hirt and Markman (1995) found that generating a plausible counterexplanation for an initial explanation of a future outcome effectively lowered participants' ratings of the likelihood of the initially explained future outcome, whereas generating an implausible counterexplanation failed to lower likelihood ratings of the initially explained outcome (see also Hirt, Kardes, & Markman, 2004; Koehler, 1991). A critical factor determining the nature of responses to projective social comparisons, then, should be the individual's perception that it was relatively easy versus difficult to construct a particular mental simulation (cf. Schwarz et al., 1991). Simulations perceived as easy to generate should encourage inclusion of comparison information in self-construals, whereas simulations perceived as difficult to generate should encourage exclusion.

CODA

The REM can be differentiated from other models of comparison processes by virtue of its guiding spirit—it focuses on the power of the imagination to alter our perceptions of present reality and our present selves, for better or for worse. The nature and vividness of the mental simulations we construct, as well as the ease with which we can conjure up these mental simulations, imbue counterfactual, social, and temporal comparisons with an emotional intensity that has consequences for motivation and behavior later on (see Markman & McMullen, 2005, for a more extensive discussion of the downstream consequences of mental simulation). We hope that the ideas presented in this chapter will stimulate further inquiries into how comparisons, and responses to comparisons, are impacted by thoughts of what was, what is, what could have been, and what yet could be.

REFERENCES

Anderson, C. A. (1983). Imagination and expectation: The effect of imagining behavioral scripts on personal intentions. *Journal of Personality and Social Psychology*, 45, 293–305.

Associated Press Online. (2003). *No 9–11 compensation for flight attendant*. Retrieved November 27, 2003, from http://www.softcom.net/webnews/wed/do/Aattacks-workers-compensation.RzIU_DNR.html

Biernat, M. (2003). Toward a broader view of social stereotyping. *The American Psychologist*, 58, 1019–1027.

Biernat, M., & Manis, M. (1994). Shifting standards and stereotype-consistent judgments. *Journal of Personality and Social Psychology*, 66, 5–20.

Biernat, M., Manis, M., & Kobrynowicz, D. (1997). Simultaneous assimilation and contrast effects in judgments of self and others. *Journal of Personality and Social Psychology*, 73, 254–269.

Blanton, H. (2001). Evaluating the self in the context of another: The three-selves model of social comparison assimilation and contrast. In G. B. Moskowitz (Ed.), *Cognitive social psychology: The Princeton symposium on the legacy and future of social cognition* (pp. 75–87). Mahwah, NJ: Lawrence Erlbaum Associates, Inc.

Brown, J. D., Novick, N. J., Lord, K. A., & Richards, J. M. (1992). When Gulliver travels: Social context, psychological closeness, and self-appraisals. *Journal of Personality and Social Psychology*, 62, 717–727.

Carroll, J. S. (1978). The effect of imagining an event on expectations for the event: An interpretation in terms of the availability heuristic. *Journal of Personality and Social Psychology*, 36, 1501–1511.

Cheng, P. W., & Novick, L. R. (1990). A probabilistic contrast model of causal induction. *Journal of Personality and Social Psychology*, 58, 545–567.

Collins, R. L. (1996). For better or worse: The impact of upward social comparison on self-evaluations. *Psychological Bulletin, 119*, 51–69.

Connolly, T., & Zeelenberg, M. (2002). Regret and decision making. *Current Directions in Psychological Science, 11*, 212–216.

Davis, C. G., Lehman, D. R., Silver, R. C., Wortman, C. B., & Ellard, J. (1996). Self-blame following a traumatic event: The role of perceived avoidability. *Personality and Social Psychology Bulletin, 22*, 557–567.

Evans, P. C. (2003). "If only I were thin like her, maybe I could be happy like her." *Psychology of Women Quarterly, 27*, 209–214.

Festinger, L. (1954). A theory of social comparison processes. *Human Relations, 7*, 117–140.

Gardner, W. L., Gabriel, S., & Lee, A. Y. (2002). When you and I are "we," you are not threatening: The role of self-expansion in social comparison. *Journal of Personality and Social Psychology, 82*, 239–251.

Green, M. C., & Brock, T. C. (2000). The role of transportation in the persuasiveness of public narratives. *Journal of Personality and Social Psychology, 79*, 701–721.

Helson, H. (1964). *Adaptation-level theory.* New York: Harper & Row.

Hilton, D. J., & Slugoski, B. R. (1986). Knowledge-based causal attribution: The abnormal conditions focus model. *Psychological Review, 93*, 75–88.

Hirt, E. R., Kardes, F. R., & Markman, K. D. (2004). Activating a mental simulation mind-set through generation of alternatives: Implications for debiasing in related and unrelated domains. *Journal of Experimental Social Psychology, 40*, 374–383.

Hirt, E. R., & Markman, K. D. (1995). Multiple explanation: A consider-an-alternative strategy for debiasing judgments. *Journal of Personality and Social Psychology, 69*, 1069–1086.

Hodges, S. D., Bruininks, P., & Ivy, L. (2002). It's different when I do it: Feature matching in self—other comparisons. *Personality and Social Psychology Bulletin, 28*, 40–53.

Holyoak, K. J., & Gordon, P. C. (1983). Social reference points. *Journal of Personality and Social Psychology, 44*, 881–887.

Hsee, C. K., Salovey, P., & Abelson, R. P. (1994). The quasi-acceleration relation: Satisfaction as a function of the change of velocity of outcome over time. *Journal of Experimental Social Psychology, 30*, 96–111.

Kahneman, D. (1995). Varieties of counterfactual thinking. In N. J. Roese & J. M. Olson (Eds.), *What might have been: The social psychology of counterfactual thinking* (pp. 375–396), Mahwah, NJ: Lawrence Erlbaum Associates, Inc.

Kahneman, D., & Miller, D. T. (1986). Norm theory: Comparing reality to its alternatives. *Psychological Review, 93*, 136–153.

Kahneman, D., & Tversky, A. (1982). The simulation heuristic. In D. Kahneman, P. Slovic, & A. Tversky (Eds.), *Judgment under uncertainty: Heuristics and biases* (pp. 201–208). New York: Cambridge University Press.

Kahneman, D., & Varey, C. A. (1990). Propensities and counterfactuals: The loser who almost won. *Journal of Personality and Social Psychology, 59*, 1101–1110.

Karniol, R., & Ross, M. (1996). The motivational impact of temporal focus: Thinking about the future and the past. *Annual Review of Psychology, 47*, 593–620.

Klinger, E. (1990). *Daydreaming: Using waking fantasy and imagery for self-knowledge and creativity.* Los Angeles: Tarcher.

Koehler, D. J. (1991). Explanation, imagination, and confidence in judgment. *Psychological Bulletin, 110*, 499–519.

Larsen, J. T., McGraw, A. P., & Cacioppo, J. T. (2001). Can people feel happy and sad at the same time? *Journal of Personality and Social Psychology, 81*, 684–696.

Lipe, M. G. (1991). Counterfactual reasoning as a framework for attribution theories. *Psychological Bulletin, 109*, 456–471.

Lockwood, P., Jordan, C. H., & Kunda, Z. (2002). Motivation by positive or negative role models: Regulatory focus determines who will best inspire us. *Journal of Personality and Social Psychology*, 83, 854–864.

Lockwood, P., & Kunda, Z. (1997). Superstars and me: Predicting the impact of role models on the self. *Journal of Personality and Social Psychology*, 73, 91–103.

Major, B., Testa, M., & Bylsma, W. H. (1991). Responses to upward and downward social comparisons: The impact of esteem-relevance and perceived control. In J. Suls & T. A. Wills (Eds.), *Social comparison: Contemporary theory and research* (pp. 237–260). Hillsdale, NJ: Lawrence Erlbaum Associates, Inc.

Markman, K. D., Elizaga, R. A., Ratcliff, J. J., & McMullen, M. N. (in press). The interplay between counterfactual reasoning and feedback dynamics in producing inferences about the self. *Thinking and Reasoning*.

Markman, K. D., Gavanski, I., Sherman, S. J., & McMullen, M. N. (1993). The mental simulation of better and worse possible worlds. *Journal of Experimental Social Psychology*, 29, 87–109.

Markman, K. D., & McMullen, M. N. (2003). A reflection and evaluation model of comparative thinking. *Personality and Social Psychology Review*, 7, 244–267.

Markman, K. D., & McMullen, M. N. (2005). Reflective and evaluative modes of mental simulation. In D. R. Mandel, D. J. Hilton, & P. Catellani (Eds.), *The psychology of counterfactual thinking* (pp. 77–93). London: Routledge.

Markman, K. D., & Tetlock, P. E. (2000). Accountability and close counterfactuals: The loser that nearly won and the winner that nearly lost. *Personality and Social Psychology Bulletin*, 26, 1213–1224.

Markus, H. R., & Nurius, P. (1986). Possible selves. *The American Psychologist*, 41, 954–969.

Martin, R., Suls, J., & Wheeler, L. (2002). Ability evaluation by proxy: Role of maximal performance and related attributes in social comparison. *Journal of Personality and Social Psychology*, 82, 781–791.

Marx, D. M., Stapel, D. A., & Muller, D. (2005). We can do it: The interplay of construal orientation and social comparisons under threat. *Journal of Personality and Social Psychology*, 88, 432–446.

McMullen, M. N. (1997). Affective contrast and assimilation in counterfactual thinking. *Journal of Experimental Social Psychology*, 33, 77–100.

McMullen, M. N., & Markman, K. D. (2000). Downward counterfactuals and motivation: The wake-up call and the Pangloss effect. *Personality and Social Psychology Bulletin*, 26, 575–584.

McMullen, M. N., & Markman, K. D. (2002). Affective impact of close counterfactuals: Implications of possible futures for possible pasts. *Journal of Experimental Social Psychology*, 38, 64–70.

McMullen, M. N., Markman, K. D., & Gavanski, I. (1995). Living in neither the best nor worst of all possible worlds: Antecedents and consequences of upward and downward counterfactual thinking. In N. J. Roese & J. M. Olson (Eds.), *What might have been: The social psychology of counterfactual thinking* (pp. 133–167). Hillsdale, NJ: Lawrence Erlbaum Associates, Inc.

Medvec, V. H., Madey, S. F., & Gilovich, T. (1995). When less is more: Counterfactual thinking and satisfaction among Olympic athletes. *Journal of Personality and Social Psychology*, 69, 603–610.

Medvec, V. H., & Savitsky, K. K. (1997). When doing better means feeling worse: A model of counterfactual cutoff points. *Journal of Personality and Social Psychology*, 72, 1284–1296.

Mellers, B. A., Schwartz, A., Ho, K., & Ritov, I. (1997). Decision affect theory: Emotional reactions to the outcomes of risky options. *Psychological Science*, 8, 423–429.

Miller, D. T., & McFarland, C. (1986). Counterfactual thinking and victim compensation: A test of norm theory. *Personality and Social Psychology Bulletin, 12*, 513–519.

Mussweiler, T. (2003). Comparison processes in social judgment: Mechanisms and consequences. *Psychological Review, 110*, 472–489.

Mussweiler, T., Rüter, K., & Epstude, K. (2004). The ups and downs of social comparisons: Mechanisms of assimilation and contrast. *Journal of Personality and Social Psychology, 87*, 832–844.

Mussweiler, T., & Strack, F. (2000). The "relative self": Informational and judgmental consequences of comparative self-evaluation. *Journal of Personality and Social Psychology, 79*, 23–38

Niedenthal, P. M., Tangney, J. P., & Gavanski, I. (1994). "If only I weren't" versus "If only I hadn't": Distinguishing shame and guilt in counterfactual thinking. *Journal of Personality and Social Psychology, 67*, 585–595.

Oettingen, G. (1996). Positive fantasy and motivation. In P. M. Gollwitzer & J. A. Bargh (Eds.), *The psychology of action: Linking cognition and motivation to action* (pp. 236–259). New York: Guilford Press.

Roese, N. J. (1994). The functional basis of counterfactual thinking. *Journal of Personality and Social Psychology, 66*, 805–818.

Roese, N. J. (1997). Counterfactual thinking. *Psychological Bulletin, 121*, 133–148.

Roese, N. J., & Olson, J. M. (1995). Counterfactual thinking: A critical overview. In N. J. Roese & J. M. Olson (Eds.), *What might have been: The social psychology of counterfactual thinking* (pp. 1–59). Mahwah, NJ: Lawrence Erlbaum Associates, Inc.

Roese, N. J., & Olson, J. M. (1997). Counterfactual thinking: The intersection of affect and function. In M. Zanna (Ed.), *Advances in experimental social psychology* (Vol. 29, pp. 1–59). San Diego, CA: Academic Press.

Ross, L., Lepper, M. R., Strack, F., & Steinmetz, J. L. (1977). Social explanation and social expectation: The effects of real and hypothetical explanation upon subjective likelihood. *Journal of Personality and Social Psychology, 35*, 817–829.

Schwarz, N., & Bless, H. (1992). Constructing reality and its alternatives: An inclusion/exclusion model of assimilation and contrast effects in social judgment. In L. L. Martin & A. Tesser (Eds.), *The construction of social judgments* (pp. 217–245). Hillsdale, NJ: Lawrence Erlbaum Associates, Inc.

Schwarz, N., Bless, H., Strack, F., Klumpp, G., Rittenauer-Schatka, H., & Simons, A. (1991). Ease of retrieval as information: Another look at the availability heuristic. *Journal of Personality and Social Psychology, 61*, 195–202.

Schwarz, N., & Clore, G. L. (1983). Mood, misattribution, and judgments of well-being: Informative and directive functions of affective states. *Journal of Personality and Social Psychology, 45*, 513–523.

Sherman, S. J., Cialdini, R. B., Schwartzman, D. F., & Reynolds, K. D. (1985). Imagining can heighten or lower the perceived likelihood of contracting a disease: The mediating effect of ease of imagery. *Personality and Social Psychology Bulletin, 11*, 118–127.

Stapel, D. A., & Koomen, W. (2000). Distinctness of others, mutability of selves: Their impact on self-evaluations. *Journal of Personality and Social Psychology, 79*, 1068–1087.

Stapel, D. A., & Koomen, W. (2001). Let's not forget the past when we go into the future: On our knowledge of knowledge accessibility. In G. B. Moskowitz (Ed.), *Cognitive social psychology: The Princeton symposium on the legacy and future of social cognition* (pp. 229–246). Mahwah, NJ: Lawrence Erlbaum Associates, Inc.

Strack, F., Schwarz, N., & Gschneidinger, E. (1985). Happiness and reminiscing: The role of time perspective, affect, and mode of thinking. *Journal of Personality and Social Psychology, 49*, 1460–1469.

Suls, J., Marco, C. A., & Tobin, S. (1991). The role of temporal comparison, social comparison and direct appraisal in the elderly's self-evaluation of health. *Journal of Applied Social Psychology, 21*, 1125–1144.

Taylor, S. E., Buunk, B. P., & Aspinwall, L. G. (1990). Social comparison, stress, and coping. *Personality and Social Psychology Bulletin, 16*, 74–89.

Taylor, S. E., & Pham, L. B. (1996). Mental simulation and action. In P. M. Gollwitzer & J. A. Bargh (Eds.), *The psychology of action: Linking cognition and motivation to action* (pp. 219–235). New York: Guilford Press.

Tesser, A. (1988). Toward a self-evaluation maintenance model of social behavior. In L. Berkowitz (Ed.), *Advances in experimental social psychology* (Vol. 21, pp. 181–227). New York: Academic Press.

Thibaut, J. W., & Kelley, H. H. (1959). *The social psychology of groups*. New Brunswick, NJ: Transaction Publishers.

Tversky, A. (1977). Features of similarity. *Psychological Review, 84*, 327–352.

Wells, G. L., & Gavanski, I. (1989). Mental simulation of causality. *Journal of Personality and Social Psychology, 56*, 161–169.

Wilson, A. E., & Ross, M. (2000). The frequency of temporal-self and social comparisons in people's personal appraisals. *Journal of Personality and Social Psychology, 78*, 928–942.

Wilson, A. E., & Ross, M. (2001). From chump to champ: People's appraisals of their earlier and present selves. *Journal of Personality and Social Psychology, 80*, 572–584.

Wood, J. V. (1989). Theory and research concerning social comparisons of personal attributes. *Psychological Bulletin, 106*, 231–248.

9

Set/Reset and Self-Regulation: Do Contrast Processes Play a Role in the Breakdown of Self-Control?

LEONARD L. MARTIN and STEVE SHIRK

A number of years ago, the first author began studying the processes underlying certain types of assimilation and contrast effects (e.g., Martin, 1986; Martin & Achee, 1992; Martin, Seta, & Crelia, 1990). More recently, in collaboration with the second author, he began studying the processes underlying certain types of self-regulation (e.g., Martin, 1999; Martin, Campbell, & Henry, 2004). In this chapter, we speculate on some connections between the two lines of research.

We begin with the observation that certain forms of self-regulation require individuals to behave in ways that are contrary to some of their authentic feelings. If individuals are to be successful at dieting, for example, then they must ignore, suppress, discount, or otherwise put out of play their genuine hunger and their continued desire to eat high calorie foods. Not surprisingly, this can be difficult to do. It can also be counterproductive. In fact, under some circumstances, attempts at self-control can facilitate breakdowns in self-control. For example, after struggling to lose weight but seeming to make no progress, individuals may rebound into self-defeating overindulgence (Cochran & Tesser, 1996; Heatherton & Baumeister, 1991; Polivy, 1998; Tice & Bratslavsky, 2000). They not only terminate their dieting, but they actually engage in behavior that works against their dieting (e.g., binging on high calorie foods).

On the surface, this kind of breakdown in self-control has some features in common with the kind of contrast effects we have studied. Both reflect a shift from one extreme to the other. In what we have termed reset contrast, individuals attempt to partial out from their judgment of the target stimulus any reactions they perceive to be coming from nontarget sources (e.g., contextual stimuli, their mood). This partialling can be difficult to calibrate precisely, so individuals sometimes overcorrect. Specifically, they partial out aspects of their genuine reaction to the target and turn what would have been a judgment biased toward the implications of the inappropriate reaction (assimilation) into one that is biased away from that reaction (contrast). In short, the shift from self-control to overindulgence and the shift from assimilation to reset contrast both reflect a kind of over-correction. In this chapter, we explore whether this similarity is more than surface deep.

We begin by describing optimal self-regulation and the conditions that lead to less than optimal self-regulation (e.g., breakdowns in self-control). Then, we dis-cuss the set/reset model of assimilation and contrast. After that, we speculate on some ways in which set/reset processes may play a role in the shift from self-control to self-indulgence. Finally, we discuss ways in which a consideration of set/reset processes might help individuals attain optimal self-regulation.

OPTIMAL SELF-REGULATION

It is useful to think of self-regulation in cybernetic or control system terms (Carver & Scheier, 1998). From this perspective, we can think of individuals as having representations of their actual state as well as their desired state and as attempting to reduce the discrepancy between the two. An individual may weigh 150 pounds, for example, but have the goal of weighing 120 pounds. The discrep-ancy between the individual's actual and desired weight would lead the individual to experience negative affect and engage in behaviors (e.g., dieting, exercise) designed to reduce the discrepancy. The faster individuals reduce the discrepancy, the more positive affect they experience. The faster they increase the discrepancy, the more negative affect they experience (Carver & Scheier, 1990).

Diener, Sandvik, and Pavot (1991) obtained evidence generally consistent with this view of self-regulation. They assessed the frequency as well as the intensity with which individuals experienced positive affect and then correlated these affective experiences with the level of subjective well-being the individuals reported. From a control system perspective, positive affect arises when indi-viduals receive feedback that they are progressing toward their goals. So, frequent positive affective may be more likely than intense positive affect to increase subjective well-being. Frequent positive affect suggests that individuals are pro-gressing rapidly toward their goals. Consistent with this hypothesis, Diener et al. found that individuals reported greater subjective well-being when they experi-enced frequent as opposed to intense positive affect. More generally, these results suggest that frequent feedback regarding goal progress can facilitate optimal self-regulation.

In addition to influencing one's affective experiences, feedback regarding goal progress can also influence an individual's level of motivation, self-efficacy, and optimism (e.g., Bandura & Schunk, 1981; Latham & Locke, 1991). The more feedback individuals receive that they are progressing toward their goals, the higher their motivation, self-efficacy, and optimism. This is especially true if the goals are moderately difficult to attain. This is because goals that are too easy or too difficult to attain do not elicit a great deal of commitment and do not provide individuals with much information regarding their competence.

Several lines of work have provided evidence consistent with this hypothesis. Bandura and Schunk (1981), for example, found that, compared to children who pursued a single, long-term goal, those who pursued a series of subgoals toward the same end displayed greater competence and self-efficacy as well as greater interest and enjoyment. The children also displayed greater congruency between their actual and perceived ability.

Goals are also more likely to facilitate optimal functioning if they are clear and proximate as compared to diffuse and distal. This is because clear, proximate goals can be achieved more quickly and provide more frequent feedback regarding progress. Emmons (1992), for example, found that individuals who defined their persistent goals in broad, abstract ways (e.g., get closer to God) reported greater negative affect and depression than those who defined their persistent goals in concrete, specific ways (e.g., go to church once a week). According to Emmons, this difference was observed because it is more difficult for individuals to monitor their progress toward higher level goals. It is easy for individuals to determine whether they have attended church, for example, but it is difficult for them to determine if they are getting closer to God. Because concrete goals provide clearer, more frequent feedback regarding goal progress, individuals with concrete goals experience less negative affect and depression.

Another aspect of goal pursuit that is relevant to optional functioning is the extent to which a goal is congruent with one's authentic values. An individual may diet, for example, because staying in shape is consistent with his or her personal values or because he or she was ordered by a doctor to lose weight. Ryan and Deci (2000) have discussed this kind of distinction in terms of their intrinsic–extrinsic continuum. When individuals perform a task for the interest or enjoyment it provides, they are said to be intrinsically motivated. When they perform a task because they believe they will obtain a reward or avoid punishment for doing so, they are said to be extrinsically motivated. Numerous studies have shown that the more intrinsically oriented individuals are, the higher their subjective well-being (Carver & Baird, 1998; Schmuck, Kasser & Ryan, 2000).

There are at least three other advantages to pursuing goals that are congruent with one's personal values (Sheldon & HouserMarko, 2001). First, doing so is associated with greater success in goal attainment. Second, doing so is associated with an increased likelihood individuals will pursue self-congruent goals in the future. Third, doing so can lead to an upward spiral of subjective well-being. Here is how it works. When individuals pursue a goal consistent with their authentic values, they experience increased commitment and motivation. This, in turn, increases the likelihood they will attain the goal, which, in turn, increases their positive affect. As a result, the next time these individuals are setting a goal, they choose one consistent with their authentic values. This leads them to experience greater commitment, motivation, goal attainment, positive affect, and so on.

Many of the features of optimal self-regulation were captured by Csikszentmihalyi (1997) in his conceptualization of flow or optimal experience. According to Csikszentmihalyi, optimal experience involves intrinsic motivation, clear goals, clear performance feedback, and positive affect. It also involves a focus on the details of one's performance rather than the implications of that performance. For example, an individual in flow would focus on climbing a mountain, rather than on the consequences of reaching or not reaching the top. In addition, while in flow, individuals tend not to be concerned about their self-worth. They are focused on the task. Nevertheless, flow experiences can lead individuals to develop a stronger, more positive self-concept. This is because individuals are more likely to experience flow when they successfully perform a task at the upper limits of their skill (i.e., high challenge plus high skill).

In sum, research from a variety of perspectives has converged to paint a fairly coherent picture of optimal self-regulation. It seems that individuals function best when they have clear goals, receive frequent feedback that they are progressing toward those goals, and are intrinsically motivated to pursue those goals. Under these conditions, individuals experience positive affect, a sense of self-efficacy, a focus on the task, a loss of concern about self-worth, and an upward spiral of subjective well-being. The research suggests, therefore, that with the right motivation and the right level of goal (e.g., not too easy or too difficult, one that provides frequent feedback), our dieter could stick with his or her diet, be successful losing weight, experience competence and positive affect as a result, and do all of this while not losing contact with his or her personal values or becoming overly concerned with self-evaluation. This would be optimal self-regulation.

WHEN SELF-CONTROL GOES BAD

The problem, of course, is that individuals cannot function optimally all of the time. Sometimes, they have to engage in behaviors that are not intrinsically motivating, that do not provide clear feedback, or that lead them to focus on their self as an object of evaluation. Although behaving under such nonoptimal conditions can sometimes pay off in the long run (e.g., studying for years to get a PhD), it may also lead to a number of negative effects.

For example, having to perform extrinsic, controlled behaviors may lead individuals to terminate their self-compatibility checks (Kazén, Baumann, & Kuhl, 2003). During these checks, individuals consult their authentic preferences and values while making a decision. In essence, they ask themselves "Is this right for me? What do I really want?" When individuals perform controlled behaviors, on the other hand, they ask themselves "What do I have to do? What do others want me to do? What will happen if I don't do this?" Under these conditions, an individual's authentic preferences or values are irrelevant because the reason for the behavior is external. Persistent failure to engage in a self-compatibility check is associated with negative affect, rumination, hesitation, difficulty in down-regulating one's negative emotions, and the adoption of goals that are not congruent with one's authentic values (Kazén et al., 2003).

A particularly interesting sort of controlled behavior is the type individuals impose on themselves. Delay of gratification is the prototype of this kind of self-regulation (Mischel, Ebbesen, & Raskoff Zeiss, 1972). A dieter, for example, may intentionally forgo the immediate gratification of eating enjoyable, high calorie foods in order to attain the long-term goal of losing weight. Although potentially productive (e.g., the person loses weight), this kind of self-control can lead individuals to miss many features of optimal experience. Specifically, delay of gratification may be associated with negative affect, delayed, uncertain performance feedback, and an intense focus on the self as an object of evaluation. These byproducts of self-control are unpleasant and may even contribute to a breakdown in self-control (Polivy, 1998; Tice & Bratslavsky, 2000).

SELF-DEFEATING BEHAVIOR AS A BREAKDOWN IN SELF-REGULATION

Given the nonoptimal possibilities inherent in engaging in controlled behavior, it is not surprising that individuals often wish to escape from conditions in which such behavior is imposed on them. In fact, after engaging in controlled behaviors, individuals often strive to engage in behaviors that are nonevaluative and that do not engage the self (Heatherton & Baumeister, 1991). Perhaps the most dramatic example of this kind of escape is self-defeating behavior. In this case, individuals not only forgo self-control but also engage in precisely those behaviors that are detrimental to the attainment of the goal they had been attempting to attain through self-control. A dieter, for example, may stop dieting and start overeating. Such breakdowns in self-control have often been explained in terms of hedonic motivations.

Polivy (1998), for example, starts with the assumption that emotions communicate to individuals the appropriateness of their actions. Generally, when individuals experience a positive emotion, they may infer that they are acting appropriately and can continue their action. When they experience a negative emotion, they may infer that they are not acting appropriately and may be motivated to change their action (Bless, Bohner, & Schwarz, 1990; Frijda, Manstead, & Bem, 2000). From this perspective, emotions are a source of wisdom. Thus, sad individuals should attend to their loss, anxious individuals should eliminate the threatening object, and so on. According to Polivy, if individuals do not act in accordance with this emotional wisdom, then they may experience more distress or discomfort than they otherwise might have experienced.

According to Polivy, one problem with self-control is that it typically involves acting against the implications of one's emotions. For example, although hungry, a dieter may not eat; although tired, a student may continue to read rather than go to sleep; and although angry, an employee may refrain from retaliating against his or her boss. Thus, successful self-control involves directing one's behavior according to a goal rather than the implications of one's emotions. Ignoring these implications, however, can be unpleasant, and individuals may attempt to reduce their discomfort by performing the inhibited behavior. As a result, there may be a rebound in performance of the inhibited behavior. In fact, several studies have shown that individuals attempting to suppress their desire to eat fattening foods are prone to bouts of excessive eating or even binge eating, especially of the foods they are trying to avoid (Polivy & Herman, 1985).

A related model of breakdowns in self-control was proposed by Tice and

Bratslavsky (2000). These authors proposed that self-defeating overindulgence can result from a shift in goal priorities. Specifically, they suggested that the negative feelings associated with self-control can arouse in individuals the motive to repair their moods. Unfortunately, many strategies individuals use to repair their moods involve performing activities they otherwise try to control or resist (e.g., overeating). If individuals are in a particularly negative mood, however, this may not matter to them. For them, at this time, mood repair may take on a greater priority than the attainment of the long-term goal. As a result, individuals may abandon self-control and indulge themselves in activities that are detrimental to the attainment of their long-term goals.

Tice and Bratslavsky (2000) obtained some evidence for this mood repair explanation of overindulgence. They had participants read either a distressing or uplifting scenario and imagine how they would feel if they were actually in that scenario. The purpose of this task was to induce in participants a negative or positive mood, respectively. Participants were then told that they had to wait 15 minutes before resuming the experiment. During this waiting period, participants were asked to eat various foods and make some ratings of those foods. The amount participants ate during the taste testing task was actually the measure of self-indulgence.

If breakdowns in self-regulation result from attempts to make oneself feel better, then participants in a negative mood might eat more in the taste testing task than participants in a positive mood—assuming, of course, that participants believed that the eating would improve their mood. Tice and Bratslavsky (2000) attempted to undermine this belief in some of their participants.

Specifically, they asked all participants to take a vitamin pill, but told some participants that this pill had an unusual side effect. It led people to continue experiencing whatever mood they were currently in. Thus, those currently in a negative mood would stay that way, even if they ate the food—or so they were led to believe. Consistent with the hypothesis that the motive to repair one's mood can initiate overindulgence, participants in negative moods ate more than participants in positive moods only when they believed they could improve their moods by eating the food. More generally, the results suggest that self-indulgent overeating occurs when individuals are in a negative mood and believe that eating can improve their mood.

So, the pattern seems pretty clear. Self-control can be productive but it can also give rise to negative effects (e.g., negative mood) that, in turn, may lead to nonoptimal self-regulation. Specifically, individuals may shift from overcontrol to overindulgence as they attempt to improve their mood.

WHY DO INDIVIDUALS NOT ESCAPE TOWARD OPTIMAL FUNCTIONING?

So far, we have suggested that there are three general classes of self-regulation: overcontrol, optimal self-regulation, and self-indulgence. Overcontrol is goal-oriented and productive, but it is also associated with extrinsic motivation, delayed, uncertain feedback, negative affect, awareness of the self as an object of evaluation, and a failure to engage in a self-compatibility check. Optimal self-regulation is also goal-oriented and productive, but, unlike overcontrol, it is associated with intrinsic motivation, clear, frequent feedback, positive affect, loss of awareness of the self as an object of evaluation, self-compatibility checks, and an increasing spiral of goal congruence and well-being.

Self-indulgence differs from both overcontrol and optimal functioning in that it is not at all productive and may even be counterproductive. If it is goal-oriented at all, it is so only in a mood repair sense. It does not lead to an increasing spiral of goal congruence and well-being. Nevertheless, self-indulgence does have some features in common with optimal experience. Both are performed out of enjoyment and interest and both are associated with clear, frequent feedback, positive affect, and loss of awareness of the self as an object of evaluation.

It is possible to represent the common and distinctive features of these three general classes of self-regulation in terms of a Venn diagram (see Figure 9.1). As can be seen, optimal self-regulation shares features with overcontrol and overindulgence. Most interesting for present purposes is the observation that optimal self-functioning is associated with positive affect. This means there is no need for individuals to shift from overcontrol to self-indulgence in order to repair their mood. They could repair their mood by engaging in optimal self-regulation. Moreover, optimal self-regulation does not have the downsides of over-indulgence. This means that if a person wishes to escape overcontrol, it would be better for him or her to engage in optimal self-functioning than to engage in self-indulgence.

A dieter, for example, could set clear, concrete, proximate subgoals in order to obtain clearer, more frequent feedback (Bandura & Schunk, 1981). He or she could also be sure to find some reason to diet that is congruent with his or her important, authentic values (e.g., personal desire to stay in shape) as opposed to

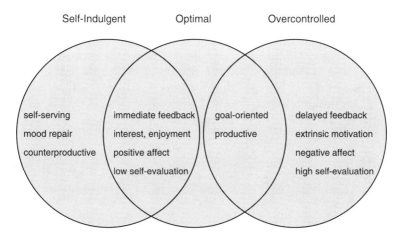

FIGURE 9.1   Common and distinctive features of three types of self-regulation.

being motivated merely for extrinsic reasons (e.g., doctor's orders). Either of these changes would move the individual closer to optimal self-regulation. Given that such options are hypothetically possible, we have to ask why individuals often bypass it in favor of self-defeating overindulgence.

According to Polivy (1998) and Tice and Bratslavsky (2000), individuals engage in self-indulgence because they believe that doing so will improve their mood. As just noted, though, optimal self-regulation is also associated with positive affect. So, additional considerations are needed to explain why individuals move past optimal self-regulation to overindulgence. We sought those considerations in the set/reset model.

THE SET/RESET MODEL OF ASSIMILATION AND CONTRAST

Before describing the model, we want to remind readers that assimilation and contrast are descriptive labels. They refer to different types of judgment effects and are mute with regard to the processes underlying those effects. Assimilation refers simply to a movement toward the contextual stimuli, whereas contrast refers simply to a movement away from those stimuli. Either effect may occur for a number of reasons and through a number of processes.

The set/reset model was designed to address one particular kind of assimilation and contrast effect. It addresses assimilation that results when individuals fail to remove from their target judgment reactions that are produced by something other than the target, and it addresses contrast that results when individuals remove these nontarget reactions but also remove aspects of their genuine reaction to the target (i.e., overcorrection). These types of assimilation and contrast effects can be distinguished from those that result from individuals comparing the target and contextual stimuli (e.g., Herr, Sherman, & Fazio, 1983; Stapel & Koomen, 2001). For example, a social psychologist may feel more intelligent after comparing him- or herself with similar, but slightly more productive, social psychology researchers (assimilation), yet feel less intelligent after comparing him- or herself to Albert Einstein (contrast). These comparison-based assimilation and contrast effects are different in a number of ways from the correction-based effects addressed by the set/reset model (Moskowitz & Skurnik, 1999).

The set/reset model begins with the assumption that individuals have many sources of information they can use at any given time to construct a judgment. When forming an impression of a target person, for example, individuals may make use of activated trait concepts, evaluative concepts, scripts, exemplars, global moods, specific emotions, or bodily states such as arousal, fatigue, or hunger. They may also consider previously formed judgments or attributions, attitudes, general world knowledge, and communication rules.

Of course, individuals do not consider all of these sources of information for each and every judgment. Individuals are selective in their use of information. This selectivity is the heart of the set/reset model. The model assumes that individuals use information in active, strategic ways. Thus, the model focuses not so much on what different kinds of stimuli do to individuals as on what individuals do with the information they have.

What determines which subset of information individuals incorporate into any given judgment? The set/reset model assumes that individuals seek information that appears appropriate (or at least not inappropriate) to their current processing objectives. When individuals take seriously the goal of forming an impression, for example, their goal is to assess their genuine reaction to the target person. To attain this goal in its strictest sense, individuals should not report on their current mood, their impression of the contextual stimuli, or their impression of the priming stimuli. Neither should they report on their impression of their neighbor, their accountant, or what they saw on television the previous night. They should also not report another person's impression of the target person. They should report on their impression of the target, and nothing else.

So, if individuals find themselves thinking negative thoughts that appear due to their exposure to negative contextual stimuli, for example, then they may avoid using these thoughts in forming their impression. After all, these thoughts pertain to the contextual stimuli, not to the target person. So, the thoughts do not help the individual fulfill his or her processing objective (i.e., give your impression of the target). Once individuals have suppressed their use of an inappropriate reaction, they search for another reaction that seems to reflect their unbiased reaction to the target information. Unbiased, in this context, refers to a reaction that does not appear to have been made accessible by something other than the target.

The suppressed use of an inappropriate reaction and the search for an appropriate one is called resetting. According to the model, individuals reset by focusing on features of the target that distinguish it from the inappropriate reaction, and then using these distinctive features to generate a new reaction. It is because of the focus on distinct features that resetting typically produces a shift in judgment away from the inappropriate reaction. For example, if a person is trying to form an impression of a target person who engages in ambiguously persistent–stubborn behavior and has been primed with the construct stubborn, the person may suppress the use of that construct and interpret the behavior as persistent (an evaluative contrast effect).

The set/reset model does not assume, however, that contrast is the inevitable outcome of resetting. There may be conditions in which individuals reset but produce judgments showing no effect of the inappropriate reaction or even a reduced assimilation effect relative to that reaction (Martin & Achee, 1992). If these alternatives are possible, then why do individuals so often contrast their final judgments away from the inappropriate reaction? The answer lies in the individual's processing objectives.

The processing objectives inherent in forming an accurate impression impose multiple, simultaneous constraints (McClelland, Rummelhart, & the PDP Research Group, 1986). For example, individuals have to (1) find a reaction in themselves that allows them to make sense of the target person's behavior and (2) they have to make sure this reaction has been elicited by the target and not by some nontarget source (e.g., contextual stimuli, the individual's own mood). When forming an impression of a target person who "never changes his mind," for example, an individual could interpret the target's actions as either persistent or stubborn. Although these constructs differ in valence, each is applicable for interpreting a behavior reflecting single-mindedness. Constructs such as flexible or wishy-washy, on the other hand, are not applicable, so only the former constructs satisfy the first processing constraint. Only the former can be used to interpret the target's behavior.

Suppose, though, that prior to learning about the target person, the individual had performed a task in which he or she had repeatedly been exposed to words related to stubbornness (e.g., stubborn, obstinate, hard-headed). In this case, the individual might be drawn to stubborn as the first interpretation of the target's single-minded behavior because of the heightened accessibility of this construct. If the individual associates his or her initial interpretation with the prior task, however, then he or she cannot use that interpretation in forming the impression of the target. Doing so would violate the second processing objective. The interpretation was elicited by a nontarget source. Thus, the individual is constrained to interpret the target's behavior as persistent. This is the only construct that is applicable to interpreting the target behavior (first processing objective) and that was not made accessible by a nontarget source (second processing objective). The result is an evaluative contrast effect.

According to the model, reset contrast involves the suppressed use of the initial, inappropriate reaction and the generation of another reaction, whereas noncorrected assimilation merely involves use of the initial reaction. These processing differences imply that reset contrast demands the expenditure of more cognitive effort than noncorrected assimilation. This does, in fact, appear to be the case. A number of studies have shown that reducing an individual's cognitive effort can eliminate reset contrast but not assimilation. Martin et al. (1990), for example, blatantly primed participants with either the construct persistent or the construct stubborn. The result of such priming is usually contrast. Participants form more favorable evaluations after being primed with stubborn than persistent. Martin et al. were able to eliminate this contrast in some participants, though, by asking the participants to perform a cognitively demanding task while forming their impression of the target. In exerting the effort needed to complete the secondary task, participants undermined their ability to complete reset contrast (Moskowitz & Skurnik, 1999). In fact, their impressions reflected assimilation. They formed more favorable evaluations of the target person after being primed with persistent than stubborn.

Although reset contrast is a function of effortful cognitive processing, it is not necessarily a function of conscious, intentional processing. A cognitive operation may be difficult to accomplish yet still be initiated automatically. In fact, in debriefing after our experiments, participants routinely denied that the contextual stimuli had any influence on their judgments or that they engaged in any sort of correction process (Martin, 1986; Martin et al., 1990).

The hypothesis that correction processes can be effortful yet still be initiated without conscious intention is consistent with the view that, with repeated association, individuals can develop knowledge structures that represent the links between goals and actions instrumental in attaining those goals (Aarts &

Dijksterhuis, 2000; Ferguson & Bargh, 2004). When this occurs, the goals can be elicited without the person's awareness and, through spreading activation, the associated instrumental action can become automatically activated. So, even if the instrumental actions demand cognitive effort to run to completion, they can still be activated automatically.

INTEGRATING SELF-REGULATION AND SET/RESET PROCESSES

Overcorrection

We begin our integration by placing self-regulation back into control system terms. Specifically, we start by assuming that individuals monitor the discrepancy between their actual state and their desired state. When they observe this discrepancy being reduced at a desired rate, they can continue engaging in their current behavior because this behavior has been successful in moving them toward their goal. When they observe the discrepancy increasing or not being reduced at a desired rate, they may change their behavior in an attempt to find some way to move closer to their goals. Thus, from a control system perspective, self-regulation can be conceptualized in terms of three broad subprocesses: (1) setting a goal, (2) monitoring one's progress toward that goal, and (3) taking actions to reduce the discrepancy between the goal and one's current state.

Although each of these subprocesses may contribute to breakdowns in self-regulation, we focus primarily on the first and the third. The role of the first subprocess is obvious. Breakdowns in self-control occur, by definition, when individuals shift from pursuit of a productive goal (e.g., diet) to a nonproductive or counterproductive one (e.g., mood repair). Thus, our first assumption is related to the Polivy (1998) and the Tice and Bratslavsky (2000) suggestion that individuals avoid self-control to pursue mood repair. Unlike these authors, however, we do not rely solely on mood repair to account for the breakdown. We also incorporate a form of overcorrection.

Consider the Venn diagram in Figure 9.1. This diagram represents the common and distinct features of three general classes of self-regulation. As noted earlier, overcontrol is goal-oriented and it is potentially productive, but individuals may attempt to escape from such behavior because overcontrol is also associated with negative affect, extrinsic motivation, and other features of nonoptimal functioning. As Figure 9.1 also makes clear, individuals can escape the undesirable features of overcontrol by engaging in either optimal self-regulation or in self-indulgence. Each of these forms of self-regulation is associated with positive affect, intrinsic motivation, clear feedback regarding goal progress, and so on. So, what is it in the avoidance of overcontrol that leads individuals to move past the optimal middle category to settle into the more extreme, less productive category of self-indulgence?

Part of the answer lies in the fact that, unlike social psychologists, individuals in the real world tend not to construe their behavior in terms of the abstract components of optimal and nonoptimal self-regulation. They think instead in terms of real behaviors and real situations. Individuals may avoid their boss in the break room, for example. They do not avoid "extrinsic control" or "immediate effort for a delayed, uncertain payoff" (at least not consciously). In other words, in the real world, individuals do not exchange one abstract feature for another. They exchange one concrete configuration of features for another.

Even if individuals were knowledgeable of specific abstract components of a situation, this does not necessarily give them control over those components. Individuals may like some aspects of their job better than others, for example, but this does not mean they have the ability to pick and choose among these aspects. Individuals either show up for work or they do not. If they show up, they experience both the desirable as well as the undesirable aspects of work. If they fail to show up, then they miss the desirable as well as the undesirable aspects of work. The latter is a form of overcorrection, and it is represented in Figure 9.2. As can be seen, this kind of overcorrection can contribute to a breakdown in self-control. In trying to avoid the undesirable components of a controlled or extrinsic situation, individuals may avoid the entire situation. This may lead them to avoid some desirable features of overcontrol (e.g., goal progress), features that overcontrol shares with optimal self-regulation.

Of course, if individuals construed their behavior in terms of specific features and were aware of which features they liked and disliked, then they might be able to be more precise in their self-regulation. Individuals tired of dieting, for example, could either avoid dieting altogether or they could avoid the features of dieting they do not like. They might set concrete, clear, proximate subgoals in order to obtain clearer more frequent feedback (Bandura & Schunk, 1981) or they might find a reason to diet that was congruent with their important, authentic values (e.g., personal desire to stay in shape). In these ways, a dieter could avoid the undesired aspects of dieting while maintaining the desirable aspects. This

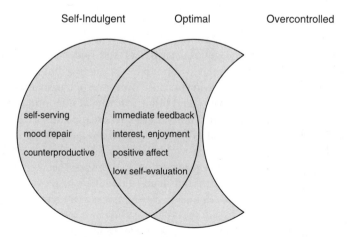

FIGURE 9.2   Overcorrection during self-regulation.

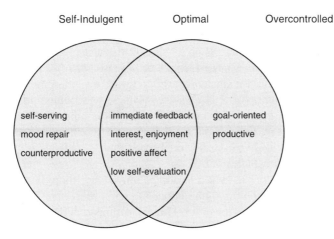

FIGURE 9.3   Optimal correction during self-regulation.

would place the dieter in the optimal self-regulation section of the Venn diagram. This option can be seen in Figure 9.3.

In short, our application of set/reset thinking to self-regulation suggests that breakdowns in self-regulation may occur, in part, because individuals tend to process situations in configural or categorical terms (e.g., my job) rather than in terms of the abstract components of those situations (e.g., extrinsic control). This tendency could lead individuals into a form of overcorrection in which they avoid the desirable (e.g., goal progress) as well as the undesirable (e,g., negative mood) aspects of their situations.

As we noted earlier, breakdowns in self-control can occur either when individuals switch goals or when they adopt new strategies to reach their goals. We have just talked about the former. Now we talk about the latter.

Self-Control Breakdowns Resulting from the Choice of Behaviors

We begin with the observation that adoption of a mood repair goal is not inherently counterproductive (Aspinwall, 1998). The value of that goal depends, in part, on the means individuals use to attain it. For example, individuals may improve their mood by smoking, overeating, socializing with friends, engaging in their hobby, donating blood, and so on. As can be seen, not all of these means of mood repair reflect self-defeating overindulgence. In fact, as a general rule, if individuals are able to obtain positive affect while staying cognizant of their self-defining goals, then they may be able to repair their mood in a way that is not self-defeating. It seems important, therefore, to keep individuals cognizant of their self-defining higher-level goals. How can we do this?

One answer can be derived from Vallacher and Wegner's (1987) action identification theory. According to that theory, individuals can identify any given action at either a high or low level. Individuals may describe brushing their teeth, for example, as moving the toothbrush (a low level identification) or as practicing oral hygiene (a high level identification). Low level identities reflect the details of an action or how the action is done. High level identities reflect the meaning, significance, or goals of an action. Higher level identities also convey information about the reasons for the action. Finally, compared to lower level identities, higher level ones are more likely to implicate one's self-concept. As Vallacher and Wegner put it "While identities at lower levels are devoid of self-defining significance, higher level identities are practically synonymous with such significance" (p. 11). Thus, individuals are more likely to stay in touch with their self-defining goals if they identify their actions at a high level.

Fortunately, according to action identification theory, there is a general tendency for individuals to identify their actions in high level terms. The main factor that moves individuals toward lower level identifications is difficulty in performing an action. If an individual is very skilled at playing the guitar, for example, then he or she is likely to identify that action as "making music" or "entertaining others," both high level identities. If the individual is not skilled, however, or if a string broke, then the individual would be more likely to describe playing the guitar as "trying to make a chord" or "putting my fingers on the right strings."

If difficulty in performing an action can lead individuals to identify that action at a lower level and if lower level identities are associated with the loss of higher-order aspects of the self, then difficulty in performing an action should lead individuals to lose contact with higher order aspects of themselves. Wegner, Vallacher, and Kiersted (1986) provided evidence that this was the case. In one study, they asked participants to drink a cup of coffee and describe what they were doing. Half of the participants were given an ordinary cup of coffee, whereas half were given an overly large, especially heavy cup. Consistent with action identification theory, participants with the normal cup described their drinking in high level terms (e.g., getting my caffeine fix), whereas participants with the large, heavy cup described their actions in low level terms (e.g., trying to keep the cup level).

More interesting for present purposes was the way in which the two groups of participants reacted to feedback from a personality test they had taken earlier in the experiment. Half of the participants received feedback that they were cooperative, whereas half received feedback that they were competitive. Then, all participants were asked to rate themselves along the cooperative–competitive dimension and they were asked if they wanted to volunteer for another experiment that involved behaving in either a cooperative or a competitive way. Wegner et al. (1986) found that participants who had previously identified their actions in low level terms (large coffee cup) were more likely than those who had identified their action in high level terms (normal coffee cup) to endorse the personality feedback they had been given and to volunteer for an experiment in which they had to behave consistently with that feedback. The results suggested that when individuals identify their actions in low level terms, they lose contact with aspects of their self-definition.

What are the implications of this research for our understanding of breakdowns in self-control? The research suggests that as long as individuals are being successful in performing their desired action, they will remain in touch with their self-defining goals and may even experience positive affect (Carver & Scheier, 1990). When individuals have difficulty performing that action, however, they may lose contact with their self-definition and may experience negative affect. The negative affect, in turn, may lead individuals to engage in mood repair, but with the loss of their self-definition, individuals may choose mood repair strategies that do not facilitate attainment of their higher-order self-defining goals. As a result, individuals may choose self-defeating overindulgence (positive, not self-defining) instead of optimal self-regulation (positive, self-defining).

Of course, difficulty in performing an activity is not the only factor that can lead individuals to lose contact with themselves. According to Heatherton, Polivy, and Herman (1989), the very act of self-control can have similar effects. These researchers noted that if individuals are to be successful at dieting, then they must suppress their feelings of hunger and their desire for high calorie food. Thus, dieting may get individuals out of touch with their own feelings. To test this hypothesis, Heatherton et al. asked participants to take a vitamin pill prior to engaging in a taste testing task. Although the pill had no effects on the participants, the researchers told half of the participants that the pill would make them feel hungry, but told the other half that the pill would make them feel full. The question, of course, was whether this false information would influence the amount of food the participants ate in the subsequent taste testing task.

Presumably, the information about the pill would have little, in any, effect on participants who really knew whether they were full or hungry. That information should influence participants only to the extent that they were not in touch with their actual feelings. According to Heatherton et al., participants who had been dieting (i.e., restrained eaters) would be more out of touch with their feelings of hunger than individuals who were not dieting. Consistent with this hypothesis, the restrained eaters consumed more food in the taste test when they had been told the pill would make them hungry than when told the pill would make them feel full. The information about the pill had no effect on the amount of food consumed by the unrestrained eater.

These results suggest that the very act of self-control can lead individuals to lose contact with themselves. The results, however, are not definitive. One reason for this is that the study examined the effects of a pre-existing individual differ- ence. The restrained and unrestrained eaters may have differed in a variety of ways prior to the experiment and any number of these differences could have contri- buted to the results. For example, it could be that an initial insensitivity to internal hunger cues led some participants to overeat, and this, in turn, led them to attempt to control their weight. Thus, the difference in sensitivity to hunger cues could have preceded and even caused the differences in eating restraint rather than vice versa. So, a different type of study would be needed if we are to make a strong claim that self-control can decrease an individual's awareness of aspects of his or her self. We attempted such a study.

Set/Reset and Suppression of the Self During Self-Control

Recall that the main assumption underlying the set/reset model is that individuals suppress reactions that are inappropriate to the current processing objectives. What reactions are inappropriate during self-control? The most obvious inappropriate reactions are an individual's authentic preferences—at least some of those preferences. For example, if dieters are to be successful, they need to put out of play their very real hunger and urge for high calorie foods. These are authentic experiences within the individual. These experiences, however, are also counterproductive to attaining the goal of losing weight, so a dieting individual may attempt to suppress those feelings when going on a diet. If this self-suppression leaves the individual's true preferences less accessible, then any subsequent decision the individual makes may not be based on his or her true preferences. In other words, self-control may foster in individuals a failure to engage in a self-compatibility check (Kazén et al., 2003).

We tested this hypothesis using a measure of self-accessibility developed by Setterlund and Niedenthal (1993). First, we had participants rate the extent to which a series of trait adjectives (e.g., sociable and intelligent) were descriptive of themselves. Then, following Baumeister Bratslavsky, and Muraven (1998), we presented participants with three bowls of food and asked them to rank order these foods in terms of their preference. One bowl contained cookies, one contained candy, and one contained radishes. Not surprisingly, participants overwhelmingly rated the cookies as the most preferable and the radishes as the least preferable.

We manipulated self-control by asking some participants to eat one of the cookies, and asking the remaining participants to eat one of the radishes. In this way, the former behaved in accordance with their authentic preferences, but the latter engaged in self-control by acting in a manner inconsistent with their authentic preferences. Next, we presented participants with descriptions of five restaurants and asked the participants to rate the extent to which they would like to eat at each restaurant. The restaurants were described in terms of the traits of the people who ate there. Restaurant H, for example, was described by the traits unconventional, intelligent, friendly, and spontaneous. Restaurant K was described by the traits sophisticated, well-mannered, sociable, and witty.

Presumably, the more the traits associated with a restaurant overlap with those participants considered to be self-descriptive, the more participants would like to eat at that restaurant. This would be true, however, only to the extent that participants were in touch with their genuine preferences (Setterlund & Niedenthal, 1993). If, in the course of self-control, individuals suppressed aspects of those preferences, then participants who ate a radish would be more likely than those who ate a cookie to be out of touch with their preferences. This would reflect itself in a weaker relation between participants' self-ratings and their liking for the restaurants when participants have eaten the radishes compared to the cookies.

The results were consistent with this prediction. There was a weaker association between participants' self-ratings and their liking for the restaurants among those who ate a radish compared to those who ate a cookie. These results suggest that individuals may accomplish self-control by designating aspects of their feelings as irrelevant. Moreover, this designation may last beyond the initial self-control task to contribute to nonoptimal performance on a subsequent self-regulation task. Specifically, after discounting their preferences in one task, participants may forgo a self-compatibility check in a subsequent task.

This suppression-induced lack of access to one's true preferences may account for some of the overshoot that leads to breakdowns in self-control. When individuals are performing overcontrolled behaviors, they may be suppressing aspects of their genuine preferences. This suppression presumably facilitates the accomplishment of the controlled behavior (e.g., ignoring one's desire for a cookie while dieting). When individuals finally seek to escape the unpleasant aspects of self-control, however, they may fail to consult their preferences to ascertain what it is they really want as an alternative. As a result, they move away from extrinsic overcontrol to self-defeating overindulgence and miss the affectively positive goal progress available in optimal functioning.

How to Avoid a Breakdown and Move Toward Optimal Functioning

We have seen how a consideration of set/reset processes may contribute to break-downs in self-control. The more important question, of course, is whether a consideration of these processes can lead us to a better understanding of optimal self-regulation. What can individuals do to avoid overcontrol or self-indulgence and arrive at optimal self-regulation? Set/reset thinking suggests at least three possibilities.

First, individuals may be more likely to attain optimal self-regulation if they adopt an approach motivation as opposed to an avoidance motivation. This is because with an approach motivation, individuals can actively seek out optimal functioning, whereas with an avoidance motivation, individuals may find them-selves settling into the byproduct of their avoidance of overcontrol. This passive byproduct is likely to be nonoptimal.

Second, individuals must also know what to approach. If, in the course of self-control, they suppress their genuine preferences, then they may be unable to choose an alternate goal or approach strategy that is compatible with their authentic values. As a result, they may devolve into nonoptimal behavior (Kazén et al., 2003; Sheldon & HouserMarko, 2001). With each choice of a new goal or approach strategy individuals should ask themselves "What do I really want? Is this right for me? How does this choice fit with my authentic values?"

Finally, individuals should learn to deconstruct their behaviors and situations. They need to determine which specific aspects of their diet or job, for example, they like or dislike. In this way, they can be more precise in their correction. They can avoid the undesirable features without also losing the desirable ones. In sum, with an approach focus on specific features chosen by means of a self-compatibility check, individuals should be able to stick with their self-control goal, be successful at attaining that goal, experience competence and positive affect as a result, and do all of this while not losing contact with their authentic values.

REFERENCES

Aarts, H., & Dijksterhuis, A. (2000). Habits as knowledge structures: Automaticity in goal-directed behavior. *Journal of Personality and Social Psychology, 78,* 5363.

Aspinwall, L. G. (1998). Rethinking the role of positive affect in self-regulation. *Motivation and Emotion, 22,* 132.

Bandura, A. & Schunk, D. H. (1981). Cultivating competence, self-efficacy, and intrinsic interest through proximal self-motivation. *Journal of Personality and Social Psychology, 41,* 586–598.

Baumeister, R. F., Bratslavsky, E., & Muraven, M. (1998). Ego depletion: Is the active self a limited resource? *Journal of Personality and Social Psychology, 74,* 1252–1265.

Bless, H., Bohner, G., & Schwarz, N. (1990). Mood and persuasion: A cognitive response analysis. *Personality and Social Psychology Bulletin, 16,* 331–345.

Carver, C. S., & Baird, E. (1998). The American dream revisited: Is it what you want or why you want it that matters? *Psychological Science, 9,* 289–292.

Carver, C. S., & Scheier, M. F. (1990). Origins and functions of positive and negative affect: A control process view. *Psychological Review, 97,* 19–35.

Carver, C. S., & Scheier, M. F. (1998). *On the self-regulation of behavior.* New York: Cambridge University Press.

Cochran, W., & Tesser, A. (1996). The "what the hell" effect: Some effects of goal proximity and goal framing on performance. In L. L. Martin & A. Tesser (Eds.), *Striving and feeling: Interactions among goals, affect, and self-regulation* (pp. 99–120). Hillsdale, NJ: Lawrence Erlbaum Associates, Inc.

Csikszentmihalyi, M. (1997). *Finding flow: The psychology of engagement with everyday life.* New York: Basic Books.

Diener, E., Sandvik, E., & Pavot, W. (1991). Happiness is the frequency, not the intensity, of positive versus negative affect. In F. Strack, M. Argyle, & N. Schwarz (Eds.), *Subjective well-being: An interdisciplinary perspective* (pp. 119–139) Elmsford, NY: Pergamon Press.

Emmons, R. A. (1992). Abstract versus concrete goals: Personal striving level, physical illness, and psychological well-being. *Journal of Personality and Social Psychology, 62,* 292–300.

Ferguson, M. J., & Bargh, J. A. (2004). Liking is for doing: The effects of goal pursuit on automatic evaluation. *Journal of Personality and Social Psychology, 87,* 557–572.

Frijda, N. H., Manstead, A. S. R., & Bem, S. (2000). *Emotions and belief: How feelings influence thoughts.* New York: Cambridge University Press.

Heatherton, T. F., & Baumeister, R. F. (1991). Binge eating as escape from self-awareness. *Psychological Bulletin, 110,* 86–108

Heatherton, T. F., Polivy, J., & Herman, C. P. (1989). Restraint and internal responsiveness: Effects of placebo manipulations of hunger state on eating. *Journal of Abnormal Psychology, 98,* 89–92.

Herr, P. M., Sherman, S. J., & Fazio, R. H. (1983). On the consequences of priming: Assimilation and contrast effects. *Journal of Experimental Social Psychology, 9,* 323–340.

Kazén, M., Baumann, N., & Kuhl, J. (2003). Self-infiltration vs. self-compatibility checking in dealing with unattractive tasks: The moderating influence of state vs. action orientation. *Motivation and Emotion, 27,* 157–197.

Latham, G. P., & Locke, E. A. (1991). Self-regulation through goal setting. *Organizational Behavior and Human Decision Processes, 50,* 212–247.

Martin, L. L. (1986). Set/reset: Use and disuse of concepts in impression formation. *Journal of Personality and Social Psychology, 51*, 493–504.

Martin, L. L. (1999). ID compensation theory: Some implication of trying to satisfy immediate-return needs in a delayed-return culture. *Psychological Inquiry, 10*, 195–208.

Martin, L. L. & Achee, J. W. (1992). Beyond accessibility: The role of processing objectives in judgment. In L. L. Martin & A. Tesser (Eds.), *The construction of social judgments* (pp. 195–216). Hillsdale, NJ: Lawrence Erlbaum Associates, Inc.

Martin, L. L., Campbell, W. K., & Henry, C. (2004). The roar of awakening: Mortality acknowledgment as a call to authentic living. In J. Greenberg, S. L. Koole, & T. Pyszczynski (Eds.), *Handbook of experimental existential psychology* (pp. 431–448). New York: Guilford Press.

Martin, L. L., Seta, J. J., & Crelia, R. A. (1990). Assimilation and contrast as a function of people's willingness and ability to expend effort in forming an impression. *Journal of Personality and Social Psychology, 59*, 27–37.

McClelland, J. L., Rummelhart, D. E., and the PDP Research Group (1986). *Parallel distributed processing, Vol. 2*. Cambridge, MA: MIT Press.

Mischel, W., Ebbesen, E. B., & Raskoff Zeiss, A. (1972). Cognitive and attentional mechanisms in delay of gratification. *Journal of Personality and Social Psychology, 21*, 204–218.

Moskowitz, G. B., & Skurnik, I. W. (1999). Contrast effects as determined by the type of prime: Trait versus exemplar primes initiate processing strategies that differ in how accessible constructs are used. *Journal of Personality and Social Psychology, 76*, 911–927.

Polivy, J. (1998). The effects of behavioral inhibition: Integrating internal cures, cognition, behavior, and affect. *Psychological Inquiry, 9*, 181–204.

Polivy, J., & Herman, C. P. (1985). Dieting and binging: A causal analysis. *The American Psychologist, 40*, 193–201.

Ryan, R. M., & Deci, E. L. (2000). Self-determination theory and the facilitation of intrinsic motivation, social development, and well-being. *The American Psychologist, 55*, 68–78.

Schmuck, P., Kasser, T., & Ryan, R. M. (2000). Intrinsic and extrinsic goals: Their structure and relationship to wellbeing in German and U. S. college students. *Social Indicators Research, 50*, 225–241.

Setterlund, M. B., & Niedenthal, P. M. (1993). "Who am I? Why am I here?" Self-esteem, self-clarity, and prototype matching. *Journal of Personality and Social Psychology, 65*, 769–780.

Sheldon, K. M., & HouserMarko, L. (2001). Self-concordance, goal attainment, and the pursuit of happiness: Can there be an upward spiral? *Journal of Personality and Social Psychology, 80*, 152–165.

Stapel, D. A., & Koomen, W. (2001). The impact of interpretation versus comparison mindsets on knowledge accessibility effects. *Journal of Experimental Social Psychology, 37*, 134–149.

Tice, D. M., & Bratslavsky, E. (2000). Giving in to feel good: The place of emotion regulation in the context of general self-control. *Psychological Inquiry, 11*, 149–159.

Vallacher, R. R., & Wegner, D. M. (1987). What do people think they're doing? Action identification and human behavior. *Psychological Review, 94*, 3–15.

Wegner, D. M., Vallacher, R. R., & Kiersted, G. W. (1986). Action identification in the emergence of social behavior. *Social Cognition, 4*, 18–38.

Section III

Motivational Perspectives

10

Contrast Effects in Automatic Affect, Cognition, and Behavior

JACK GLASER

A utomatic mental processes have captured the attention of cognitive and then social psychologists, and even more recently, the general public (e.g., Gladwell, 2005). These processes are known to operate outside of conscious awareness and control, be triggered spontaneously by the mere perception of even the most minimal stimulus, and proceed to completion without effort or attention (e.g., Bargh, 1994, 1997; Neely, 1977; Schiffrin & Schneider, 1977). Of particular interest and importance to social psychologists, fundamental intergroup processes also have automatic components. Compelling demonstrations have been made of the automaticity of attitude activation—that evaluations of objects, concepts, people, and even social groups occur rapidly, spontaneously, and unintentionally (e.g., Bargh, Chaiken, Govender, & Pratto, 1992; Bargh, Chaiken, Raymond, & Hymes, 1996; Fazio, Jackson, Dunton, & Williams, 1995; Fazio, Sanbonmatzu, Powell, & Kardes, 1986). On the cognitive side, research building on theories and methodologies relating to memory and mental construct activation (Higgins, Rholes, & Jones, 1977; Meyer & Schevaneveldt, 1971; Neely, 1977) has revealed that beliefs, and specifically stereotypes, can be activated automatically (e.g., Banaji & Hardin, 1996; Bargh & Pietromonaco, 1982; Blair & Banaji, 1996; Dovidio, Evans, & Tyler, 1986). Automatic components of behavior too have been demonstrated, some behaviors being more benign (e.g., Bargh, Chen, & Burrows, 1996, found that subliminally priming people with thoughts of the elderly caused them to walk more slowly) than others (e.g., Correll, Park, Judd, & Wittenbrink, 2002; and Greenwald, Oakes, & Hoffman, 2003, found that people tend to shoot Black men holding guns faster than White men holding guns in a speeded computer simulation).

Through most of the history of automaticity theory and research, there has been a presumption of "inescapability" (Devine, 1989) that has led one expert to muse about the "cognitive monster" inherent in our automatic tendencies (Bargh, 1999; see Blair, 2002, for a thorough review about presumptions of the inevitability of automatic effects). In fact, *automaticity* has been used synonymously with *uncontrollability*. The relevance of automaticity to issues of assimilation and contrast, therefore, is that automatic reactions to stimuli lend themselves well to assimilation, but the types of adjustments needed for comparison—or correction—contrast effects to occur are precluded in most theories of automaticity. There is a widely held presumption that awareness of the influence (or at least the potential influence) of a biasing stimulus (a "prime") is needed to engender contrast effects. It is only once one notices a difference and/or exerts some form of conscious control over one's judgments that the influence of extraneous stimuli can be adjusted, and, indeed, overadjusted for.

The theory that conscious awareness of the potential influence of an extraneous stimulus (a prime) is necessary for contrast effects (either via comparison or correction) to occur is empirically based (e.g., Lepore & Brown, 2002; Lombardi, Higgins, & Bargh, 1987; Martin, Seta, & Crelia, 1990; Newman & Uleman, 1990; Strack, Schwarz, Bless, Kübler, & Wänke, 1993) and clearly articulated (e.g., Jacoby, Kelley, & McElree, 1999; Strack & Hannover, 1996; Wilson & Brekke, 1994). It may be, however, that conscious awareness is sufficient but not necessary to give rise to contrast effects, and that automatic vigilance for biasing information allows for the possibility of contrast occurring without conscious awareness. Another area of research on nonconscious mental processes supports this idea. Specifically, research on implicit goals and motives (e.g., Bargh & Barndollar, 1996; Bargh & Chartrand, 1999; Bargh & Ferguson, 2000; Bargh, Gollwitzer, Lee-Chai, Barndollar, & Trötschel, 2001; Chartrand & Bargh, 1996; Shah & Kruglanski, 2003) has demonstrated that they can be activated and influential without conscious awareness or control.

Pushing this idea to its extreme, Kihlstrom and I (Glaser & Kihlstrom, 2005) have argued for entertaining the possibility of the seemingly oxymoronic "unconscious awareness," borrowing from Hilgard's (1977) conceptions of "divided consciousness" and a "hidden observer." Moskowitz, Gollwitzer, Wasel, and Schaal (1999) have made a similar argument: that automatic compensatory processes can result, without conscious activation, from deeply internalized chronic goals. It appears from recent social neuroscience research that efforts to control prejudiced responding can, indeed, originate preconsciously (Amodio, Harmon-Jones, & Devine, 2003; Amodio et al., 2004). These ideas will be discussed in greater detail below with regard to inhibition of automatic stereotype activation (Moskowitz et al., 1999) and correction processes in reverse priming (Glaser & Banaji, 1999).

EVIDENCE FOR CONTROL OF AUTOMATIC PROCESSES

In response to the growing consensus that automatic processes are uncontrollable (Bargh, 1999), and the attendant concerns about the inevitability of unintended bias and discrimination, social psychologists have begun to explore the possibility that nonconscious biases are indeed "malleable." Some of this literature has created unnecessary confusion because malleability has been taken to mean controllability, when in fact many of the relevant studies have revealed that underlying implicit associations (e.g., stereotypes, evaluations) are malleable (i.e., changeable), rather than that their activation can be controlled. Nevertheless, some of the investigations being described under this rubric of malleability do indeed appear to indicate that the automatic activation of mental processes can be *controlled*, through automatic inhibition, correction, and distraction.

Blair (2002) provides a thorough review of this line of research, so it need not be reiterated fully here, but some of her conclusions are worth highlighting in the context of assimilation and contrast in automatic affect, cognition, and behavior. Specifically, some studies of automatic stereotyping and prejudice reveal that stereotype and prejudice activation and/or application can be altered due to a number of different types of factors. These factors, according to Blair, include: *self-image motives*—employing or inhibiting stereotypes that support or undermine, respectively, positive self-image (e.g., Sinclair & Kunda, 1999); and *social motives*—moderating stereotypes or prejudice to achieve social relations goals, such as getting along with outgroup members (e.g., Richeson & Ambady, 2001).

Blair (2002) also identifies *specific strategies* that have been shown to moderate automatic stereotyping and prejudice, including: *suppression*, although such effects are very limited (e.g., Gollwitzer & Schaal, 1998) and have been shown to have rebound effects (i.e., leading to especially strong stereotyping) once the initial suppression effort is lifted (e.g., Macrae, Bodenhausen, Milne, & Jetten, 1994); and *promotion of counterstereotypes*, e.g., by expecting counterstereotypes (Blair & Banaji, 1996) or invoking counterstereotypic imagery (e.g., strong women; Blair, Ma, & Lenton, 2001). Blair also notes that manipulating the perceiver's *focus of attention* can attenuate the impact of automatic biases. For example, cognitive busyness (i.e., distraction, perhaps due to retaining a long number in memory) reduces stereotype activation (e.g., Gilbert & Hixon, 1991). Whether such distraction leading to reduced automatic activation of implicit associations reflects real "control" is perhaps a philosophical question. To the extent that preventing the perceiver from perceiving (even subliminally) the triggering stimulus at all—to take the argument to its logical extreme—will prevent the automatic activation of the related construct, one has to question whether this reflects *control* on the part of the perceiver so much as *interference* on the part of the environment.

Not surprisingly, then, another factor Blair (2002) identifies as moderating the automatic activation of stereotypes or prejudice is the *configuration of stimulus cues*. Blair cites a Macrae, Bodenhausen, and Milne (1995) study in which female or Chinese stereotypes were activated when a Chinese woman target stimulus was pictured applying makeup versus using chopsticks, respectively. Those who saw the woman applying makeup were faster to recognize female-related trait words, and those who saw the woman eating with chopsticks were faster to recognize Chinese-related trait words, in a subsequent, ostensibly unrelated task. Although this may represent another example of environmental determinants of what gets activated, more than individual *control*, the implication is that individuals may be able to *choose* the category to which they wish to attend, in the service of circumventing unintended bias.

Other research that has been characterized as reflecting the control of automatic bias more clearly represents the malleability of implicit associations. For example, Kawakami, Dovidio, Moll, Hermsen, and Russin (2000) had participants relearn stereotypes by "just saying no," repeatedly responding negatively to stereotypic pairings of stimuli (and affirmatively to counterstereotypic pairings). Consequently, these participants exhibited less automatic stereotyping on a subsequent reaction time task. This strategy resulted in short- (immediate) and long- (24 hours) term reduction in automatic stereotyping effects. Similarly, Dasgupta and Greenwald (2001) presented examples of liked minority and disliked majority group members to participants, resulting in reduced automatic stereotyping that persisted 24 hours later. Results of tests such as these offer reason for hope that automatic stereotyping and prejudice is not as inevitable as it was believed to be in the wake of earlier research on the subject (e.g., Devine, 1989). To the extent that individuals take steps to alter their implicit biases, those biases are alterable, and contextual factors (such as which of multiple possible categories a person is perceived as belonging to) can determine whether or not a bias is activated. In the absence of such influences, however, controlling automatic feelings, thoughts, and behaviors (including prejudice, stereotypes, and discrimination) will require nonconscious vigilance. Conscious vigilance will not suffice because, once activated, automatic processes cannot be deliberately interrupted. Evidence for nonconscious vigilance, present in findings of contrast in automatic effects, described below, appears to be growing.

CONTRAST IN AUTOMATIC AFFECT, COGNITION, AND BEHAVIOR

Assimilation effects, covered so thoroughly in this volume, appear to be the resounding norm in studies of automatic construct activation. This is perhaps due to the need for a secondary adjustment, either correction or comparison, that is necessary for contrast effects and that, logically, is less likely to occur under the kinds of conditions typically employed to study automatic processes (e.g., time pressure, cognitive load, unobtrusiveness). Nevertheless, a nontrivial number of studies have emerged wherein the mental activity being investigated most certainly reflects automaticity, but contrastive results have been obtained. Many of these will be considered here, divided into affect, cognition, and behavior, and their related intergroup constructs—prejudice, stereotyping, and discrimination—respectively. I will also consider studies of automatic processes that yield noncontrastive (and nonassimilative) results, which nevertheless appear to reflect the type of automatic adjustments that, if stronger, could yield contrast.

Contrast in Automatic Affect

Adopting a highly nonreactive method for studying automatic evaluation developed by Bargh, Chaiken, et al. (1996), Glaser and Banaji (1999) employed a sequential priming procedure with a short prime presentation and latency to pronounce the target word as the dependent variable. In a sequential priming procedure, two stimuli (in this case, words), a "prime" and a "target," are pre-sented in rapid succession (e.g., the prime is typically presented for 200 ms or less) and a response is given to the second stimulus. The speed of response is taken as a measure of the strength of association between the concepts represented by the two stimuli. Fazio et al. (1986) demonstrated that when the target is preceded by an evaluatively congruent prime it is evaluated more quickly. Bargh, Chaiken, et al. (1996) replicated this finding when the response task was simply to read the target word aloud. Fazio et al. (1995) also demonstrated that such procedures could be used to measure implicit racial attitudes, varying the race of the prime and finding White participants to be faster, on average, to respond to positive targets preceded by White primes and negative targets preceded by Black primes.

By employing the word pronunciation task and manipulating the evaluative valence (positive/negative) and the race-relatedness (Black/White) of the prime *and* the target, Glaser and Banaji (1999) could assess automatic evaluation (faster reading of targets preceded by evaluatively congruent primes), automatic race categorization (faster reading of race targets preceded by same-race primes), and automatic prejudice (faster reading of Black and White targets preceded by negative and positive race-neutral primes, respectively).[1] All of our hypotheses were supported, but with some interesting moderators, which became the focus of subsequent experiments and the basis for much of the following discussion.

We used two distinct sets of race-neutral, evaluatively valenced (positive/negative) stimulus words that serendipitously differed in their extremity. With the more moderately valenced words, our hypotheses were supported. But with the very extremely valenced words serving as primes, we obtained results that were strong and in the opposite direction (faster responding to target words—regardless of target extremity—preceded by evaluatively incongruent primes). We replicated this result a number of times, under several procedural variations. We dubbed this pattern of results "reverse priming," and because other explanations were not reconcilable with our results and various post hoc analyses, we concluded that the reversed effects resulted from correction. The procedure exceeded basic condi-tions (e.g., timing of stimulus presentation) for precluding controlled processing explaining the reaction time differences (Neely, 1977). This necessitated that the results reflected *automatic* evaluation, and because participants were unaware that their evaluations of the stimuli were being assessed, any correction for such bias was most likely automatic as well.

We further speculated that such a correction would most likely result from an unconscious motivation to respond accurately, and a direct test of this hypothesis, manipulating accuracy motivation, yielded supportive results (Glaser, 2003). This study also provides a plausible explanation for the discrepancies in the findings of Glaser and Banaji (1999) and those of Bargh, Chaiken, et al. (1996), who had employed very similar procedures and obtained equal levels of assimilative prim-ing with moderate and extreme primes (i.e., no reverse priming as in Glaser & Banaji, 1999; and no weaker priming with weaker primes, as in Fazio et al., 1986).

I (Glaser, 2003) adopted the stimuli and procedures used by Bargh, Chaiken, et al. Perhaps most important, the use of target word sets that were different than the prime sets, and generally more moderate than the extreme words used by

Glaser and Banaji, may have led participants to be less concerned (however non-consciously) with the possibility of primes interfering with the responses to the targets, thereby weakening any reverse priming effects. I manipulated accuracy motivation by informing only half the participants (as all participants had been instructed in the Glaser & Banaji, 1999, experiments) that trials on which they mispronounced words would be repeated later in the procedure. Those in the "low accuracy" condition exhibited assimilative priming effects with extreme primes but not with moderate primes (consistent with Fazio et al., 1986). Those in the "high accuracy" condition exhibited priming with the moderate primes but not with the extreme primes. It seems likely that the absence of priming with extreme primes under "high" (but admittedly subtly manipulated) accuracy motivation reflects some correction (but not enough to yield full reverse priming), the extreme primes having been shown to be capable of eliciting automatic evaluation under low accuracy motivation.

Adopting the Glaser and Banaji (1999) procedure (without race stimuli, as in Experiments 4–6, because they were not interested in automatic prejudice), Maier, Berner, and Pekrun (2003; see also Berner & Maier, 2004) replicated the reverse priming effect with high trait anxiety participants only, and among moderate trait anxiety participants when they manipulated prime activation level by using two extreme primes per trial. These findings are consistent with the idea that concern over making errors (i.e., accuracy motivation), perhaps higher among anxious people, leads to reverse priming, and that stimulus salience (i.e., through extremity or repetition) triggers a correction.

Reverse priming with extreme primes in automatic evaluation measured with a pronunciation task has also been replicated by Simmons (2004), but only for participants who were instructed to ignore the primes. This could be seen as consistent with the theory that accuracy motivation moderates the direction of affective priming because instructions to ignore the prime may have a similar effect as an exhortation to avoid bias in the response to the target.

Banse (2001) found reverse priming with an evaluation task using picture and name primes of liked and disliked people, when primes were masked (subliminal) but not when they were supraliminal. While this result makes a stronger case for the automaticity of contrast in affective priming, it does pose a puzzle with regard to the effect of prime salience on inducing correction, and stands in contrast to other research indicating that usually prime obtrusiveness engenders contrast (e.g., Stapel, Koomen, & Ruys, 2002), not the other way around.

In addition to reverse priming, related paradigms have produced contrast effects in automatic affect. Underwood (1994), in a very large sample employing a BBC broadcast, found subliminal presentation of a happy face led to higher frequency of judgments of a subsequent target face as sad, compared to control. Interestingly, Underwood speculated that if this result is due to comparison contrast, it would have to be attributable to the primes not being truly subliminal for some viewers. This reflects, and illustrates the pervasiveness of, the assumption discussed above that contrast effects necessitate awareness, an assumption that the research discussed here should challenge.

Underwood (1994) also tested the subliminal affective priming effect in a laboratory-based experiment, informing only half of the participants that they would be exposed to a subliminal prime. While not increasing the chances of them actually consciously recognizing the prime, the warning did increase the likelihood that they would rate the target stimulus in a contrastive manner. In fact, those who were not given a warning were equally likely to rate the target face as happy or sad after being subliminally exposed to a happy face prime, while those who received the warning were more than four times as likely to rate the target face as sad after being subliminally exposed to the happy face prime. This may reflect that the warning instigated a vigilance for bias that did not help them to consciously recognize the prime, but did change the manner in which they nonconsciously processed it.[2]

Shapiro and Spence (2005) demonstrated that even people who do not have explicit memory for the quality of a comparison standard exhibit contrast effects, despite conscious efforts to avoid bias. Having participants rate the quality of a music recording after hearing a superior recording that was presented sufficiently far in advance to preclude explicit memory of the quality of the recording, they found that ratings of the second recording were contrasted away from the quality of the first. They did not use strict measures of automaticity (i.e., subliminal priming nor reaction time dependent measures) that would have conclusively precluded conscious, deliberate adjustment away from the comparison stimulus. Nevertheless, their findings are strongly suggestive that comparison contrast can occur without conscious awareness of the potential biasing influence of the prime, in contradiction to common beliefs that awareness is necessary for contrast to occur.

A more direct demonstration of automatic contrast in implicit evaluation was provided by Stapel and Blanton (2004) who found that extreme (in age, attractiveness, and intelligence) primes presented subliminally elicited contrasted self-evaluations in their participants. Even though participants were unaware of the primes or their influence, they compared and contrasted themselves to them. Furthermore, they found these effects were present on an indirect measure of self-regard (signature size) and an implicit, reaction time measure of self-esteem.

Stapel et al. (2002), building on Murphy and Zajonc's (1993) demonstrations that affective reactions precede cognitive appraisals, provide clear conditions for automatic contrast effects in affective priming. Specifically, they demonstrated that when subliminally presented faces exhibiting emotion appeared for very brief intervals (30 ms) only diffuse affective reactions occurred, yielding assimilative appraisals of the emotions of subsequent target stimuli. When primes appeared for somewhat longer intervals (100 ms), albeit still presented subliminally, Stapel et al. argued that they allowed for more distinct perceptions of features, which engendered comparisons with targets of the same type (faces), leading to contrast effects. This finding is bolstered by a post hoc appraisal of Murphy and Zajonc's findings. As Glaser and Banaji (1999) pointed out, Murphy and Zajonc obtained a fairly clear, but only marginally significant ($p < .08$, two-sided) contrast effect in their "optimal" (supraliminal) priming condition that they did not consider meaningful. In retrospect, this result parallels Stapel et al.'s finding and extends it to supraliminal priming.

In sum, there is ample evidence that contrastive affective judgments can occur when controlled processing is unlikely or even precluded. This trend is further borne out in research on intergroup bias (i.e., stereotyping and prejudice), where researchers have been looking for conditions under which automatic prejudice (i.e., intergroup attitudes that operate outside of conscious awareness or intent) can be moderated.

One promising set of findings with regard to control of automatic prejudice involves the consideration of context effects. For example, Maddux, Barden, Brewer, and Petty (2005) found that those high in an individual difference measure of motivation to control prejudiced responses (MCPR; Dunton & Fazio, 1997) showed automatic evaluative bias in favor of Blacks when the background was a jail cell (vs. a church interior). The opposite was true for low MCPR participants. This indicates that one's personal motivation to be nonprejudiced interacts with the effect of context, such that those high in MCPR appear to actually correct their automatic anti-Black bias when the context (a jail cell, reflecting anti-Black stereotypes of criminality) triggers the potential for stereotype influence.

Similarly, Wittenbrink, Judd, and Park (2001) found that the presentation of a film clip that presented a positive depiction of African Americans led to a significant decline in automatic anti-Black prejudice as measured by an Implicit Association Test (IAT).[3] In a second study, they found that the immediate context (e.g., church interior vs. street corner) in which a Black person prime was presented elicited opposite automatic evaluations (positive vs. negative, respectively) as assessed by a speeded (i.e., with time pressure) sequential priming task with a response latency measure. These findings, while reminiscent of the research showing the malleability of implicit associations (e.g., Dasgupta & Greenwald, 2001), indicate that the immediate context, rather than prior relearning, can affect automatic evaluation.

Inhibition and Contrast in Automatic Cognition/Stereotyping

With regard to nonconscious control of automatic cognition, the relevant research published to date appears to be limited to the specific case of stereotyping. Much of the interest in stereotype control and inhibition can be traced to Devine's (1989) influential study differentiating automatic and controlled processes in stereotyping and prejudice. Devine demonstrated that although most people have knowledge of, and automatic access to, group stereotypes, their efforts to control the application or utilization of those stereotypes are what distinguishes those who behave in more or less biased and discriminatory ways. The question that has arisen for many researchers in this area has to do with the extent to which people can inhibit the activation of stereotypes in the first place.

The most obvious strategy for inhibiting stereotype activation might be *suppression* (see Monteith, Sherman, & Devine, 1998, for a review). However, a profound problem exists with attempting to suppress stereotypes. Most notably, Macrae et al. (1994) found that, consistent with Wegner's (1994) theory of ironic processes, people instructed to suppress a stereotype exhibited greater stereotyping in subsequent tasks (a contrast effect), including a measure of automatic stereotype activation. This "just say no" to stereotyping approach, unlike Kawakami et al.'s (2000) strategy involving many repetitions and relearning (described earlier), appears to be counterproductive.

A more passive strategy for blocking stereotype activation may be found in Gilbert and Hixon's (1991) cognitive busyness manipulation, wherein participants who held an eight-digit number in their memory while doing a task were less likely to have a stereotype activated in the presence of an outgroup member. However, the danger inherent in this strategy is that, if the stereotype is activated, those who are cognitively busy are more likely to *apply* it to judgments of an outgroup target (Gilbert & Hixon, 1991, Study 2). It is not clear that the effect of cognitive busyness on stereotype activation can be described as "control" so much as "preclusion."

Making good on her challenge (Devine, 1989) to find methods to control stereotyping and prejudice, Devine and colleagues (Devine, Plant, Amodio, Harmon-Jones, & Vance, 2002; Plant & Devine, 1998) have, like Fazio and colleagues (Dunton & Fazio, 1997; Fazio et al., 1995), pursued a measure of individual differences in motivation to control prejudice. Devine and Plant parse this construct into two distinct components: *internal* motivation, representing intrinsic, self-relevant goals to be non-prejudiced; and *external* motivation, representing extrinsic concerns about others' appraisals of oneself. They find that those high in internal *and* low in external motivation to control prejudice exhibit lower levels of automatic stereotyping, presumably because they are truly and viscerally motivated to control it (Devine et al., 2002). Similarly, Hausman and Ryan (2004) found that those high in internal motivation alone exhibited less automatic stereotyping. These findings suggest that those who are highly (and chronically) intrinsically motivated to control their bias can do so even with regard to automatic stereotyping. However, although Devine and colleagues demonstrated that high internal/low external motivation individuals have the same explicit knowledge of the stereotypes in question, it remains possible that their implicit stereotypes are less strong, as opposed to being controlled.

In parallel to context effects on automatic *prejudice* (e.g., Maddux et al., 2005), Lowery, Hardin, and Sinclair (2001) found that White participants exhibited less automatic anti-Black *stereotyping* on an IAT when in the presence of a Black experimenter than when in the presence of a White experimenter, an effect that had been previously demonstrated only on an explicit measure of prejudice (Fazio et al., 1995). In this case, the lower levels of implicit bias resulting from being near a member (not to mention one in an authority position) of the stigmatized group cannot be attributed to differential levels of pre-existing implicit bias. Although motivation was not directly measured or manipulated, it does seem a likely cause of the change in attitudes, although it could also be the case that the Black experimenter serves as a positive exemplar (cf. Blair et al., 2001).

Perhaps the most direct evidence of automatic control of stereotype activation comes from Moskowitz et al.'s (1999) demonstration that those with chronic egalitarian goals (i.e., consistent, internalized motivation to be nonprejudiced) exhibited lower levels of automatic gender stereotype activation. Moskowitz and colleagues assessed chronic egalitarianism indirectly, by forcing participants to violate their egalitarian ideals and assessing whether or not participants sub-sequently displayed extra egalitarianism when given the opportunity. Those who did were deemed high in chronic egalitarianism, and they, in turn, exhibited less automatic stereotype activation on a sequential priming task. One of Moskowitz et al.'s experiments employed a negative priming paradigm, which assesses inhibi-tory processes to the extent that it detects slower responses to targets that had served as primes in recent trials—hence the inhibition of the prime slows the response to the same word when it subsequently serves as the target. Using this method, they provided persuasive evidence that the lower stereotype activation among high egalitarians resulted from active inhibition of the stereotypes. These results are compelling with regard to automatic stereotype inhibition, though they do need to be considered in light of Wasel and Gollwitzer's (1997) finding that priming of the sort employed in the Moskowitz et al. test of stereotype activation had to be supraliminal (i.e., consciously perceptible) for stereotype inhibition to occur. Similarly, de Houwer, Hendrickx, and Baeyens (1997) found that awareness of primes led to contrast effects in implicit learning (i.e., learning associations, through repeated pairings, without awareness). These findings only suggest that on some level there may need to be conscious awareness of the possibility of stereotype activation for some form of automatic control (inhibition, correction) to occur.

The studies described above are relevant to the present discussion to the extent that they provide evidence for control of automatic stereotyping, implying some degree of adjustment that may be related to the type of processes that yield contrast. None of these studies, however, involve actual contrast effects. Lepore and Brown (2002), on the other hand, found that awareness of a possible relation between (supraliminal) group priming and judgments of targets led to contrastive results—low prejudice individuals showed less stereotyping when unaware and more when aware; high prejudice individuals showed more stereotyping when unaware and less when aware. Lepore and Brown postulate a correction mechan-ism operating for those participants who suspect that the priming affects their judgments. Because conscious awareness of the possibility of displaying bias was necessary, and the dependent variable involved a deliberative judgment, we cannot say with confidence that these results reflect automatic correction, but it is a reasonable inference. Lepore and Brown's results, in combination with those of other experiments demonstrating inhibition, indicate that the mechan-isms necessary for correction and contrast exist in the domain of automatic stereotyping.

Contrast in Automatic Behavior/Discrimination

Recent research indicates that behaviors can unfold automatically, even with a minimal triggering stimulus (e.g., marginally perceived prime). In the realm of intergroup relations, such findings promise to help explain the impact of implicit biases on intergroup behavior. For example, Fazio et al.'s (1995) finding that the strength of an automatic negative evaluation of Blacks predicted the quality of nonverbal (i.e., unintended) behavior during interaction with a Black confederate suggests that implicit biases may be influential in this way. A better understanding of automatic behavior, and the conditions that may give rise to contrastive effects, could be useful, and a number of researchers have begun exploring this area.

Findings that priming of an outgroup causes automatic behavior consistent with outgroup stereotypes (e.g., college students walk more slowly when unobtrusively primed with thoughts of the elderly; Bargh, Chen, & Burrows, 1996) are somewhat puzzling because one might expect such behavior to occur only if the stereotype is relevant to the self-concept. Accordingly, Spears, Gordijn, Dijksterhuis, and Stapel (2004) demonstrated that ingroup–outgroup ("us–them") priming led to contrast in automatic behavior (e.g., coloring pictures neatly vs. messily, carrying out tasks more or less quickly) when the primed stereotypes (e.g., neatness, speed, respectively) were associated with outgroups. Similarly, Schubert and Hafner (2003) demonstrated that stereotypes of outgroups elicit a contrast effect in automatic behavior if the self is subliminally primed. These results almost certainly reflect comparison contrast (as opposed to correction), given that thoughts of self and group identity naturally invite social comparison.

Dijksterhuis, Spears, and Lépinasse (2001), replicating similar findings by Dijksterhuis et al. (1998), found that people asked to form an impression of a group exhibited automatic behavior that was assimilative to the group's stereotype (e.g., those primed with elderly behaved more slowly), while those who formed an impression of a specific exemplar behaved in a contrastive manner. Specifically, they performed slower or faster, respectively, on a lexical decision task (i.e., deciding quickly if a stimulus is a real word or a nonword). This reflects automatic behavior to the extent that participants were unaware of the potential influence of the group stereotype priming on their performance. Furthermore, the dependent measure, response speed, is unlikely to reflect deliberate intent.

There is also emerging evidence that more clear automatic behavior is subject to control and perhaps contrast effects. Specifically, Glaser and Knowles (2006; Park, Glaser, & Knowles, 2006) have adopted the "shooter task," a procedure developed by Correll et al. (2002), to test for *implicit motivation to control prejudice* (IMCP) and have found some evidence of contrast. The shooter task involves a computer simulation of police target practice where a series of men are presented and the task is to "shoot" (with a button press, or, in the Glaser & Knowles procedure, pulling a trigger) as fast as possible any man who is holding a gun. Half of the men are holding guns and the other half are holding harmless objects. Within those two groups of target stimuli, half are Black and half are White. Correll et al. have found repeatedly that participants are faster and more likely to shoot Black men holding guns than White men holding guns, and that this tendency correlates with the strength of a stereotype (measured explicitly) associating Blacks with weapons. Glaser and Knowles have also found the shooter bias to be prevalent in our sample, and found it to be correlated with an implicit race-weapons stereotype.

Shooter bias is an excellent measure of automatic behavior because, in addition to being measured using response latency in a speeded task, the bias (i.e., shooting Blacks faster) clearly reflects an *unintended* behavior that the vast majority of participants would control if they could. Furthermore, because shooter bias correlates with the implicit race-weapons stereotype, it represents a good opportunity to test for nonconscious control of the impact of implicit biases on automatic behavior, which is precisely the goal of our research. However, directly measuring an implicit motive is not straightforward and there is no existing precedent for it. Moskowitz et al. (1999) have identified an efficacious proxy (compensatory behaviors after forced defiance of egalitarianism) for a related construct (chronic egalitarianism), but developing a direct measure of an implicit motive is another matter. Accordingly, we have hypothesized that those who are high in both an implicit *belief in one's own prejudice* and an implicit *negative attitude toward prejudice*, both measurable with IATs, should be high in IMCP.

The strong test of the existence of IMCP would not be so much that those high in both belief in their own prejudice and negative attitude toward prejudice show relatively low levels of shooter bias, because they may indeed have less bias, but not necessarily be inhibiting it. Rather, those high in IMCP should exhibit a weaker relation between their implicit race-weapons stereotype and the shooter bias, because they are controlling the impact of the stereotype. Indeed, we find that those who are not high in both belief in their own prejudice and negative attitude toward prejudice (i.e., those not high in IMCP) have positive correlations between implicit race-weapons stereotype and shooter bias. Those high in both belief in their own prejudice and negative attitude toward prejudice (i.e., those high in IMCP) show a weak, nonsignificant relation between the race-weapons stereotype and shooter bias. The negative slope of the correlation is suggestive of a contrast effect resulting from overcorrection.

In sum, research like that of Moskowitz et al. (1999) and Glaser and Knowles (2005) indicates that stereotypes operating outside of conscious awareness or control do not inevitably lead to automatic discriminatory behavior. Rather, some people are able, however nonconsciously, to inhibit the effects of these stereotypes. It appears that, in addition to affect, cognition, and behavior operating outside of conscious awareness and control (i.e., automatically), the mechanisms necessary to compensate for resulting biases may also transpire automatically.

CORRECTION VERSUS COMPARISON CONTRAST

The reverse priming findings stand apart from most contrast findings because the proposed mechanism is automatic correction (Glaser, 2003; Glaser & Banaji, 1999; Glaser & Kihlstrom, 2005) as opposed to the more common comparison-contrast explanations (e.g., Stapel et al., 2002). Stapel, Koomen, and Zeelenberg (1998) articulate the importance of this distinction and it is amply covered elsewhere in this volume. But it is worth briefly considering what accounts for this difference across studies of automatic processes.

Perhaps the most critical feature of studies of automatic contrast with regard to differentiating between comparison and correction is the nature of the dependent variable. Specifically, reaction time dependent variables, particularly in sequential priming paradigms, virtually necessitate that contrast effects result from correction instead of comparison. Indeed, this was the primary rationale for Glaser and Banaji's (1999) conclusion that reverse priming was due to correction, and, in fact, it was concern over confusion with the more common comparison-contrast effects that led us to coin a new term (reverse priming) and call it something other than "contrast."

With a sequential priming task using a reaction time dependent measure, a contrast effect describes when responses are slower to congruent prime–target pairs than to incongruent pairs (and, ideally, to a neutral prime condition). In order for comparison processes to yield such a contrast effect, both the prime and target would have to first be recognized, then one would have to be compared to and contrasted from (perhaps due to being very disparate) the other. Subsequently, the prime and target would have to be re-considered, as a pair, and the process of facilitation or inhibition due to similarity or difference between prime and target that leads to differential response times would have to take place. This multistage process (depicted in the second row of Figure 10.1) seems highly improbable, especially given that such reaction time studies typically involve responses that take little more than half of a second. Furthermore, in the case of the Glaser and Banaji (1999) reverse priming results, the reaction times were comparable with the numerous studies that had yielded only congruent effects (e.g., Bargh et al., 1992; Bargh, Chaiken, et al., 1996; Fazio et al., 1986), suggesting that the extra processing stages required of a comparison-contrast account would not be allowed for. Additional evidence against a comparison-contrast explanation for reverse priming comes from the fact that, in the Glaser

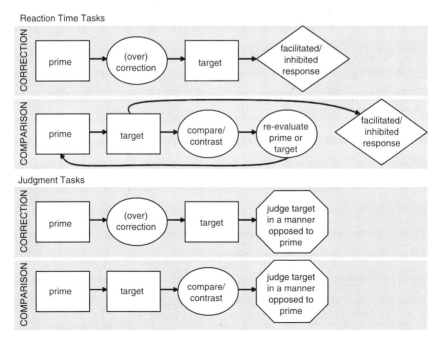

FIGURE 10.1 Likely sequences for correction- versus comparison-contrast effects with reaction time versus judgment measures.

and Banaji experiments, target words varied in extremity as well, but this had no effect on the direction of the priming (reverse priming occurs only when the *prime* is extreme), suggesting that the cause of the contrast resided in the prime alone, not the comparison of the prime and target.

Figure 10.1 is intended to portray the temporal sequence most likely in correction- and comparison-contrast effects with reaction time versus judgment task dependent measures. This model as presented here is restricted to sequential priming procedures, which are common in studies of automatic processes. The first row, involving a reaction time dependent variable and a posited correction mechanism, reflects Glaser and Banaji's (1999) account of their reverse priming effects. A prime is perceived and, perhaps due to its obtrusiveness, a corrective response is made (e.g., an inherently negative prime elicits a positive response tendency). The response to a subsequent target stimulus is facilitated if it is incompatible with the inherent valence of the prime and inhibited if it is compatible.

The second row in Figure 10.1, as noted above, reflects a comparison-contrast account of reverse priming. In it there is no direct path from prime and target presentation to response. Rather, there is the multistage, iterative process. The curved arrows reflect the need for a reconsideration of the prime and target after one of them has been contrasted from the other in the first stage. Without this second stage, reaction time differences could not emerge. The process is cumbersome and unlikely to be able to unfold in the same time frame as the typical, direct path. This model also begs the question of when and why the comparing and contrasting would stop.

While comparison processes appear unable to explain contrast effects with reaction time dependent measures (a.k.a. reverse priming), they are much more plausible, and in fact common when the dependent measure is a continuous rating (e.g., an evaluation on a scale). This is not to say that contrast effects in rating measures cannot also result from correction. To the contrary, this is what Stapel et al. (1998) found. Rather, it is comparison that cannot explain contrast effects in sequential priming reaction time measures, not the other way around. As Figure 10.1 (bottom two rows) depicts, correction and comparison are both feasible routes to contrast effects with judgment rating dependent variables. What determines whether or not correction or comparison occurs with priming and judgment tasks has more to do with processing goals (as operationalized through experimental instructions, e.g., to correct for bias) (Stapel et al., 1998) than with any inherent limitations of either mechanism.

It should be noted that not just any reaction time procedure will preclude a comparison-contrast account. Rather, this applies to tasks that involve a direct facilitative effect of the prime on the speed of response to the target, as in the sequential priming paradigm. In these cases, the construct activation resulting from the perception of the prime facilitates (if congruent) or inhibits (if incongruent) the processing, and therefore the speed of responding to the target. As a counterexample, the study by Dijksterhuis et al. (2001) involved priming and a reaction time measure that were two separate tasks. Priming thoughts of the elderly in the first task led to slower speed on the subsequent reaction time task, but this was due to the activation of the slow stereotype, not to any facilitation or inhibition of the processing of the targets. Consequently, a reaction time task of this sort is coincidental, and the contrast effect could, and probably does, result from comparison.

CONCLUSION

As noted at the outset of this chapter, the preponderance of automatic priming or context effects appear to be assimilative. There has long been a presumption that, in order for contrast effects to occur, via some adaptation or correction, a degree of awareness of the potentially biasing prime or context is necessary. But findings of contrast effects in measures of automatic processes challenge this presumption and provide evidence of a sophisticated and comprehensive unconscious.

The implications of contrast (i.e., reverse priming) effects in sequential priming automatic evaluation studies are profound. Because a comparison account, which may entail relatively passive processing (i.e., *perceiving* the target differently in relation to the prime), is not plausible, correction is the most likely explanation (Glaser & Banaji, 1999). That people are correcting for an evaluation (of the prime) that they are not consciously aware they are making strongly suggests that humans are capable of being nonconsciously vigilant for biasing information and taking proactive and yet unconscious action to redress such bias. We have long known that humans automatically categorize (Neely, 1977) and evaluate (Fazio et al., 1986) stimuli. More recently, psychologists have demonstrated that behavior can have automatic, unintended components (e.g., Bargh, Chen, & Burrows, 1996; Correll et al., 2002). If affect, cognition, and behavior can operate automatically, why not the other pillar of human mentality: motivation? Indeed, recent investigations have compellingly demonstrated the existence and qualities of nonconscious motivation (e.g., Chartrand & Bargh, 1996; Shah & Kruglanski, 2003). Research evidencing automatic control of automatic cognitions (Moskowitz, et al., 1999), affect (Glaser & Banaji, 1999), and behavior (Glaser & Knowles, 2005) implicates implicit goals to be unbiased, in terms of mundane information processing, but also social egalitarianism.

NOTES

1. We also found evidence for automatic race prejudice by testing the prime race by target valence interaction (i.e., race-neutral positive and negative targets were pronounced faster when preceded by White- and Black-related primes, respectively).

2. It should also be noted that with the larger BBC viewing sample, due to the constraints of the television broadcast medium for manipulating the independent variable, Underwood confounded the priming variable (presence vs. absence of subliminal smiling prime) with geographic region. This cannot, however, explain the contrast effect found in the lab.

3. The Implicit Association Test (IAT) is a well-validated, computerized reaction time measure of nonconscious associations (Greenwald, McGhee, & Schwartz, 1998;

Nosek, Greenwald, & Banaji, 2005). The procedure involves having participants make paired categorizations of stimuli (e.g., Black with bad and White with good, and vice versa) and comparing the differential speed at which they can make these categorizations.

REFERENCES

Amodio, D. M., Harmon-Jones, E., & Devine, P. G. (2003). Individual differences in the activation and control of affective race bias as assessed by startle eyeblink response and self-report. *Journal of Personality and Social Psychology, 84*, 738–753.

Amodio, D. M., Harmon-Jones, E., Devine, P. G., Curtin, J. J., Hartley, S. L., & Covert, A. E. (2004). Neural signals for the detection of unintentional race bias. *Psychological Science, 15*, 88–93.

Banaji, M. R., & Hardin, C. D. (1996). Automatic stereotyping. *Psychological Science, 7*, 136–141.

Banse, R. (2001). Affective priming with liked and disliked persons: Prime visibility determines congruency and incongruency effects. *Cognition and Emotion, 15*, 501–520.

Bargh, J. A. (1994). The four horsemen of automaticity: Awareness, intention, efficiency, and control in social cognition. In R. S. Wyer & T. K. Srull (Eds.), *Handbook of social cognition* (2nd ed., pp. 1–40). Hillsdale, NJ: Lawrence Erlbaum Associates, Inc.

Bargh, J. A. (1997). The automaticity of everyday life. In R. Wyer (Ed.), *Advances in social cognition* (Vol. X, pp. 1–62). Mahwah, NJ: Lawrence Erlbaum Associates, Inc.

Bargh, J. A. (1999). The cognitive monster: The case against the controllability of automatic stereotype effects. In S. Chaiken & Y. Trope (Eds.), *Dual-process theories in social psychology* (pp. 361–382). New York: Guilford Press.

Bargh, J. A., & Barndollar, K. (1996). Automaticity in action: The unconscious as repository of chronic goals and motives. In P. M. Gollwitzer & J. A. Bargh (Eds.), *The psychology of action* (pp. 457–481). New York: Guilford Press.

Bargh, J. A., Chaiken, S., Govender, R., & Pratto, F. (1992). The generality of the automatic attitude activation effect. *Journal of Personality and Social Psychology, 62*, 893–912.

Bargh, J. A., Chaiken, S., Raymond, P., & Hymes, C. (1996). The automatic evaluation effect: Unconditional automatic attitude activation with a pronunciation task. *Journal of Experimental Social Psychology, 32*, 104–128.

Bargh, J. A., & Chartrand, T. L. (1999). The unbearable automaticity of being. *The American Psychologist, 54*, 462–479.

Bargh, J. A., Chen, M., & Burrows, L. (1996). The automaticity of social behavior: Direct effects of trait concept and stereotype activation on action. *Journal of Personality and Social Psychology, 71*, 230–244.

Bargh, J. A., & Ferguson, M. J. (2000). Beyond behaviorism: On the automaticity of higher mental processes. *Psychological Bulletin, 126*, 925–945.

Bargh, J. A., Gollwitzer, P. M., Lee-Chai, A., Barndollar, K., & Trötschel, R. (2001). The automated will: Nonconscious activation and pursuit of behavioral goals. *Journal of Personality and Social Psychology, 81*, 1014–1027.

Bargh, J. A., & Pietromonaco, P. (1982). Automatic information processing and social perception: The influence of trait information presented outside of conscious awareness. *Journal of Personality and Social Psychology, 43*, 437–449.

Berner, M. P., & Maier, M. A. (2004). The direction of affective priming as a function of trait anxiety when naming target words with regular and irregular pronunciation. *Experimental Psychology, 51,* 180–190.

Blair, I. V. (2002). The malleability of automatic stereotypes and prejudice. *Personality and Social Psychology Review, 6,* 242–261.

Blair, I. V., & Banaji, M. R. (1996). Automatic and controlling processes in stereotype priming. *Journal of Personality and Social Psychology, 70,* 1142–1163.

Blair, I. V., Ma, J. E., & Lenton, A. P. (2001). Imagining stereotypes away: The moderation of implicit stereotypes through mental imagery. *Journal of Personality and Social Psychology, 81,* 828–841.

Chartrand, T. L., & Bargh, J. A. (1996). Automatic activation of impression formation and memorization goals: Nonconscious goal priming reproduces effects of explicit task instructions. *Journal of Personality and Social Psychology, 71,* 464–478.

Correll, J., Park, B., Judd, C. M., & Wittenbrink, B. (2002). The police officer's dilemma: Using ethnicity to disambiguate potentially threatening individuals. *Journal of Personality and Social Psychology, 83,* 1314–1329.

Dasgupta, N., & Greenwald, A.G. (2001). On the malleability of automatic attitudes: Combating automatic prejudice with images of admired and disliked individuals. *Journal of Personality and Social Psychology, 81,* 800–814.

De Houwer, J., Hendrickx, H., & Baeyens, F. (1997). Evaluative learning with "subliminally" presented stimuli. *Consciousness and Cognition, 6,* 87–107.

Devine, P. G. (1989). Stereotypes and prejudice: Their automatic and controlled components. *Journal of Personality and Social Psychology, 56,* 5–18.

Devine, P. G., Plant, E. A., Amodio, D. M., Harmon-Jones, E., & Vance, S. L. (2002). The regulation of explicit and implicit race bias: The role of motivations to respond without prejudice. *Journal of Personality and Social Psychology, 82,* 835–848.

Dijksterhuis, A., Spears, R., & Lépinasse, V. (2001). Reflecting and deflecting stereotypes: Assimilation and contrast in impression formation and automatic behavior. *Journal of Experimental Social Psychology, 37,* 286–299.

Dijksterhuis, A., Spears, R., Postmes, T., Stapel, D. A., Koomen, W., van Knippenberg, A., & Scheepers, D. (1998). Seeing one thing and doing another: Contrast effects in automatic behavior. *Journal of Personality and Social Psychology, 75,* 862–871.

Dovidio, J. F., Evans, N., & Tyler, R. B. (1986). Racial stereotypes: The contents of their cognitive representations. *Journal of Experimental Social Psychology, 22,* 22–37.

Dunton, B. C., & Fazio, R. H. (1997). An individual difference measure of motivation to control prejudiced reactions. *Personality and Social Psychology Bulletin, 23,* 316–326.

Fazio, R. H., Jackson, J. R., Dunton, B. C., & Williams, C. J. (1995). Variability in automatic activation as an unobtrusive measure of racial attitudes: A bona fide pipeline? *Journal of Personality and Social Psychology, 69,* 1013–1027.

Fazio, R. H., Sanbonmatsu, D. M., Powell, M. C., & Kardes, F. R. (1986). On the automatic activation of attitudes. *Journal of Personality and Social Psychology, 50,* 229–238.

Gilbert, D. T., & Hixon, J. G. (1991). The trouble of thinking: Activation and application of stereotypic beliefs. *Journal of Personality and Social Psychology, 60,* 509–517.

Gladwell, M. (2005). *Blink: The power of thinking without thinking.* New York: Little, Brown.

Glaser, J. (2003). Reverse priming: Implications for the (un)conditionality of automatic evaluation. In J. Musch & K. C. Klauer (Eds.), *The psychology of evaluation: Affective processes in cognition and emotion.* Mahwah, NJ: Lawrence Erlbaum Associates, Inc.

Glaser, J., & Banaji, M. R. (1999). When fair is foul and foul is fair: Reverse priming in automatic evaluation. *Journal of Personality and Social Psychology, 77*, 669–687.

Glaser, J., & Kihlstrom, J. F. (2005). Compensatory automaticity: Unconscious volition is not an oxymoron. In R. Hassin, J. S. Uleman, & J. A. Bargh (Eds.), *The new unconscious* (pp. 171–195). New York: Oxford University Press.

Glaser, J., & Knowles, E. D. (2006). *Implicit motivation to control prejudice.* Unpublished manuscript, University of California, Berkeley.

Gollwitzer, P. M., & Schaal, B. (1998). Metacognition in action: The importance of implementation intentions. *Personality and Social Psychology Review, 2*, 124–136.

Greenwald, A. G., McGhee, D. E., & Schwartz, J. L. K. (1998). Measuring individual differences in implicit cognition: The implicit association test. *Journal of Personality and Social Psychology, 74*, 1464–1480.

Greenwald, A. G., Oakes, M. A., & Hoffman, H. (2003). Targets of discrimination: Effects of race on responses to weapons holders. *Journal of Experimental Social Psychology, 39*, 399–405.

Hausmann, L. R. M. & Ryan, C. S. (2004). Effects of external and internal motivation to control prejudice on implicit prejudice: The mediating role of efforts to control prejudiced responses. *Basic and Applied Social Psychology, 26*, 215–225.

Higgins, E. T., Rholes, W. S., & Jones, C. R. (1977). Category accessibility and impression formation. *Journal of Experimental Social Psychology, 13*, 141–154.

Hilgard, E. R. (1977). *Divided consciousness.* New York: John Wiley.

Jacoby, L. L., Kelley, C. M., & McElree, B. D. (1999). The role of cognitive control: Early selection versus late correction. In S. Chaiken & Y. Trope (Eds.), *Dual-process theories in social psychology* (pp. 383–400). New York: Guilford Press.

Kawakami, K., Dovidio, J. F., Moll, J., Hermsen, S., & Russin, A. (2000). Just say no (to stereotyping): Effects of training in the negation of stereotype associations on stereotype activation. *Journal of Personality and Social Psychology, 78*, 871–888.

Lepore, L., & Brown, R. (2002). The role of awareness: Divergent automatic stereotype activation and implicit judgment correction. *Social Cognition, 20*, 321–351.

Lombardi, W. J., Higgins, E. T., & Bargh, J. A. (1987). The role of consciousness in priming effects on categorization: Assimilation versus contrast as a function of awareness of the priming task. *Personality and Social Psychology Bulletin, 13*, 411–429.

Lowery, B. S., Hardin, C. D., & Sinclair, S. (2001). Social influence effects on automatic racial prejudice. *Journal of Personality and Social Psychology, 81*, 842–855.

Macrae, C. N., Bodenhausen, G. V., & Milne, A. B. (1995). The dissection of selection in person perception: Inhibitory processes in social stereotyping. *Journal of Personality and Social Psychology, 69*, 397–407.

Macrae, C. N., Bodenhausen, G. V., Milne, A. B., & Jetten, J. (1994). Out of mind but back in sight: Stereotypes on the rebound. *Journal of Personality and Social Psychology, 67*, 808–817.

Maddux, W. W., Barden, J., Brewer, M. B., & Petty, R. E. (2005). Saying no to negativity: The effects of context and motivation to control prejudice on automatic evaluative responses. *Journal of Experimental Social Psychology, 41*, 19–35.

Maier, M. A., Berner, M. P., & Pekrun, R. (2003). Directionality of affective priming: Effects of trait anxiety and activation level. *Experimental Psychology, 50*, 116–123.

Martin, L. L., Seta, J. J., & Crelia, R. A. (1990). Assimilation and contrast as a function of people's willingness and ability to expend effort on forming an impression. *Journal of Personality and Social Psychology, 59*, 27–37.

Meyer, D. E., & Schevaneveldt, R. W. (1971). Facilitation in recognizing pairs of words:

Evidence of a dependence between retrieval operations. *Journal of Experimental Psychology, 90*, 227–234.

Monteith, M. J., Sherman, J. W., & Devine, P. G. (1998). Suppression as a stereotype control strategy. *Personality and Social Psychology Review, 2*, 63–82.

Moskowitz, G. B., Gollwitzer, P. M., Wasel, W., & Schaal, B. (1999). Preconscious control of stereotype activation through chronic egalitarian goals. *Journal of Personality and Social Psychology, 77*, 167–184.

Murphy, S. T., & Zajonc, R. B. (1993). Affect, cognition, and awareness: Affective priming with optimal and suboptimal stimulus exposures. *Journal of Personality and Social Psychology, 64*, 723–739.

Neely, J. H. (1977). Semantic priming and retrieval from lexical memory: Roles of inhibitionless spreading activation and limited-capacity attention. *Journal of Experimental Psychology: General, 106*, 225–254.

Newman, L. S., & Uleman, J. S. (1990). Assimilation and contrast effects in spontaneous trait inference. *Personality and Social Psychology Bulletin, 16*, 224–240.

Nosek, B. A., Greenwald, A. G., & Banaji, M. R. (2005). Understanding and using the Implicit Association Test: II. Method variables and construct validity. *Personality and Social Psychology Bulletin, 31*, 166–180.

Park, S. H., Glaser, J., & Knowles, E. D. (2006). *Implicit motivation to control prejudice moderates the effect of cognitive depletion on automatic discrimination.* Unpublished manuscript, University of California, Berkeley.

Plant, E. A., & Devine, P. G. (1998). Internal and external motivation to respond without prejudice. *Journal of Personality and Social Psychology, 75*, 811–832.

Richeson, J. A., & Ambady, N. (2001). Effects of situational power on automatic racial prejudice. *Journal of Experimental Social Psychology, 39*, 177–183.

Schubert, T. W., & Hafner, M. (2003). Contrast from social stereotypes in automatic behavior. *Journal of Experimental Social Psychology, 39*, 577–584.

Shah, J. Y., & Kruglanski, A. W. (2003). When opportunity knocks: Bottom-up priming of goals by means and its effects on self-regulation. *Journal of Personality and Social Psychology, 84*, 1109–1122.

Shapiro, S., & Spence, M. T. (2005). Mind over matter? The inability to counteract contrast effects despite conscious effort. *Psychology and Marketing, 22*, 225–245.

Shiffrin, R. M., & Schneider, W. (1977). Controlled and automatic human information processing: II. Perceptual learning, automatic attending, and a general theory. *Psychological Review, 84*, 127–190.

Simmons, J. P. (2004). *Attention to the primes determines the nature and extent of priming within the attitude activation paradigm: Implications for indirect attitude assessment.* Unpublished doctoral dissertation, Princeton University, Princeton, NJ.

Sinclair, L., & Kunda, Z. (1999). Reactions to a Black professional: Motivated inhibition and activation of conflicting stereotypes. *Journal of Personality and Social Psychology, 77*, 885–904.

Spears, R., Gordijn, E., Dijksterhuis, A., & Stapel, D. A. (2004). Reaction in action: Intergroup contrast in automatic behavior. *Personality and Social Psychology Bulletin, 30*, 605–616.

Stapel, D. A., & Blanton, H. (2004). From seeing to being: Subliminal social comparisons affect implicit and explicit self-evaluations. *Journal of Personality and Social Psychology, 87*, 468–481.

Stapel, D. A., Koomen, W., & Ruys, K. I. (2002). The effects of diffuse and distinct affect. *Journal of Personality and Social Psychology, 83*, 60–74.

Stapel, D. A., Koomen, W., & Zeelenberg, M. (1998). The impact of accuracy motivation on interpretation, comparison, and correction processes: Accuracy × knowledge accessibility effects. *Journal of Personality and Social Psychology, 74*, 878–893.

Strack, F., & Hannover, B. (1996). Awareness of influence as a precondition for implementing correctional goals. In P. M. Gollwitzer & J. A. Bargh (Eds.), *The psychology of action: Linking cognition and motivation to behaviour* (pp. 579–595). New York: Guilford Press.

Strack, F., Schwarz, N., Bless, H., Kübler, A., & Wänke, M. (1993). Awareness of the influence as a determinant of assimilation versus contrast. *European Journal of Social Psychology, 23*, 53–62.

Underwood, G. (1994). Subliminal perception on TV. *Nature, 370*, 103.

Wasel, W., & Gollwitzer, P. M. (1997). Willful control of "automatic" stereotype activation: The role of subliminally vs. supraliminally presented stimuli. *Sprache und Kognition, 16*, 198–210.

Wegner, D. M. (1994). Ironic processes of mental control. *Psychological Review, 101*, 34–52.

Wilson, T. D., & Brekke, N. (1994). Mental contamination and mental correction: Unwanted influences on judgments and evaluations. *Psychological Bulletin, 116*, 117–142.

Wittenbrink, B., Judd, C. M., & Park, B. (2001). Spontaneous prejudice in context: Variability in automatically activated attitudes. *Journal of Personality and Social Psychology, 81*, 815–827.

11

Complementary Contrast and Assimilation: Interpersonal Theory and the Social Functions of Contrast and Assimilation Effects

LARISSA Z. TIEDENS, ROSALIND M. CHOW, and
MIGUEL M. UNZUETA

*T*he notion that judgments are frequently relative is central to the research and theory on contrast and assimilation effects. Objects and people can rarely be evaluated in a vacuum and are instead compared and related to other aspects of the environment. In the case of judgments about people, contrast and assimilation effects demonstrate that people are assessed by the degree to which they are similar and different from salient others. We often evaluate ourselves by comparing ourselves with others (Festinger, 1954), and we evaluate others by comparing them to ourselves (Dunning & Hayes, 1996) or to a third party (Herr, 1986; Ostrom & Upshaw, 1968). In this sense, contrast and assimilation effects underscore the social nature of person perception. Specifically, people are evaluated *vis-à-vis* other people.

In this chapter, we suggest an additional way in which contrast and assimilation effects can be social. People's lives are filled with interactions with others that range from short-lived exchanges on the subway, to coordinating with co-workers, to the long-term commitments involved in marriages and parenting. In all of those contexts, people generally want positive social interactions. They want conversations to go smoothly; they want to feel comfortable, and to enjoy themselves when interacting with others. This desire for positive relationships can be categorized as a social motive because it is a goal revolving around the quality of social interactions with others, and can be contrasted with individualistic motives (such as the desire for food or the desire to see oneself in a positive light) that disregard others. The need for positive social relationships is basic to human nature and can guide human behavior, cognition, and emotion (Baumeister & Leary, 1995; Maslow, 1968). We argue that contrast and assimilation effects can be the product of this social motive. Because certain patterns of contrast and assimilation can facilitate and promote satisfying relationships, we propose that contrast and assimilation can be based on expectations and desires for positive relationships. We suggest a unique form of contrast and assimilation, which we call "complementary contrast and assimilation." Further, we contend that complementary contrast and assimilation facilitates social interactions. Thus, people are motivated to engage in complementary contrast and assimilation in part to fulfill their needs for social connection.

Our arguments arise from integrating a concern with the bases and consequences of contrast and assimilation effects with a classic theoretical construct in personality psychology called "interpersonal complementarity," which was defined and discussed in the context of Interpersonal Theory (Carson, 1969; Kiesler, 1983; Leary, 1957; Sullivan, 1953; Wiggins, 1982). This chapter begins with a description of Interpersonal Theory and the notion of interpersonal complementarity. We define interpersonal complementarity and explain how it can be conceptualized as a form of contrast and assimilation. The second part of the chapter focuses on the attributes of complementary contrast and assimilation and pays particular attention to the interpersonal rewards associated with complementary contrast and assimilation. In the final part of the chapter, we consider the possibility that people desire complementary contrast and assimilation as a way to promote positive relationships. In that section, we review evidence supporting the idea that people are motivated to produce complementary contrast and assimilation, we suggest specific kinds of relationship motivations that guide complementary contrast and assimilation, and we consider the effects of complementary contrast and assimilation on the products of social relationships. Our general aim is to suggest that contrast and assimilation can serve relationship goals. As such, we suggest that contrast and assimilation are not merely social in the sense that they involve at least two people, but are much more fundamentally social in the sense that they are intricately tied to people's desire for and ability to achieve positive relationship outcomes.

INTERPERSONAL THEORY

Interpersonal Theories (IT) were first suggested in the 1950s (Leary, 1957; Sullivan, 1953) and were discussed mainly in clinical and personality psychology (Carson, 1969; Kiesler, 1983; Wiggins, 1982). They have primarily been used as a framework for understanding therapist/client relationships (Kiesler, 1988; Leary, 1957; Tracey & Sherry, 1993) and psychological dysfunction (Kiesler, 1991; Leary, 1957), as well as an approach for conceptualizing and measuring individual differences in social behavior (LaForge, 1977; Wiggins, 1982). However, IT provides propositions about the basic dynamics of interpersonal interactions, and thus also has the potential to inform social and organizational psychologists about questions pertinent to those fields.

The Affiliation and Control Dimensions

The most basic principle of IT is that humans are social animals. In Leary's early work, he stated, "Man [sic] is viewed as a uniquely social being, always involved in crucial interactions with his family members, his contemporaries, his predecessors, and his society. All these factors are seen as influencing and being influenced by the individual" (1957, p. 3). That is, in IT, the social attributes of humans are the fundamental ones. In no uncertain terms Leary said, "interpersonal behavior defines the most important dimension of personality" (p. 12).

IT suggests that there are two primary dimensions of social interaction: affiliation and control. The affiliation dimension is anchored by agreeableness and quarrelsomeness and refers to the degree to which a person or behavior is friendly and warm versus aloof and cool. The control dimension is anchored by dominance and submission and refers to the degree to which a person or behavior is controlling and self-confident versus controlled by others and self-doubting. When intersected at their origins, a two-dimensional space that is typically divided into octants (each quadrant split in half) results. For the purposes of this chapter, the layout of the two-dimensional space is not particularly important, but the idea that the control and affiliation dimensions are central and basic dimensions of human social life is critical. These dimensions have also been described as fundamental to human social interaction by a number of theorists including Bales (1950), Brown (1986), Fiske (1992), Foa (1961), and Sullivan (1953).

Quite a few empirical studies have explored the notion that human behavior can be meaningfully organized along these two theoretically orthogonal dimensions (Markey, Funder, & Ozer, 2003; Moskowitz, 1994; Tracey, 1994; Wiggins, 1982). In addition, some individual difference scales measuring affiliation and control have been validated (Horowitz, Alden, Wiggins & Pincus, 2000; Horowitz, Rosenberg, Baer, Ureno, & Villasenor, 1988; LaForge & Suczeck, 1955; Locke, 2000; Wiggins, Trapnell, & Phillips, 1988), suggesting that these dimensions can describe people's chronic ways of behaving. However, for our purposes, it is important to emphasize that the initial renditions of IT did not conceptualize these dimensions as only relevant to individual differences. To the contrary, it was assumed that most people's repertoire includes behavior in all sectors of the two dimensional space created by the intersection of affiliation and control. According to Carson, "We would expect reasonably well-adjusted persons to be capable . . . of displaying behaviors across the entire range" (1969, p. 112). Recent research has established that indeed, on top of individual differences in behavioral patterns, people demonstrate situational sensitivity such that their behavior along these dimensions varies according to situational demands (Markey et al., 2003; Tiedens & Fragale, 2003).

Complementarity

The dimensions of control and affiliation are not just interpersonal in the sense that they describe behavior that an individual could display in an interpersonal setting, but also because IT makes predictions about how these dimensions are involved in the way that one person's behavior influences another person's behavior. Leary described IT as "dynamic behaviorism" because it is concerned with "the impact one person has or makes in interaction with others" (1957, p. vi). Specifically, IT predicts that the affiliativeness of one person's behavior requests or invites a similar level of affiliativeness on the part of the interaction partner. According to IT, someone who behaves in a highly agreeable fashion will likely be met with highly agreeable behavior from interaction partners. Similarly, IT predicts that someone who behaves in a highly quarrelsome manner will be met with highly quarrelsome behavior from interaction partners. In contrast, the control dimension is considered to function quite differently. The control dimension is expected to invite opposite responses. When one person acts dominantly, they are inviting the other to submit, and when an individual submits, he or she is requesting that the other take control or dominate. This interpersonal dynamic is called "complementarity" (Carson, 1969). Thus, a dyad is complementary when they are similar in terms of affiliation and different in terms of control.

Although IT theorists have not typically used the terms "contrast" and "assimilation" in their discussions of complementarity, complementarity can be seen as a particular pattern of contrast and assimilation. Since the affiliation dimension pulls for similarity in behavior and the control dimension for opposition in behavior, we have argued that one way of conceptualizing complementarity is as contrast for control and assimilation for affiliation (Tiedens & Jimemez, 2003). Thus, here we use the phrase "complementary contrast and assimilation" to refer to contrast for the control dimension and assimilation for the affiliation dimension. Just like other forms of contrast and assimilation, complementary contrast and assimilation can be expressed behaviorally (Tiedens & Fragale, 2003) or in perceptions of the self and others (Stapel & van der Zee, 2006; Tiedens & Jimenez, 2003).

Complementary contrast and assimilation is interesting for both theoretical and practical reasons. First, other theories do not make predictions about whether contrast or assimilation will occur predicated on the dimension on which a target is being judged. Rather, it is typically assumed (and rarely tested) that if an effect occurs for one trait dimension, it will generalize to any other trait dimension. That is, many approaches to understanding contrast and assimilation imply that contrast and assimilation effects are not dependent on whether an evaluation is about dominance or affiliation. In contrast, the notion of complementary contrast and assimilation suggests that whether contrast or assimilation occurs depends on the trait dimension. Contrast effects are expected for the control dimension and assimilation for the affiliation dimension. Behavior associated with the affiliation dimension conveys desires and expectations about warmth and closeness, whereas behavior associated with the control dimension conveys information about desires and expectations about who will be in charge. The notion of complementary contrast and assimilation suggests that people pay attention to these social messages and modulate their responses. Thus, in our view, the social meaning associated with the dimension on which behavior or evaluation occurs plays an important role in the psychology of contrast and assimilation. In this way, complementary contrast and assimilation poses a challenge to theoretical approaches to contrast and assimilation effects that are insensitive to trait dimensions.

Second, although there is overwhelming evidence of the degree to which people engage in self-enhancing judgment (Baumeister, 1998; Kunda, 1990; Sedikides, Gaertner, & Toguchi, 2003; Taylor & Brown, 1988; Wood, 1989), complementary contrast and assimilation suggests that people are willing to engage in contrast and assimilation processes that are not particularly flattering to the self. Complementary contrast and assimilation suggests that an individual confronted with a dominant person will portray himself in a submissive fashion and an individual confronted with a quarrelsome person will portray herself in a quarrelsome manner. Since submissiveness and quarrelsomeness are generally regarded as negative attributes (Locke, 2003), this pattern of responding requires that individuals overcome their tendencies to self-enhance. Thus, complementary contrast and assimilation proves a challenge to approaches that emphasize the self-serving functions of contrast and assimilation (Cialdini et al., 1976; Snyder, Lassegard, & Ford, 1986; Stapel & Koomen, 2001; Wood, 1989).

Finally, the particular pattern of contrast and assimilation that defines complementarity is also of interest. Contrast on the control dimension is akin to hierarchical differentiation. That is, whenever people contrast on the control dimension, the result is that one person is dominant and the other submissive. A dominant individual paired with a submissive individual constitute a social hierarchy where one person has more control than the other. Thus, understanding the principles of complementarity may be a useful lens for understanding the emergence, maintenance, and ubiquity of social hierarchical relationships. Similarly, conceptualizing contrast effects along the control dimension as hierarchy emergence may help us understand the nature of complementarity.

THE ATTRIBUTES OF COMPLEMENTARITY

Prevalent

Complementarity (i.e., assimilation for affiliation and contrast for control) was considered by IT researchers to be the most likely outcome of social interaction. Carson claimed, "complementary responses have a statistically higher probability of occurrence than do other kinds of responses" (1969, p. 144). According to IT, people would choose to associate with those who complement their personal inclinations on control and affiliation and they would shift their behavior to complement relationship partners. Such responses were suggested to occur frequently and habitually. Numerous studies have provided support for this contention (Markey et al., 2003; Sadler & Woody, 2003; Strong et al., 1988; Tiedens & Fragale, 2003; Tracey, 1994; however, see Orford, 1986). A recent meta-analysis suggests that across studies, the overall effect size for complementary relations between two individuals is large, indicating that interpersonal complementarity is consistent and robust (Acton, n.d.).

Easily Induced

Complementarity was also considered to be easy to induce, requiring only subtle and minimal behavioral displays to set it into place. Indeed, Leary (1957) discussed complementarity as a "reflex" to connote how quickly and easily it occurs. Tiedens and Fragale (2003) provide a demonstration of the facile nature of complementarity. In one study, when a confederate merely adopted a dominant body posture, participants engaged in submissive behavior. When the confederate adopted a subtly submissive posture, the participants were more likely to behave in a dominant fashion. These responses occurred within a matter of minutes.

An Accepted Invitation

The ease with which complementarity was hypothesized to occur and its postulated prevalence have resulted in it often being discussed in a quite deterministic fashion, as if people can do nothing but respond to dominance with submission and quarrelsomeness with quarrelsomeness, regardless of what they might like to do. Following Horowitz et al. (2006), we reject this deterministic framing of complementarity and intentionally use the terminology of "invitations" and "requests" as opposed to "causes" and "evokes." Dominant behavior invites the other to be submissive, but this invitation can be accepted or rejected by the other. Thus, the other can opt to engage in the expected contrast effect or opt to assimilate.

We prefer conceptualizing complementarity as an accepted invitation for several reasons. For one, it reflects the empirical reality that complementarity does not always occur (Orford, 1986), and it points toward variables that are likely to moderate complementarity and the contrast and assimilation it connotes. In addition, conceptualizing complementarity as an accepted invitation allows us to more easily see the connection between the prevalence of complementary behavior and its interpersonal functions and roots.

Moderators of Complementarity

If interpersonal behavior acts as an invitation to the other, and complementarity is an instance of an accepted invitation, then we can make predictions about when complementarity is more likely and when it is unlikely. Specifically, we should expect that when the invitation is inappropriate or undesirable, the invitation will be rejected. For example, some skepticism about the prevalence of complementarity (particularly the contrast effect for the control dimension) was based on studies examining interpersonal behavior among therapists and their clients, which showed that therapists do not respond to their client's dominance with submission (Orford, 1986). Yet, as has been discussed elsewhere (see Tracey, 1994), the therapy context has social norms that may override complementary responding. Viewed from the invitation perspective, clients may invite their therapist to submit, but therapists likely feel a stronger obligation to their professional duties than to the immediate desires of their client, and thus they reject that particular invitation. In general, social roles can moderate complementarity because they can influence one party's desire to accept or reject an invitation, particularly if that invitation requests behavior that is contrary to role expectations.

Attributes of the relationship may also determine whether an invitation is accepted or rejected. People are more likely to accept invitations from those who they care about, want to impress, like, need to cooperate with, identify with, etc., and are more likely to reject invitations from those they dislike, consider to be an outgroup member, are competing with, or generally want distance from. Thus, we would expect contrast effects for the control dimension and assimilation effects for the affiliation dimension in the former kinds of relationships but less so in the latter type. Note that this proposal differs significantly from the suggestion made by earlier research on contrast and assimilation in relationships, which argued that when comparison targets are close friends, desired friends, or ingroup members, assimilation (regardless of dimension) will ensue (Brewer & Weber, 1994; Brown, Novick, Lord, & Richards, 1992; Pelham & Wachsmuth, 1995). Yet, consistent with our reasoning, there is evidence that when people have a relationship with the other, they perceive themselves as similar to the other in terms of affiliation but different in terms of control, but this does not occur when there is no relationship with the target (Tiedens & Jimenez, 2003). In addition, complementary perceptual patterns also occur, and are acted upon, when individuals are in a relational frame of mind (Stapel & van der Zee, 2006). Further, when first meeting a target with whom a relationship is forthcoming, people perceive that target as similar to themselves in terms of affiliation, but different in terms of control. These complementary perceptions do not occur when no relationship is expected or desired with the target (Tiedens, Unzueta, & Young, 2006).

Automatic

Tiedens and Fragale (2003) argued that complementarity occurs automatically, by which we meant without intention or awareness and very quickly. Indeed, in that paper, we showed that participants responded to a confederate by posing their body in a complementary fashion quickly and without having any awareness of having done so. In fact, in extensive debriefing interviews we established that participants did not notice the subtle dominance or submission of the confederates' posture nor were they aware that their own posture took on a dominant or submissive tone in a complementary response to the confederate. This result could be seen as contradicting the notion that complementarity is an instance of an invitation accepted if accepting an invitation requires conscious processing. However, we do not think accepting an invitation can only be done intentionally and consciously. As has been well demonstrated in the literature on the acquiescence bias, demand effects, placebo effects, and mindlessness, people have a tendency to accept or agree to requests (Knowles & Condon, 1999; Langer, Blank, & Chanowitz, 1978; Orne, 1962; Ray, 1983), particularly when acceptance or agreement will please another person (Leary & Kowalski, 1990; Lenski & Leggett, 1960). Such appeasement occurs quickly and automatically. People need to be jolted out of this kind of response, which might happen through salient role obligations or particular dislike or distance from the other. Thus, conceptualizing complementarity as an accepted interpersonal invitation is suggestive of the instances in which it is not likely to occur (e.g., conflicts with social role, disliked other) but is also highly consistent with complementarity being prevalent, easily induced, and sometimes unconscious.

Interpersonally Functional

Most important to the idea that complementarity is an accepted invitation is that it underscores the most fundamental attribute of complementarity: complementarity facilitates social relationships. We accept invitations from those whom we care about and by accepting their invitation we build a stronger bond. And so, when we respond to others' affiliative behavior with assimilation and their control behavior with contrast, the relationship between ourselves and the other becomes better. "It is more rewarding and/or less costly for persons to make complementary rather than noncomplementary responses to the prompts offered by their fellows" (Carson, 1969, p. 144). In fact, in IT, complementarity is considered so essential to the functioning of relationships that unwillingness or inability to complement others or to select relationship partners who complement oneself was thought to be a cause and symptom of mental illness (Kiesler, 1991; Leary, 1957)

The prediction that complementarity facilitates relationship success is different than the age-old and well supported doctrine of similarity enhancing relationships (Byrne, 1971) because complementarity entails contrast or difference in terms of control. Yet, the relationship-enhancing effect of complementary responses has been demonstrated in the lab several times. For example, in one study, Dryer and Horowitz (1997) found that participants reported higher levels of satisfaction when they had a personal conversation with a confederate who had been trained to complement the participants' self-reported style than when the confederate tried to be similar to the participant. In another study, participants who worked on the desert survival task (Lafferty & Eady, 1974) in complementary pairs enjoyed the relationship more than those who worked with noncomplementary partners. Also, Tiedens and Fragale (2003) showed that participants working on a picture description task with a confederate enjoyed their relationship with the confederate more when the two were opposite in terms of control than when they were similar. Interestingly, in both the Dryer and Horowitz and Tiedens and Fragale studies there was no difference in comfort with the relationship and liking of the partner between participants who displayed dominant behaviors with a submissive partner and participants who displayed submissive behavior with a dominant partner. The participants in these conditions enjoyed the relationship equally, and better than those participants who had behavior similar to the confederate. Thus, in terms of participants' perceptions of relationship success, it did not matter whether they were dominant or submissive, but just that they were complementary to their interaction partner.

As more evidence of the interpersonal rewards of complementarity, Tiedens et al. (2006) found that when people perceived a stranger in a complementary manner, they predicted that they would have a better relationship with that person. Finally, Tiedens and Unzueta (2005, unpublished data) asked first-year college students to rate themselves and their first-year college roommates' personalities in terms of affiliation and control. These ratings were taken at the end of the year when students were making decisions about whether to live with their roommate again in the following school year. Among the students who had made plans to live with their roommate again, we found positive correlations in their perception of the degree to which they and their roommates were affiliative (an assimilation effect) and negative correlations in their perceptions of the degree to which they and their roommate were dominant (a contrast effect). Among students not planning to live with their roommate again, these complementary perceptions did not occur. Thus, complementary perceptions were associated with the sustainability of the relationship.

WHY COMPLEMENTARITY IS SO PLEASANT

It is worthwhile to consider why complementary contrast and assimilation is experienced so positively. This seems particularly true since complementarity can conflict with two basic principles of pleasure. As already mentioned, the contrast for control aspect of complementarity runs counter to the robust and highly replicable finding that similarity between people facilitates relationships and leads to relationship satisfaction. In addition, as discussed above, at times, attaining complementarity can be ego damaging. Since submissiveness and quarrelsomeness are considered negative attributes, complementing a dominant or quarrelsome other requires voluntarily embodying negative traits. Therefore, we turn next to consider each component of complementarity and why it is appealing. In general, in an interpersonal context, the behavior of one person communicates the type of relationship they desire. A complementary response is the response that best cooperates with that request.

Assimilation for Affiliation

Assimilation for affiliation is consistent with the notion that similarity is associated with relationship satisfaction. It is particularly easy to see why two people who behave in a highly agreeable fashion would enjoy that interpersonal interaction. Beyond being similar, both parties express friendly warm behavior associated with feeling close and good. Thus, the pleasure associated with agreeableness paired with agreeableness is probably multiply determined; it is consistent with the principles of complementarity and similarity and it involves friendly positive behavior.

It is also easy to understand why agreeableness met with quarrelsomeness results in dissatisfaction. It not only conflicts with the similarity-attraction principle, but it also evokes anxiety because an attempt to become closer has been met with a rejection or a cold shoulder. However, it might be difficult to see how an argumentative relationship can be a pleasurable experience; yet quarrelsomeness paired with quarrelsomeness should, according to complementarity, also result in relationship satisfaction. One way to understand the appeal of quarrelsome relationships can be taken from Leary's (1957) argument that much of interpersonal dynamics results from peoples' need to avoid and reduce anxiety. For an individual who behaves in a quarrelsome manner, a warm and agreeable response from the other conveys that the other is not respecting the boundaries set in place by the quarrelsome individual. The agreeable individual is coming too close, provoking anxiety for the quarrelsome one. Quarrelsome behavior communicates a desire for some distance in the relationship and only a quarrelsome response can show understanding and cooperation with that desire. Thus, while dyads in which both individuals are quarrelsome are likely to be less satisfying than a dyad in which both individuals are agreeable, the quarrelsome–quarrelsome dynamic is more satisfying than a pairing of agreeableness and quarrelsomeness.

Contrast for Control

Why is contrast for control so pleasant? When interacting with a submissive other, contrast for control may just indicate self-enhancement. People may contrast from undesirable submissiveness and take on the desirable dominant trait in order to feel good about themselves. However, this explanation clearly does not elucidate why contrast also occurs in response to dominant relationship partners. This phenomenon is particularly puzzling when one considers that although many people claim to want egalitarian, hierarchy-free relationships (Regan & Berscheid, 1997; van Lange & Rusbult, 1995), contrast for control results in the establishment of a hierarchical relationship. There are three ways to reconcile our contention that people desire complementary relationships with the finding that people say they prefer egalitarian relationships. First, the desire for equality is central to American ideology as well as other Western contexts (Fiske, 1992). Thus, explicit self-report may rely more on this ideology and what is considered culturally appropriate than the true desires of people. People may produce and enjoy hierarchy without their realizing it (Tiedens & Fragale, 2003). In addition, the data about relational preferences are primarily in regard to romantic relationships. We believe that people may have different preferences for relational forms depending on the type of relationship in question. Although people might desire and enjoy equality in the context of romantic love, it may be less appealing in the context of a task-oriented relationship. After all, hierarchies are an effective relational form for coordinating, allocating resources, deciding who will be responsible for what, increasing accountability, acknowledging expertise, and efficiently executing a plan. All of these benefits are much more relevant to and useful in contexts in which a task needs to be accomplished than in relationships entered purely for social connection. Finally, a person acting dominantly is communicating to the other that they want to be in control. Submitting to that person cooperates with their relationship goal. Thus, contrast on the control dimension can produce relationship satisfaction even from the submitting partner because they know they are cooperating with relationship formation rather than rejecting the invitation of the other.

COMPLEMENTARY CONTRAST AND ASSIMILATION AS MOTIVATED COGNITION

So far in this chapter, we have tried to establish the interpersonal consequences of complementary contrast and assimilation. Now, we will consider the possibility that the interpersonal rewards associated with complementary perceptions and behaviors are also a cause of complementary perceptions and behavior. Given that people seem to experience contrast for control and assimilation for affiliation positively, it is possible that people desire complementarity and will engage in strategies that make it more likely to occur. It may be that people are motivated to achieve complementarity in their relationships and thus perceive themselves and relationship partners in a complementary fashion. We suggest that perceiving the self as complementary to another person or the other as complementary to the self is like any other motivated perception: we come to see other people and ourselves in a way that satisfies our desires. Since people have the desire for positive relationships (Baumeister & Leary, 1995) and since they have experienced the positive effects of complementarity, they will perceive people with whom they want relationships and themselves as complementary. That is, we expect to see a contrast effect in regard to the control dimension and assimilation for affiliation in situations where this relational motivation is salient.

Conceptualizing complementary contrast and assimilation as motivated departs in an important way from other motivational approaches to contrast and assimilation. Typically, when motivational accounts are provided, they focus on people's motivations to enhance and protect their self-esteem. This approach predicts contrast to undesirable targets and assimilation to desirable ones (Stapel & Koomen, 2001). Since dominance and agreeableness are both perceived as positive traits (Tiedens & Jimenez, 2003), people motivated to self-enhance should assimilate to targets who exemplify these traits. Similarly, given that submission and quarrelsomeness are both perceived in a negative light (Tiedens & Jimenez, 2003), a self-enhancement motivation would result in contrast to targets who exemplify these traits, a pattern quite distinct from complementarity (see Stapel & van der Zee, 2006). Thus, the motive referred to in most motivational accounts is an individualistic one where the target functions to make the individual feel better about him- or herself.

Some early renditions of complementarity also emphasized a quite individualistic motive similar to more recent conceptualizations of self-verification (Swann, 1987; Swann, Rentfrow, & Guinn, 2003). As originally conceived by Carson (1969), complementarity was a strategy that was undertaken in an effort to increase individuals' security in their own self-perceptions. By using the strategy of complementarity, individuals could restrict the behaviors of others such that their own behaviors would remain in line with their self-perceptions. Yet, this does little to explain the ease with which people change their behavior and self-perceptions to complement others.

We propose that the motive underlying complementary contrast and assimilation is a relational one. Rather than affirming one's sense of self, a relational motive revolves around trying to have good relationships. Obviously, in many cases, these two motives are not in competition; in fact, having good relationships is one way to feel good about oneself. But, as can be seen in the case of contrast and assimilation effects, there are instances in which these different motives may lead to different outcomes. We suggest that when the desire to have a good relationship is stronger than the individualistic desire to think highly of oneself, complementary patterns of contrast and assimilation will result. Some support for this comes from a series of studies by Stapel and van der Zee (2006) who found that when they made the individual self salient through the use of individual pronouns (such as "I" and "me"), participants confronted with dominant, submissive, agreeable, or quarrelsome targets appeared to follow the principles of self-enhancement in their self-ratings and behaviors. That is, participants in an individualistic frame of mind contrasted themselves from submissive and quarrelsome targets and assimilated to dominant and agreeable targets. However, when the relational self (i.e., knowledge of relationships with other) was activated through the use of words associated with relationships such as "others" and "interpersonal roles," complementarity occurred. People contrasted to dominant and submissive targets and assimilated to agreeable and quarrelsome targets.

Tiedens et al. (2006) more explicitly tested the notion that complementary perceptions have a motivational underpinning by comparing ratings of people with whom a relationship was expected or desired with ratings of people with whom no relationship was expected or desired. We reasoned that a motive for good relationships could color people's perceptions of potential relationship partners such that they perceive others in a way that implies that a good relationship is forthcoming. We found support for this idea by demonstrating a general tendency for perceiving others as complementing oneself. Further, we found that contrasting the other with the self on the control dimension and assimilating others with the self on the affiliation dimension only occurred when participants expected a relationship with the other. For example, in one study, some participants in a class were asked to provide their first impressions of another student in the class (actually a confederate) whom they were told they would be working with on a course project. Other students also provided an impression of the confederate, but were told that he was a confederate whom they would not see again. All students also provided ratings of their self-perceptions of affiliation and control. Among students who believed they would be working with the confederate later, there was a positive correlation between self and other ratings of affiliation (i.e., assimilation) and a negative correlation between self and other ratings of control (i.e., contrast). Among students who did not anticipate a relationship with the target, these relationships did not exist.

Although some might argue that a relational motive is secondary to an individualistic motive, we do not think so. In part, this is because successful relationships are such an important route through which self-esteem is served. Enhancing one's relationships usually does enhance the self, so if one is presented with a choice between enhancing oneself or the relationship, it only makes sense to choose the relationship as the other need will likely ultimately be served as well. Further, although many laboratory studies present participants with targets with whom no relationship will ever be possible, many of the targets we encounter in our daily lives are either current or potential relationship partners. As such, we think that complementary patterns of contrast and assimilation may occur far more frequently than the current literature suggests.

Specific Relationship Goals

Although people generally want positive relationships, they also probably have more specific goals for particular types of relationships. That is, what constitutes a positive relationship may vary to some extent from relationship to relationship. For example, in some relationships people want to socialize and have fun; in others they want to coordinate with one another so that they can accomplish a task. In the former case, the success of the relationship will be evaluated in terms of how much fun the relationship partners had, and in the latter case, the relationship will be evaluated as good and enjoyable if coordination occurred and the task was completed quickly and effectively. These two motivations might be differentially related to the two components of complementarity. Friendship goals could be linked to assimilation for affiliation and coordination goals to contrast for control.

We have some evidence for the idea that different types of relationship goals exist and are differentially tied to complementarity. For example, Tiedens and Jimenez (2003) found that individuals assimilated perceptions of themselves to a target on the affiliation dimension when the target was from a relationship defined around socializing and having fun. Contrast for control did not occur for these targets. However, when the target was from a relationship defined around working on a task together, contrast for control occurred and assimilation for affiliation did not. In another study, Tiedens et al. (2006) queried new college students in their first week of school about their goals for their relationships with their new roommates as well as their chronic perceptions of themselves and their initial perceptions of their roommates. From these data, we were able to divide the participants up into those who prioritized coordination with their roommates and those who prioritized friendship with their roommate. Among those who prioritized friendship, initial perceptions of roommates assimilated to perceptions of the self in terms of affiliation. The more agreeable they thought they themselves were, the more agreeable they thought their roommates were. There was no relationship between self-perceptions and roommate perceptions in terms of control. However, among those who prioritized coordination, there was a contrast effect for control. The more dominant participants perceived themselves, the less dominant they perceived their roommate to be. These participants also demonstrated an assimilation effect for affiliation.

The connection of contrast for control to coordination as opposed to friendship goals could lead some to conclude that contrast for control is less relational than assimilation for affiliation. We dispute this perspective. Although social psychologists have tended to focus on romantic relationships in their study of interpersonal relationships, we would suggest that the majority of people's interpersonal interactions and relationships involve nonromantic relationship partners. Consider the number of hours people spend working and the number of people with whom they interact and have relationships at work. Further, long-term romantic relationships are not always purely oriented toward friendship, nor are they unconcerned with coordination. Long-term romantic partners who are married, cohabit, and/or raise children certainly face a number of coordination challenges and demands. As such, we imagine that in many romantic relationships, especially long-term ones, coordination goals loom as large as friendship ones. Although not exactly parallel to long-term romantic partners, it is worth noting that in our study of first-year college students' perceptions of their roommates, the majority of students were concerned more with coordinating with their roommates than with becoming friends with them. Thus, it may be that many relationships that are frequently conceptualized as oriented around friendship may be just as much, if not more, concerned with coordination.

If the pleasure of contrast from control is based on its association with increased coordination, then spontaneous contrast on the control dimension among work partners should lead to better task performance, particularly for tasks the require coordination, in addition to being more enjoyable. One study by Estroff and Nowicki (1992) provides preliminary support for this contention. They compared the performance of complementary dyads to anticomplementary dyads on two tasks: a jigsaw puzzle and a word generation task. Complementary partners completed significantly more of the jigsaw and generated marginally more words. We suggest that the stronger effects associated with the jigsaw puzzle task occurred because the jigsaw puzzle required greater coordination than the word generation task. Tasks that require even more coordination should be even more facilitated by complementarity, particularly the contrast for control component of complementarity. As an example, Tracey and Sherry (1993) studied supervision, which is a task that clearly requires a high level of coordination, among clinical psychologists and their trainees. They found that when complementarity occurred, better training resulted.

We should note that Dryer and Horowitz (1997) did not find enhanced task performance in complementary dyads; indeed, the dyads who performed best in their study were anticomplementary. That study required participants to work on the famous "Desert Survival Problem" (Lafferty & Eady, 1974). Critical to succeeding on that task is a willingness to argue effectively for one's perspective and to recognize when the other has a better argument than oneself. Thus, it is a task where too much cohesion and too little argumentation is the impediment to success. If one conceptualizes this task in this way, it is no surprise that complementarity hampered performance. Complementary pairs got along too well. Thus, complementarity is likely to be particularly effective in facilitating task performance on tasks where coordination and cohesion is conducive to high performance but not on those tasks that require disagreement and dissent.

CONCLUSIONS

Contrast and assimilation effects can be seen as the result of a purely cold cognitive process in which attributes of two targets are examined for similarities and dissimilarities, or they can be seen as strategies that function to help individuals achieve their goals. In this chapter, we have discussed a way in which contrast and assimilation effects can be conceptualized as goal directed. By connecting the notions of contrast and assimilation to the phenomenon of interpersonal complementarity, we argued that contrast and assimilation can serve social functions. Specifically, when people engage in perceptual or behavioral complementary contrast and assimilation (contrast for control and assimilation for affiliation), their relationships are facilitated. The relationship becomes more enjoyable, more comfortable, and more sustainable, and coordination between relationship partners is facilitated.

The phenomenon of complementary contrast and assimilation and its social motivational underpinnings are important for basic theoretical work on contrast and assimilation effects as well as having applied implications about interpersonal relationships. For one, the complementary contrast and assimilation effect should call researchers' attention to the fact that contrast and assimilation can be influenced by the dimension on which evaluation occurs. All too often researchers assume that, by showing a contrast effect under particular conditions on a dimension such as assertiveness, the same contrast effect would occur in those same conditions for a judgment about warmth. Complementarity effects call such leaps of inference into question. Again and again, we find participants thinking quite differently about constructs related to dominance and constructs related to affiliation. A second interesting aspect of complementary contrast and assimilation, which has been highlighted throughout this chapter, is that engaging in complementary contrast and assimilation requires that individuals, at times, adopt characteristics that are not entirely flattering. This may be surprising given the large literature on self-enhancement; however, as we have argued in various places in this chapter, we believe that this less than flattering portrayal of the self is in service of the relationship in which it occurs. By complementing relationship partners, individuals cement the relationship and facilitate coordination on joint tasks. In many cases, we believe, this relationship function is more appealing than simple self-flattery, in part because the relationships themselves are important to the individual and in part because successful relationships provide a way to feel good about oneself.

Complementary contrast and assimilation may also provide a useful lens for understanding the processes and mechanisms through which people's relationship dynamics are formed in interpersonal, group, and organizational contexts. One often noted aspect of social life is the omnipresence of hierarchies as well as the spontaneity through which these hierarchies come to exist (Bales, 1950; Brown, 1986; Fiske, 1992). We see the contrast on the control dimension aspect of complementarity as an embodiment of informal social hierarchy creation in the sense that it captures instances in which people act and/or perceive themselves in such a way that one person is dominant and the other submissive. As described in this chapter, our research has uncovered situations in which such spontaneous hierarchy formation is likely to happen as well as when it is less likely. Our proposal that complementary contrast and assimilation facilitates relationship and task success and that people engage in it in order to fulfill their social relationship goals could easily be used to generate more hypotheses about situational and individual moderators. In this way, we believe that research on complementary contrast and its relationship enhancing characteristics may be critical to understanding some of the questions central to group life, such as who becomes a leader, when, and why.

Although the formation of hierarchies is often conceptualized as a competitive process in which the winner forces the loser to submit, our perspective questions how well this view characterizes the spontaneous, everyday hierarchies that emerge through social interaction. Certainly, throughout history and in the present day, there are many instances of hostile declarations of power that result in the utter oppression of a large number of people, but our research leads us to question whether that same psychology plays out in the more banal yet omnipresent hierarchical differentiation that characterizes people's experience in the workplace, at home, and in other group settings. In our view, many of these informal hierarchies are created and maintained through a cooperative and mutually enjoyable process. Those who submit do so willingly, and both parties find the relationship rewarding as a consequence. Further, rather than being motivated by an individual desire to control others and get access to resources, we see some hierarchies as motivated by a social desire to get along with others and cooperate with others' goals. This is not the kind of dynamic that attracts newspaper headlines, yet we suspect that it underlies everyday behavior that does, such as how a debate in congress is settled, who is chosen as the next CEO of a company, and whether a defendant is found guilty or innocent in a trial.

Since hierarchies can be, from this perspective, a voluntary and positive relationship, our approach also predicts that these kinds of hierarchical arrangements can shift fairly easily; however, such shifts require that individuals either insert their own invitation into a dynamic rather than mindlessly responding to others' invitations or that they reject the importance of a particular relationship. Obviously, context will affect how possible those options are. Thus, our research on complementary contrast and assimilation provides a novel perspective on how and why hierarchies form, survive, and change.

In sum, early Interpersonal Theorists argued that affiliation and control were central and defining aspects of human social life. In this chapter, we have suggested that, as such, they are dimensions that researchers interested in contrast and assimilation should be concerned with. Indeed, the phenomenon of complementarity is simultaneous assimilation for the affiliation dimension and contrast for the control dimension. By thinking about complementarity as a form of contrast and assimilation, we hope to have contributed to both the literature on contrast and assimilation and to the literature on complementarity. By combining these literatures and through our own empirical investigations we have come to believe that contrast and assimilation can be entirely social phenomena. That is, complementary contrast and assimilation are not just social in their use of others as reference points, but they are engaged in to fulfill humans' basic social needs.

REFERENCES

Acton, G. S. (n.d.). *The interpersonal principle of complementarity: A meta-analysis.* Retrieved June 27, 2005, from http:www.personalityresearch.org/acton/meta-analysis.html

Bales, R. (1950). *Interaction process analysis: A method for the study of small groups.* Cambridge, MA: Addison-Wesley.

Baumeister, R. (1998). The self. In D. Gilbert, S. Fiske, & G. Lindzey (Eds.), *The handbook of social psychology* (pp. 680–740). Boston: McGraw-Hill.

Baumeister, R. F., & Leary, M. R. (1995). The need to belong: Desire for interpersonal attachments as a fundamental human motivation. *Psychological Bulletin, 117,* 497–529.

Brewer, M. B., & Weber, J. G. (1994). Self-evaluation effects of interpersonal versus intergroup social comparison. *Journal of Personality and Social Psychology, 66,* 268–275.

Brown, J. D., Novick, N. J., Lord, K. A., & Richards, J. M. (1992). When Gulliver travels: Social context, psychological closeness, and self-appraisals. *Journal of Personality and Social Psychology, 62,* 717–727.

Brown, R. (1986). *Social psychology* (2nd ed.). New York: Free Press.

Byrne, D. (1971). *The attraction paradigm.* New York: Academic Press.

Carson, R. C. (1969). *Interaction concepts of personality.* Chicago: Aldine.

Cialdini, R. B., Borden, R. J., Thorne, A., Walker, M. R., Freeman, S., & Sloan, L. R. (1976). Basking in reflected glory: Three (football) field studies. *Journal of Personality and Social Psychology, 39,* 406–415.

Dryer, D. C., & Horowitz, L. M. (1997). When do opposites attract? Interpersonal complementarity versus similarity. *Journal of Personality and Social Psychology, 72,* 592–603.

Dunning, D., & Hayes, A. F. (1996). Evidence for egocentric comparison in social judgment. *Journal of Personality and Social Psychology, 69,* 58–68.

Estroff, E., & Nowicki, S. (1992). Interpersonal complementarity, gender interactions, and performance on puzzle and word tasks. *Personality and Social Psychology Bulletin, 18,* 351–356.

Festinger, L. (1954). A theory of social comparison processes. *Human Relations, 7,* 117–140.

Fiske, A. P. (1992). The four elementary forms of sociality: Framework for a unified theory of social relations. *Psychological Review, 99,* 689–723.

Foa, U. G. (1961). Convergences in the analysis of the structure of interpersonal behavior. *Psychological Bulletin, 68,* 341–353.

Herr, P. M. (1986). Consequences of priming: Judgment and behavior. *Journal of Personality and Social Psychology, 51,* 1106–1115.

Horowitz, L. M., Alden, L. E., Wiggins, J. S., & Pincus, A. L. (2000). *Inventory of interpersonal problems.* San Antonio, TX: Psychological Corporation.

Horowitz, L. M., Rosenberg, S. E., Baer, B., Ureno, G., & Villasenor, V. (1988). Inventory of Interpersonal Problems: Psychometric properties and clinical application. *Journal of Consulting and Clinical Psychology, 56,* 885–892.

Horowitz, L. M., Wilson, K. R., Turan, B., Zolotsev, P., Constantino, M. J., & Henderson, L. (2006). How interpersonal motives clarify the meaning of interpersonal behavior: A revised circumplex model. *Personality and Social Psychology Review, 10,* 67–86.

Kiesler, D. (1983). The 1982 interpersonal circle: A taxonomy for complementarity in human transactions. *Psychological Review, 90,* 185–214.

Kiesler, D. (1988). *Therapeutic metacommunication: Therapist impact disclosure as feedback in psychotherapy*. Palo Alto, CA: Consulting Psychologists Press.

Kiesler, D. (1991). Interpersonal methods of assessment and diagnosis. In C. R. Snyder & D. R. Forsyth (Eds.), *Handbook of social and clinical psychology: The health perspective* (pp. 438–468). Elmsford, NY: Pergamon Press.

Knowles, E. S., & Condon, C. A. (1999). Why people say "yes": A dual-process theory of acquiescence. *Journal of Personality and Social Psychology, 77*, 379–386.

Kunda, Z. (1990). The case for motivated reasoning. *Psychological Bulletin, 108*, 480–498.

Lafferty, J., & Eady, P. (1974). *The desert survival problem*. Plymouth, MI: Experimental Learning Methods.

LaForge, R. (1977). *Using the ICL*. Mill Valley, CA: Author.

LaForge, R., & Suczeck, R. (1955). The interpersonal dimension of personality: III. An interpersonal checklist. *Journal of Personality, 24*, 94–112.

Langer, E., Blank, A., & Chanowitz, B. (1978). The mindlessness of ostensibly thoughtful action: The role of placebic information in interpersonal interaction. *Journal of Personality and Social Psychology, 36*, 635–642.

Leary, M. R., & Kowalski, R. M. (1990). Impression management: A literature review and two-component model. *Psychological Bulletin, 107*, 34–47.

Leary, T. (1957). *Interpersonal diagnosis of personality*. New York: Ronald.

Lenski, G. E., & Leggett, J. C. (1960). Caste, class, and deference in the research interview. *American Journal of Sociology, 65*, 463–467.

Locke, K. D. (2000). Circumplex Scales of Interpersonal Values: Reliability, validity, and applicability to interpersonal problems and personality disorders. *Journal of Personality Assessment, 75*, 249–267.

Locke, K. D. (2003). Status and solidarity in social comparison: Agentic and communal values and vertical and horizontal directions. *Journal of Personality and Social Psychology, 84*, 619–631.

Markey, P. M., Funder, D. C., & Ozer, D. J. (2003). Complementarity of interpersonal behaviors in dyadic interactions. *Personality and Social Psychology Bulletin, 29*, 1082–1090.

Maslow, A. H. (1968). *Toward a psychology of being*. New York: Van Nostrand.

Moskowitz, D. S. (1994). Cross-situational generality and the interpersonal circumplex. *Journal of Personality and Social Psychology, 66*, 921–933.

Orford, J. (1986). The rules of interpersonal complementarity: Does hostility beget hostility and dominance, submission? *Psychological Review, 93*, 365–377.

Orne, M. (1962). On the social psychology of the psychological experiment. *The American Psychologist, 17*, 776–783,

Ostrom, T. M., & Upshaw, H. S. (1968). Psychological perspective and attitude change. In A. G. Greenwald, T. C. Brock, & T. M. Ostrom (Eds.), *Psychological foundations of attitudes* (pp. 217–242). New York: Academic Press.

Pelham, B. W., & Wachsmuth, J. O. (1995). The waxing and waning of the social self: Assimilation and contrast in social comparison. *Journal of Personality and Social Psychology, 69*, 825–838.

Ray, J. J. (1983). Reviving the problem of acquiescence response bias. *Journal of Social Psychology, 121*, 81–96.

Regan, P., & Berscheid, E. (1997). Gender differences in characteristics desired in a potential sexual and marriage partner. *Journal of Psychology and Human Sexuality, 9*, 25–37.

Sadler, P., & Woody, E. (2003). Is who you are who you're talking to? Interpersonal style and complementarity in mixed-sex interaction. *Journal of Personality and Social Psychology, 84*, 80–96.

Sedikides, C., Gaertner, L., & Toguchi, Y. (2003). Pancultural self-enhancement. *Journal of Personality and Social Psychology, 84,* 60–79.

Snyder, C. R., Lassegard, M. A., & Ford, C. E. (1986). Distancing after group success and failure: Basking in reflected glory and cutting off reflected failure. *Journal of Personality and Social Psychology, 51,* 383–388.

Stapel, D. A., & Koomen, W. (2001). I, we, and the effects of others on me: How self-construal level moderates social comparison effects. *Journal of Personality and Social Psychology, 80,* 766–781.

Stapel, D. A., & van der Zee, K. I. (2006). The self salience model of other-to-self effects: Integrating principles of self-enhancement, complementarity, and imitation. *Journal of Personality and Social Psychology, 90,* 258–271.

Strong, S. R., Hills, H. I., Kilmartin, C. T., DeVries, H., Lanier, K., Nelson, B. N., et al. (1988). The dynamic relations among interpersonal behaviors: A test of complementarity and anticomplementarity. *Journal of Personality and Social Psychology, 54,* 798–810.

Sullivan, H. S. (1953). *The interpersonal theory of psychiatry.* New York: Norton.

Swann, W. B., Jr. (1987). Identity negotiation: Where two roads meet. *Journal of Personality and Social Psychology, 53,* 1038–1051.

Swann, W. B., Jr., Rentfrow, P. J., & Guinn, J. (2003). Self-verification: The search for coherence. In M. Leary & J. Tangney (Eds.), *Handbook of self and identity* (pp. 367–383). New York: Guilford Press.

Taylor, S. E., & Brown, J. D. (1988). Illusion and well-being: A social psychological perspective on mental health. *Journal of Personality and Social Psychology, 103,* 193–210.

Tiedens, L. Z., & Fragale, A. R. (2003). Power moves: Complementarity in dominant and submissive nonverbal behavior. *Journal of Personality and Social Psychology, 84,* 558–568.

Tiedens, L. Z., & Jimenez, M. C. (2003). Assimilation for affiliation and contrast for control: Complementary self-construals. *Journal of Personality and Social Psychology, 85,* 104–1061.

Tiedens, L. Z., Unzueta, M. M., & Young, M. J. (2006). The desire for hierarchy: The motivated perception of dominance complementarity. *Unpublished manuscript.*

Tracey, T. J., & Sherry, P. (1993). Complementary interaction over time in successful and less successful supervision. *Professional Psychology: Research and Practice, 24,* 304–311.

Tracey, T. J. G. (1994). An examination of the complementarity of interpersonal behavior. *Journal of Personality and Social Psychology, 67,* 864–878.

Van Lange, P. A. M., & Rusbult, C. E. (1995). My relationship is better than—and not as bad as—yours is: The perception of superiority in close relationships. *Personality and Social Psychology Bulletin, 21,* 32–44.

Wiggins, J. S. (1982). Circumplex models of interpersonal behavior in clinical psychology. In P. C. Kendall & J. K. Butcher (Eds.), *Handbook of research methods in clinical psychology* (pp. 183–221). New York: Wiley.

Wiggins, J. S., Trapnell, P., & Phillips, N. (1988). Psychometric and geometric characteristics of the Revised Interpersonal Adjective Scales (IAS-R). *Multivariate Behavioral Research, 23,* 517–530.

Wood, J. V. (1989). Theory and research concerning social comparisons of personal attributes. *Psychological Bulletin, 106,* 231–248.

12

Contrast Effects in Knowledge Activation: The Case of Inhibition Effects Due to Competing Constructs or Goal Fulfillment

JENS FÖRSTER and NIRA LIBERMAN

*I*n the present chapter we would like to present inhibition after goal fulfillment and due to competing constructs, which, we believe, is distinct from other processes that create contrast-like effects. For that, however, we would like to start by introducing the basic paradigm of priming.

Higgins, Rholes, and Jones (1977) invited participants to an experiment that consisted of two apparently unrelated studies. The first study was a verbal learning task in which participants had to memorize words; for some participants these were positive words (adventurous, self-confident, independent, persistent); for other participants these were negative words (reckless, conceited, aloof, stubborn). The second study was an impression formation task in which participants were asked to read a description of a person called Donald who performed a series of ambiguous behaviors that could be regarded as reckless or adventurous (e.g., Donald thought about crossing the Atlantic in a sailboat). Participants then wrote a free description of Donald and indicated how much they liked him on a rating scale. Results showed that he was rated as more adventurous and less reckless by the positive priming group than by the negative priming group. Since then research evidence for such accessibility or priming effects amassed (for reviews see Decoster & Claypool, 2004; Förster & Liberman, in press; Higgins, 1996; Wyer, 2004).

A typical priming experiment has two major phases: a priming phase in which participants are exposed to some information and an ostensibly unrelated perception, memory, or judgment task in which participants' responses towards a target stimulus are examined. The *afferent stage* of a priming experiment consists of a stimulus presentation (e.g., reckless or adventurous) that leads to activation of associated memory structures. The *efferent stage* of a priming experiment consists of activation of a memory structure in the process of responding to a target stimulus (Fiedler, 2003).

Priming does not always lead to assimilation. That is, perception or memory during the second phase does not always directly reflect the primed construct, but sometimes reflects the opposite, giving rise to a contrast effect. There are many different processes that produce contrast, and many factors are involved in determining whether assimilation or contrast would ensue from priming. In the present chapter, we will argue that contrast can occur at both the afferent and efferent stages and look more closely at inhibition, which is one of the mechanisms that can produce contrast and has received relatively little attention in the social psychological literature. Our aim is to show that inhibition is a powerful and very simple mechanism which renders information accessible below baseline. We will then summarize some empirical evidence for inhibition effects in the cognitive and social psychological literature. We will show that the fundamental mechanism of inhibition is involved in tasks that from the outside look very differently and have different research traditions in psychological research. In this chapter we aim to bring them together to provide a basis for further research questions. We will begin, however, with defining the terms that we will use through the chapter.

The effect whereby a measure that is applied at the second phase of a priming experiment reflects the implication of the prime is termed an *assimilation effect*; if the measure applied at the second stage of a priming experiment reflects the opposite of the prime's implication, it is termed a *contrast effect*. Several mechanisms of contrast have been distinguished in the literature (see DeCoster & Claypool, 2004; Förster & Liberman; in press). Consciously or unconsciously avoiding using the prime or correcting its influence will be called a *correction effect*. Primes can also serve as standards of comparison, and we call the process of contrasting away the target from the prime an *anchoring effect*. Finally, if a process reduces knowledge accessibility before the efferent stage, it will be called *inhibition*.

A few important aspects should be noted: Correction often, but not always, results in a contrast effect. Such contrast should be distinguished from contrast that results from anchoring. The main difference is that correction, by definition, is a second-stage, metacognitive process that operates on a presumed previous influence of a prime. Correction may or may not occur. Anchoring is a primary cognitive process that may happen by default, that is, as the first process upon encountering a target (DeCoster & Claypool, 2004). Inhibition is distinct from both correction and anchoring, because it operates at the efferent stage, before encountering a target. Inhibition may reduce activation below a no-priming baseline. Thus, inhibited primed knowledge will not be used, because it cannot be used—neither as a standard nor as a basis for judgment or correction. Therefore, after inhibition assimilation is unlikely and contrast is possible. In other words, priming will tend to have no effect or produce a contrast if inhibition of the prime occurred.

The previous discussion emphasizes that the distinction between *effects* and *processes* is of central importance for understanding contrast effects. Let us consider an example. Suppose that, after having been primed with "reckless," people judge a target person to be *less* reckless than an unprimed control group. This contrast effect could have been produced by various processes. For example, the participants might have been suspicious about the prime and decided not to use it or attempt to counteract its effect (judged the prime as unusable). Notably, this process of correction may lead not only to contrast but also to assimilation if the person has an incorrect theory about the direction of the influence or if the correction was insufficient (Strack, 1992). Contrast may also occur if a prime is used as a standard of comparison, or an anchor. For example, if a person thinks that, compared to the prime, the target does not seem reckless, the person might judge the target to be "careful." Research on social comparisons convincingly demonstrated such effects and identified the conditions under which these effects occur. For example, anchoring tends to occur if the standards are distinct (the primes are exemplars as opposed to traits) or extreme (Stapel & Koomen, 2000). It is also possible that the prime information is simply made inaccessible because, for example, the priming task has been completed and anything relevant to it has already been "cleared" from the mental system, or, in other words, inhibited. Note that correction takes place *after* knowledge activation at the time of applying it to the target (the efferent response stage), whereas it appears that anchoring effects occur at both the afferent and the efferent stage, although more research is needed to clarify this question. Inhibition seems to take place immediately after the activation state, regardless of whether or not a new target is encountered (before the efferent perceptual stage). Thus, inhibition can be distinguished from correction by the stage of its occurrence. We will return later to this distinction, when we demonstrate inhibition effects in procedures that were formerly assumed to produce contrast due to correction.

Research in social psychology focused mainly on assimilation, correction, and anchoring effects, and inhibition processes have been largely neglected. To close this theoretical gap, we would like to focus in the present chapter on inhibition effects in social judgment and memory. We first present a general overview of inhibition effects, and then look more closely at inhibition from goal fulfillment and its consequences for person perception and for postsuppressional rebound.

INHIBITION DUE TO COMPETING CONSTRUCTS

Very generally, inhibition seems to occur when a construct or an action is expected to interfere with subsequent mental processes. This expectation does not need to be conscious, and we will present some demonstrations of such inhibition processes in cognitive and social psychology. We will pay special attention to inhibition after goal fulfillment, as we believe that this type of inhibition is particularly relevant to social psychology. We will then argue that these effects are functional in that they help to perform experimental or everyday tasks (e.g., person perception) successfully.

Inhibition of Return

The basic experimental paradigm that demonstrates inhibition of return (IOR; Posner & Cohen, 1984) presents to participants visual targets that they need to detect. For example, they might be asked to press a key whenever they see the letter "T" appear on the screen. Most targets are presented at a fixation point that is located at the center of the visual field, but occasionally a target may appear at one of two peripheral locations. A precue (e.g., the sign "°") is presented near one of the two peripheral locations at varying temporal intervals before the appearance of the target. This precue does not convey any information as to where the target would appear (that is, the precue does not help to predict the location of a subsequent target). When the cue precedes the target by a short temporal interval (i.e., a short cue–target stimulus–onset asynchrony, or SOA), subjects detect the target faster when it appears at the cued location. In contrast, after about 200–300 ms this effect reverses and targets at the uncued location are detected more rapidly. Apparently, over longer SOAs people inhibit responses (or attention) to a previously attended location if that location is judged uninformative with respect to the task (see also Klein & Taylor, 1994). Notably, IOR does not occur following peripheral cues which do convey information about the subsequent target.

Inhibition of Habitual Semantic Associates by an Active Set

In Neely's classic study (1977), participants performed lexical decisions in which the target words were preceded by signal words. In one condition, the signal "body" appeared consistently with targets that signified building parts (e.g., door) and, therefore, was reasoned to semantically prime body parts and simultaneously induce an "active set" for building parts. The study found that at longer delays (1000 ms) between the prime and the target (SOA), the prime inhibited decisions about semantic associates (e.g., body parts) and facilitated decisions related to the active set (e.g., building parts). However, at shorter delays (250 ms), it facilitated decisions about the semantic associates but not about the active set. These results indicate that novel associations have longer onset times, whereas more habitual associations are faster to exert influence.

Similarly, in linguistic processing, it has been found that homonyms initially activate all the semantic meanings (e.g., the word "bank" activates both the meaning of a financial institution and the meaning of a riverside). However, once a context is determined, the context-irrelevant meanings become inhibited (Swinney, Prather, & Love, 2000).

Inhibition Across Modalities

It seems that modalities can compete with each other, too. Ratcliff and McCoon (1996) presented participants with pictures of mundane objects (e.g., a light bulb) and recorded naming latencies after being primed 1 week earlier with the same object or a graphically similar but semantically different object (e.g., a balloon). A no-priming control group was also included. The authors found that, whereas semantically similar primes produced facilitation, graphically similar primes produced inhibition by increasing the response time relative to the control group.

Inhibition of Competing Stereotypes

In the social domain, Macrae, Bodenhausen, and Milne (1995) exposed participants to targets that belonged to multiple stereotyped groups (e.g., an Asian woman). Prior to that exposure, participants were subliminally primed with one of the category labels (women or Chinese). Using a lexical decision task, the study showed that such priming led to higher accessibility of the primed category and at the same time inhibited concepts that were related to the other, nonprimed category.

Part-Set Cuing Inhibition and Retrieval-Induced Forgetting

Part-set cuing inhibition refers to inhibition processes in memory retrieval (for reviews of the empirical findings, see Anderson & Neely, 1996; Nickerson, 1984; Roediger & Neely, 1982). The paradigm typically requires participants to memorize a list of words from a small number of semantic categories (e.g., 40 words comprised of colors, trees, fish, and musical instruments). At recall, participants are presented with a different number of words from each category (e.g., one musical instrument, four colors, four trees) as cues. The classic finding is that participants recall fewer of the remaining items in a given category when *more* words from that category are presented as cues (see e.g., Rundus, 1973; Slamecka, 1968; Watkins, 1975). Anderson and colleagues (Anderson & Neely, 1996; Anderson & Spellman, 1995) have suggested that selective attention toward the rehearsed items inhibits accessibility of the other competing items.

Retrieval-induced forgetting refers to a related phenomenon. Here, during the study phase, participants study several categories, each composed of several exemplars in a category–exemplar format (e.g., fruit–orange). After the study phase, participants engage in directed "retrieval practice" for half of the items from half of the studied categories. In this phase, they complete category-plus-exemplar stem cue tests (e.g., fruit–or____). After a retention interval, a final and unexpected category-cued recall test is administered in which participants are cued with each category name and they are asked to reproduce any exemplar of that category that they remember from any point in the experiment. It is typically found that performance on practiced items improves relative to the baseline condition (i.e., items from unpracticed categories), whereas performance on the unpracticed items from practiced categories falls below this baseline. Anderson and Bjork (1994) explained these effects by suggesting that during the retrieval practice phase the practiced items compete with the unpracticed items from the same category and thus inhibit them (see also Anderson & Neely, 1996; Anderson & Spellman, 1995).

GOAL SHIELDING

Goal shielding occurs when alternative goals are inhibited by pursuit of a focal goal. Shah, Friedman, and Kruglanski (2002) demonstrated that priming chronic (concerns that one holds across situations) or situation-specific goals (goals that are elicited in a specific situation) inhibited the accessibility of conflicting goal constructs compared to goal-unrelated concepts. In some of their experiments, goals were activated by presenting goal concepts suboptimally at a computer screen so that participants were neither aware of the fact that goals were activated nor did they know their content. Thus self-regulatory tactics might be automatically engaged prior to conscious awareness. Moreover, a variety of motivational variables mediated the effect. More specifically, inhibition increased with commitment to the goal and to the extent to which its attainment could substitute for the attainment of the alternatives. Inhibition also increased with need for closure and level of anxiety and decreased with level of depression. Presumably, these variables are related to a motivation to achieve closure on active goals.

Inhibition Effects—Summary

It seems from all these examples of different types of inhibition that constructs are inhibited if they have a potential to interfere with a focal task, or may compete with constructs that help to perform the focal task. There are different reasons for the presumed competition or interference: In inhibition of return, inhibition serves to prevent attending to an irrelevant location; active sets inhibit stronger but currently irrelevant habitual responses (or equally strong alternative responses), which seems to be the case also in inhibition of homonyms in semantic understanding and alternative social groups in social perception. In retrieval-induced forgetting, inhibition prevents interference with the retrieval of constructs that the "retrieval practice" task demands. Finally, in goal shielding, goals inhibit potentially interfering alternative goals. In all those cases, inhibition serves a function—by inhibiting incorrect or competing but viable alternative responses, it helps to perform the task at hand, be it an experimental task or a daily task of pursuing goals or understanding language and social stimuli.

In a social context, it may be important whether knowledge is activated or inhibited. To reiterate, people can use accessible knowledge for their judgments, with accessible knowledge providing a basis for both assimilation and contrast effects, whereas inhibited knowledge necessarily leads to contrast effects. We turn now to discuss inhibition after goal fulfillment, which, we would like to argue, follows the same functional logic—we would like to demonstrate that goal-related constructs are inhibited after goal fulfillment, and argue that this serves, as in other cases of inhibition, the function of reducing interference with other processes. We then examine some implications of this notion for social psychology.

INHIBITION AFTER GOAL FULFILLMENT

Motivational states, such as needs, goals, intentions, and concerns, are characterized by enhanced accessibility of motivation-related constructs (Ach, 1935; Anderson, 1983; Bruner, 1957; Gollwitzer 1996; Gollwitzer & Moskowitz, 1996; Goschke & Kuhl, 1993; Higgins & King, 1981; Kruglanski et al., 2002; Kuhl, 1983, 1987; Kuhl & Kazén-Saad, 1988; Shah & Kruglanski, 2002, 2003; Wyer & Srull, 1989). To give an example, if you are searching for your keys, motivation-related constructs such as the typical location, special features of the keys, and related associations become accessible. This is said to be functional because it may help you to find the keys (see Förster & Liberman, in press; Liberman & Förster, 2005).

Inhibition after goal fulfillment was first described by Zeigarnik (1938), who demonstrated that people remembered interrupted tasks better than completed tasks (for reviews see Butterfield, 1964; Heckhausen, 1991). Based on Lewin's (1951) field theory, she explained these findings by suggesting that unfinished goals leave the actor in a state of tension (a state that preserves thoughts about the tasks), which is reduced only after the focal goal or a substitute goal are completed, when thoughts of the task are inhibited. In these studies, it is impossible to determine whether the enhanced memory for the unfinished task relative to the completed task is due to prefulfillment activation or rather due to postfulfillment inhibition. More recently, Marsh, Hicks, and Bink (1998, 1999) used a lexical decision task to examine the accessibility of action-related constructs both before and after completion of the action. Replicating former findings by Goschke and Kuhl (1993), they found that before completion, accessibility of intended actions was enhanced relative to nonintended (i.e., to-be-observed) actions. In addition, they found that after completing the action, accessibility of action-related constructs dropped below the level of the control, no-goal group, demonstrating postfulfillment inhibition.

Rothermund (2003) argued that positive feedback signifies a completed goal, whereas negative feedback signifies an incomplete goal. Consistent with this idea, he found inhibition of goal-related constructs after success feedback and increased accessibility after failure feedback. He used an interference paradigm in which participants had to read out loud a nonprimed word that is presented together with a primed word or another nonprimed word. In this task, longer reading times of the target word indicate more interference by and therefore a higher accessibility of the nontarget word. The results indicated enhanced accessibility of goal related constructs after failure feedback and inhibition after success feedback. Presumably, unsuccessful performance kept the goal active and maintained accessibility at a high level, whereas successful performance signaled goal completion and led to inhibition.

Interestingly, in social settings, it has been found that people tended to remember arguments in which they think that they lost better than arguments in which they think that they won (Ross & Holmberg, 1992). Likewise, chess players tend to remember games in which they lost better than games in which they won.

It is possible that these situations create rumination because they induce an open set—a state of an unfulfilled goal that promotes attempts at symbolic or real goal fulfillment, and leaves goal-related constructs highly accessible.

Förster, Liberman and Higgins (2005) found that goal-related accessibility and postfulfillment inhibition increased with the motivation to achieve a goal. In their experiments, participants were instructed to search through a presented series of pictures for a target combination (glasses followed by scissors) and report it to the experimenter. Participants had to watch four blocks of slides and the target combination was presented in Block 3. After each block, lexical decision times for words related (e.g., read, professor, sun) and unrelated to glasses were assessed. Increase of accessibility of goal-related words was found before goal fulfillment (i.e., before Block 3, lexical decisions were faster for words related than for words unrelated to glasses) and inhibition after goal fulfillment (i.e., after Block 3, lexical decisions were faster for words unrelated to glasses than for words related to glasses). No such effects were observed within the control, no-goal condition. Förster et al. manipulated the expectancy of achieving the goal (by telling participants that the target combination was present in 90% of the cases vs. only in 5% of the cases), the value of the goal (by telling participants that they would receive $1.00 vs. only $0.05 for finding the combination), or both expectancy and value. The experiments also included a no-goal, control group that merely saw the pictures without the goal of finding the target combination. As predicted, accessibility of goal-related words prior to fulfillment and inhibition after fulfillment were found in the high-expectancy and high-value conditions but not in the low-expectancy and low-value conditions. The combination of high-value and high-expectancy enhanced the effects. These findings indicate that the effects of expectancy and value on goal-related accessibility and on postfulfillment inhibition were interactive (i.e., multiplicative) and similar to the effects of expectancy and value on motivation (e.g., Atkinson, 1964; Fishbein & Ajzen, 1974; Vroom, 1966). It therefore appears that goal-related accessibility and postfulfillment inhibition are motivational phenomena that are proportional to the strength of the motivation.

Fiedler, Schenck, Watling, and Menges (2005), presenting participants with film clips that showed two people interacting (e.g., a man beating a woman), asked participants to focus on one of the people (the man or the woman) and to indicate whether a verb (e.g., attack, follow) was consistent with the scene. Both scene-consistent verbs (e.g., attack) and scene-inconsistent verbs (e.g., follow) were presented. The authors reasoned that encoding a scene-inconsistent verb would keep participants' minds busy, because it would create an open mindset as a result of an unfulfilled goal to interpret the scene. Encoding a scene-consistent verb, on the other hand, would close the set (i.e., the goal of interpreting the scene would be attained). After watching the films, participants were asked to identify trait words that were related or unrelated to the scene. These words were masked, and speed of recognition served as a measure of accessibility. The authors found facilitation for related traits after both scene-consistent and scene-inconsistent verbs for the focal person. They argued that this reflected two different processes: Whereas after scene-inconsistent verbs accessibility was high because of an unfulfilled goal, after encoding a scene-consistent verb, semantic activation took place—processing a scene-consistent verb with respect to the focal person strongly activated it, and thus enhanced the accessibility of semantically related constructs. For the nonfocal person, however, the facilitation effect was only found after the scene-inconsistent verbs. The authors argued that the nonfocal person condition disentangled goal fulfillment from semantic activation better than the focal person condition. Specifically, in the nontarget person condition, the open mindset due to nonfitting verbs led to facilitation of semantically related concepts; a closed mindset due to scene-consistent verbs, however, created inhibition.

In sum, it appears that goal fulfillment can lead to inhibition of goal-related constructs and the strength of the motivation moderates the size of the effect. We think, furthermore, that the logic underlying postfulfillment inhibition is the same as with other types of inhibition, namely, constructs are inhibited that might interfere with efficient performance of current tasks. Specifically, we think that inhibiting goal-related constructs upon goal fulfillment is functional because goal-related constructs can interfere with other tasks. Clearing them from the system allows other goals to be more easily pursued after fulfillment. In cybernetic models of goal hierarchies (Carver & Scheier, 1999; Vallacher & Wegner, 1987) goal attainment (e.g., watering plants) is followed by a reinstatement of a higher-order, superordinate goal (e.g., arranging the room for a romantic dinner) that was the reason for pursuing the original, subordinate goal. In this view, constructs related to the fulfilled goal (e.g., water, watering can, fertilizer) are clearly irrelevant and could potentially interfere with successful performance of the next task at hand (e.g, cooking or cleaning). "Clearing up" the mental system from such constructs thus may be highly instrumental (see also Gollwitzer, 1999; Kuhl, 1983; Mayr & Keele, 2000).

It is interesting to think about the potential functionality of the increase of postfulfillment inhibition produced by strength of motivation. One possibility would be that highly motivating goals are more likely than less motivating goals to suppress (or put "on hold") other important alternative goals. For example, a high motivation to respond to sexist remarks in a conversation with a colleague may suppress the important goal of self-presentation, but a weak motivation would not suffice to produce such suppression. Therefore, as a rule, turning to the next goal pursued after completion of a previous goal is likely to be more important if the previously fulfilled goal was highly motivating. Attending to this important goal is then facilitated by strong inhibition of the constructs related to the previous goal. Thus, the more motivating the initial goal was, the more functional it is to inhibit its related constructs after goal fulfillment in order to turn back to the important alternative goal that was suppressed (for a more detailed analysis on the functionality of inhibitory mechanisms in goal pursuit see Förster & Liberman, in press; Liberman & Förster, 2005).

We will now turn to examine the relevance of goal-related inhibition processes for social judgments. First we will focus on priming, and argue that fulfillment of the priming tasks can lead to inhibition so that the knowledge is not used any more and judgments are contrasted away from the prime. Second, we will show how our model can be applied to explain rebound after suppression of thoughts.

INHIBITION AND SOCIAL JUDGMENT: THE CASE OF COMPLETED PRIMING TASKS

By the logic of the Zeigarnik effects, which we discussed above, one might assume that completed priming tasks should lead to inhibition of the primed concept and thus to contrast on a subsequent task. Contrast caused by completed priming was first shown in Martin's (1986) now classic study, in which participants performed a priming task in which they decided whether two different traits characterized a number of behavioral descriptions In the positive priming condition, the phrases conveyed either boldness or self-confidence, whereas in the negative priming condition the phrases conveyed either foolhardiness or conceitedness. Participants always classified eight phrases. In the interrupted task condition, they had the goal to complete twelve phrases and were interrupted after the first eight phrases. In the completed task condition, participants had the goal to complete eight phrases and fulfilled that goal. Martin then examined the effect of priming on people's impressions of an ambiguous social target.

Borrowing Higgins et al.'s (1977) paradigm, participants read a paragraph about Donald in which one of the sentences could be interpreted as either adventurous or reckless (e.g., "Donald thought perhaps he might do some skydiving or maybe cross the Atlantic in a sailboat") and another sentence could be interpreted as either self-confident or conceited (e.g., "Donald was well aware of his ability to do things well"). Participants rated Donald on a scale ranging from "reckless" to "adventurous" and on a scale ranging from "conceited" to "self-confident." The data showed assimilation effects when the priming task was interrupted and contrast effects when the priming task was completed.

To explain these results, Martin (1986) suggested that after completing a task people "reset" their mental states and refrain from using the accessible construct in subsequent judgments (see also Martin & Achee, 1992). Specifically, set/reset theory proposes that an interrupted task leaves the cognitive system in the "set of the interrupted task, and causes an enhanced accessibility of the activated construct during formation of the target impression" (p. 502). That is, an interrupted priming task caused an assimilation of the target to the constructs activated by the prime. Completed tasks, however, were theorized to cause the cognitive system to "reset" the previously activated construct. According to Martin (1986), "Reset refers to the suppressed use of a contextually primed concept and the encoding of the stimulus in terms of an independently activated one. Resetting may be most likely to occur when use of the initially primed concept would appear to bias an independent judgment or the target . . . or when there are demands to exclude from consideration information that has activated a concept" (p. 502).

Notably, as discussed above, a contrast effect in impression formation and the notion of resetting allow for the possibility that, at the time of judging the target, the primed construct remains highly accessible but is suppressed because it is considered irrelevant or inappropriate to use (i.e., a "judged usability" effect; see Higgins, 1996). Using our definitions above, Martin interpreted these effects as unconscious or conscious correction effects. Or, in other words, resetting is a secondary process which happens at the efferent stage: Knowledge is activated and thus highly accessible but nevertheless it is not used because of a secondary, metacogntiive process. An operation such as resetting occurs upon encountering a new target and involves suppressing or refraining from using a construct whose accessibility could remain high. However, it is also possible to assume that a completed priming phase would instigate inhibitory mechanisms due to goal fulfillment, which could explain the contrast effect in the studies. How can one disentangle the two processes?

Based on the distinction between inhibition and resetting, we argued that postfulfillment inhibition, but not resetting, would be revealed in an implicit task such as a lexical decision task. If, as we propose, a primed construct is inhibited following goal fulfillment, i.e., following mere completion of a task, then a lexical decision task should reveal its reduced accessibility. In contrast, resetting needs a decision not to use an accessible construct. This would be unlikely with an implicit task that is characterized by a lack of awareness of the potential effects of accessibility. Accessibility that is measured with a lexical decision task should be unaffected by resetting or attempts at not using a construct because participants would not consider the potential relevance or appropriateness of the primes when making lexical decisions. Moreover, accessibility in a lexical decision task has a desirable effect of enhancing the speed and the efficiency of one's performance, and thus there is no strategic reason to reset primed constructs. More generally, reduced accessibility on a lexical decision task, after a completed priming task (indicated by slower lexical decisions on prime-related words), cannot be explained by a model that assumes strategic suppression of accessible constructs upon encountering a new target (e.g., to avoid biased responding). Factors that rely on judged usability, or comparison of the target to the prime, could not account for such results.

In a recent study, Liberman, Förster, and Higgins (in press) examined this prediction by replicating Martin's (1986) original study with the addition of a lexical decision task between the priming task and the impression formation task. On both the lexical decision task and the impression formation task, they found enhanced accessibility after the interrupted priming task and reduced accessibility after the completed priming task. The study by Förster et al. suggests the possibility that some contrast effects in the literature may in fact reflect inhibition at the afferent stage rather than correction due to judged unusability.

One might ask why in many experiments assimilation effects were found when the priming task was presumably completed. Does the present framework suggest that contrast effects should have been obtained in all studies in which a priming task was completed? We think not. Task completion probably had a very strong impact in the experimental procedure used by Martin (1986) that we also used. Specifically, lexical decision and impression formation were the fifth and sixth tasks, respectively, among a series of clearly unrelated tasks. The participants were likely to try to be as efficient as possible in performing these tasks because they were introduced as speed relevant and achievement related. Inhibition of constructs related to a completed task before moving to a new one would be an especially effective strategy in such circumstances but would be less so under the circumstances of the typical priming study in the literature. For example, the above cited study by Fiedler et al. (2005) showed that a verb that was consistent with a scene led to facilitation of constructs associated with it when the verb pertained to the behavior of the focal protagonist. However, when considering the nonfocal person in the same scene, an open mindset, created by considering a scene-inconsistent verb, resulted in an enhanced accessibility of semantically related constructs that led to facilitation; no facilitation was found after encoding fitting behavioral descriptions, which presumably induced a closed mindset. These results suggest that even after completing the priming procedure, some accessibility can be found for focal aspects of the goal, if goal attainment is more subtle, as seems to be the case in Fiedler's studies.

It is also interesting to consider whether some types of tasks create a stronger experience of completion than others. For example, standards could be thought of as a subtype of goals that can be instantiated but cannot be entirely fulfilled. We would expect less inhibition after an instantiation of standards than after fulfillment of goals (see Förster & Liberman, in press, for a related discussion). From our perspective, it is interesting to consider inhibition as a basic mechanism that can produce contrast by rendering information inaccessible. Methodologically, the data suggest that the priming task should be designed in a way that the participant perceives it as uncompleted in order to avoid unwanted contrast or null effects. Researchers in the area of social cognition that seek to demonstrate assimilation effects might be advised against giving their participants feedback (and especially positive feedback) about their performance in the priming task. In fact, failures to replicate priming effects might have been due to this factor. These findings also suggest that assimilation effects are less prevalent than social cognition researchers thought. For example, the possibility that a newspaper article that you read in the morning would influence your buying behavior is reduced if a reader experiences this as a completed task. In the domain of learning, it is interesting to investigate whether positive feelings (I did well) or positive feedback after completion would lead to less recollection of the learning material than a negative feeling or negative feedback.

INHIBITION AND SOCIAL JUDGMENT: THE CASE OF POSTSUPPRESSIONAL REBOUND

Many times, attempts to suppress one's thoughts not only fail but also produce the opposite effect (Wegner, 1992, 1994; Wegner, Shortt, Blake, & Page, 1990). Wegner, Schneider, Carter, and White (1987) were the first to demonstrate both the fallibility of suppression and the existence of postsuppressional rebound (PSR)—the tendency of the suppressed construct to become even more accessible than it would be without having attempted to suppress the construct. In the classic study by Wegner et al. (1987), participants were instructed to not think of white bears for a period of 5 minutes and to ring a bell each time the thought of a white bear crossed their minds. Following this initial suppression period, the authors introduced another 5-minute phase (the so-called expression phase) during which participants could think of anything they wanted, including white bears, and continued to ring a bell each time the thought of a white bear appeared. This group was compared to another group of participants who performed the expression phase first, without initial suppression. The results showed that suppression in the first phase was difficult for the participants—most of them thought of white bears despite instructions not to think of them—and that thoughts of white bears rebounded after suppression in the second, free expression phase. Thus, the rate of white bear thoughts during the expression phase was higher in the suppression-first group than in the expression-first group.

In order to explain PSR, Wegner (1994) introduced his ironic monitoring model of suppression (Wegner & Wenzlaff, 1996). According to this model, suppressing a thought or a response involves a controlled search for distracters (i.e., mental contents other than the one being suppressed) and automatic monitoring for suppression failures, or thoughts of the suppressed construct. The automatic monitor "reviews potentially conscious material, noting items that imply failed control and increasing their activation. This increases the likelihood that the items will surface in consciousness so that the operating process can renew its work" (Wegner, 1994, p. 38). For example, when trying to suppress thoughts of white bears people try to think about other things (e.g., last weekend) and at the same time monitor for occurrences of thoughts of white bears. This monitoring process notes suppression failures (e.g., "Ooops I thought about the zoo and they had polar bears there! I should not have thought about the zoo.") and directs thoughts to a new subject upon detecting a failure (e.g., "Let's try to think of museums instead. Oops! There was a flower bear by Jeff Koons! Let me try my last visit to the gay fathers' chess club!"). Although this process successfully pushes thoughts of white bears out of consciousness, the ironic monitor remains sensitized to the construct of white bears through the entire period of suppression, and thereby makes it accessible. Consequently, when the suppression period is over, the accessibility of the suppressed construct is manifested in faster and more frequent use.

Thus, one reason for PSR is that the ironic monitor makes the suppressed construct accessible through the act of thought suppression. Whereas ironic monitoring theory is not specific with respect to the question of how exactly accessibility is produced, Macrae, Bodenhausen, Milne, and Jetten (1994) theorized that the ironic monitor produces semantic priming. According to the logic of conceptual priming, activation of a concept enhances its accessibility, with frequent and recent priming being the major determinants of the strength of the resulting accessibility. Because the suppression phase is extended, and the ironic monitor operates during that entire period of suppression, relatively intense and lasting accessibility is produced. This type of *priming-related accessibility* might be distinguished from *motivation-related accessibility*.

Recently, Liberman and Förster (2000, 2005; Förster & Liberman, 2001, 2004) proposed that *inferences about motivation* and *motivation-related accessibility* underlie PSR. Their Motivational Inference Model of PSR (MIMO) proposes that people may infer from the difficulty they experience during suppression or from suppression failures that they are motivated to use the suppressed construct.

For example, in Macrae et al.'s (1994) experiment participants were asked to write a story about a day in the life of a skinhead presented on a photograph. Those participants could have found the task difficult and thought, "If it is so hard for me not to use stereotypes of skinheads, then it must be because I really want to use them." We propose that this attribution of difficulty to motivation enhances the motivation to think of the suppressed construct, thereby also enhancing its accessibility. The inference process proposed by MIMO has been supported by some recent findings (Förster & Liberman, 2001, 2004) showing that when suppression is easy or when difficulty is attributed to external sources, participants do not even seem to activate unwanted concepts. MIMO also predicts that inasmuch as expressing thoughts after periods of suppression fulfills a goal, it should lead to inhibition of those constructs.

Two studies examined this hypothesis about the effect of expression after suppression of stereotypes. One study used the stereotype of African-Americans in the US (Liberman & Förster, 2000), which includes, among other traits, hostility. Borrowing the Macrae et al. (1994; Macrae, Bodenhausen, & Milne, 1998) paradigm, the experiment had two phases: In the first phase, participants received a portrait of a smiling young African-American man. Participants in the no-suppression condition were simply asked to write a story about a day in the life of this person; participants in the suppression condition were instructed, in addition, to not use the stereotype of African-Americans in their stories. Participants in the expression condition were asked to write a second story. They were shown a second photograph of another young African-American man and instructed, again, to write a story about a day in the life of that person. In order to manipulate expression of racist thoughts, they were instructed to take the perspective of a racist person and write the story by using stereotypes of African-Americans. The authors reasoned that such expression instructions would fulfill the goal of using racist stereotypes, which were presumably activated or enhanced during suppression. However, it was argued that writing the racist story, with no suppression before, would make the stereotype highly accessible and this activated knowledge would serve as a prime. After both phases, all the participants proceeded to an ostensibly unrelated study in which they were asked to read a story about Donald and form an impression about him. Donald's actions were ambiguous and could be interpreted as either hostile or assertive (Srull & Wyer, 1979).

Participants rated Donald's hostility among other trait dimensions. The results revealed that the hostility ratings in the baseline, no-suppression, no-expression condition were lower than both the suppression alone condition and the expression alone condition, demonstrating PSR and the knowledge activation effect, respectively. When expression followed suppression, hostility ratings dropped to the level of the baseline (i.e., they were lower both relative to the suppression alone condition and relative to the expression alone condition). Accordingly, introducing expression after suppression reduced rebound, and this is consistent with MIMO's suggestion that rebound stems from a need to express the suppressed construct, a need that may be fulfilled by expression. Note that semantic priming accounts would have predicted an increase rather than a decrease in accessibility following expression because the accessibility from the suppression and the expression phases should have added up.

Another study replicated the same results with the stereotype of women (Liberman & Förster, 2000). Again, participants were instructed to describe a picture of a scene involving two women in stereotypical situations under suppression or no-suppression instructions. Only the expression groups received a second picture to describe and expression instructions (i.e., take the perspective of a sexist writer). After that, participants proceeded with an unrelated task on people's conceptions about traits, in which they were asked to type three trait terms into the computer as fast as they could. Judges rated the traits on their degree of femininity. The mean degree of femininity of what participants wrote served as the main dependent measure in our study. The results showed that relative to the no-suppression, no-expression baseline, accessibility of the female stereotype was enhanced by both suppression only (which was, in essence a replication of PSR), and expression only (which was, in essence, a replication of knowledge accessibility effects). Most importantly, when expression followed suppression, accessibility of the stereotype was *reduced* relative to both the suppression alone condition and the expression alone condition. Thus, in both studies, introducing expression after suppression eliminated PSR, showing that the logic of goal fulfillment can also be applied to thought suppression. Suppression attempts appear to activate a motivation that can be fulfilled, inhibiting motivation-related thoughts, thus causing a reduced accessibility and a reduced tendency to exhibit an assimilation effect.

CONCLUSIONS

We demonstrated that, like correction and anchoring, inhibition is an important route by which contrast effects may occur. We tried to distinguish the effects of inhibition from those of correction by suggesting that the former operates at the afferent stage, after priming but before encountering a new target, whereas the latter occurs at the time of encountering a new target. We examined the implications of goal-related inhibition for the effects of completed versus interrupted priming tasks, and for explaining (and controlling) postsuppressional rebound effects on social judgments. We believe that because inhibition may produce contrasts in a very simple and automatic way at a relatively early stage of information processing, it is important to consider it when trying to explain assimilation versus contrast effects in judgment, evaluation, and perception. Importantly, inhibition has different moderators than anchoring or correction and many unpublished failures to replicate priming or assimilation effects in the laboratory may be due to the fact that the process of inhibition was poorly understood. For example as described above, the strength of the motivation to work on a task, the completion of a goal, or the parallel operation of competing goals can render information inaccessible. Knowledge that is made inaccessible cannot be used any more for judgments and behavior. For research it is important to understand that completed priming tasks, positive feedback, and parallel goals (does the participant have to do a priming task and also want to impress the experimenter?) may inhibit information and thus prevent assimilation effects. Although disappointing for a researcher interested in priming effects, the implications for real life may be relieving—after all, assimilation effects due to priming often constitute an unwanted contamination of judgment and perception. We may often have one focal goal and thus will not be influenced by goal irrelevant primed information, because the latter would be efficiently inhibited.

ACKNOWLEDGMENTS

This research was supported by a grant from the Deutsche Forschungsgemein-schaft to Jens Förster (FO244/8–2). We thank Martin Denzler, Stefanie Kuschel, Katrin Schimmel, and Amina Özelsel for invaluable discussions and Ashleigh Ferris for editing the manuscript.

REFERENCES

Ach, N. (1935). Analyse des Willens. In E. Abderhalden (Ed.), *Handbuch der biologischen Arbeitsmethoden, Bd. VI*. Berlin, Germany: Urban & Schwarzenberg.

Anderson, J. R. (1983). *The architecture of cognition*. Cambridge, MA: Harvard University Press.

Anderson, M. C., & Bjork, R. A. (1994). Mechanisms of inhibition in long-term memory: A new taxonomy. In D. Dagenbach & T. H. Carr (Eds.), *Inhibitory processes in attention, memory and language* (pp. 265–326). San Diego, CA: Academic Press.

Anderson, M. C., & Neely, J. H. (1996). Interference and inhibition in memory retrieval. In E. L. Bjork & R. A. Bjork (Eds.), *Memory* (pp. 237–313). New York: Academic Press.

Anderson, M. C., & Spellman, B. A. (1995). On the status of inhibitory mechanisms in cognition: Memory retrieval as a model case. *Psychological Review, 102*, 68–100.

Atkinson, J. W. (1964). *An introduction to motivation*. Princeton, NJ: Van Nostrand.

Bruner, J. S. (1957). On perceptual readiness. *Psychological Review, 64*, 123–152.

Butterfield, E. C. (1964). The interruption of tasks: Methodological, factual and theoretical issues. *Psychological Bulletin, 62*, 309–322.

Carver, C. S., & Scheier, M. F. (1999). Themes and issues in the self-regulation of behavior. In R. S. Wyer, Jr. (Ed.), *Advances in social cognition* (Vol. 12, pp. 1–106). Mahwah, NJ: Lawrence Erlbaum Associates, Inc.

DeCoster, J., & Claypool, H. M. (2004). A meta-analysis of priming effects on impression formation supporting a general model of informational biases. *Personality and Social Psychology Review, 8*, 2–27.

Fiedler, K. (2003). The hidden vicissitudes of the priming paradigm in evaluative judgment research. In J. Musch & K. C. Klauer (Eds.), *The psychology of evaluation: Affective processes in cognition and emotion* (pp. 109–137). Mahwah, NJ: Lawrence Erlbaum Associates, Inc.

Fiedler, K., Schenck, W., Watling, M., & Menges, J. I. (2005). Priming trait inferences through pictures and moving pictures: The impact of open and closed mindsets. *Journal of Personality and Social Psychology, 88*, 229–244.

Fishbein, M., & Ajzen, I. (1974). Attitudes toward objects as predictors of single and multiple behavioral criteria. *Psychological Review, 81*, 59–74.

Förster, J., & Liberman, N. (2001). The role of attribution of motivation in producing post-suppressional rebound. *Journal of Personality and Social Psychology, 81,* 377–390.

Förster, J., & Liberman, N. (2004). How motivational inferences influence post-suppressional rebound. In S. Shohov (Ed.), *Advances in psychology research* (Vol. 34, pp. 63–88). New York: Nova Science Publishers.

Förster, J., & Liberman, N. (in press). Knowledge activation. In E. T. Higgins & A. W. Kruglanski (Eds.), *Social psychology: Handbook of basic principles* (2nd ed.). New York: Guilford Press.

Förster, J., Liberman, N., & Higgins, E. T. (2005). Accessibility from active and fulfilled goals. *Journal of Experimental Social Psychology, 41,* 220–239.

Gollwitzer, P. M. (1996). The volitional benefits of planning. In P. M. Gollwitzer & J. A. Bargh (Eds.), *The psychology of action* (pp. 287–312). New York: Guilford Press.

Gollwitzer, P. M. (1999). Implementation intentions: Strong effects of simple plans. *The American Psychologist, 54,* 493–503.

Gollwitzer, P. M., & Moskowitz, G. B. (1996). Goal effects on action and cognition. In E. T. Higgins & A. W. Kruglanski (Eds.), *Social psychology: Handbook of basic principles* (pp. 361–399). New York: Guilford Press.

Goschke, T., & Kuhl, J. (1993). Representation of intentions: Persisting activation in memory. *Journal of Experimental Psychology: Learning, Memory, and Cognition, 19,* 1211–1226.

Heckhausen, H. (1991). *Motivation and action.* Berlin, Germany: Springer.

Higgins, E. T. (1996). Knowledge activation: Accessibility, applicability and salience. In E. T. Higgins & A. W. Kruglanski (Eds.), *Social psychology: Handbook of basic principles* (pp. 133–168). New York: Guilford Press.

Higgins, E. T., & King, G. (1981). Accessibility of social constructs: Information processing consequences of individual and contextual variability. In N. Cantor & J. Kihlstrom (Eds.), *Personality, cognition, and social interaction* (pp. 69–121). Hillsdale, NJ: Lawrence Erlbaum Associates, Inc.

Higgins, E. T., Rholes, W. S., & Jones, C. R. (1977). Category accessibility and impression formation. *Journal of Experimental Social Psychology, 13,* 141–154.

Klein, R. M., & Taylor, T. L. (1994). Categories of cognitive inhibition with reference to attention. In D. Dagenbach & T. H. Carr (Eds.), *Inhibitory processes in attention, memory and language* (pp. 113–150). San Diego, CA: Academic Press.

Kruglanski, A. W., Shah, J. Y., Fishbach, A., Friedman, R., Chun, W., & Sleeth-Keppler, D. (2002). A theory of goal systems. In M. P. Zanna (Ed.), *Advances in experimental social psychology* (Vol. 34, pp. 331–378). San Diego, CA: Academic Press.

Kuhl, J. (1983). *Motivation, Konflikt und Handlungskontrolle.* New York: Springer.

Kuhl, J. (1987). Action control: The maintenance of motivational states. In F. Halisch & J. Kuhl (Eds.), *Motivation, intention, and volition* (pp. 279–291). New York: Springer.

Kuhl, J., & Kazén-Saad, M. (1988). A motivational approach to volition: Activation and deactivation of memory representations related to unfulfilled intentions. In V. Hamilton, G. H. Bower, & N. H. Frijda (Eds.), *Cognitive perspectives on emotion and motivation* (pp. 63–85). Dordrecht, The Netherlands: Martinus Nijhoff.

Lewin, K. (1951). *Field theory in social science.* New York: Harper.

Liberman, N., & Förster, J. (2000). Expression after suppression: A motivational explanation of post-suppressional rebound. *Journal of Personality and Social Psychology, 79,* 190–203.

Liberman, N., & Förster, J. (2005). Motivation and construct accessibility. In J. P. Forgas,

K. D. Kipling, & S. M. Laham (Eds.), *Social motivation: Conscious and unconscious processes (Sydney Symposium of Social Psychology)* (pp. 228–248). Cambridge, UK: Cambridge University Press.

Liberman, N., Förster, J., & Higgins, E. T. (in press). Set/reset or inhibition after goal fulfillment? A fair test between two mechanisms producing assimilation and contrast. *Journal of Experimental Social Psychology.*

Macrae, C. N., Bodenhausen, G. V., & Milne, A. B. (1995). The dissection of selection in person perception: Inhibitory processes in social stereotyping. *Journal of Personality and Social Psychology, 69,* 397–407.

Macrae, C. M., Bodenhausen, G. V., & Milne, A. B. (1998). Saying no to unwanted thoughts: Self focus and the regulation of mental life. *Journal of Personality and Social Psychology, 72,* 578–589.

Macrae, C. N., Bodenhausen, G. V, Milne, A. B., & Jetten, J. (1994). Out of mind but back in sight: Stereotypes on the rebound. *Journal of Personality and Social Psychology, 67,* 808–817.

Marsh, R. L., Hicks, J. L., & Bink, M. L. (1998). Activation of completed, uncompleted and partially completed intentions. *Journal of Experimental Psychology: Learning, Memory, and Cognition, 24,* 350–361.

Marsh, R. L., Hicks, J. L., & Bryan, E. S. (1999). The activation of unrelated and canceled intentions. *Memory and Cognition, 27,* 320–327.

Martin, L. L. (1986). Set/reset: Use and disuse of concepts in impression formation. *Journal of Personality and Social Psychology, 51,* 493–504.

Martin, L. L., & Achee, J. W. (1992). Beyond accessibility: The role of processing objectives in judgment. In L. L. Martin & A. Tesser (Eds.), *The construction of social judgments* (pp. 195–216). Hillsdale, NJ: Lawrence Erlbaum Associates, Inc.

Mayr, U., & Keele, S. W. (2000). Changing internal constraints on action in role of backward inhibition. *Journal of Experimental Psychology: General, 129,* 4–26.

Neely, J. H. (1977). Semantic priming and retrieval from lexical memory: Roles of inhibition less spreading activation and limited-capacity attention. *Journal of Experimental Social Psychology: General, 106,* 226–254.

Nickerson, R. S. (1984). Retrieval inhibition from part-set cuing: A persisting enigma in memory research. *Memory and Cognition, 12,* 531–552.

Posner, M. I., & Cohen, Y. (1984). Components of visual orienting. In H. Bouma & D. G. Bouwhuis (Eds.), *Attention and performance X: Control of language processes* (pp. 531–556). Hillsdale, NJ: Lawrence Erlbaum Associates, Inc.

Ratcliff, R., & McCoon, G. (1996). Bias effects in implicit memory tasks. *Journal of Experimental Psychology: General, 125,* 403–421.

Roediger, H. L., & Neely, J. H. (1982). Retrieval blocks in episodic and semantic memory. *Canadian Journal of Psychology, 36,* 213–242.

Ross, M., & Holmberg, D. (1992). Are wives' memories for events in relationships more vivid than their husbands' memories? *Journal of Social and Personal Relationships, 9,* 585–604.

Rothermund, K. (2003). Automatic vigilance for task-related information: Perseverance after failure and inhibition after success. *Memory and Cognition, 31,* 343–352.

Rundus, D. (1973). Negative effects of using list items as retrieval cues. *Journal of Verbal Learning and Verbal Behavior, 12,* 43–50.

Shah, J. Y., Friedman, R., & Kruglanski, A. W. (2002). Forgetting all else: On the antecedents and consequences of goal shielding. *Journal of Personality and Social Psychology, 83,* 1261–1280.

Shah, J. Y., & Kruglanski, A. W. (2002). Priming against your will: How goal pursuit is affected by accessible alternatives. *Journal of Experimental Social Psychology, 38,* 368–383.

Shah, J. Y., & Kruglanski, A. W. (2003). When opportunity knocks: Bottom-up priming of goals by means and its effects on self-regulation. *Journal of Personality and Social Psychology, 84,* 1109–1122.

Slamecka, N. J. (1968). An examination of trace storage in free recall. *Journal of Experimental Psychology, 76,* 504–513.

Srull, T. K., & Wyer, R. S., Jr. (1979). The role of category accessibility in the interpretation of information about persons: Some determinants and implications. *Journal of Personality and Social Psychology, 37,* 1660–1672.

Stapel, D. A., & Koomen, W. (2000). Distinctness of others and malleability of selves: Their impact on social comparison effects. *Journal of Personality and Social Psychology, 79,* 1068–1087.

Strack, F. (1992). The different routes to social judgments: Experiential versus informational strategies. In L. L. Martin & A. Tesser (Eds.), *The construction of social judgments* (pp. 249–275). Hillsdale, NJ: Lawrence Erlbaum Associates, Inc.

Swinney, D., Prather, P., & Love, T. (2000). The time-course of lexical access and the role of context: Converging evidence from normal and aphasic processing. In Y. Grodzinsky, L. P. Shapiro, & D. A. Swinney (Eds.), *Language and the brain: Representation and processing* (pp. 273–294). New York: Academic Press.

Vallacher, R. R., & Wegner, D. M. (1987). What do people think they're doing? Action identification and human behavior. *Psychological Review, 94,* 3–15.

Vroom, V. H. (1966). Organizational choice: A study of pre- and post-decision processes. *Organizational Behavior and Human Performance, 1,* 212–225.

Watkins, M. J. (1975). Inhibition in recall with extralist "cues." *Journal of Verbal Learning and Verbal Behavior, 14,* 294–303.

Wegner, D. M. (1992). You can't always think what you want: Problems in the suppression of unwanted thoughts. In M. Zanna (Ed.), *Advances in experimental social psychology* (Vol. 25, pp. 193–225). San Diego, CA: Academic Press.

Wegner, D. M. (1994). Ironic processes of mental control. *Psychological Review, 101,* 34–52.

Wegner, D. M., Schneider, D. J., Carter, S., & White, L. (1987). Paradoxical effects of thought suppression. *Journal of Personality and Social Psychology, 53,* 5–13.

Wegner, D. M., Shortt, J. W., Blake, A. W., & Page, M. S. (1990). The suppression of exciting thoughts. *Journal of Personality and Social Psychology, 58,* 409–418.

Wegner, D. M., & Wenzlaff, R. M. (1996). Mental control. In E. T. Higgins & A. W. Kruglanski (Eds.), *Social psychology: Handbook of basic principles* (pp. 466–492). New York: Guilford Press.

Wyer, R. S. (2004). *Social comprehension and judgment: The role of situation models, narratives, and implicit theories.* Mahwah, NJ: Lawrence Erlbaum Associates, Inc.

Wyer, R. S., & Srull, T. K. (1989). *Memory and cognition in its social context.* Hillsdale, NJ: Lawrence Erlbaum Associates, Inc.

Zeigarnik, B. (1938). On finished and unfinished tasks. In W. D. Ellis (Ed.), *A source book of gestalt psychology* (pp. 300–314). New York: Harcourt, Brace, & World.

13

Contrast and Assimilation in Upward Comparison: The Intragroup Dimension

MICHAEL L. W. VLIEK, COLIN WAYNE LEACH, and RUSSELL SPEARS

A s this volume attests, the assimilation–contrast model continues to be of great use to scholars interested in human judgment and its psychological and social implications. Assimilation–contrast models have been particularly important in helping us understand how people use other individuals as standards of comparison in order to evaluate themselves (for reviews see Suls & Wheeler, 2000). As individuals' evaluations of themselves are central to their psychological experience and social behavior, assimilation–contrast models have illuminated the processes and mechanisms behind individual self-esteem, emotion, motivation to achieve, and cooperation and competition with others (for a review see Buunk & Gibbons, 1997; Suls & Wheeler, 2000). Assimilation–contrast models have also been used to examine the more macro-social phenomena that are linked to evaluation of the group-level self. Thus, assimilation–contrast models have also formed the building blocks in the processes underlying adherence to group norms, polarization of group opinion, group identity, and intergroup competition and conflict (for reviews see Pettigrew, 1967; Turner, 1991; Turner, Hogg, Oakes, Reicher, & Wetherell, 1987).

Unfortunately, the disparate uses of assimilation–contrast models of social comparison has meant not only that insights in the different domains of application have somewhat isolated them from each other, but that points of connection are not always apparent (for a review, see Leach, 2005). Thus, work on interpersonal assimilation–contrast and its role in individual self-evaluation seems to share little in common with work on intergroup assimilation–contrast and its role in group self-evaluation (Pettigrew, 1967). In this chapter we take a step toward a reintegration of these traditions by focusing on a level of analysis at which interpersonal and intergroup assimilation–contrast may meet—the intragroup dimension. We think that attention to this meso level of analysis between the interpersonal and intergroup helps to illustrate how individuals assimilate and contrast themselves to the successful others who are most relevant to self-evaluation. The aim of this chapter is to provide some argument and empirical evidence that there is a distinctive (and neglected) meso level of assimilation and contrast, the intragroup dimension, that is not reducible to either the interpersonal or intergroup level and is more than the sum of these, albeit important, parts.

The chapter is structured as follows. We begin with a theoretical discussion of assimilation and contrast processes in self-evaluation. Based in our review of previous assimilation–contrast models of self-evaluation, we suggest that the intragroup context is an important but neglected dimension. Consistent with a classic reference group theory approach, we suggest that it is at the intragroup level that the interpersonal and intergroup dynamics of self-evaluation determine whether individuals are likely to assimilate or to contrast themselves to individual others. Intergroup models of assimilation and contrast such as self-categorization theory (SCT; Turner et al., 1987) state that salient intergroup relationships lead individuals to assimilate themselves to their fellow ingroup members. This process is referred to as depersonalization. In essence, assimilating oneself to fellow group members serves to "denote" one as a group member by shifting self-definition to the group level. Like most models of assimilation and contrast that have been applied to self-evaluation in group contexts (e.g., Brewer, 1991), SCT presumes that a *denoting* assimilation within a group precludes contrast between individual members of the group.

Similarly, at the interpersonal level, Tesser's (1988) self-evaluation maintenance model argues that individuals who face a potentially "demoting" contrast between themselves and a more successful other may use a *denoting* assimilation in an effort at self-protection. By defining both the individual and the more successful other as a group, a *denoting* assimilation is expected to preclude the deleterious effects that a *demoting* contrast can have on individual self-evaluation. A number of recent studies have applied this model of assimilation and contrast to examinations of how individual members of low status groups assimilate or contrast themselves to referents with high or low group status (e.g., Blanton, Crocker, & Miller, 2000; Mussweiler, Gabriel, & Bodenhausen, 2000; Schmitt, Silvia, & Branscombe 2000). In contrast, we suggest a second kind of assimilation might occur, which is more motivational and which we will refer to as *promoting* assimilation. Here assimilation involves a process of striving to be like the comparison other (e.g., inspiration) as a way to cope with the threat of a possible "demoting" contrast that might otherwise ensue (e.g., Lockwood & Kunda, 1997, 1999). Thus, ingroup members are suggested to be highly relevant as proxies for individual's own behavior (e.g., Wheeler, Martin, & Suls, 1997) and can therefore serve as motivating and inspiring role models through whom an individual can learn to improve his or her own abilities (e.g., Burleson, Leach, & Harrington, 2005; Leach & Smith, 2006).

We then review an empirical program of research that attempts to demonstrate the importance and utility of an intragroup analysis of assimilation and contrast in upward social comparison. This work addresses how the group frames what otherwise appear to be interpersonal comparisons. In all these cases the basic issue confronting the individual is the *potentially demoting* contrast to another person who is better off than the individual. We show that the intragroup context provides different ways of assimilation and contrast that help individuals to cope with the "problem" of a potentially *demoting* contrast.

In the first line of research discussed, we consider how the individual can use his or her ingroup to protect individual self-evaluation against a potentially *demoting* contrast with a more successful other. More specifically, we show how individuals may assimilate the ingroup's average performance to their individual performance to cope with a potentially *demoting* "upward" contrast. In this case, the potentially deleterious effects of a *demoting* contrast at the intragroup level lead individuals to make a *denoting* assimilation at the intragroup level. In the second line of research discussed, we consider how membership in a group enables individuals to assimilate themselves to a more successful member of their ingroup. However, different to work that suggests that ingroup membership leads to a *denoting* assimilation to more successful ingroup members, we show that group membership enables a *promoting* assimilation of the individual to the more successful other. Thus, this line of research differentiates the process of *denoting* assimilation that has been emphasized in work on self-evaluation in intergroup contexts from a *promoting* assimilation that occurs between individuals within a group. In the third line of research discussed, we move to an explicit intergroup context to show that the intragroup level remains important even here. Here the point is that intergroup *status* is also likely to affect how individuals assimilate or contrast themselves to a more successful individual with whom they share a group membership. We show that a *denoting* assimilation to a more successful ingroup member protects against the negative implications of a *demoting* contrast. Importantly, we show that this *denoting* assimilation at the intragroup level affects individuals' self-evaluation at the group, rather than the individual, level.

CONCEPTUAL BACKGROUND

Assimilation and contrast always take place within a "frame of reference" that makes entities comparable to each other (Hyman, 1942; Marsh & Parker, 1984; Ruys, Spears, Gordijn, & de Vries, 2006). According to both reference group theory and SCT, individual self-evaluation always operates within the frame of reference given by the next higher level of self-categorization—a group (Hyman, 1942; Hyman & Singer, 1968; Turner et al., 1987). The importance of the group as a frame of reference is also illustrated by Miller and Prentice (1996, p. 815), who argue that "people do not typically view themselves in terms of their standing on attributes that may or may not be related to their performance or treatment; they more typically view themselves in terms of their identity." Thus, the intragroup level forms a natural frame of reference for what otherwise appear to be interpersonal processes of assimilation and contrast. One could even argue that a "pure" interpersonal level of assimilation and contrast, devoid of an intragroup frame of reference, cannot exist (see Deschamps & Devos, 1998; Tajfel & Turner,

1979). Thus, we argue that the intragroup frame of reference provides the context in which individuals assimilate and contrast themselves to others who are better or worse off than they.

Although the intragroup dimension of assimilation–contrast is not emphasized in most contemporary approaches, some of the earliest statements of social comparison presumed that interpersonal assimilation and contrast necessarily occurred within the frame of reference provided by group membership (e.g., Festinger, 1950; Heider, 1958; for reviews see Cartwright, 1951; Cartwright & Zander, 1968; Turner, 1991). For example, Festinger's (1954) influential paper presumed that interpersonal comparison occurred within "cohesive groups." He argued that a "pressure toward uniformity in groups" encouraged individuals to assimilate their opinions and self-evaluations to that of fellow group members. This process of intragroup assimilation was presumed to maintain the cohesiveness of the group. Thus, Festinger (1954) viewed intragroup assimilation and group cohesiveness as constituting a positively reinforcing cycle—where each reinforced the other (for a discussion, see Singer, 1990). Where individuals contrasted themselves to their fellow group members, Festinger (1954) believed they would face even greater pressure toward uniformity. As a result, he suggested that contrast within groups would force individuals to either assimilate or leave the group (for general discussions, see Asch, 1952; Cartwright & Zander, 1968). Thus, like SCT, SEM, and other contemporary approaches to assimilation and contrast within groups, Festinger (1954) viewed intragroup assimilation as precluding intragroup contrast.

Some years before Festinger's (1954) more influential treatment, reference group theory offered an assimilation–contrast model of self-evaluation that also emphasized the intragroup dimension (see Hyman, 1942; Hyman & Singer, 1968; Sherif, 1936; for a review, see Leach, 2005). As mentioned above, this approach was based on the view that individuals' assimilation and contrast of themselves to other individuals necessarily occurred within a frame of reference provided by shared membership in a group or social category. For example, Davis (1966) used reference group theory to argue that individuals' self-evaluation was better served by being "a big frog in a small pond, than a small frog in a big pond." Because reference group theory states that other members of one's reference group provide the most relevant standards by which individuals can evaluate themselves, Davis argued that being in a very successful reference group hurt individual's self-evaluation. He believed that belonging to a highly successful group increased individuals' potential of *demoting* contrasts between themselves and more successful ingroup members (for a review, see Marsh & Craven, 2001). However, given that more successful others are part of an individual's reference group, assimilation to their success should also be possible (Hyman, 1942).

Consistent with this, Burleson et al. (2005) recently showed that individuals in a highly successful group can also make a *promoting* assimilation between themselves and more successful members of their reference group (see also Leach & Smith, 2006). They found adolescent artists who were "inspired" by the most successful individuals in an advanced summer arts program to show positive improvements in their self-concept and aspirations regarding art. As reference group theory suggests that it is fellow group members who offer the most relevant standard for individual self-evaluation, individuals' assimilation or contrast to fellow group members should have the greatest effect on self-evaluation (Hyman, 1942; for a review, see Leach, 2005). Thus, unlike most other approaches, reference group theory suggests that it is intragroup assimilation *and* contrast that explain what appear to be intergroup or interpersonal processes.

Despite the importance placed on the intragroup level of analysis in early assimilation–contrast models of self-evaluation, more recent work has tended to give it little attention (for a discussion, see Miller & Prentice, 1996). Although recent research has examined individual assimilation and contrast to in- and out-group members in intergroup settings (e.g., Blanton et al., 2000; Brewer & Weber, 1994; Martinot, Redersdorff, Guimond, & Dif, 2002; Schmitt, Branscombe, Silvia, Garcia, & Spears, 2006; Schmitt et al., 2000), a systematic approach to assimilation and contrast at the *intragroup* level is still in its infancy. Indeed, contemporary work that addresses group-level processes has tended to emphasize the intergroup dimension of assimilation and contrast, rather than the intragroup dimension we wish to emphasize here. The social identity tradition, for example, offers a decidedly intergroup model of assimilation and contrast in the evaluation of the group self. According to self-categorization theory (Turner et al., 1987), where intergroup relations lead an individual to perceive himself as a group member, this individual comes to perceive himself as "depersonalized" and thus interchangeable with fellow group members.

This perceptual process is akin to what we refer to as a *denoting* assimilation. Thus, SCT suggests that a contrast between groups at the intergroup level relies upon a depersonalizing, *denoting* assimilation at the intragroup level. Although self-categorization theory does not argue that the individual self completely disappears when group membership is salient, it does argue that the individual self is necessarily less salient when the group self is activated by a relevant intergroup relation (Spears, 2001; Turner, Reynolds, Haslam, & Veenstra, 2006; see also Smith & Spears, 1996; Smith, Spears, & Oyen, 1994). Thus, SCT suggests that relevant intergroup relations promote *denoting* assimilation at the intragroup level, which serve to make salient the group-level self and group-level self-evaluation. As such, SCT presumed that relevant intergroup relations preclude *promoting* assimilation or *demoting* contrast at the intragroup level (for a discussion, see Turner, 1991).

Making the Ingroup a Reference Group: Intergroup Distinctiveness

Tajfel (1972) argued that being different from another group is necessary for a group identity to acquire meaning. Based in this, self-categorization theory argues that people are more likely to categorize themselves as a group as the ratio of intergroup to intragroup differences increases, and thus when the ingroup is perceived as relatively *distinct* from an outgroup (i.e., the metacontrast principle: see for example Turner et al., 1987). Other researchers have also pointed to distinctiveness as an important determinant for the creation of a meaningful group identity (Brewer, 1991; Vignoles, Chryssochoou, & Breakwell, 2000; Spears, Jetten, & Scheepers, 2002). Thus, other things being equal, group membership becomes most salient when there is enough intergroup difference to ensure the distinctive-ness of the ingroup from a relevant outgroup. However, both groups should at the same time be sufficiently close to be able to generate some comparative relevance between groups, thereby keeping group identity salient (Jetten, Spears, & Manstead, 1998). Previous research has shown that members of distinctive ingroups see their fellow members as more psychologically close and similar (Brewer, 1991; Turner et al., 1987). For example, Miller, Turnbull, and McFarland (1988) found that participants see themselves as more similar to people with whom they shared a distinctive attribute.

We agree with the basic tenet of SCT and the other approaches that argue that intergroup distinctiveness makes ingroup membership salient. However, we do not think that this kind of intergroup relation necessarily leads to a *denoting* assimilation at the intragroup level. Indeed, as intergroup distinctiveness means that only ingroup members share the distinctive qualities of the self (e.g., Miller et al., 1988; for discussions, see Brewer, 1991; Turner et al., 1987), intergroup distinctiveness should make fellow ingroup members the most relevant standard of comparison for individuals (see also Miller et al., 1988). In this way, intergroup distinctiveness should make intragroup processes of assimilation *and* contrast most important to individual and group self-evaluation. Indeed, reference group theory may be seen as suggesting that ingroups that are highly distinctive from outgroups are most likely to serve as a reference for individual self-evaluation (Hyman, 1942; Merton, 1957). As such, membership in a distinctive ingroup should make the possibility of a *demoting* contrast with a more successful ingroup member espe-cially threatening, as it is a fellow ingroup members' success that provides the most meaningful standard of comparison for the individual self. Thus, individuals may be most likely to make active attempts to cope with a potentially *demoting* contrast within their ingroup by making a *denoting* assimilation instead. This *denoting* assimilation would thus result from concern for the individuals' standing at the intragroup level, rather than concern for the group's standing at the inter-group level. As the success of fellow ingroup members should provide the most relevant and meaningful standard for individual self-evaluation, it should also be the case that a *promoting* assimilation to more successful ingroup members will be especially beneficial to individuals.

In order to investigate these claims, in the first two empirical studies reported below we tried to make an intragroup frame of reference salient by presenting the ingroup as distinct from but proximal to an outgroup. These studies used a quasiminimal group paradigm. Participants were told that research had revealed that people could be characterized as having one of two perceptual styles: "global" and "detailed" (see also Jetten et al., 1998). Ostensibly based on their performance on a "dot-estimation" and "dice recognition" task (Jetten et al., 1998), all partici-pants were categorized as "detailed perceivers." Participants then had to perform a series of difficult "visual intelligence" tasks (pilot tests confirmed that participants thought they performed well below 50%). The ostensible goal of the experiments was to discover whether the styles of perception mattered for performance on visual intelligence tasks (see also Miller et al., 1988). After participants had completed the tasks, we manipulated *intergroup distinctiveness* by showing a distribution of each group's introversion–extraversion (Jetten et al., 1998). In the condition of low intergroup distinctiveness, the outgroup's introversion–extroversion closely overlapped that of the ingroup. In the condition of high intergroup distinctiveness, the outgroup hardly overlapped with the ingroup. Thus, only under high intergroup distinctiveness did the ingroup's level of introversion–extroversion clearly distinguish them from the outgroup, while the proximity of the outgroup served to maintain the salience of ingroup identity.

Although introversion–extroversion is not an attribute likely to be seen as related to visual perception, sharing this distinctive psychological characteristic should make ingroup membership more meaningful (Miller et al., 1988; for a review, see Wood, 1989). When such an attribute makes the ingroup of "detailed perceivers" distinct from the outgroup of "global perceivers" it should make intragroup comparisons with fellow "detailed perceivers" especially relevant (e.g., Miller et al., 1988; for a discussion, see Turner et al., 1987).

That high intergroup distinctiveness had the effect we expected was confirmed by participants' apparent self-categorization. For example, participants perceived significantly more overlap between themselves and the ingroup (using the circle overlap measures of Schubert & Otten, 2002). Conversely, participants perceived less overlap between themselves and the outgroup when the ingroup was highly distinctive. Participants also perceived less overlap between the ingroup and the outgroup when the ingroup was highly distinctive. Furthermore, consistent with our suggestion that high intergroup distinctiveness makes an ingroup member a more relevant standard for the self, participants saw more overlap between their individual self and an ingroup referent (Study 1 and 2) and less overlap between their individual self and an outgroup referent (Study 2) when intergroup distinctiveness was high.

We investigated the impact of intergroup distinctiveness manipulated in this way on intragroup comparisons in two separate lines of research. However, intergroup relations in naturally occurring settings are often also asymmetrical, with groups often occupying distinct status positions within a system of shared social values (see, for example, Deschamps, 1982). These kinds of features also endow groups with distinctive characteristics that define group boundaries. We therefore also investigated the effects of intergroup status on intragroup social comparison in a third line of research. We now proceed to describe these three lines of research.

EMPIRICAL INVESTIGATIONS

The following studies were designed to provide evidence of the added value of an intragroup level of analysis to assimilation and contrast in individual and group self-evaluation. The focus here was mostly on participants' reactions to a more successful individual who either was or was not a member of the participants' distinctive ingroup (i.e., upward social comparison). We find this an especially useful approach for examining the importance of the intragroup dimension to self-evaluation because most theoretical approaches assume that membership in a distinctive ingroup precludes the possibility of a *demoting* contrast or a *promoting* assimilation to a fellow ingroup member (for reviews see Collins, 1996; Leach, 2005). For example, Tesser's (1988) influential self-evaluation maintenance model argues that a self-categorization that includes the self and a more successful other in a single "unit" (or category, see Figure 13.1a and 13.1b) allows the less success-ful individual to "bask in the reflected glory" of the other's success. This kind of *denoting* assimilation therefore eliminates the possibility that the less successful individual can use the more successful ingroup member as a standard for their individual self-evaluation. Thus, in addition to precluding a *demoting* contrast, SEM suggests that a *promoting* assimilation is not possible at the intragroup level.

Most research on intragroup comparison in intergroup contexts has extrapo-lated the SEM model to the intergroup level. Therefore, it is assumed that indi-viduals engage in a process of *denoting assimilation* with highly successful ingroup members in an effort to positively compare their ingroup to outgroups (e.g., Blanton et al., 2000; Brewer & Weber, 1994; Mussweiler et al., 2000). As detailed above, this is broadly consistent with self-categorization theory (see Turner et al., 1987). We think there is good conceptual reason, and empirical evidence, for the notion that individuals *can* engage in a *denoting* assimilation when confronted with a highly successful ingroup member in an intergroup context. However, we think there is little reason to assume that the intergroup context necessarily eliminates the possibility of contrast (or of a more comparative, *promoting* assimilation) at

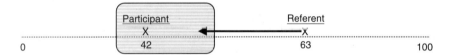

FIGURE 13.1a   Perceiving a unit—relationship I: Denoting assimilation.

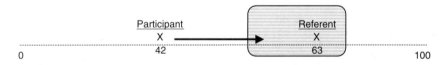

FIGURE 13.1b   Perceiving a unit—relationship II: Denoting assimilation.

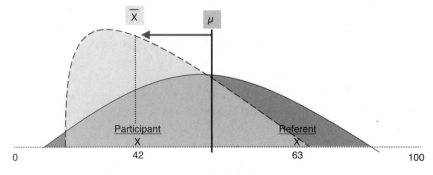

FIGURE 13.1c   Intragroup function of denoting assimilation: "No worse than average."

the intragroup level. Indeed, we think that self-categorization theory allows for the possibility that the intergroup context can operate as a background for the intragroup level. As such, intergroup distinctiveness may not always make intergroup standards of self-evaluation central. Where intergroup distinctiveness establishes the ingroup as a reference group, this intergroup context may make intragroup standards the most relevant to individual self-evaluation (for a discussion, see Turner, 1991).

Using the Intragroup Level to Manage Upward Comparison in the Context of Individual Failure

In a recent study (Vliek, Leach, Spears & Wigboldus, 2004, Study 2), we examined how individuals' membership in a distinctive ingroup alters how they cope with their own failure in the context of a potentially *demoting* contrast with a more successful ingroup member. As described above, we believe that intergroup distinctiveness should make the ingroup a highly relevant reference group. As such, individual failure and a potentially demoting contrast to a more successful ingroup member should encourage individuals to redefine the discrepancy between themselves and the highly relevant referent (see Vliek et al., 2004, Study 1). However, instead of focusing on the interpersonal or intergroup strategies that individuals have to cope with a potentially *demoting* contrast at the intragroup level, the current study sought to provide evidence of a decidedly intragroup coping strategy.

Thus, we assumed that when a potentially *demoting* contrast occurs within the context of ingroup membership, the interpersonal discrepancy must be interpreted within the larger frame of ingroup performance (e.g., Miller et al., 1988). To be outperformed by an ingroup member in the context of a poor performing ingroup should have less detrimental implications than to be outperformed by an ingroup member in the context of a group that performs well (e.g., Seta & Seta, 1996). Within a poor performing group, the more successful referent is framed as unusually successful, whereas within a well performing group, it is the less successful individual that is framed as unusually unsuccessful. Thus, given that the ingroup's overall performance provides a frame of reference for evaluating the self in comparison to a more successful ingroup member, we expected that participants would cope with a potentially *demoting* intragroup contrast by altering the intragroup frame of reference. By seeing themselves as "no worse than average" within their group, participants could use the intragroup frame of reference to frame a more successful ingroup member as unusually successful. This *denoting* assimilation of the individual participant to a modest group standard should serve to protect against the deleterious effects of what would otherwise be a demoting contrast between the participant and the more successful ingroup member (see Figure 13.1c). Indeed, research has shown individuals are capable of reconstructing social reality in a manner that can serve to protect their self-evaluation (e.g., Goethals, 1986) and, as already suggested by Buckingham and Alicke (2002), the "aggregate" of others within a group can serve as a potent standard for self-evaluation.

Most previous work has assumed that in the context of individual failure, those with sufficient psychological resources (e.g., self-esteem) protect themselves against a *demoting* contrast with more successful referents (for a review see Wood, 1989). In addition, those high in self-esteem appear to be especially good at interpreting others' success in a self-serving manner (e.g., Mussweiler et al., 2000; Reis, Gerrard, & Gibbons, 1993). Thus, we expected participants higher in self-esteem to be especially likely to use the intragroup strategy of seeing themselves as "no worse than average." We hypothesized that this *denoting* assimilation at the intragroup level should serve to protect those higher in self-esteem against the potentially deleterious effects of a *demoting* contrast with a more successful member of a distinctive, and thus highly relevant, ingroup.

In this study, we presented participants with feedback that they had performed poorly on the visual intelligence tasks described above (i.e., 42% correct answers: relative failure). After telling them that a randomly chosen ingroup member had performed better (i.e., 63%: relative success), participants were asked to estimate the *average score* of the ingroup, followed by items measuring negative affect. Thus, the seemingly objective feedback regarding individual performance in this study made estimates of the ingroup average the more malleable standard for self-evaluation. As we expected high intergroup distinctiveness to heighten the threat of a *demoting* contrast with the more successful ingroup member, we predicted that individuals high in self-esteem should most use the intragroup strategy of self-protection in this condition. Thus, to protect themselves against the potentially demoting contrast with a more successful member of a distinctive ingroup, participants should assimilate the ingroup's average performance to their own individual performance. This *denoting* assimilation would enable them to see their own score as "no worse than average." If perceiving themselves as no worse than average serves as self-protection, then the lower their estimates of the ingroup average, the less negative affect participants should experience in reaction to the potentially *demoting* contrast.

Results supported our predictions. In line with previous research on the use of self-protective strategies after failure feedback, participants high in self-esteem seemed most capable of protecting themselves against the potentially *demoting* contrast with a more successful member of a distinctive ingroup. However, given the intragroup context of comparison, this self-protective strategy took an intragroup form. Thus, when the ingroup was highly distinctive, higher self-esteem predicted lower estimates of the ingroup's average performance. The lower these estimates of ingroup performance, the less negative affect participants experienced (see Figure 13.2a). In contrast, participants' self-esteem was unrelated to estimates of their own or the ingroup referents' performance. Thus, there was no evidence that participants used an interpersonal strategy of self-protection aimed at negating the discrepancy between themselves and the more successful member of their ingroup. That seeing themselves as no worse than average was an intragroup strategy of comparison was further evidenced by the fact that the mediation model described above was not observed under low intergroup distinctiveness. Thus, when ingroup membership was not especially relevant, individuals' estimates of the ingroup's average performance did not reduce their negative affect (see Figure 13.2b).

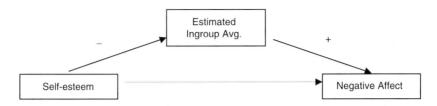

FIGURE 13.2a   Mediating role of ingroup average estimate under high intergroup distinctiveness.

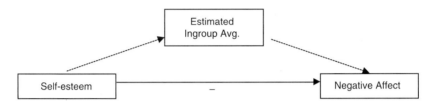

FIGURE 13.2b   Mediating role of ingroup average estimate under low intergroup distinctiveness.

Importantly, the above research indicated that the *intragroup* strategy of seeing oneself as "no worse than average" did not require participants to underestimate the success of the ingroup referent (see Figure 13.1c). Interestingly, by perceiving themselves as average for their ingroup, participants may have been able to perceive the upward referent as an exemplar of success. This may have served to reinforce the value of group membership or to provide a model for their own future success (e.g., Lockwood & Kunda, 1997). We examine both of these possibilities next.

Defining an Interpersonal Discrepancy at the Intragroup Level

As described earlier, most of the work on assimilation and contrast at the intragroup level has focused on what we call *denoting* assimilation. This kind of assimilation seems most likely in contexts where individuals are themselves unsuccessful and face potentially demoting contrasts with more successful members of a relevant reference group. We illustrated a particularly intragroup variety of this kind of *denoting* assimilation in the study above. However, under other circumstances, a successful ingroup member can provide a model that "inspires" individual members of the group to improve their own performance (e.g., Burleson et al., 2005; Lockwood & Kunda, 1997). Indeed, more successful ingroup members may serve as especially good proxies of an individual's own behavior (Wheeler, Martin, & Suls, 1997). This is likely why Festinger (1954) postulated that people generally prefer to compare with superior others because more can be learned from similar, slightly superior, others.

Recent research shows that, under some circumstances, individuals feel more positively, evaluate themselves more highly, and see their chance of future improvement as more likely when exposed to others who are more successful than they (e.g., Aspinwall & Taylor, 1993; Leach et al., 2005; Lockwood & Kunda, 1997, 1999). Although individual-level factors such as self-esteem, perceived control, and interpersonal similarity appear important to this kind of promoting assimilation (for reviews, see Collins, 1996; Wood, 1989), we think there may also be an intragroup dimension at work. Indeed, reference group theory suggests that it is the success of fellow members of one's reference group that should most encourage a *promoting* assimilation that inspires and motivates better performance (see Hyman, 1942; for a review, see Leach, 2005). Although most of the research illustrating *promoting* assimilation has not explicitly addressed the group context, it *has* examined interpersonal assimilation within what appear to be highly relevant reference groups. For example, Lockwood and Kunda (1997) examined the degree to which beginning university students studying accounting were inspired by the success of a senior student in accounting. And Burleson et al. (2005) examined university students' *promoting* assimilation to highly successful students in a similar course of study. Thus, these studies showed individuals to assimilate themselves to the success of members of fairly distinctive reference groups.

Successful ingroup referents are likely to provide more relevant standards for self-evaluation than successful outgroup referents (Festinger, 1954; Hyman, 1942; Major, 1994). Leach and Smith (2006) provided some recent evidence of this in a 7-day diary study of ethnic minority university students' comparisons to others. Although the minority or majority status of a comparison other had no effect on participants' perceived prospect of future improvement, the comparison other's group status *did* determine the affective implications of this perception. Thus, no matter how much the participants thought they might improve in the future after comparison with an ethnic majority referent, these comparisons did not alter their affect. In contrast, participants' positive affect increased dramatically when a comparison with a fellow ethnic minority suggested they might improve in the future. Thus, only the future improvement suggested by these ethnic minorities' comparisons with other ethnic minorities appeared to be psychologically relevant and affecting. Only their fairly distinctive ingroup served as a reference group for their perceived future prospect of improvement.

Inspiration: *Promoting* Assimilation at the Intragroup Level   In a recent study, we used the group distinctiveness paradigm described above to examine the intragroup dimension to a promoting assimilation to more successful referents (Vliek, Leach, & Spears, 2005a). As in our previous study, we argue that intergroup distinctiveness makes the ingroup a reference group that provides highly relevant standards for self-evaluation. More specifically, membership in a distinctive ingroup is presumed to promote a sense of we-ness (e.g., Brown, Novick, Lord, & Richards, 1992; Stapel & Koomen, 2001, Study 1), which should make the ingroup member a highly relevant referent for the individual's future prospect of improvement (e.g., Leach & Smith, 2006). Thus, we expected that exposure to a more successful member of a distinctive ingroup should be able to promote inspiration through a *promoting* assimilation.

It is important to note that our expectation of a *promoting* assimilation to more successful members of a distinctive ingroup is quite different than what is predicted by models such as SCT and SEM. For example, the SEM model suggests that exposure to a more successful member of distinctive ingroup should lead to a *demoting* contrast when individuals want to be successful themselves. Only where individuals are uninterested in success for themselves does the SEM model expect assimilation to a close and similar other's success (for a review, see Tesser, 1988). And, this assimilation is expected to be of the type that denotes the self as part of a social category rather than promoting the individual self by inspiring greater individual success within an intragroup frame of reference. Our expectation of a promoting assimilation to a more successful member of distinctive ingroup is also distinct from previous work in intragroup assimilation in the context of intergroup relation differences (e.g., Brewer & Weber, 1994; Blanton et al., 2000; Mussweiler et al., 2000). This work presumes that a *denoting* assimilation to a successful member of a distinctive ingroup serves as self-protection against a potentially *demoting* intergroup contrast.

For example, extrapolating from SEM, Blanton et al. (2000) examined average performing African-American students' self-evaluation in response to a highly successful in- or outgroup member. They argued that the more positive self-evaluation that African Americans showed in response to a highly successful ingroup member resulted from individuals emphasizing their group membership and thereby "basking in the reflected glory" of the successful ingroup member (see also Martinot et al., 2002). This denoting assimilation was believed to protect group members against a potentially demoting contrast at the intergroup level. However, in the absence of individual failure (as in Vliek et al., 2004) and low group status, we think that individuals may be enabled to make a *promoting* assimilation with more successful members of a distinctive ingroup. Rather than serving as self-protection against a potentially demoting intergroup contrast, this *promoting* assimilation would be a decidedly intragroup reaction to the ingroup frame of reference introduced by intergroup distinctiveness.

The method used in Vliek et al. (2005a) was the same as in our previous studies, with two exceptions. First, rather than giving participants feedback that they had performed poorly, we asked them to *estimate* how well they did on the difficult (visual intelligence) tasks described earlier. Thus, in contrast to the studies in Vliek et al. (2004), we let peoples' estimate of their *own* performance be the more malleable standard of self-evaluation. Second, we introduced an outgroup referent to make the intergroup context even more salient. In the "moderate ingroup success" condition, the ingroup referent was shown to score 52%. As the difficulty of the tasks led participants to expect to perform poorly, a score of 52% represented moderate success. Furthermore, the presence of the outgroup referent who was shown to score 74% reinforced that the ingroup referent's score was only moderately successful. In the "high ingroup success" condition, the ingroup referent scored 74%. Here the outgroup referent was shown to score 52%, which reinforced that the ingroup referent was highly successful. We then asked participants to estimate their own performance on the tasks. We also asked participants to indicate to what degree they assimilated or contrasted themselves to the ingroup and the outgroup referent. This was assessed with circle overlap measures, which presented the relevant parties (self vs. ingroup and outgroup referent) as two circles with various degrees of overlap (see Schubert & Otten, 2002). We predicted that when presented with a referent from a highly distinctive ingroup, participants would take the ingroup referent's performance as the best proxy for their own performance. Thus, where the ingroup referent was highly successful, participants should estimate their own performance more highly. Where the referent was a member of a less distinctive ingroup or part of an outgroup, participants' estimate of their own performance should not be assimilated to the referent's in this promoting way.

Results supported our predictions. When participants had been exposed to a highly successful referent from a distinctive ingroup, participants estimated their own performance relatively highly. Our suggestion that ingroup distinctiveness enabled participants to engage in a *promoting* assimilation was supported by a mediation analysis. It showed that high ingroup distinctiveness led participants to perceive themselves as overlapping more with the ingroup referent. This assimilation predicted participants' estimate of their own performance. Thus, the more participants assimilated themselves to the highly successful ingroup referent, the higher their estimates of their own performance. Not surprisingly, the higher individuals' estimated their performance, the greater their satisfaction with their performance.

Importantly, there was little sign that participants engaged in a *denoting* assimilation with the highly successful referent from the distinctive ingroup. Thus, participants did not report greater similarity, closeness, or affection for the ingroup referent or for the ingroup as a whole. Thus, none of the processes presumed to indicate the kind of *denoting* assimilation suggested by SEM and SCT could explain why participants' estimated performance was increased by exposure to a highly successful member of their distinctive ingroup. This further corroborates our view that, rather than *denoting* participants as a group member indistinguishable from the successful referent, intergroup distinctiveness allowed participants to engage in a *promoting* assimilation of themselves to the highly relevant intragroup standard presented by a successful member of a distinctive ingroup. That intergroup distinctiveness made salient an intragroup frame of reference was also suggested by what occurred when intergroup distinctiveness was low. A mediation analysis showed that *low* intergroup distinctiveness led to greater perceived overlap between the participant and the highly successful referent from an indistinctive *outgroup*. This apparently interpersonal promoting assimilation led participants to increase their estimated performance, which led them to feel more satisfied. Thus, only when intergroup distinctiveness was low did participants use the highly successful outgroup referent as a standard for a *promoting* assimilation. This interpersonal level assimilation with an outgroup member was only possible where the ingroup was not a reference group that provided highly relevant intragroup standards.

Taken together, the results of this study offer further support for our suggestion that intergroup distinctiveness can make important the intragroup dimension of assimilation–contrast. The focus on the intragroup level is important partly because it enables a clearer distinction between the *denoting* and the *promoting* type of assimilation to successful ingroup members. Here we showed that exposure to a highly successful member of a highly distinctive ingroup led individuals to increase their estimates of their performance on a difficult task. Rather than denoting the individual as part of a successful group, this assimilation process appeared to promote greater expectations of individual performance. This suggests that intragroup assimilation can serve self-improvement rather than simply being focused on self-enhancement or self-protection. When exposed to highly successful others, we not only want to feel better, we want to be better.

Intergroup Status and the Intragroup Dimension

A third line of investigation into the intragroup dimension of assimilation–contrast comes from a recent study where we manipulated the ingroup's status relative to an outgroup. Whereas in our other research we used intergroup distinctiveness to make the ingroup a relevant reference group, here we used intergroup status to accomplish this. As low group status clearly differentiates the ingroup from higher status outgroups, it serves to make the ingroup distinctive (e.g., Brewer & Weber, 1994; Jetten et al., 1998; Miller et al., 1988; Turner et al., 1987). However, the ingroup distinctiveness that results from low group status has more clearly evaluative implications for group members. This is likely why a good deal of previous research at the intragroup level has (explicitly or implicitly) examined the role of assimilation and contrast in the self-evaluation of low status groups.

Social psychology has an abiding interest in the psychological effects of low group status (e.g., ethnic minorities, women, lower status universities or courses of study). As mentioned above, most of this research argues that, when their low group status is salient, individuals engage in a *denoting* assimilation at the intragroup level when exposed to a successful referent from the ingroup (e.g., Blanton et al., 2000; Martinot et al., 2002; Marx, Stapel, & Muller, 2005; Mussweiler et al., 2000). Consistent with the previously described extrapolation of the SEM model to the intergroup level, it is argued that members of low status groups use a denoting assimilation to a successful ingroup referent to protect themselves against potentially demoting contrasts with members of higher status outgroups. This presumes that members of low status groups use successful ingroup referents to self-categorize at the group rather than individual level. Presumably, by emphasizing their membership in an ingroup that contains a successful referent, individuals can evaluate their low status group more positively. This positive group level self-evaluation should conceivably provide the basis for more positive individual self-evaluation as the individual can see him- or herself as part of the positively evaluated ingroup. Although this model of a denoting assimilation at the intragroup level is fairly clear, it has not been examined directly. Mainly as a result of the fact that little work conceptually or empirically distinguishes between what we call *denoting* and *promoting* intragroup assimilation, there is little direct evidence that a *denoting* assimilation serves to increase group-level self-evaluation and protect against a *demoting* intergroup contrast to a high status outgroup. Thus, we used this conceptual approach to examine these issues in Vliek, Leach, and Spears (2005b).

We thought that our conceptual model could be best addressed by examining the precise way in which the intragroup assimilation–contrast made by members of a low status group differs from that of members of a high status group. Although intergroup work based in the SEM model implies that members of high status groups will not engage in a *denoting* intragroup assimilation, it does not make explicit what sort of social comparisons should arise. Although group identity may still frame comparison for high status groups (in keeping with the intragroup analysis), members of this group may be less likely to see themselves in terms of their group identity than low status group members, as low status can threaten group identity and enhance group homogeneity (Doosje, Ellemers, & Spears, 1995). If correct, we suggest that members of high status groups are therefore more likely to make more purely interpersonal comparisons with upward referents in their group (cf. Deschamps & Devos, 1998; Doise, 1978; Doise & Lorenzi-Cioldi, 1989). As successful members of a high status group are likely to present a *demoting* intragroup contrast to other members of the high status group (e.g., Seta & Seta, 1996), such a standard should lower individual self-evaluation. Thus, where we expect low group status to encourage a *denoting* intragroup assimilation with more successful ingroup members, we expect high group status to encourage a demoting intragroup contrast with more successful ingroup members.

In this investigation, we manipulated ingroup status in an ostensibly independent "first study." This was accomplished with a fake newspaper article in which psychology students at the University of Amsterdam were described as having higher or lower academic status than students at a neighboring university (Free University). After a number of bogus questions about the article we introduced the "second" study, which had a completely different layout and was introduced as an investigation into intuitive knowledge. After completion of the task, which consisted of 32 general knowledge questions with limited time for answering, participants received feedback on their own score (59% correct answers) and that of a more successful (76%) or less successful (42%) ingroup referent. This resulted in a 2 (ingroup status: high, low) × 2 (ingroup referent position: upward, downward) factorial design.

After exposure to the ingroup member, participants completed a number of dependent measures. First participants were asked to indicate to what extent they were satisfied with their performance, in order to ascertain their individual-level self-evaluation. We expected that members of high status groups' *individual-level* self-evaluation should suffer from a demoting contrast with a more successful ingroup referent. Next, items from the collective self-esteem scale were included to measure participants' group-level self-evaluation (see Luhtanen & Crocker, 1992). We expected that members of low status groups' *group-level* self-evaluation should benefit from a denoting assimilation with a more successful ingroup referent. Finally participants completed the Rosenberg (1965) self-esteem scale, modified to assess participants' state (i.e., temporary), rather than trait (or general), well-being. We used state self-esteem as a measure of the psychological implications of the individual- and group-level processes of self-evaluation we examined.

Our predictions were generally supported. For members of the high status group, the intragroup dimension affected their well-being through its effect on participants' *individual-level* self-evaluation (see Figure 13.3a). However, for members of the low status group, the intragroup dimension affected well-being through its effect on participants' *group-level* self-evaluation (see Figure 13.3b). More specifically, members of the high status group showed much lower satisfaction with their individual performance after exposure to the more successful ingroup member. This lower self-evaluation was consistent with the *demoting* contrast we expected among members of the high status group. That this apparent contrast was demoting was further evidenced by the fact that a mediation model showed that participants' lower individual-level self-evaluation led to a decrease in their self-esteem. Thus, members of the high status group had lower well-being when their individual-level self-evaluation was lowered by a demoting contrast with a more successful ingroup member. Although it was participants' individual-level self-evaluation that was lowered by a *demoting* contrast between themselves and another individual, this contrast occurred within the context of a shared group membership. Thus, the intragroup dimension provided an implicit frame of reference for what participants were likely to have experienced as an interpersonal contrast between themselves and the more successful ingroup member (see also Leach & Smith, 2006; Smith & Leach, 2004).

As expected, those with low group status produced a very different pattern of results. For them, exposure to the more successful ingroup referent had no effect on their *individual-level* self-evaluation. Instead, for members of the low status group, exposure to a more successful ingroup member led to higher *group-level* self-evaluation. This is consistent with the process of assimilation we expected. That participants' apparent assimilation to the more successful ingroup member led them to evaluate their entire group more positively suggested that the assimilation was of the denoting variety that we expected. Thus, individuals evaluated their

FIGURE 13.3a High intergroup status: Mediating role of individual-level self-evaluation for high status group members after intragroup comparison.

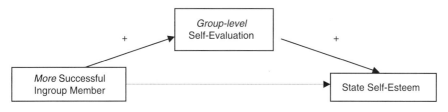

FIGURE 13.3b Low intergroup status: Mediating role of group-level self-evaluation for low status group members after intragroup comparison.

group more positively in response to the success of a fellow group member with whom they were associated. This increased group-level self-evaluation augmented participants' well-being. Indeed, a mediation model showed participants' more positive group-level self-evaluation to lead to increased self-esteem.

To provide additional evidence for the process of *denoting* assimilation we believe is central to increased group-level self-evaluation after exposure to a more successful ingroup member, we conducted additional analyses. A mediation analysis showed that low status group members had higher group-level self-evaluation *because* exposure to a more successful ingroup member led them to perceive themselves as more *prototypical* of their ingroup. This suggests that members of the low status group emphasized their membership in the group of which this successful other was a part. In so doing, they deemphasized their poor individual performance and instead emphasized the positive value of their group. We think this is some of the clearest evidence yet obtained of the intragroup assimilation previous approaches have described as "upward reflection," or "basking in reflected glory" (cf. Blanton et al., 2000; Mussweiler et al., 2000) Importantly, our conceptual distinction between this kind of *denoting* assimilation and the *promoting* assimilation we illustrated in the above described studies enabled us to show precisely how low group status leads individuals to emphasize their membership in a group and its positive evaluation (as a group) over the concern for individual self-evaluation emphasized by members of the high status group.

CONCLUSION

The research presented here presents some of our first steps into discerning some of the very different types of assimilation and contrast at work in self-evaluation in intragroup contexts. Although we have focused on individuals' assimilation and contrast of themselves to more successful others, we believe that the process of *denoting* assimilation, *promoting* assimilation, and *demoting* contrast may be of more general use to studies of self-evaluation. Differentiating a *denoting* assimilation from a *promoting* assimilation seems especially important in work that aims to understand why individuals may evaluate themselves more positively after exposure to more successful others. This distinction followed from our emphasis of the intragroup dimension in self-evaluation.

We suggested assimilation and contrast approaches to self-evaluation might benefit from greater attention to the intragroup level of analysis. Although we do not deny the independent conceptual status of the interpersonal and intergroup levels of analysis, we have tried to argue that focusing on these two extremes has important limitations. That is why we suggested the intragroup dimension as an intermediary, meso level of analysis, where interpersonal and intergroup processes of assimilation and contrast meet and mingle. For example, in the first two lines of research we discussed, we aimed to show that distinctiveness at the *intergroup* level can serve to make *intragroup* processes of assimilation and contrast the most relevant to individual self-evaluation. In the third line of research we discussed, we aimed to show that *intergroup* status can emphasize *intragroup* contrast for those high in status while emphasizing *intragroup* assimilation for those low in status.

We believe that attention to the intragroup dimension of self-evaluation may offer one way of integrating a broad field in which sometimes diverging results seem contradictory. Future research will need to look further into people's perception of similarity and identification with the group and comparison referents on the focal as well as the surrounding dimensions of comparison. In the meantime, we hope to have made clear that the intragroup dimension forms an important meso level of comparison that includes important parts of both individual and group, without being reducible to either. In this respect the intragroup dimension offers the true integration of research on the individual within the group and the group within the individual (Postmes & Jetten, 2006). If assimilation–contrast approaches to self-evaluation have tended to be divided by the two poles of interpersonal versus intergroup levels in the past, we hope to have shown the value of keeping both of these in the frame, and in focus, of the intragroup dimension.

ACKNOWLEDGMENTS

We thank Diederik Stapel and Jerry Suls for their helpful and insightful comments on an earlier draft of this chapter. The research described herein was supported by The Netherlands Organization for Scientific Research (NWO).

REFERENCES

Asch, S. E. (1952). *Social psychology*. Englewood Cliffs, NJ: Prentice Hall.

Aspinwall, L. G., & Taylor, S. E. (1993). Effects of social comparison direction, threat, and self-esteem on affect, self-evaluation and expected success. *Journal of Personality and Social Psychologyy*, 64, 708–722.

Blanton, H., Crocker, J., & Miller, D. T. (2000). The effects of in-group and out-group social comparison on self-esteem in the context of a negative stereotype. *Journal of Experimental Social Psychology*, 36, 519–530.

Brewer, M. B. (1991). The social self: On being the same and different at the same time. *Personality and Social Psychology Bulletin*, 17, 475–482.

Brewer, M. B., & Weber, J. G. (1994). Self-evaluation effects of interpersonal versus intergroup social comparison. *Journal of Personality and Social Psychology*, 66, 268–275.

Brown, J. D., Novick, D., Lord, K. A., & Richards, J. M. (1992). When Gulliver travels: Social context, psychological closeness, and self-appraisals. *Journal of Personality and Social Psychology*, 62, 717–727.

Buckingham, J. T., & Alicke, M. D. (2002). The influence of individual versus aggregate social comparison and the presence of others on self-evaluations. *Journal of Personality and Social Psychology*, 83, 1117–1130.

Burleson, K., Leach, C. W., & Harrington, D. M. (2005). Upward social comparison and self-concept: Inspiration and inferiority among art students in an advanced programme. *British Journal of Social Psychology*, 44, 109–123.

Buunk, B. P., & Gibbons, F. X. (Eds.). (1997). *Health, coping and well-being: Perspectives from social comparison theory*. Hillsdale, NJ: Lawrence Erlbaum Associates, Inc

Cartwright, D. (Ed.). (1951). *Field theory in social science: Selected theoretical papers by Kurt Lewin*. New York: Harper & Row.

Cartwright, D., & Zander, A. (1968). Origins of group dynamics. In D. Cartwright & A. Zander (Eds.), *Group dynamics: Research and theory* (3rd ed., pp. 3–21). New York: Harper & Row.

Collins, R. L. (1996). For better or worse: The impact of upward comparison on self evaluations. *Psychological Bulletin, 119*, 51–69.

Davis, J. A. (1966). The campus as a frog pond: An application of the theory of the relative deprivation to career decisions of college men. *American Journal of Sociology, 72*, 17–31.

Deschamps, J. C. (1982). Social identity and relations of power between groups. In H. Tajfel (Ed.), *Social identity and inter-group relations* (pp. 85–98). Cambridge, UK: Cambridge University Press.

Deschamps, J. C., & Devos, T. (1998). Regarding the relationship between social identity and personal identity. In S. Worchel, J. F. Morales, D. Paez, & J.-C. Deschamps (Eds.), *Social identity: International perspectives* (pp. 1–12). London, UK: Sage Publications.

Doise, W. (1978). *Groups and individuals: Explanations in social psychology*. Cambridge, UK: Cambridge University Press.

Doise, W., & Lorenzi-Cioldi, F. (1989). Patterns of differentiation within and between groups. In J. P. van Oudenhoven & T. M. Willemsen (Eds.), *Ethnic minorities: A social psychological perspective* (pp. 43–57). Amsterdam: Swetz & Zeitlinger.

Doosje, B., Ellemers, N., & Spears, R. (1995). Perceived intra-group variability as a function of group status and identification. *Journal of Experimental Social Psychology, 31*, 410–436.

Festinger, L. (1950). Informal social communication. *Psychological Review, 57*, 271–282.

Festinger, L. (1954). A theory of social comparison processes. *Human Relations, 7*, 117–140.

Goethals, G. R. (1986). Fabricating and ignoring social reality: Self-serving estimates of consensus. In J. M. Olson, C. P. Herman, & M. P. Zanna (Eds.), *Relative deprivation and social comparison: The Ontario Symposium* (Vol. 4, pp. 135–158). Hillsdale, NJ: Lawrence Erlbaum Associates, Inc.

Heider, F. (1958). *The psychology of interpersonal relations*. New York: Wiley.

Hyman, H. H. (1942). The psychology of status. *Archives of Psychology, 269*.

Hyman, H. H., & Singer, E. (1968). *Readings in reference group theory and research*. New York: Free Press.

Jetten, J., Spears, R., & Manstead, A. S. R. (1998). Defining dimensions of distinctiveness: Group variability makes a difference to differentiation. *Journal of Personality and Social Psychology, 74*, 1481–1492.

Leach, C. W. (2005). *Toward a unified theory of social comparison*. Unpublished manuscript, University of Sussex, UK.

Leach, C. W., & Smith, H. J. (2006). By whose standard? The affective implications of ethnic minorities' comparison to ethnic minority and majority referents. *European Journal of Social Psychology, 36*, 747–760.

Leach, C. W., Smith, R. H., Webster, J. M., Iyer, A., Kelso, K., & Garonzik, R. (2005). *Inferiority and inspiration: Distinguishing the phenomenology of upward comparison*. Unpublished manuscript.

Lockwood, P., & Kunda, Z. (1997). Superstars and me: Predicting the impact of role models on the self. *Journal of Personality and Social Psychology, 73*, 91–103.

Lockwood, P., & Kunda, Z. (1999). Increasing the salience of one's best selves can undermine inspiration by outstanding role models. *Journal of Personality and Social Psychology*, 76, 214–228.

Luhtanen, R., & Crocker, J. (1992). A collective self-esteem scale: Self-evaluation of one's social identity. *Personality and Social Psychology Bulletin*, 18, 302–318.

Major, B. (1994). From social inequality to personal entitlement: The role of social comparisons, legitimacy appraisals, and group membership. In M. P. Zanna (Ed.), *Advances in experimental social psychology* (Vol. 26, pp. 293–355). San Diego, CA: Academic Press.

Marsh, H. W., & Craven, R. (2001). The pivotal role of frames of reference in academic self-concept formation: The big fish little pond effect. In F. Pajares & T. Urdan (Eds.), *Adolescence and education* (Vol. II, pp. 83–123). Greenwich, CT: Information Age.

Marsh, H. W., & Parker, J. W. (1984). Determinants of student self-concept: Is it better to be a relatively large fish in a small pond even if you don't learn to swim as well? *Journal of Personality and Social Psychology*, 47, 213–231.

Martinot, D., Redersdorff, S., Guimond, S., & Dif, S. (2002). In-group versus out-group comparisons and self-esteem: The role of group status and identification. *Personality and Social Psychology Bulletin*, 28, 1586–1600.

Marx, D. M., Stapel, D. A., & Muller, D. (2005). We can do it: The interplay of construal orientation and social comparisons under threat. *Journal of Personality and Social Psychology*, 88, 432–446.

Merton, R. K. (1957). *Social theory and social structure* (2nd ed.). Glencoe, IL: Free Press.

Miller, D. T., & Prentice, D. A. (1996). The construction of social norms and standards. In A. Kruglanski & E. T. Higgins (Eds.), *Social psychology: Handbook of basic principles* (pp. 799–829). New York: Guilford Press.

Miller, D. T., Turnbull, W., & McFarland, C. (1988). Particularistic and universalistic evaluation in the social comparison process. *Journal of Personality and Social Psychology*, 55, 908–917.

Mussweiler, T., Gabriel, S., & Bodenhausen, G. V. (2000). Shifting social identities as a strategy for deflecting threatening social comparisons. *Journal of Personality and Social Psychology*, 79, 398–409.

Pettigrew, T. F. (1967). Social-Evaluation Theory: Convergences and applications. In D. Levine (Ed.), *Nebraska Symposium on Motivation* (Vol. 15, pp. 241–311). Lincoln, NE: University of Nebraska Press.

Postmes, T., & Jetten, J. (Eds.). (2006). *The puzzle of individuality and the group*. In T. Postmes & J. Jetten (Eds.), *Individuality and the group: Advances in social identity* (pp. 258–269). London: Sage.

Reis, T. J., Gerrard, M., & Gibbons, F. X. (1993). Social comparison and the pill: Reactions to upward and downward comparison of contraceptive behaviour. *Personality and Social Psychology Bulletin*, 19, 13–20.

Rosenberg, M. (1965). *Society and the adolescent self-image*. Princeton, NJ: Princeton University Press.

Ruys, K. I., Spears, R., Gordijn, E. H., & de Vries, N. K. (2006). Two faces of (dis)similarity in affective judgments of persons: Contrast or assimilation effects revealed by morphs. *Journal of Personality and Social Psychology*, 90, 399–411.

Schmitt, M. T., Branscombe, N. R., Silvia, P. J., Garcia, D. M., & Spears, R. (2006). Categorizing at the group level in response to intra-group social comparisons: A self-categorization theory integration of self-evaluation and social identity motives. *European Journal of Social Psychology*, 36, 297–314.

Schmitt, M. T., Silvia, P. J., & Branscombe, N. R. (2000). The intersection of self-evaluation maintenance and social identity theories: Intra-group judgement in interpersonal and inter-group contexts. *Personality and Social Psychology Bulletin*, *26*, 1598–1606.

Schubert, T. W., & Otten, S. (2002). Overlap of self, in-group, and out-group: Pictorial measures of self-categorization. *Self and Identity*, *1*, 353–376.

Seta, J. J., & Seta, C. E. (1996). Big fish in small ponds: A social hierarchy analysis of inter-group bias. *Journal of Personality and Social Psychology*, *71*, 1210–1221.

Sherif, M. (1936). *The psychology of social norms*. New York: Harper.

Singer, E. (1990). Reference groups and social evaluations. In R. H. Turner & M. Rosenberg (Eds.), *Social psychology: Sociological perspectives* (pp. 66–93). New Brunswick, NJ: Transaction Publishers.

Smith, H. J., & Leach, C. W. (2004). Group membership and everyday social comparison experiences. *European Journal of Social Psychology*, *34*, 297–308.

Smith, H. J., & Spears, R. (1996). Ability and outcome evaluations as a function of personal and collective (dis)advantage: A group escape from individual bias. *Personality and Social Psychology Bulletin*, *22*, 690–704.

Smith, H. J., Spears, R., & Oyen, M. (1994). "People like us": The influence of personal deprivation and group membership salience on justice evaluations. *Journal of Experimental Social Psychology*, *30*, 277–299.

Spears, R. (2001). The interaction between the individual and the collective self: Self-categorization in context. In M. B. Brewer & C. Sedikides (Eds.), *Individual self, relational self, collective self* (pp. 171–198). New York: Psychology Press.

Spears, R., Jetten, J., & Scheepers, D. (2002). Distinctiveness and the definition of collective self: A tripartite model. In A. Tesser, D. A. Stapel, & J. V. Wood (Eds.), *Self and motivation: Emerging psychological perspectives* (pp. 147–171). Washington, DC: American Psychological Association.

Stapel, D. A., & Koomen, W. (2001). I, we, and the effects of others on me: How self-construal level moderates social comparison effects. *Journal of Personality and Social Psychology*, *80*, 766–781.

Suls, J., & Wheeler, L. (Eds.). (2000). *Handbook of social comparison theory and research*. New York: Kluwer Academic/Plenum Publishers.

Tajfel, H. (1972). Social categorization [English manuscript of "La categorisation sociale"]. In S. Moscovici (Ed.), *Introduction à la psychologie sociale* (Vol. 1, pp. 272–302). Paris: Larousse.

Tajfel, H., & Turner, J. C. (1979). An integrative theory of inter-group conflict. In W. G. Austin & S. Worchel (Eds.), *The social psychology of inter-group relations* (pp. 33–47). Monterey, CA: Brooks/Cole.

Tesser, A. (1988). Toward a self-evaluation maintenance model of social behavior. In L. Berkowitz (Ed.), *Advances in experimental social psychology* (Vol. 21, pp. 181–227). San Diego, CA: Academic Press.

Turner, J. C. (1991). *Social influence*. Milton Keynes, UK: Open University Press.

Turner, J. C., Hogg, M. A., Oakes, P. J., Reicher, S. D., & Wetherell, M. S. (1987). *Rediscovering the social group: A self-categorization theory*. Oxford, UK: Blackwell.

Turner, J. C., Reynolds, K. J., Haslam, S. A., & Veenstra, K. E. (2006). Reconceptualizing personality: Producing individuality by defining the personal self. In T. Postmes & J. Jetten (Eds.), *Individuality and the group: Advances in social identity* (pp. 11–36). London: Sage.

Vignoles, V. L., Chryssochoou, X., & Breakwell, G. M. (2000). The distinctiveness principle: Identity, meaning, and the bounds of cultural relativity. *Personality and Social Psychology Review*, *4*, 337–354.

Vliek, M. L. W., Leach, C. W., & Spears, R. (2005a). Upward social comparisons in an intra-group context: Feeling better and being better. *Manuscript in preparation*.

Vliek, M. L. W., Leach, C. W., & Spears, R. (2005b). Intragroeps sociale vergelijkingen: Procesmatige verwerking van sociale vergelijkingen binnen hoge en lage status groepen [Intragroup social comparisons: Processing social comparison information within high and low status groups]. In R. W. Holland, J. Ouwerkerk, C. van Laar, R. Ruiter, & J. Ham (Eds.), *Jaarboek sociale psychologie*. Groningen, The Netherlands: Aspo Pers.

Vliek, M. L. W., Leach, C. W., Spears, R., & Wigboldus, D. H. J. (2004, September). *No worse than average: Shifting the in-group average as protection against an unflattering upward comparison*. Paper presented at the first European workshop on Social Comparison, Cassis, France.

Wheeler, L., Martin, R., & Suls, J. (1997). The proxy model of social comparison for self-assessment of ability. *Personality and Social Psychology Review, 1*, 54–61.

Wood, J. V. (1989). Theory and research concerning social comparisons of personal attributes. *Psychological Bulletin, 106*(2), 231–248.

14

Several Answers to Four Questions:
Reflections and Conclusions

DIEDERIK A. STAPEL and JERRY SULS

As the chapters in this volume attest, research on assimilative and contrastive context effects in social judgment and behavior was thriving in the 20th century, and still is in the 21st century. Interest in the determinants of the direction and magnitude of context effects has waxed and waned since the beginnings of experimental psychology, but especially in the domain of social psychology it has never waned out of existence (see Suls & Wheeler, chapter 1, this volume). In fact, the past few decades have seen the rise of several new approaches to and perspectives of the study of context effects. The chapters in this volume are the stirring witnesses of that resurgence. The question of what determines the (assimilative, null, or contrastive) effects of cognitively accessible information on cognitions, emotions, judgments, and behaviors is now considered to be a relevant and worthwhile topic of study in research domains as diverse as counterfactual thinking, stereotyping, self-evaluation, emotion regulation, and intergroup relations.

This long and ongoing interest in the determinants of assimilation and contrast effects does not mean, of course, that all the important questions have been solved. Although the experimental study of perceptual and psychological assimilation and contrast effects is almost a century old, there is still a plethora of unanswered questions and much more to be investigated. Thus, it is unlikely that, with this final chapter, the book on assimilation and contrast effects is closed. We hope that with bringing together divergent models, perspectives, and theories of assimilation and contrast in one volume, the rich diversity of research on assimilation and contrast effects is given a stage that is at the same time comprehensive and provocative.

Each of the chapters in this volume speaks for itself and gives a clear and insightful perspective on what determines whether assimilation or contrast occurs in the chosen domain of study. Readers can do the math and compare and contrast (or assimilate) the different perspectives, approaches, conjectures, and conclusions. Anyone who has read two or more chapters in this volume is likely to have engaged in spontaneous (but perhaps unaware) comparisons between chapters. In this final chapter, we have made these comparisons between approaches and perspectives more explicit by bringing together the contributors to this volume in their answers to four questions. After they had finished the final draft of their chapters, we asked the contributors to this volume to give us their (spontaneous and uncontrolled) thoughts on four questions, felt by the editors to be core to the issues and findings discussed in all of the chapters. Thus, all contributors were given the following four questions:

1. Is there a default context effect? That is, is assimilation or contrast more likely to be the most frequent outcome? Explain why.
2. Are separate models or theories needed to explain assimilation and contrast effects in different domains? Should there be separate models for emotions, groups, social comparison, behavior, counterfactuals, or is an all-encompassing model possible?
3. How can models and theories of assimilation and contrast be usefully applied to understanding and correcting real-life social problems?
4. What are the greatest impediments to advancing the understanding of assimilation and contrast?

In short, the contributors to this volume were asked to reflect on the issues of natural occurrence (Is there a natural context effect?), theoretical universality (Can there be one model that explains all?), relevance (Does it matter to the real world?), and progress (How can we do better?). The editors also explicitly asked contributors to give their intuitive, spontaneous, unedited responses. In their chapters, contributors presented their own well-reasoned, empirically grounded views on the determinants of assimilation and contrast effects. In the answers to the four questions, they could be more opinionated and less diplomatic (if they wanted to). In the remainder of this chapter, we will discuss, compare, assimilate, and contrast the answers contributors gave to the four questions. It is important to note that what follows is an (edited) selection of the answers to the questions. Because of page limits and because we did not want this final chapter to be a laundry list of answers, thoughts, and ruminations, we selected excerpts from contributors' answers. What follows is a selective (and thus, by definition, biased) sample of contributors' answers to our four questions. We invite any reader who wants to check our interpretation, or know more, to Google the contributors and contact them directly.

NATURAL OCCURRENCE?

Is There a Default Context Effect? That Is, Is Assimilation or Contrast More Likely To Be the Most Frequent Outcome? Explain Why

According to most contributors, the answer to this question is: No, there is no default context effect, it all depends on what processes and stimuli one is studying and under what conditions one does so. Thus, what the default context effect is depends on the context. As Markman puts it: "In order to support the notion of a default context *effect*, one needs to believe that there is such a thing as a default *context*. As for the types of domains that social psychologists typically study (e.g., social comparison, priming, stereotyping, etc.), the elicitation of assimilation versus contrast effects seems to depend almost completely upon the cognitive (e.g., abstract vs. concrete exemplars, prime extremity, etc.) and/or motivational contextual elements (e.g., self-enhancement needs, self assessment needs, etc.) that are present at the time of judgment."

Martin and Shirk note that assimilation and contrast are effects, not processes, and that therefore the effects are mute with regard to processes. "In fact, the literature has indicated that several processes could underlie assimilation and contrast. Given that there are multiple processes underlying different types of assimilation and contrast, then there is no need to assume a default context effect. It seems more likely that there will be different defaults with different types of stimuli, different judgmental settings, different processing objectives, and so on." As Förster and Liberman note in agreement with Martin and Shirk, assuming a default process overlooks "the essentials" of the categorization process is part and parcel of any comparison. They introduce a nice metaphor to argue and illustrate that whether assimilation or contrast is what one "sees" naturally is a matter of categorization or inclusion/exclusion:

> One can visualize the underlying metaphor with the prime and the target as two blots and the question of assimilation versus contrast as whether they are seen as one blot or as two distinct blots. Fuzzier boundaries of either of the blots and a shorter distance between them would promote assimilation. Moreover, a detailed, close look that concentrates on the differences may foster a perception of two blots (i.e., exclusion, contrast), whereas a more general, distal perspective and concentration on similarities may make them seem as one entity (i.e., inclusion, assimilation). Zooming in on the two blots is likely to produce a contrast effect, whereas placing both in a much wider context is more likely to result in viewing them as closer to each other and thus produce an assimilation effect.

Perhaps, then as Mussweiler writes, the default question is "a question of secondary importance. Empirical evidence clearly demonstrates that assimilation and contrast are both frequent context effects. A multitude of studies demonstrates that contextual influences lead to assimilation and a multitude of studies demonstrates that contextual influences lead to contrast. In light of this state of empirical affairs, it seems somewhat arbitrary to call the one or the other the default outcome."

However, even though most contributors tend to agree that it is unlikely that there is one, universal, automatic, natural context effect that occurs most of the time, ceteris paribus, at the same time there is also a tendency to afford assimilation effects more "naturalness" than contrast effects. The reasoning is then that logically assimilation must be more natural because it should take less time. As Glaser writes:

> I think that a purely probabilistic argument can be made that assimilation effects are more common because they involve fewer processes, specifically, the mere application of qualities of the context to the target. To the extent that contrast effects require a comparison between the context and the target or a correction of/for the context, and to the extent that anything that might inhibit or interrupt the processing would favor the simpler process, parsimony dictates that assimilation effects should occur more often. Having said that, depending on one's model of comparison contrast, it could be seen as being as simple as assimilation. If this is the case, then only correction contrast would be less common.

In a similarly intuitive vein, Markman writes: "On a completely intuitive level, I do believe that our brains have an 'easier' time assimilating than contrasting, as assimilation seems to rely somewhat less on intentional processing and motivational needs such as uncertainty reduction than does contrast."

In fact, it may be argued that there is enough reason to assume that assimilation is somewhat more of a default process, given that one defines such processes as processes that demand less cognitive resources (see also Stapel, chapter 6, this volume). As Schwarz and Bless note in this context, "time pressure and cognitive resources interfere with many exclusion operations, making assimilation more likely." And as Ric and Niedenthal write, "many models of affect and judgment assume that assimilation is the default context effect. People's affect colors their judgment in a congruent way unless mood regulation and/or other additional processes (e.g., accuracy motivation guided) take place and counteract the assimilative effects of affect. This idea is consistent with findings indicating that contrast effects are less likely (assimilation effects are more likely) when people's processing resources are limited." Thus, the state of the art in the affect literature seems to be that assimilation is a more natural effect than contrast.

Biernat and Manis indicate that a similar conclusion is warranted when reviewing the relevant stereotyping literature—assimilation is more natural than contrast: "Well, if you go by the chapter we wrote, we'd have to say that assimilation is the default context effect. Note that here we are talking primarily about the influence of stereotypes on judgment, and our model does suggest that there is a general tendency to assimilate what we encounter to stereotyped representations. In Kunda and Thagard's review of the stereotyping literature, they describe contrast effects as being extremely rare. We are not sure we would use that description, but we would agree that assimilation is the most typical outcome."

Based on the Selective Accessibility Model, Mussweiler also posits that

> assimilation is closest to being the default effect. From the perspective of this model, assimilation is closer to being the default effect. This is the case, because when comparing the target to a context stimulus judges are more likely to focus on similarities, which leads to assimilation. Why then, have so many studies demonstrated contrastive context effects? Part of the answer is methodological in nature. Many of the studies showing contrastive context effects have used extreme context stimuli and have thus established boundary conditions that explicitly foster contrast. By definition, however, most stimuli

people encounter in their daily routines are not extreme. Thus, contrast may be more frequent in the psychological lab than in people's real lives. Furthermore, most of the studies showing contrast effects have used subjective judgment scales as their outcome measure. Because such subjective judgment scales tend to be anchored on contextual stimuli they are not only sensitive to changes in the perception and representation of the target stimulus but also to changes in response language. Many of the contrast effects that are reported in the literature are thus likely to reflect mere changes in response language rather than actual changes in the perception or representation of the target. If this contrastive layer of response language which overlays actual context effects is removed, assimilation surfaces more frequently.

Mussweiler's point on methodology raises the issue of the paradigm-contingent nature of assimilation and contrast effects as touched upon in several of the chapters in this volume (see especially the chapters by Stapel, Suls & Wheeler, and Tiedens—chapters 6, 1, and 11, respectively, this volume). Whether assimilation or contrast on (subjective or objective) judgments, emotions, or behaviors is perceived as the most logical, most frequent, most natural effect seems to be dependent on the research paradigm (stimuli, procedure, measures) one is using.

As Biernat puts it "it strikes me that if you look at other areas of research, e.g., psychophysical judgments, *contrast* is the more typical outcome. There are lots of differences between judging people based on stereotypes and judging physical attributes of objects, but one key difference may be that the judgment task itself orients the judge more to comparison or to interpretation. . . . So on this question, I'd ultimately have to say no—that the 'default' context effect may depend on the type of judgment, the nature of the object of judgment, the strength of the context, etc."

Similarly, Ric and Niedenthal note that although models of affect and judgment assume assimilation is the default context effect, "models based on comparison processes do not assume that contrast and assimilation require a different amount of cognitive effort." The notion that it all depends on the paradigm one is working with is also voiced by Vliek, Leach, and Spears, in their discussion of the issue of natural occurrence in the domain of group research:

> The answer to this question depends in part on the process we wish to investigate. Recent research, using assimilation–contrast models to explain social comparison effects in intergroup contexts, would seem to suggest that there is indeed a default context effect. That is, where an intergroup context is made salient, results seem to point to the occurrence of assimilation after comparison with ingroup members. However, this kind of (denoting) assimilation precludes actual interpersonal *comparison* within groups, and is more akin to the process described by Tesser as *reflection*. Therefore, we would suggest that if an actual comparison *does* take place between group members, and theory and research on social comparison processes suggest this to be the rule rather than the exception, the occurrence of assimilation or contrast would depend in part on the characteristics of the group, and not easily defined in terms of a single *default* context effect.

In sum then, the conclusion must be that there is no default context effect. And even though there seem to be intuitive, logical, empirical reasons to assume that assimilation is a more frequent, more natural outcome of contextual influences on judgments and behaviors, it is very well possible that these intuitions and empirical results are biased by the paradigms and methodologies that have been used. Therefore, as Mussweiler notes, it is relatively "arbitrary" to call either assimilation or contrast the default context effect.

This conclusion is nicely stated by Wedell, Hicklin, and Smarandescu, when they discuss the default issue in relation to their model:

> While there may well be a default contextual process for a given circumstance, we do not believe that a single process is the default across all circumstances. Within our framework, processing takes place under two fundamental processing goals, generalization and discrimination. Often both goals may be active, as during the process of categorization. When categorizing, one would like to place similar objects together in the same category (generalization aided by assimilation) and dissimilar objects into different categories (discrimination aided by contrast). Thus, assimilation and contrast may be occurring simultaneously (see this volume). When one goal dominates, then the default process corresponding to that goal may likewise dominate (contrastive processes for discrimination goals and assimilative processes for generalization). A single default process might seem reasonable if one type of effect was more likely to be based on automatic processing and the other more likely to be based on effortful processing. However, we believe both assimilation and contrast can be generated automatically or effortfully, so that either one can serve as a default or as a corrective process.

THEORETICAL UNIVERSALITY?

Are Separate Models or Theories Needed to Explain Assimilation and Contrast Effects in Different Domains? Should There Be Separate Models for Emotions, Groups, Social Comparison, Behavior, Counterfactuals, or Is an All-Encompassing Model Possible?

Is it possible to design an all-encompassing model of assimilation and contrast effects? Is it good or desirable to have one model that explains everything? Again, when it concerns these questions, most of the contributors to this volume tend to agree. Most of them believe that it is good to strive for theoretical universality and that it should be possible to come up with one overarching theory or model that covers most if not all possible processes and effects. At the same time, however, many note that such a "unimodel" comes with a cost. By necessity and by definition, such an all-encompassing model is relatively abstract and general. One can only achieve theoretical generality by forgetting about the details. And sometimes, these details are what makes psychological research (and life) interesting and fascinating. A focus on very specific, content-oriented models and theories may therefore yield the most interesting and relevant results.

Biernat and Manis are clear in what the goal of the assimilation and contrast enterprise should be. "We don't think separate models are necessary. Although it's tempting to develop and refer to our mini-, domain-specific models, we think we gain a lot by pointing to general processes that apply across domains." Mussweiler has a similar opinion and argues quite persuasively that searching for general models of assimilation and contrast is preferable over developing specialized models. Furthermore, he argues that the development of such models is possible:

> Developing specialized models that explain assimilation and contrast in specific domains entails the risk of fostering a compartmentalization of psychological theory and research. It seems more desirable to identify broad psychological principles and mechanisms that can be usefully applied to a variety of different domains and phenomena. In fact, many of the models that have been proposed to explain assimilation and contrast effects are quite broad in focus. They identify general psychological principles and mechanisms that explain assimilation and contrast effects across a variety of different domains. Mechanisms of inclusion/exclusion, interpretation/comparison, similarity/dissimilarity testing are all cases in point. The Selective Accessibility Model attempts to explain assimilation and contrast across different domains. We proposed that the two alternative effects result from the operation of two alternative comparison mechanisms. Similarity testing leads to assimilation, whereas dissimilarity testing leads to contrast. Both of these mechanisms are quite general in nature and operate in a variety of different domains.

Förster and Liberman welcome the development of general, abstract models, especially when such models do not only integrate past research, but also (and especially) lead to the construction of new, provocative predictions. As Förster and Liberman note, however, it is important to note that generality can come with certain costs. Whether general or specific models are to be preferred "depends on the level of analysis, and there are advantages to both general and domain-specific levels. To the extent that all content phenomena share some underlying fundamental cognitive mechanisms (such as categorization, inclusion and exclusion) and motivational mechanisms (such as self-esteem concerns, inhibition after goal completion, preserving effort, etc.), one comprehensive model may have relevant insights about each of the domains, but such a general model should not detract from the informativeness of domain-specific models."

Markman focuses on the costs of general, abstract theorizing. He applauds the development of general models, "I think it is extremely useful to develop models of assimilation and contrast that identify general sets of processes that operate across a wide variety of domains," but at the same time he wonders whether the development of general models is necessarily useful and desirable, because specific domains of research demand specific mini-theories because they are *special*:

> It appears that we are passing through a "mini-era" of research and theory that is attempting to identify commonalities between these types of comparisons. However, given that we are presently accomplishing the goal of getting these disparate areas to talk to each other, I am now particularly looking forward to a new mini-era where we see a rigorous attempt to delineate the *differences*

between these processes—what makes counterfactual versus social versus temporal comparisons *special*, and worthy of separate study? The proposal of an all-encompassing model of assimilation and contrast would seem to impede this sort of investigation.

Vliek et al. also note that although general models of assimilation and contrast seem to be possible, disagreement and confusion enter the picture when researchers try to apply general principles to specific phenomena:

> Thus, when the abstract model of assimilation and contrast is applied to specific phenomena, such as self-esteem, category perception, affective contagion, and the like, specific theories are required to explain when, why, and in what form assimilation and contrast occur. These theories of assimilation and contrast must, of necessity, relate to other conceptualizations of the phenomenon of interest. Thus, work on assimilation and contrast requires a general, widely agreed upon, conceptual model *as well as* more specific, and more contentious, theories of phenomena. The similarities and the differences between applications of the assimilation–contrast model would be clearer if researchers differentiated their use of the general model from the specific theory they wish to apply to their phenomenon of interest.

In a similar vein, Ric and Niedenthal note that because "assimilation and, to an even greater degree, contrast effects of affect can be produced by a variety of processes (e.g., subtraction, adjustment, and comparison processes for contrast effects) . . . we are not inclined to think that an integrative model for all the assimilation and contrast effects is likely."

Several contributors argue that by definition an all-encompassing model is too general and abstract to have hermeneutic value and that therefore it may be best to consider separate (relatively general) middle-range models for different phenomena. As Glaser writes, "It may be prudent to consider separate models for different domains. Some contrast effects, particularly those due to correction, may be due to very different kinds of motivations, such as accuracy versus self-enhancement, which would vary in prevalence across domains. Some may be purely perceptual. Since Petty and Wegener's research shows that assimilation and contrast effects vary as a function of people's implicit theories about how they make judgments, it seems that this could be sensitive to different domains and motivations as well."

Similarly, Schwarz and Bless write in answer to this question, "An all-encompassing model is possible for cognitively mediated effects, including social comparison, counterfactuals, and judgments of groups and emotions. However, emotional assimilation and contrast can also refer to online emotional experience (rather than judgments of emotion); these experiential processes require a different conceptualization that takes their psychophysiological components into account."

The main reason why several general models may seem necessary—so seems to be the opinion of most of the contributors—is that there are different types of assimilation and contrast effects. As Wedell et al. note:

> We feel that separate models or theories of the processes producing assimila-
> tion and contrast are needed, but that these models may apply across different
> domains. . . . We would argue that contrast and assimilation effects arise out of
> basic cognitive processes that are generally applicable, but there is no single
> theory of either assimilation or contrast that can account for the various
> demonstrations of these effects. If there were, then these processes would
> have to be at the same time stimulus-based and response-based or automatic
> and effortful.

In conclusion then, the development of a general theoretical model of assimilation and contrast seems possible. In fact, in the relevant literature (and in the
current volume) there have been several attempts at developing such an all-
encompassing model. An important question is, however, whether the development of such "big" models is desirable because they are either relatively abstract
or relatively complicated. As Martin and Shirk put it,

> we need to make a distinction between theoretical models and underlying
> psychological processes. Different psychological processes may underlie dif-
> ferent forms of assimilation and contrast. One of our jobs as researchers,
> therefore, is to find out which particular processes operate in which particular
> domains. Once we have done this, we might find that some domains cluster
> together because they share similar underlying processes but that these
> domains differ from others that, in turn, share similar underlying processes.
> There is no reason to assume that one general psychological process will even-
> tually account for all instances of assimilation and contrast. On the other hand,
> it seems likely that theorists could develop a general theoretical model. Such a
> model, however, would have to incorporate a variety of underlying processes
> along with the factors that moderate the occurrence of those processes.

RELEVANCE?

How Can Models and Theories of Assimilation and Contrast Be Usefully Applied to Understanding and Correcting Real-Life Social Problems?

In the current volume, the focus was on delineating and discussing the basic
principles and processes that are thought to underlie assimilation and contrast
effects in a variety of domains. The general idea behind this basic, fundamental
focus on processes and mechanisms over specific practical, applied questions
is Lewin's famous dictum that there is nothing as practical as a good theory.
The best applications of (social) psychological knowledge are those that are
based on experimentally meticulous, methodologically rigorous, basic studies.
But what then, after all those decades of basic research (see Suls & Wheeler,
chapter 1, this volume), are the lessons to be learned from models and theories of
assimilation and contrast? How can those theories and models be employed to
further our understanding of real-life phenomena and to solve social problems and
conflicts?

Several of the contributors to this volume have attempted to answer these questions in their chapters. Martin and Shirk (chapter 9); Mussweiler (chapter 7); Schwarz & Bless (chapter 5); Stapel (chapter 6); Tiedens, Chow, and Unzueta (chapter 11); and Wedell, Hicklin, and Smarandescu (chapter 2) have all provided readers with examples of how their theories and models apply to emotion and self-regulation, stereotyping and prejudice, survey methodology, advertising strategies, political campaigning, juridical decision making, conflict resolution, and investment decisions. As Förster and Liberman note, "since making judgments is a fundamental human skill and all judgments depend on some accessible knowledge," the list of possible applications of assimilation–contrast models is potentially endless. Förster and Liberman go on to argue that the mechanisms underlying context effects are so basic that they can be used to illuminate any real-life phenomenon or problem. As an example, they adopt the inclusion/exclusion logic to understand prejudice:

> To illustrate, consider the animosity of some people in the USA toward illegal Mexican immigrants. Such intergroup conflict, although it is often referred to as examples of a "realistic conflict" (the immigrants compete on jobs and make wages go down), heavily depends on construal, categorization, and assimilation versus contrast processes. Perceiving the group of immigrants as distinct, and the boundaries between them and US citizens as fixed, would result in contrast and lead to prejudice. However, people may also apply other, broader categorizations. For example, while walking in the zoo, a person may think of herself as a human being (as opposed to an animal). Possibly, such broader categorization would diminish her animosity toward immigrants.

Förster and Liberman's discussion of the US-Mexican immigrant issue attests to the power and potential impact of assimilation and contrast research that goes beyond the psychology laboratory and 2×2(×2) designs. As do some of the examples given in the main chapters of this volume, this shows that the basic principles underlying assimilation and contrast effects can readily be used to understand (and perhaps solve) real-life phenomena. As Mussweiler notes, the applied success of assimilation and contrast models is probably related to their generality (see also the Universality section above): "To the extent that models of assimilation and contrast identify general psychological principles and mechanisms that transcend specific paradigms, they can be readily applied to real-life phenomena."

But is there anything to be learned from assimilation and contrast models that go beyond understanding the mechanisms that lead to categorization (inclusion, assimilation) and particularization (exclusion, contrast) in real life? Vliek et al. are pretty clear in their answer to this question: Any knowledge is to be preferred over no knowledge. Ignorance is not bliss: "In so far as theoretical analyses involving assimilation and contrast (and other processes for that matter) increase our understanding of the basic processes of social comparison and the evaluation of self and others, then of course this knowledge is useful (and preferable to a state of ignorance, or lack of knowledge). Such understanding is clearly a precursor to useful applications with regard to real-life social problems outside the lab."

On perhaps an even more abstract, epistemological level, Glaser notes that perhaps the most important and obvious implication of research on context effects is that it "suggests that few judgments are *pure*, most if not all are influenced by contextual factors."

Biernat and Manis make a similar point, when they discuss the application value of their work on the assimilative and contrastive effects of stereotypes:

> We have shown that stereotypes can affect our judgments of others, often in an assimilative fashion, but that their effects can sometimes appear counterintuitive or contrastive. This complexity in the effects of stereotypes may sometimes lead to wrong conclusions about how much of a problem stereotyping is. For example, if women are placed on shortlists, this might lead observers to conclude that gender stereotyping is not a problem (even though this very placement may be a direct manifestation of gender stereotyping). I guess I believe that awareness of these assimilative and contrastive processes may be a benefit in itself—as individuals we might come to acknowledge and perhaps resist (or correct for) subtle influences of our stereotypes.

Ric and Niedenthal also point to the consciousness-raising potential of knowledge about how contexts may affect choices and decisions, "Knowing that their current affective state has been induced by some irrelevant factor may help people to resist assimilation, even though contrast may sometimes ensue as a result of inaccurate naïve theories of affective states. Therefore the 'mere' dissemination of social psychology research on assimilation and contrast effects of affect on judgment could help to reduce the impact of these factors on judgment and decisions."

Markman notes that for assimilation and contrast models to be truly successful in the applied arena, a change of focus (from antecedent to consequences of context effects) seems to be needed: "Although formal models of assimilation and contrast effects tend to focus on antecedents to assimilative and contrastive responses (i.e., what produces them), much is to be gained from developing models that predict and explain the potential downstream consequences of assimilation and contrast effects (i.e., motivation and subsequent behavior)."

Martin and Shirk raise a related issue when it concerns the potential impact of assimilation and contrast models in real-life settings. They argue that to be successful it is essential that assimilation and contrast models are construed as models of information use rather than models of judgmental shifts: "Applications might be easier to identify if researchers think in terms of the factors that lead individuals to bring information to bear on a judgment or remove that information from their judgment rather than in terms of a shift in the judgment of a target stimulus toward or away from a context. The more general view seems to expand the number of ways in which research on assimilation and contrast could be applied, and it seems to foster application to more central, real-life phenomena (self-control, existential issues, mindfulness)."

In sum then, we can conclude that assimilation and contrast models do have relevance and can be applied in understanding real-life phenomena. The basic principles underlying assimilation and contrast effects (e.g., anchoring, categorization, interpretation, comparison, (dis)similarity testing) may even be used to design clinical interventions and societal change. Research on assimilation and contrast effects touches upon the core of social psychology by showing that few judgments and behaviors are "pure" or represent a "true" context-free response. The main applied lesson of assimilation and contrast models then is that life is not lived in a social vacuum. The value of assimilation and contrast models is that they do more than posit that "everything is relative." As the chapters in this volume show, each of these models go beyond this postmodernist relativism and attempt to delineate the basic processes and specific mechanisms causing life's relative nature.

PROGRESS?

What Are the Greatest Impediments to Advancing the Understanding of Assimilation and Contrast?

In the last question we posed to the contributors to this volume we asked them to reflect on the things they thought might be impeding progress in this research area. Of course, the chapters in this volume should be viewed as support for the optimistic notion that assimilation and contrast research is alive and thriving and that the past decade or so a lot of progress has been made in our understanding of the processes causing the magnitude and direction of context and/or accessibility effects. However, scientists should never sit back for too long and enjoy their accomplishments too intensely. Although it is comfortable to focus on what has been achieved and on the problems that have been solved, it is better to have a future-oriented focus and to focus on what is needed to improve our understanding of assimilation and contrast effects (even more).

It is striking to learn that there is a lot of consensus among the contributors to this volume as to what may be impeding the advancement of our understanding of assimilation and contrast effects. Most of the contributors mention what could be called "theoretical provincialism" and "methodological provincialism" as the main impediments to progress in this research area. That is, there is a concern that most researchers stay too much within the realm of their "pet" research paradigm to test their "pet" theory. As Markman notes, "This creates conceptual ambiguity when we attempt to develop general models of assimilation and contrast."

Theoretical Provincialism Schwarz and Bless write: "Many conceptual analyses stay overly close to the specific manipulation used, resulting in a proliferation of highly specific mini-theories that clouds the generality of the underlying processes. In fact, nearly every variable that we discuss as a determinant of inclusion/exclusion operations comes with its own special theory."

Similarly, Vliek et al. write: "The greatest impediment to advancement is the fact that most of the applications of the assimilation–contrast model are isolated from each other. For example, work on social comparisons of people is rarely integrated with work on judgment, category boundaries, or affective assimilation and contrast, etc. Indeed, even work on the social comparisons that people make with individual people is isolated from the work on comparisons within groups and work on comparisons between groups. Our understanding of assimilation and contrast models might well benefit from a step toward the integration of the many different uses of this conceptual approach."

Förster and Liberman note that researchers should try harder to relate their new insights to earlier findings: "We think that when a new variable or concept is introduced, it is helpful to relate it to previous concepts and variables—what are the similarities and differences between the newly introduced concept and previous ones? Do they follow from the same overall theory? What are the advantages of introducing the new construct?"

Martin and Shirk also stress the importance of historical awareness and point to the risk that so-called new theories may actually be reruns of older but not-so-well-known models (see also Stapel, chapter 6; Suls & Wheeler, chapter 1, this volume). Martin and Shirk suggest that to avoid the further proliferation of mini-theories and isolated solutions, researchers should try to adopt a multiprocess view (assimilation and contrast may occur through a various processes) and try to integrate and reconcile various findings:

> If one study finds that assimilation occurs under cognitive load, whereas another finds that contrast occurs under cognitive load, it is not clear that one study contradicts the other. If there were meaningful differences between the kinds of context and target stimuli used and in the judges' processing objectives, then it is likely that studies elicited different types of processes. If so, then the studies are complementary, not contradictory. The task of researchers in such a case would be to identify the different processes that produced the different effects as well as the conditions that, in turn, gave rise to these processes. The end result would be a more general theoretical model that would allow for the operation of a variety of different psychological processes that underlie the simple judgmental effects we refer to as assimilation and contrast.

Theoretical provincialism may impede the development not only of more general models of assimilation effects, but also of more specific models. As, Ric and Niedenthal note in their discussion of impediments to the advancement of comprehensive models of affective assimilation and contrast effects: "We think that a better understanding of assimilation and contrast effects of affect on judgment would benefit from research exploring the effects of the different components of the affective experience. Until recently, affect has been equated with affective feelings. It could be useful to further explore the effects of other aspects of affect, as activation of cognitions (emotion concepts and appraisals) or action tendencies."

In a similar vein, Glaser points to the closed-mindedness when it concerns the preconditions for subliminal contrast effects (see, for more detail, Glaser, chapter 10, this volume): "One of the greatest impediments is the presumption that correction occurs only with conscious awareness of the 'context.' Dual process models can be great, but they can also give rise to false dichotomies, and I think that's the case with this application."

Methodological Provincialism

Related to the concern that theory development seems to occur too in local and temporal isolation is the concern that some methodological open-mindedness and adventurousness is needed to take assimilation and contrast research to its next level.

Mussweiler argues that the use of subjective judgment scales (e.g., "How aggressive is Donald on a scale from 1 to 9?") is an important methodological impediment to progress in this research area:

> the almost exclusive use of subjective judgment scales in the study of context effects adds a lot of ambiguity to the existing literature. For most contrast effects that were obtained on subjective judgment scales, it is difficult to determine whether they are "real" in that they reflect actual changes in the perception or representation of the target or whether they merely reflect changes in response language use.
>
> A cure to this problem is the use of objective judgment scales (e.g., "How often did Donald yell at a friend last month?") that are more directly anchored in objective reality. . . . As a consequence, assimilation and contrast effects that are obtained on objective judgment scales can be more directly attributed to actual changes in the perception or representation of the target. A more widespread use of such objective judgment scales is likely to resolve many of the apparent inconsistencies in the literature on assimilation and contrast effects.

Biernat and Manis point to the difficulty of assessing what anchor or standard people use when constructing judgments and to the problem of adequately and experimentally testing complex mediational models:

> some of the things we want to get at are difficult to measure. To give an example, in our studies adequately measuring judgment standards has been difficult—participants can provide answers to direct questions, but it is unclear whether these responses are quite capturing the phenomenon at hand. For example, though one might generally expect a negative correlation between standards and subjective judgments (lower standards produce higher subjective judgments), we often find positive or null relationships instead. It is unclear whether people can introspect on and adequately represent the standards they use. Furthermore, for testing complex mediational models, too, we have the problem of measurement order—we want to get at the critical judgment without first measuring the key mediator, for fear that the measurement itself will disrupt the judgment. I think this makes it difficult to provide full tests of complex models.

Wedell et al. see the dominance of the experimental method in the study of (social psychological) assimilation and contrast effects as an impediment and make a plea for methods that will lead to the development of richer and more fine-grained models:

We feel that one of the greatest impediments to advancing the understanding of assimilation and contrast is the use of simplistic designs and analytic methods that demonstrate an effect but do little to constrain models of the processes underlying the effect. The 2×2 design is popular because it is easily communicated and understood, but it has only three degrees of freedom and hence cannot constrain models adequately. Parametric research is often maligned as boring, but it provides a clear basis for understanding behavior at the fine-grain level necessary for distinguishing among models. The use of a series of 2×2 designs strung together is typically inadequate as well, for it assumes a continuity of processing that may not apply across the task and contextual manipulations. Modeling an extensive database is a good beginning for developing richer theories of contextual processing. These analyses are bolstered by use of additional dependent variables, such as reaction time, looking time, judgment, and choice. There are a host of tools in the toolbox of social cognition researchers that can provide theoretical leverage concerning the nature of the processes producing the effects, and these need to be used in good measure to progress our knowledge of contextual effects.

Thus, the contributors to this volume give clear advice as to what needs to be done in the next generation of assimilation and contrast research. What is needed is more explicit historical awareness, open-mindedness to and appreciation of divergent theories and methodologies, and a willingness to abandon one's own "pet" paradigm and venture into research fields where no one has gone before. There probably is enough to discover.

Author Index

Subject Index